ELEGANT NEW YORK
The Builders and the Buildings 1885–1915

ESSENTIAL NEW YORK
A Guide to the History and Architecture of
Manhattan's Important Buildings

SEEING NEW YORK
The Official MTA Travel Guide

# THE EMPIRE STATE BUILDING

## THE MAKING OF A LANDMARK

## JOHN TAURANAC

### SCRIBNER
NEW YORK LONDON TORONTO SYDNEY TOKYO SINGAPORE

SCRIBNER
1230 Avenue of the Americas
New York, NY 10020

Designed by SONGHEE KIM

Manufactured in the United States of America

    2    3    4    5    6    7    8    9    10

Library of Congress Cataloging-in-Publication Data is available.

ISBN 0-684-19678-6

The preparation of this book was based in large measure on the Empire State
Building Archive and related collections of the Avery Architectural and Fine
Arts Library at Columbia University. All the illustrations in this book—except
the photographs of St. Gabriel's Park in 1939 and the mooring mast in 1995—
are from the Avery Architectural and Fine Arts Library, and are copyrighted by
the Trustees of Columbia University.

FOR MAGGIE

# CONTENTS

# ACKNOWLEDGMENTS

I could not have written this book without Avery Library, Columbia University's great architectural library. If there is any single reason to be a Columbia graduate, aside from receiving a pretty good education, the generosity of the university in opening all its libraries to its graduates without encumbrance is it. In addition to Avery's great collection of books on architecture, Avery also has The Archives, where a researcher on the Empire State Building finds paradise—not just elevations and photographs of the building, but the building's own archives and scrapbooks. My unabashed thanks to Janet Parks and Dan Kany for all their help and encouragement, and to Avery Library's director, Angela Giral, for generously supporting this book.

I am also indebted to *The New York Times Index*, a treasury no less great than Avery's catalog. A good role for the National Endowment on the Humanities, it seems, would be to underwrite comparable indexes for other newspapers.

My third major debt, one that everyone interested in the history and architecture of New York City also shares, is to Elliot Willensky, coauthor of the *AIA Guide*. He was an exemplar of everything good in New York, and a dear friend.

There are countless other individuals and institutions to whom I am indebted. My thanks to Peter L. Malkin, the managing partner of Empire State Building Associates, for telling me some wonderful tales out of school, and Alex Smirnoff, for showing my family and me the "guts" of the mooring mast; Bobbie Klaw for her memories of the horrors of the airplane crash, and Spencer Klaw for his "Talk of the Town" pieces; Amos Landman for his tale of the army's public relations expert; Peter Hollander for his critical eye; Monsignor Andrew Landi of the Catholic Relief Services for his help in tracking down information on Al Smith's relationship to the agency; Ellen Stern for her encyclopedic knowledge of the city and what makes it tick; Bruce Smith for his ability to translate business jargon into comprehensible English; Rolf Ohlhausen for his remembrances of parties past; Willa Hutner for setting me straight on certain planning issues; the Department of City Planning's David Woodward for enlightening me on shadows; Harold Smith, now retired to Boca Raton, for his memories of the seventy-ninth floor; Jeffrey Blyth, who introduced me to the Great Atlantic Air Race; Douglas Leigh, who related the great story that took place around Pearl Harbor Day; Deborah Walk of The Ringling Museum in Sarasota for her story on the Waldorf's bar and doors; Catha Grace Rambusch for her information on the family's design studios, and the Archives of American Art for their attempts at tracking down some of the original work; Herb Squire, director of engineering for WQXR, for his story about Stan Lomax; Louis Phillips for his wonderful letter writing; Philip Freund for having "ghosted" an important contribution; the Indiana Limestone Institute for its information on that state's most important export; the Landmark Society of Western New York for its information on the Genesee Valley Trust Company Building; Jonathan Kuhn of the Parks Department for knowing about the photograph of the Empire State Building from St. Gabriel's Park; E. Fredy Warns, now of Hialeah, Florida, for his Howdy Doody story; Wayne Carhart, for his conjurings; Laura Fries and Lydia Ruth; the Cornwall (Connecticut) Library for coming through in the occasional pinch and for maintaining me while I suffered cabin fever; NYU's Bobst Library for some critical books; the branch library system of the New York Public Library for tracking down a book that neither Columbia nor NYU had, and the Main Branch of the New York Public Library, because it is there; and the Library of the Performing Arts for providing me with a steady supply of compact disks—ten at a clip, most of them multiple sets—filled with glorious music "to soften rocks, or bend a knotted oak."

At Scribner, past and present, I want to thank Bill Goldstein, who conceived the project, and Ted Lee, Hamilton Cain, and Nan Graham for their good shepherding. I also want to thank my agent, Lisa Bankoff, for her exemplary work.

The family's two cats exerted their kitties' bill of rights to the fullest. They sat on every note I was reading, toppled every pile I made, and always seemed to manage a nuzzle just as I was about to hit "Save As" on my Mac.

I thank my wife, Jane Bevans, who juggled her already crowded schedule to provide the time I needed to do the work. She kept her concerns to herself regarding my slow and painful progress, and only sometimes in the middle of the night would I become privy to them. She provided me with the love and encouragement—and the necessary fear—to fulfill the task.

And then there is Maggie, our daughter, the ten-year-old kid who walked around the parapet of the Empire State Building's 102nd floor with me. I knew that Maggie was a fan of the building from the time she and I walked up the BMT Subway stairs at Union Square one evening during the Christmas season in 1992. I pointed out the Metropolitan Life Tower, which was bedecked in all its Christmas finery, and I told her that at one time it had been the tallest building in the world. Maggie was eight at the time, and was accustomed to having another former record holder pointed out to her whenever and wherever we were provided a view of it, and she wasn't impressed with Met Life one bit. We walked west on Sixteenth Street to Fifth Avenue, where we turned uptown, and there it was, the object of her admiration, her very own cynosure. "Now that's a real building. It's not as if these aren't real buildings," she said, dismissing the neighboring buildings with a wave of her hand, "because of course they are. But that," she said, regarding the Empire State Building, "that's what I call a real building."

# 1

# THE BUILDING

The Empire State's
        Ambitious mass
Is, take it from
        The critics, class.

—Price Day, *The New Yorker*, 1932

**B**efore we set out on the story of the Empire State Building, I want to make one point perfectly clear: This book is about the building in Manhattan at 350 Fifth Avenue, on the west side of the avenue between Thirty-third and Thirty-fourth Streets, block number 835, lot number 41. The building is 102 stories high, 1,250 feet tall—1,454 feet if you include the television antenna. You might think me oddly pedantic to point out these facts, but I want to reduce the chance for any misunderstandings.

There was, and still is, another Empire State Building in Manhattan, the existence of which, never very widely known in the first place, was eclipsed by the glory of the mighty structure at Thirty-fourth Street. The other Empire State Building, at 640 Broadway on the southeast corner of Bleecker Street, is a far different structure from its uptown namesake. A *New York Sun* reporter stumbled upon the building in 1932, and described it as a rather drab, gray stone structure of nine stories, extending some distance east on Bleecker Street. Its chief occupants were two firms of pants manufacturers, a window-cleaning company, and the Millinery Workers Union. A candy and cigar store occupied the ground-floor corner. Why the Broadway building was called the Empire State when it was built in 1897 is a mystery—perhaps the builder simply wanted to celebrate the state the building was in—but the name was carved in stone above the doorway until the building was "improved." The name is now obliterated by a piece of greenish material. Although the accident of names seems the only link between the two Empire State Buildings, the superlatives *biggest, largest* tenuously link them as well. The building on Broadway at Bleecker Street was designed by De Lemos & Cordes, the architects of two of the "biggest, largest" department stores in the world—the Siegal-Cooper Store on Sixth Avenue and Eighteenth Street, and the Macy's at Herald Square. For the record, this story is not about the building on Broadway at Bleecker Street. It is about the landmark building on Fifth Avenue between Thirty-third and Thirty-fourth Streets.

*The* Empire State Building is a landmark in both meanings of the word—it is a lowercase *l* landmark in that it marks the land, and it is a landmark in what some people regard as a higher order of landmark. In its geographic sense, the building stands majestically alone in the mountain range of New York's skyscrapers. It serves to provide your bearings, acting as a mark you can use to triangulate. You can see it from SoHo and Little Italy, from Broadway and Seventy-fifth Street or from Adams Street in downtown Brooklyn, from the New Jersey Turnpike or the upper deck of the George Washington Bridge. It became a designated New York City landmark in 1981, the year of the building's golden jubilee; it was listed on the State and National Register of Historic Places in 1982; and, in 1986, the National Parks Service recognized it as a National Historic Landmark.

As an uppercase *L* landmark, it fulfills all the qualifications for designation as set down by the New York City Landmarks Preservation Commission—it has special historical, cultural, and aesthetic value, and is an important part of the city's historical and architectural heritage. In the frequently cantankerous world of landmark designation, no witness spoke against designation at the hearing.[1] More important, perhaps, the Empire State was designated for some of the most elemental reasons. The report prepared by the commission's Anthony W. Robins began by saying that the building was "the best-known symbol of New York City," and

---

[1] One of the organizations endorsing the designation of the building as a landmark was the local community planning board. The chair at the time was Dan Biederman, who went on to head the Thirty-fourth Street Partnership, perhaps the single most important force for improving the district in the 1990s.

ended by saying that it "remains New York's preeminent landmark." The building has no competition. It is peerless.

In both uses of *landmark*, the Empire State Building looms large in the legend of New York. No longer the world's tallest building, or even the city's tallest, it proudly wore the title of World's Tallest Building from the day it opened in 1931 until it was relegated to second place with the coming of the first of the World Trade Towers in 1972. With the completion of the second tower in 1973, it dropped to third place. The construction of the Sears Tower in Chicago has since dropped the Empire State Building another notch in the ratings.

None of this has diminished the affection people feel for the building. It still swells the breasts of New Yorkers and makes hearts beat faster, and it still attracts more than 2 million visitors a year. The building's splendor and lift, its very being remains a magical presence, a cynosure for the city's residents, a mecca for visitors. Language barriers and social inhibitions evaporate as tourists ask complete strangers to take their pictures in the Empire State's lobby. Their joy is manifest, their obvious eagerness to record their visit for posterity breaking down all hesitancies. The stranger smilingly obliges.

People still go to the top to admire the view, they still snatch up little replicas of the building with thermometers stuck in the façades, they still marvel at the building's power and glory. From its inception, that was the whole idea—the power and the glory. I don't want to give away the plot, but titanic forces were at play in the building's conception, design, and construction. Planned in the expansive twenties, it opened in the constrictive thirties. The building suffered, but it endured, and it endures still.

People felt comfortable with the building from the first time they saw it, as if the building had become a fast friend at first meeting. Praise for the building's architects poured in from peers, press, and the public from opening day. "Its appeal to the layman is palpably enormous," said *The New Yorker*. "In spite of Frank Lloyd Wright's characteristically sweeping statement that our modern skyscrapers are all the same, we claim that this one is distinctly different, its difference and distinction lying in the extreme sensitiveness of its entire design." Architects Shreve, Lamb & Harmon "endowed it with such clean beauty, such purity of line, such subtle uses of material, that we believe it will be studied by many generations of architects, a hazardous prophecy in these days of change."

Just as the Empire State Building rose above every other structure in New York, so it towered over its competitors at the exposition of the Architectural League of New York in 1931. "No other work exhibited received more comment, either from laymen or members of the profession," said *The New York Times*.

For his work, "for his masterful treatment of an office building," architect William F. Lamb was awarded the Architectural League's Medal of Honor in Architecture for 1931. The jury included architects Ely Jacques Kahn and John W. Root, Jr., and sculptors Adolph Alexander (A. A.) Weinman and Herbert Adams. Lamb insisted on sharing the honor with his partners, Richmond H. Shreve and Arthur Loomis Harmon, although both Shreve and Harmon gave Lamb full credit for the design from day one. Lamb had faced the necessity of meeting "the impossible demand for speed in construction," Shreve said, and for that alone Lamb deserved the laurels.

The New York Chapter of the American Institute of Architects awarded their Medal of Honor to the designers for 1931, given for "distinguished work and high professional standing." The citation reads, "In the monumental design of a great office building they have made a genuine contribution to architecture. The noble simplicity of this outstanding structure makes it an inspiring landmark in our city." According to Stephen F. Voorhees, president of the chapter and chairman of the jury, the award was not customarily based on work performed on any one building, but in this case the jury specifically recognized the accomplishment in the Empire State.

The Fifth Avenue Association awarded the Empire State Building its gold medal for design, which was "architecturally excellent from top to bottom."[2] The association's architectural committee, including architects Joseph H. Freedlander, Charles S. Peabody, and Chester Aldrich, was unanimous in its estimation of the Empire State Building's worth, which spoke "eloquently of the high regard with which not only laymen but architects and builders view this great structure," said Captain William J. Pedrick, the association's president in 1931.

In 1955, the American Society of Civil Engineers selected the Empire State Building as one of the seven greatest engineering achievements in America's history—the only wonder conceived, financed, owned, and managed by private industry.[3]

---

[2]This gave Shreve, Lamb & Harmon the second gold medal in a row from the Fifth Avenue Association. The firm had been awarded the gold in 1930 for its design of the Hollander Building at 3 East Fifty-seventh Street, a nine-story fireproof store and office structure.

[3]The other wonders: the Colorado River Aqueduct, Grand Coulee Dam, Hoover Dam, Panama Canal, San Francisco–Oakland Bay Bridge, and Chicago's sewage-disposal system.

The Empire State Building was the biggest building anyone had ever known and one of the most pleasing aesthetically, and in all likelihood the building would have received laurels on its own merits. But carefully placed press releases from the day former governor Al Smith held a press conference in 1929 to announce the building's coming resulted in one positive news story after another. Its size and scale could not be readily put into perspective, so its promoters sought a way. The building was immediately billed as the Eighth Wonder of the World, with the original Seven Wonders of the Ancient World faring poorly in comparison. A later generation of owners continued the hyperbole with claims that more people visited the Empire State Building in a single year than visited the original Seven Wonders throughout recorded history. For the lobby floor's north aisle, in 1963 they commissioned eight "original artworks" depicting the seven original wonders plus the eighth. The endurance of the Empire State Building sets it apart from the ancient wonders. Of the seven, no trace remains of four of them, a few fragments remain of two of them, and only the Great Pyramid remains, although it is missing some of its top stones. The Eighth Wonder remains in all its glory, and then some.

In 1931, *Washington Star* writer Israel Klein included the building as one of the seven wonders of the *new* world. He thought the Empire State represented "the climax of skyscraper construction" and placed it in a league with the flood-prevention work on the Mississippi, with Boulder Dam, the two-hundred-inch telescope for Mount Wilson Observatory, the electrified Cascade Tunnel system in Washington, the Panama Canal, and the George Washington Bridge. A story in a 1958 issue of *Holiday* magazine compared the building to both modern and ancient wonders: If the Eiffel Tower were piled atop the great pyramid of Cheops, the writer claimed, the Empire State Building would exceed their combined height by thirty-eight feet.

The Empire State Building is *the* twentieth-century New York building. The Chrysler Building might be glitzier, Lever House might be a purer example of modernism, and two of the city's most banal buildings might be taller. But for the true heartbeat of a New Yorker, it's the Empire State Building.

It became an instant icon for the city and its age. In 1931, a Macy's shop window exhibited the history of men's clothes from 1812. Saying that "clothes follow the demands of progress," the window dressers backdropped each style with a symbol for its age. The iconographic chronology began with City Hall and ended with the Empire State Building.

The construction job was celebrated on Broadway the week the building opened in May 1931. Major Edward Bowes celebrated the construction of the building in a stage show at the Capital Theater that he believed ranked as more than a great complement to Marion Davies's Cosmopolitan production, *It's a Wise Child*. In a special series of sets designed by Arthur Knorr, the production told the story of the rise of the Empire State Building in music, dance, and pantomime. Beginning with the barren site and working up through the various stages of girders pushing their way upward to form a new skyline for Manhattan, the production ended with a dirigible moving across stage.

The Short Line Motor Coach Service, whose local bus terminal was in the Dixie Hotel on Forty-third Street, used the image of the building on the cover of its New York schedule (Philadelphia was represented by its City Hall; Washington, D.C., by the Capitol Building). The New York Central Railroad used the building in posters advertising its Saturday excursion fares to the city. The copy plugged the building as the city's latest attraction and urged passengers to visit it on their trip to the Boston Braves–Brooklyn Dodgers game at Ebbets Field or to the Giants–Philadelphia game at the Polo Grounds in Upper Manhattan.

When the Museum of the City of New York opened its doors on Fifth Avenue in 1932, a diorama by Dwight Franklin showed the erection of the Empire State's steel framework, a scene that remained on view until the early 1990s and is probably etched as deeply in the minds of New York kids as the image of the bare-breasted Indians at the American Museum of Natural History was to Holden Caulfield.

The substantive facts of the building strain credulity in their enormity and precision. According to one of the Empire State's architects, Richmond H. Shreve, a wind blowing at 4,500,000 pounds pressure would be required to knock it over; the building was vertical to within five-eighths of an inch; its weight was 365,000 tons, but its great load was distributed so evenly that the weight on any given square inch was no greater than that normally borne by a French heel. There are 10 million bricks in the building, 27 miles of main and counterweight rails used for the tracks of the elevators, about 200,000 cubic feet of Indiana limestone, and 6,400 windows. The completed building contains 37 million cubic feet. The 210 columns at the base support the entire weight of the building.

Some of these statistics might reinforce the commonly expressed fear that Manhattan Island would give way under the strain of supporting so many skyscrapers and would collapse into the surrounding waters. However, engineers point out that the city is built upon solid rock, and the great amount of stone removed in excavations is heavier than the completed skyscrapers. The stone excavated for the Chrysler Building, for instance, weighed twice as much as the building itself. Architect Shreve computed that the Empire State weighed no more than a forty-five-foot rock pile that might cover the site.

By virtue of its size, records were set up like standing dominoes and fell just as easily, and some of the records were taken very seriously by promoters. It ranked, for instance, as New York Telephone Company's largest single installation, which the telephone company touted. In the building's first stage of occupancy, about six thousand pairs of house cables and four thousand sets of wires to the central office were installed, as well as more than five thousand station telephones and more than three thousand trunk-line switchboards.

As the tallest building in the world, the Empire State Building was used as a yardstick for everything from Fleischmann's yeast to great ocean liners. First, the ocean liners.

A custom had grown up in the early twentieth century of illustrating the latest queen of the seas stacked up against the reigning queen of the sky, with the *Lusitania*, for instance, illustrated standing bow-up next to the Singer Tower. Although the flack for the French Line did not depict the *Normandie* next to the Empire State to demonstrate the length of the 1,020-foot-long ship, at the ship's launch in 1935 they claimed that if the ship were placed on Fifth Avenue it would stretch from Thirtieth Street to the northern side of Thirty-fourth Street, and, if stood on end, it would reach "almost to the top" of the Empire State Building (it still had 230 feet to go, or about another quarter, but who's counting?).

In attempts at relating the height of New York skyscrapers, some foreign publications made legitimate comparisons with commonly known monuments back home. The *London Daily Mail* said in 1931 that the Empire State was nearly nine times higher than Nelson's Column in Trafalgar Square. (A multiple of the height of St. Paul's Cathedral might have made more sense, but it was an honest effort.) And for years, *The Michelin Green Guide to New York* stacked the Eiffel Tower against the Chrysler Building, since the Chrysler Building was the first building taller than the Eiffel Tower.

Sometimes the building was used as the basis for showing the enormity of something unfathomable. *Modern Mechanics and Inventions* held that if the thickness of a postage stamp represented the record of human history, the Empire State Building would not be high enough to represent the rest of astronomical time. To show the strength of the new two-hundred-inch telescope at Mount Wilson, the *Philadelphia Inquirer* said that the "point of a needle, held some yards away from the lens, would appear as large as the great 102-story Empire State Building from a distance of a few blocks." Critical information was a little vague in the newspaper's statement, and the illustration that showed the building standing next to a needle its size was not much more precise. Some comparisons were even more specious, however. One had the Empire State Building more than four times as high as the Tower of Babel.

Manufacturers, hoping to cash in on the building's celebrity status, frequently made comparisons between the building and their product. Kelvinator advertised that it used nearly 6 million square feet of porcelain in 1933—enough porcelain to cover the Empire State Building seven times! Kellogg's Cereals claimed that once every eight hours the company used enough Waxtite paper to encase the entire Empire State Building in the same airtight, moisture-proof Waxtite bag that protected the delicate flavor and crispness of Kellogg's Corn Flakes, Rice Krispies, and the company's other famous cereals!

Childs Restaurants almost apologetically advertised in 1938 that one of their "data hounds" had "figured out that two days' servings of its pancakes (each cake was three-eighths of an inch thick) would make a stack as high as the Empire State Building."

*Scribner's Magazine* combined two of the most popular cultural events of the 1930s into one enormous bit of useless information. *Gone with the Wind* was published June 30, 1936, and by Christmas of that year a million copies had been sold, setting a record as the fastest-selling volume in history. *Scribner's* claimed that if all the copies of the 1,037-page bestseller were piled one atop another, the stack would be 250 times taller than the Empire State Building.

Clay Morgan, publicity director of the French Line, who had probably come up with the old saw that had the *Normandie* stacked up against the Empire State Building, claimed that all the linens stocked aboard the *Normandie*—tablecloths, napkins, sheets, etc.—could completely cover the Empire State Building. To show the nonsense of Morgan's dispatch, *Harper's Bazaar* whimsically illustrated the building wrapped with the *Normandie*'s linens stitched together, with a bow tied around it.

The Wizette Corset Company cashed in on the famous shape of the Empire State Building in an effort to plug a new device that enabled women to get into and out of their product more comfortably. Wizette depicted the building magically unzipped to reveal within the "new smart girdle with the Improved Slide Fastener."

Ads that bore a remarkable similarity in design to Ripley's "Believe It or Not" ran as Don Byrd's "Amazing But True." One "Amazing But True" was an ad for Oxydol detergent, which showed a woman pulling the Empire State Building by a rope. The caption read: "The energy women use in a year to wash clothes would move the Empire State Building a block if translated into moving power. Oxydol would save nearly half this energy."

An ad for Sinclair Gasoline showed the building being picked up by a crane. The headline came complete with asterisk: ONE GALLON COULD LIFT THE EMPIRE STATE BUILDING 1 3/4 INCHES. 99 MILLION FOOT-POUNDS* PER GALLON. "Amazing as it may seem," the copy claimed, "there is enough energy stored up in a single gallon of the powerful new H-C gasoline, if it could be fully utilized, to hoist the world's tallest building 1 3/4 inches in the air." The asterisk noted that "Foot-pound [was] the amount of work required to lift one pound one foot. Due to friction and other losses, no machine yet built can convert into useful work all the potential energy in any gasoline . . ."

People have been compared with the building. Heavyweight boxer Primo Carnera was described as being "built like the Empire State Building" in 1931, but then, a few months later, Leo Pinetzki, "the world's mountain-weight wrestling champion and his Empire State Building physique—283 pounds, six feet nine inches tall, with a 96-inch reach," superseded Primo Carnera as "sport's largest mammoth."

The capacity of other buildings has been compared with it. Virginia's Harry F. Byrd in 1937 claimed that the federal government was paying rent for office space equal to fifty-two buildings the size of the Empire State.

A car card in the subways that ran under the title OUR TOWN ODDITIES in March 1942 contained a startling bit of information: The Empire State's mooring mast—just the mooring mast atop the building—was higher than any office building in Europe. (It wasn't, I hope, just because it was sitting atop a 1,050-foot base.)

Then there was the entry made by Fleischmann's yeast: From the small tube of live yeast plants that Charles Fleischmann brought from Europe in 1868 had grown "enough yeast to fill eleven Empire State Buildings solid."

The building has been a favorite subject for model builders in various media. A Tacoma, Washington, man used 135 decks of cards to build his house of cards in the shape of the Empire State Building. A four-foot-high model of the building was carved in soap. T. B. Wu, a twenty-six-year-old student, spent six months making a ten-foot-high model out of plaster and powdered sugar. Fourth and fifth graders from the Kelvedon Hatch Primary School in Brentwood, England, built a seven-foot, eight-inch model of the building from 3,212 matchboxes. And a two-foot model of it was made entirely out of anthracite coal. A model kit in book form that only required the model maker to cut and paste to build his own Em-

pire State Building ("so easy even an adult can do it") was published by
Perigee Books in the 1980s, and in the 1990s Milton Bradley produced a
"super challenging" three-dimensional puzzle whose 902 foam-backed
pieces created a model of the building over three feet tall.

A fairly common practice among architects and developers was to have
reasonably exact plaster of paris models show how the structure would
look when completed, and the Empire State's team was no exception. A
seven-foot-high, 525-pound model was built that was valued at $3,000. It
was photographed for publicity shots, and it was used as a stand-in for
the real thing in 1931 when the Fox Film Company shot the talking picture *Skyline*. Models of the Empire State, Chrysler, and Irving Trust
Buildings were shown in 1931 at the American pavilion—itself a reproduction of Mount Vernon—at the International Colonial Exhibition in
Paris. A model of the Empire State Building was shown in an exhibit illustrating the development of buildings throughout the ages at the Museum of Science and Industry in the Daily News Building in 1932. A
model was shown at the 1939 World's Fair. And, of course, it is depicted
in the "Little Apple," the model of the entire city in the New York City
Building at the Queens Museum of Art.

Tony Lordi, an art professor at County College in Morris, New Jersey,
views the building as *the* icon for New York. The six-foot models of the
building that he created in the late 1980s were either found objects that
Lordi assembled to create the armature of the building—wondrous structures built of bits and pieces of old metal that he somehow put together
in the form of the building—or models that he built of plywood and then
covered with all sorts of whimsical objects. One model was covered in
mink, another was covered in mirrors, and a third was covered in tacky
souvenirs available at tourist attractions, a wonderfully convoluted statement. He was inspired to make his own interpretations of the Empire
State in part because of his visit to the building when he was five. His parents bought him a model of the building that doubled as a pencil sharpener.

*Life* magazine's Walter McQuade was convinced that the building was
designed to make a good souvenir in miniature to be carried away by
tourists. The miniatures have been the biggest sellers over the years.
Fifty years after the building opened, the manager of the building's souvenir shop estimated that the anniversary year would see sales of eighty
thousand miniatures in various versions—a two-inch paperweight, a six-
inch piggybank, a nine-inch thermometer—but there was no mention of
the pencil sharpener that Tony Lordi had as a child.

Perhaps the earliest fictionalized account of the Empire State Building appeared in *Swiss Family Manhattan*, a children's fantasy by Christopher Morley published in 1932. The family escapes a wrecked dirigible in a balloon raft that sets them down atop the Empire State Building, which is still under construction. Muddle-headed father construes the structure as a great, giant tree "set amidst stony clefts and sierras, sometimes topped with floating plumes of steam, suggesting either fires for cooking or sacrifice, or perhaps that these peaks were of volcanic origin." They find builders' materials that prove useful in constructing a shelter for themselves, and they hide from the "anthropoids"—the workers—whose tastes in humor the father divined "were primitive . . . from certain rough drawings on plastered walls where they were working." One of the boys is more circumspect and holds that the family had landed in a great "edifice that showed all evidences of a careful plan."

The Empire State Building has appeared in about ninety movies, but no doubt the most famous is *King Kong*. Just as the building was billed as "The Eighth Wonder of the World," so was the movie's tragic hero, whose only real flaw was that he fell in love with beauty, and it was beauty that killed the beast. A Frank Buck–like character named Carl Denham sets off to shoot a movie on an island where prehistoric creatures roam about behind a wall, where he realizes that "if this picture had a love interest it would gross twice as much." The blonde who is to appear in his movie provides it. In the denouement, a manacled Kong is on display on a stage in New York.[4] The lovesick beast breaks loose, finds the blonde, and tries to escape to safety with her atop the Empire State Building, where he symbolically and literally makes a defiant stand against our civilization. A squadron of combat planes finally shoots him off the tower, but not before he has gently and lovingly placed the hysterically screaming blonde on the rooftop platform.

The movie still looms large in legend. A January 1995 *New Yorker* cover by Bruce McCall showed three great apes sitting around on rooftops reading *Variety* and playing cards while awaiting their turn to audition at the top. The cover was called "King Kong Call."

Like Will Rogers, screenwriters in the 1930s might have learned all they knew from what they read in the newspapers. *The Jersey City Journal* reported that the first marriage performed in the tower was in April 1932, when Doris Averell Welchangs, of Springfield, Massachusetts, married William Holmes, of Weehawken, New Jersey. They chose what they

---

[4]*King Kong* was shown, appropriately enough, at Radio City Music Hall and the RKO Roxy, which, with the Hippodrome, might have been the only New York theaters with stages big enough to accommodate the real King Kong.

described as "the nearest place to heaven they could find," a phrase that might sound familiar. And *The Brooklyn Eagle* told of a young woman in December 1935 who was seen pacing restlessly up and down the eighty-sixth-floor promenade. The guards were worried that she was about to jump. She was upset, but not suicidal. She had met a young man on the tower the year before and they had promised to meet again on that particular day. He had not shown up. Another familiar ring.

Here was the stuff of *Love Affair, An Affair to Remember I, An Affair to Remember II*, and, by extension, *Sleepless in Seattle*. The plot to the first of them is basically the plot to the first three: boy (Charles Boyer) meets girl (Irene Dunne). Each is to marry another for money. They fall in love onboard ship, and as they sail up the Hudson, they decide that each has to prove himself worthy of the other and get real jobs. To see what progress has been made toward unassisted solvency, they decide to meet in six months in the "nearest place we have in New York to heaven," the top of the Empire State Building. On the day, Dunne does not look at the traffic light on Fifth Avenue but instead glances at the top of the building in her excitement at seeing him there. She is hit by a cab. Boyer waits 'til midnight, pacing anxiously, and departs, disillusioned.

People have succeeded in vanquishing the building's verticality: They have walked up it. Sources disagree on who the first walker was, but building guard Pete McGuire was generally acknowledged as the first to make the climb. Next to do it were two small boys who arrived at the top unannounced after slipping past guards. Although they had properly trespassed and created a hazard to themselves, everyone secretly admired their gumption and derring-do.

Publicists soon learned to exploit such feats. In 1937, the observatory's manager, Julia Chandler, heard that the forty-nine-year-old A. W. Aldrich, a Vermont farmer and mountain climber, volunteered to make the climb, and she made arrangements for the first officially sanctioned climb to the top, which Aldrich performed in the full glare of publicity. He climbed the 1,860 steps, each one with a seven-inch rise, in thirty-six minutes. He plodded flat-footed, Indian-style, insisting it was easier on the leg muscles. He neither drank nor smoke, because "it don't do nobody any good." He had not married, either, but *The New York American* pointed out that there did not seem any correlation between that fact and his Alpine technique. Two Morris High School juniors from The Bronx, Marilyn Milstein and Helen Broan, were the next to climb it. They distinguished themselves as the first of their gender to accomplish the feat, in September 1940. One of them was photographed after the climb, soaking her feet. The feat had made them sore.

Walking up had become old hat by 1978, when the New York Road Runner Club started an annual footrace to the top. The first was won by August Gary Muhrcke, a former New York City fireman, who ran up the eighty-five flights in twelve minutes, thirty-two seconds. He did not, however, enter the race in 1979 to defend his title. Muhrcke had drawn fire for his feat—he was drawing a tax-free disability pension of $11,822 a year from the fire department for a back injury. *The Times* editorialized that the least he could do for his pension was run up and down stairs warning people of danger by yelling "Fire! Fire!"

The Empire State was the goal of another kind of race—the Great Atlantic Air Race, now memorialized by a plaque at London's Post Office Tower, the other end of the thirty-five-hundred-mile dash. The plaque reads: "Transatlantic Air Race. This plaque marks the starting and finishing point of the Daily Mail Transatlantic Air Race, 4th–11th May, 1969, in which 360 competitors travelled between the Post Office Tower and the Empire State Building in New York. The Air Race commemorated the 50th anniversary of the first Transatlantic flight in 1919 by Captain John Alcock and Lieutenant Arthur Whitten Brown." Competitors used everything from regularly scheduled commercial airline flights to Royal Navy Phantom jets, jump-jet Harriers, Piper Comanches, hot-air balloons, and World War II Spitfires. Prince Michael, the queen's cousin, entered the race, as did race-car driver Sterling Moss, neither of whom won their categories. Clement Freud took the honors for the London–New York race on a scheduled Aer Lingus flight (eight hours, four minutes, eighteen seconds). According to the *Daily Mail*'s New York bureau chief Jeffrey Blyth, the Empire State Building set aside a section of the eighty-sixth-floor observatory as a check-in area, the building dedicated elevators to the competitors, and when Sir John Alcock's niece Anne arrived, she was bearing a package for Building Manager Bob Tinker. She had been appointed a licensed mail-carrier by the British postal system for the express purpose of delivering a block of fiftieth-anniversary Alcock and Brown stamps, which were then to be sent on to the postmaster general.

The building had its own post office, but telephones had replaced the mails for speedy communication by the early 1930s, when the exchanges, which took neighborhood or institutional names, served as true area codes. The building's management office, its luncheon club, and its public relations office all had LOngacre numbers (Longacre was the original name of Times Square). The building's advertising agency, the Andrew Cone Agency (no relation to the advertising agency Foote, Cone & Belding), the pharmacy within the building, and the office of the Travelers In-

surance Company in the building had PEnnsylvania numbers (named for
the railroad station on Seventh Avenue).[5] The exchange for the Empire
State Building's renting office at Madison Avenue between Thirty-fifth
and Thirty-sixth Streets was CAledonia. This is a mystery number that
the telephone company could not identify in 1995 as one of the recognized
exchanges, and there is no apparent reason for CAledonia to be an exchange for numbers in the east thirties (there was a Caledonian Club at
846 Seventh Avenue, which had a CIrcle number because of its proximity
to Columbus Circle). In addition to the renting office at CAledonia 5-
8347, the Schrafft's at 4 East Thirty-sixth Street had a CAledonia number, as did the Empire State (probably no relation to the building)
Hunting and Fishing Club at 22 East Thirty-eighth Street.

The designers of the building were not superstitious and gave the building a thirteenth floor, not an unusual thing for an office building at the
time. Only one major 1930s office building was not given a thirteenth
floor, and it was Cross & Cross's building at 570 Lexington Avenue, at
Fifty-first Street.[6] Abolition of the thirteenth floor was not ordinarily a
concession to the superstition of the landlord or designer, but to that of
tenants, and it occurred most frequently in buildings where you might lay
your head or be dealing with life and death. Many apartment houses had
floor numbers that skipped from twelve to fourteen. The Roosevelt Hotel
had no thirteenth floor, and although there had been a thirteenth floor in
the old Waldorf-Astoria and there was a thirteenth floor in the new one,
the new hotel eliminated all room numbers ending in thirteen. Perhaps the
most confusing floor-numbering system occurred at the Presbyterian Hospital. The floor numbering was normal from one to twelve, but then suddenly numbers stopped and letters were substituted for the floor
"numbers," beginning with $M$, the thirteenth letter.

Perhaps the thirteenth floor brought the Empire State bad luck. Its
fans certainly felt unlucky in the early 1970s, as they stood by and
watched helplessly as the World's Tallest record went to the World Trade
Towers. It was like a Brooklyn Dodger fan watching his beloved team go
to Los Angeles. If the Empire State Building wasn't going to remain the

[5]People have often wondered if John O'Hara's *BUtterfield 8* would have been a hit if it had
been called 288, or if people would have been dancing to Glen Miller's "736-5000," the
number of the Pennsylvania Hotel two blocks away from the Empire State Building.
Somehow, those numbers don't have the same ring.
[6]The building was designed as the RCA Building but was called the GE Building for most
of its commercial life. To confuse things more, by the 1990s Rockefeller Center's RCA
Building was the GE Building.

champ—and it had won the record fair and square, just as the Dodgers had finally won the Series—why did it have to lose to something so big, so boring, so banal? It was as if the Yankees—a machine for winning when the Dodgers were in Brooklyn—had won again.

The Empire State's eccentric fans might not have mourned so if the title had gone to an interesting structure such as the conelike, 2,296-foot concrete tower planned for the Paris Exposition of 1937, which would have been more than a thousand feet higher than the Empire State Building and a worthy successor to the Eiffel Tower. Spiral ramps climbed the outside of the tower, the inside lane of the ramp for descending cars, the outside lane for ascending. Automobiles could climb to a height of 1,640 feet, where there would be a garage for five hundred cars and a restaurant for two thousand guests, as well as an inexplicable thing called a "sun-cure station." The structure would have been called "Phare du Monde," or "Lighthouse of the World," with a beacon twenty-three thousand feet high. Or the building's fans might have graciously relinquished the title to the Palace of the Soviets, upon which work was scheduled to begin in December 1938. It would have been twenty-three feet taller than the Empire State Building and topped with the world's largest statue, a statue of Lenin that would have been three times the size of the Statue of Liberty. The patent impracticality doomed one proposal, and the coming of World War II doomed the other.

The Empire State was luckier. The building was boldly planned, and although the exigencies of the stock market crash halted other projects, work on the Empire State went forward at a record pace. The skyscraper is a slice of architectural and planning history, a slice of the history of the city, and worthy of being called a landmark. It is the city's—and the world's—greatest skyscraper.

# 2

# THE SKYSCRAPER

As an unabashed New York booster,
I find it hard to admit something,
but Chicago was the cradle of
the American skyscraper.

—Architect Harvey Wiley Corbett

**I**f you ask the man in the street to define *skyscraper*, he will no doubt wonder what kind of jerk you are. "It's a very tall building," he would probably say, which is a perfectly acceptable answer. Inherent in the word *skyscraper*, after all, is the essence of the building—it has to be tall, it has to "scrape the sky."

Campaniles, steeples, and minarets are tall, but ordinarily there is only enough space within the structures for staircases. The rest is the structure itself. The reverse is the case with domes. They are shells, with vast interiors for effect. By contrast, a skyscraper is designed to be filled with space that can be used to commercial advantage. The structure has to be functional and remunerative. You find floors every twelve feet or so, floors that house desks and filing cabinets, lathes and sewing machines, factory and office workers. You find colonies of industry.

Richard Morris Hunt's 260-foot Tribune Building was considered very tall when it was built in 1874. It had interior space that could be used to commercial advantage, and it scraped the sky, so you would think that it would qualify for skyscraperdom. By the 1890s, however, the Tribune Building would not be considered a skyscraper by strict definition. The standards for skyscrapers had changed. Technological advances, not the man-in-the-street's perception, were defining them.

The Tribune Building had masonry walls that were load bearing—the walls helped to support the weight of the building. Every additional floor the building rose contributed that much weight for the walls below to bear, so the lower walls had to be made that much thicker. The thicker the walls, the less rentable space, a problem exacerbated by the fact that, in extreme cases, windows—a critical selling point—had to be made smaller. The goal of the skyscraper builder is to create bright and airy space, not to have it diminished. No sensible developer will sacrifice valuable rental space on the altar of height.

A skyscraper is a tall building whose weight is supported by a frame of steel or poured-in-place concrete with steel reinforcements. Unlike the load-bearing walls of a masonry structure, walls do not help support the average skyscraper.[1] The walls are attached to the frame in various ways, and do little more than keep in heat and keep out cold and dampness. Since the walls in a skyscraper are equally thin, top and bottom, they do not occupy a greater percentage of valuable space on the lower floors.

So long as the walls are impermeable, they can be made of just about any permanent material. Early skyscrapers might have had façades of brick or terra-cotta, both of which were ideal as fire retardants. Both were readily available and inexpensive. Grander buildings might have had stone façades, with ashlar—large blocks of stone cut to size at a quarry—that could be installed at the site. Later skyscrapers might have been given panels of metal, of steel or aluminum, even of glass to face the building.

A skyscraper and the human form are somewhat analogous. Your body is supported by a skeleton of bone, with muscle and cartilage holding it together. Your skin does not support the weight of your body; it simply hangs there. When your skin is pricked, you leak blood but you do not fall down. The average skyscraper is likewise supported by a skeleton, of steel. Its skin, or walls, are supported by the frame; they do not support the building. When the wall of a skyscraper is pricked, it leaks air, and unless its skeleton has suffered a seriously deleterious blow, the building does not fall down.

In the opinion of architects such as Harvey Wiley Corbett, skyscrapers were America's great gift to architecture, the first new structural form since the ancient Romans invented the arch. Egypt had built with only one fundamental structural principle: the post and lintel. The clear span under the roof was limited by the length of a stone lintel supported on

---

[1] A major exception is the World Trade Center Towers.

columns. Greece might have achieved a perfection of detail and refinement of proportion, but no new building principles were added to the basic Egyptian design. It was the Romans who devised the second new structural element—the masonry arch and dome—and used it on a grand scale. Not until the masonry arch came into being, and the consequent Gothic variations on the theme during the Middle Ages, could architects produce enclosed spaces of impressive vastness. However, if you weren't interested in building vast interior spaces such as the nave of a cathedral, but wanted a tall commercial building, you found yourself in an architectural pickle if you used masonry walls to support the building.

Stone and wood had been the coin of the building realm until the arrival of cast iron in the middle of the nineteenth century. Until then the weight of buildings had been borne by their walls, but in 1848 James Bogardus used a skeleton of cast-iron posts and beams to support a building from within. Since the walls no longer bore the load, they could be freed from their former obligations.

Builders who used cast iron built essentially in the same manner as the builders of the Empire State Building. The posts and beams, and the windows and window frames were prefabricated in a factory and assembled at the site. A foundation was dug, then a cast-iron sill was set into a base. A hollow, cylindrical column was bolted perpendicular to the sill, just as later builders would set steel posts in concrete at the bedrock level. When a pair of adjoining posts was in place, a lintel was bolted to link them. The process continued horizontally and vertically, floors were laid, and a new style of building resulted. Interior spaces were a series of self-contained boxes, each an island, entire of itself. Since the units were self-supporting, there was no need for thick walls to support the load of the building. As a result, large expanses of windows punctuated by delicate cast-iron columns created a rhythmic balance outside and well-lit spaces inside.

But there were limits as to how high pure cast-iron buildings could rise, even how high masonry buildings could rise that incorporated iron to reinforce masonry. The material framing and supporting a building higher than seven or eight stories has to combine both compression and flexibility. Wrought iron has greater tensility than cast iron, but even wrought iron is rigid, ungiving, incapable of stretching compared with steel, whose properties include tensility and compression as well as resistance to fatigue. The likelihood of structural steel losing its strength, even under tremendous heat, is pretty slim. It yields very slowly. It bends and stretches, but it doesn't break.

Henry Bessemer's process of making steel was perfected by 1860, and soon steel was being used to reinforce stone and brick in buildings. In the

1880s, it occurred to architects that they could do with steel what had been done with cast iron: They could frame buildings.

Steel produced in the late nineteenth century already had qualities that made it the favored material of bridge builders such as John Roebling, who used it for the span and cables of the Brooklyn Bridge.[2] When engineers began to use steel for skyscraper construction, they ordered from the same shops—the steel-bridge shops that had supplied Roebling—because the ordinary steel mills rolled only standard and uniform shapes. The structural steel for a skyscraper called for columns and girders of hundreds of different lengths and strengths. Only bridge shops could fabricate the posts and beams to the specifications of the drawings; only they could fabricate the shapes required for girders and columns.

The development first of box columns and then of the I beam for use as posts and beams was critical to the skyscraper's development. The thrust of an I beam as a post is toward its center, where the beam is thickest, the axis where opposing forces meet and neutralize each other. The post does not buckle. Used as a lintel, the thrust is down the I, and since that again is where the greatest thickness lies, again the beam does not buckle. Pressure, tension, and compression exist in varying degrees, but steel's tensility will keep the I beam from buckling, cracking, or failing.

By the turn of the twentieth century, good wrought iron was rated as having a strength of about 50,000 pounds per square inch; steel's rating was a conservative 65,000 pounds. Wrought iron was given an elastic limit of 25,000 pounds, steel 40,000. Within three decades, the estimates on steel were revised, a result of improved steel, granted, but more importantly, because tests were more scientific. Authorities by then claimed that not only was steel twenty times as strong as wood, it was four to five times as strong as iron.

One of the great differences between cast-iron construction and steel-frame construction, as the great builder Colonel William A. Starrett points out, was literally nuts and bolts. The elements of cast-iron buildings were bolted, but no bolt has the strength of a rivet. Steel-framed buildings were riveted. Driven red-hot into the punch holes, rivets fill up every interstice. When they cool, they are one with beam and column, an integral part, and beam and column become one with each other.

Of equal importance with these developments, no builder could reasonably hope to rent space above the sixth or seventh floor unless there was a way to get upstairs that was more convenient than stairs—you can

---

[2] Although the great French engineer Gustave Eiffel used iron for his most famous undertaking, he used steel in the frame of the Statue of Liberty.

only expect tenants and visitors to climb so many flights, a fact with which cathedral builders did not have to concern themselves. Elisha Graves Otis had demonstrated an elevator at the Crystal Palace in 1853 that had a safety device that prevented it from falling if the cable broke.[3] In the cast-iron Haughwout Building on Broadway at Broome Street, where china and cutlery were sold, Otis installed the first of his passenger safety-elevators.[4]

Elevator engineering is based on the simple hoist. Suspended by cables (called "ropes" by elevator men) and counterbalanced by a counterweight, the car is drawn upward on its rails by a motor-driven drum ("sheave") at the top of the shaft. The first elevators were powered by steam. By the 1870s, elevators were being operated by hydraulic systems, and "high livers" started paying higher rents for higher floors. This phenomenon was first exploited at the Equitable Building on Broadway at Pine Street, which was built in 1870 and was the first office building to install an elevator.

Otis installed the world's first successful electric elevator in 1889, soon after electricity had become commercially available, and by the 1890s elevators that were being powered by the more efficient and dependable medium of electricity were widespread. The hydraulic elevators in use at the time required bulky, heavy equipment and were expensive to install and operate. The electric elevator, more compact and easier to install, made elevator service economical and practical for buildings of every size.

Otis held a near monopoly on the elevator business in the mid-1920s, at which time the company controlled about 75 percent of the elevator installations in the United States. Otis's only real competitor was Alonzo Bertram See's company, A. B. See, which specialized in medium-height elevators. See presented no real competition in buildings like the Empire State, and it would be Otis's company that would reign as the standard of the world for tall structures from the Eiffel Tower to the Empire State Building.[5]

Before skyscrapers could exist, cities had to provide essential services that included sewage and garbage disposal, and a dependable water sup-

---

[3]The Crystal Palace was a cast iron and glass structure built on today's Bryant Park. It was America's first World's Fair.

[4]If any building in New York deserves to be preserved in aspic, the Haughwout Building is it. With its skeleton of cast iron and its Otis elevator, this building is the best example of skyscrapers' roots.

[5]See's name rates as one of the greatest metaphors in corporate history, a great bit of fortuitous symbolism. Operating his products was as easy as "A. B. See."

ply; private sources had to provide gas and electricity, and, in the days of privatism, transportation.

By the 1840s, New York City had a safe and dependable water-delivery system, without which tall buildings would be sanitary nightmares as well as firetraps. New Yorkers might have wanted to take their ablutions more regularly or even to drink fresh water, but the Croton Reservoir system was specifically designed to keep fires from turning into conflagrations. The very real danger of fire and the dangers of an inadequate water-delivery system had been burned into the memory of New Yorkers after the great fire of 1835. From its ashes the Croton Reservoir, an abundance of fresh water for the city, emerged.

Electricity was replacing gas for illumination by the 1890s. Although the incandescent bulb had not yet reached the state where it rivaled sunlight, there was, nevertheless, steady artificial light produced by New York's Edison Company.

The plants producing electricity had a by-product in steam that was quickly put to use. The New York Steam Company started delivering steam via an elaborate underground distribution system to buildings for heating purposes in 1882. Steam heat obviated the need for boilers and coal bins, and liberated space for more remunerative ends. At the same time, the mess associated with deliveries was abrogated, as was the resulting smoke and soot.

By the 1890s, buildings were being erected that were safer, although some of the claims of being "fireproof" were far-fetched. The criterion for a safe building was whether a fire would spread. The contents of a contained space might be reduced to ashes, but at issue was whether the fire traveled horizontally on the same floor, or traveled vertically to other floors by leaping from window to window, by finding a perfect flue in a stairwell or airshaft, or by burning its way through.

The ironically named Asch Building on Washington Place, site of the infamous Triangle Shirtwaist fire in 1911, met the standards for a safe building when it was built in 1901. In buildings as high as 150 feet, the city permitted floors of wood instead of concrete, and wood window frames instead of metal. One hundred and forty-six people died as a result of the local law. Reformers such as State Assemblyman Alfred E. Smith (more about him later), Senator Robert F. Wagner, Sr., and Frances Perkins would later enact laws mandating fire-retardant materials, adequate fire escapes, sprinklers, and regular inspections and fire drills.

Buildings were made safer by encasing structural elements in brick or terra-cotta, and by using treated wood if not marble or tiling for hallways and public spaces. This allowed builders to erect taller buildings in good conscience. Fireproof, however, the buildings were not. "Fireproof" floorings and windows were only as good as their ability to retard heat and fire. They weren't burn-proof. They were designed to burn slowly and provide time enough for people to escape a burning building.

The basic technological know-how was coming together in the 1880s to provide the ingredients necessary for the perfection of the skyscraper. Chicago's William Le Baron Jenney is usually accorded the honors for specifying the first skyscraper. His design was the first to support the wall on a shelf angle fixed to a spandrel girder and the first to use steel in the building frame. It is clear, however, that Jenney did not invent the method. It was Leroy S. Buffington who, in 1880, inspired by Viollet-le-Duc's *Discourses on Architecture*, recognized the great problem in construction methods of the day—that steel-reinforced masonry walls still did not distribute weight evenly in taller buildings, even when the bulk of the structure was supported by a frame. His solution was a "seated wall": Masonry rested on a steel shelf that projected from each story. The weight of the walls would be borne by the lintels, or beams. The walls at the base would support only their own weight, thus eliminating heavy masonry at the base to carry the load. Buffington's walls could be as thin at the bottom as at the top, resulting in more rentable space and a more practical building.

The step from using steel for strengthening masonry to using steel to carry the masonry might not seem enormous, but, as Harvey Wiley Corbett pointed out in *The New York Times*, Buffington's step was the single most momentous discovery in the history of building since the days of Rome. Architecture was freed from the shackles of stone weight and was made flexible. Buildings could become great soaring things. Calling his building a "cloudscraper," Buffington patented his plans, and by 1883 he was ready with a design. His plans, however, came to naught. Derided as a crank and a dreamer for his "cloudscrapers," he remains a footnote to history.[6]

---

[6]Although Buffington went on to design several perfectly creditable buildings, including some at the University of Minnesota, Minnesota's old State Capitol, the Union Station in St. Paul, and the West Hotel in Minneapolis, his contribution to skyscraper design was forgotten until 1929 when Rufus Rand, the grandson of a friend of Buffington, was erecting a new building in Minneapolis. Rand said he would pay the one-eighth of 1 percent royalty on steel-skeleton buildings that the architect had been demanding in suits started more than thirty years before. The estimated $2,000 that Buffington would collect was the first recognition he had ever received for his work on skyscrapers.

The glory fell to William Le Baron Jenney. In the fall of 1883, the Home Insurance Company of New York commissioned Jenney to design a building for the company's Chicago office. Other architects had strengthened walls by building cast iron into their masonry walls as posts and by using wrought-iron floor beams, but Jenney went a long, daring step further: He bolted the beams to the columns with angle-iron brackets, thereby taking the dead load off his walls and placing it on the framework of iron concealed inside the masonry.

By the time construction of the framework for the Home Insurance Company Building had reached the sixth floor, the Carnegie-Phipps Steel Company informed Jenney that they had begun rolling Bessemer steel beams. Carnegie-Phipps said they would happily renegotiate their contract and substitute steel beams for the wrought-iron beams for the remaining floors, an offer that Jenney could not refuse. To the Home Insurance Building, built in 1885, goes the honor of being the first of all skyscrapers.

Two years later, Chicago had the fourteen-story Tacoma Building, whose outer walls were pure curtains of brick and terra-cotta that were carried at each floor by steel spandrel beams attached to cast-iron columns. These beams served a double function: The beams linked the posts, supporting the weight of the floor, but they also extended from the frame to support the weight of the windows and wall for that story, the same design Buffington had devised and the architects of the Empire State Building would use.[7] Bricklayers did not have to build from the ground up but could start midway between the sidewalk and the roof, giving passing pedestrians good cause to be startled at the spectacle they saw.

New York City had been in the vanguard of tall buildings with load-bearing walls, but the city was slow to enter the skyscraper race according to the technical definition of a skyscraper. The Tower Building, often regarded as the city's first skyscraper, is more a transitional building than a true skyscraper. Bradford Gilbert designed the Tower Building at 50 Broadway in 1888 to fulfill the demands of a developer who needed a building taller than the usual five or six stories to make a return on an expensive twenty-one-and-a-half-foot-wide plot. The walls of a conservatively designed thirteen-story building with load-bearing walls would have consumed too much potential rental space on the lower floors. Gilbert decided to support the first seven stories with cast-iron columns encased

[7]Henry H. Saylor's definition of a spandrel beam is used here.

within brick walls and linked to each other across the width of the building by wrought-iron girders, much as Jenney had done. Above the seventh
floor, however, Gilbert built a standard six-story building with load-bearing walls that rested on a set of extra-heavy girders atop the seven-story
iron framework. It was as if a traditional six-story building had been
plopped on top of a then-state-of-the-art seven-story building.

"When the actual construction of the building began," said Gilbert,
"my troubles increased tenfold. The mere suggestion of a building 21.5
feet wide, rising to the height of 160 feet above its footings, filled everybody who had no particular concern in the matter with alarm [that] the
building would blow over. . . . One Sunday morning, when the walls of the
building were ready for the roof, . . . the wind [was] blowing a hurricane.
. . . I secured a plumb-line and began to climb the ladders that the workmen had left in place when they quit work the previous evening. . . . When
I reached the thirteenth story, the gale was so fierce I could not stand upright. I crawled on my hands and knees along the scaffolding and dropped
the plumb-line. There was not the slightest vibration. The building stood
as steady as a rock in the sea. . . ."

By the 1890s, New York was catching up with Chicago, and true skyscrapers were being erected. The city had the twenty-four-story St. Paul
Building on Broadway at Fulton Street, and the twenty-six-story American Surety Building at 100 Broadway (the Bank of Tokyo Building in
1995, and still standing). By the end of the 1890s, New York City had the
tallest skyscraper in the world, the now largely ignored Park Row Building at 15 Park Row—a 29-story building, 390 feet high, housing over
14,000 workers on a 15,000-square-foot plot of land.

From the first, skyscrapers were erected as speculative ventures by real
estate developers or as offices by corporations, which frequently occupied
some of the space for their own purposes and rented out the rest. The
flagship corporate skyscrapers—the Singer and Metropolitan Life Towers and the Woolworth Building, for instance—were usually designed
with more panache than speculatively built ventures, and a few speech-
makers might have gone slightly overboard in their praise for them. Met
Life stockholders were told in 1915 that "you and your directors were well
advised in the choice of your symbol. For a tower, with its light and its bel-
fry, has always been a source of inspiration. . . . Thus your Tower partakes
of the character of the ancient towers of refuge and defense. . . . Your high
tower should, therefore, be a symbol of God to you and others, standing
out boldly and erect as a plea for righteousness and purity in business corporations, and as a monumental protest against the exploitation of the

poor." The president of Met Life regarded the tower as a different kind of godsend. He said "the tenants footed the bill."

The financial return on a skyscraper could be extraordinarily rewarding, but sites were expensive to acquire, and construction costs were comparably high. In the early twentieth century, structural steel cost about $50 a ton at the mills and another $25 a ton to install. The average fifteen-story skyscraper on a fifty-by-one-hundred-foot plot required about a thousand tons of steel, four thousand barrels of cement, and 1.25 million bricks. The construction of the biggest buildings required as many as fourteen hundred workers. Besides the architect, who was responsible over all, there were engineers for weights, wind pressures, and superstructures, for brickwork, terra-cotta, plumbing, and elevators. Financiers often had to be called in to help, syndicates were frequently formed, mortgages were taken, and securities were sold.

Not all office buildings were skyscrapers, of course. The run-of-the-mill office buildings in the 1890s were not much higher than six or eight stories. A building on a good-sized plot was ordinarily a squarish dough-nutlike building in plan with a courtyard in the hole. Corridors ringed the court; surrounding the corridors and extending about twenty-five feet front and back was office space. With an increase in land value, buildings started to be built deeper, and courts were made smaller; offices started being built overlooking the courts, and corridors were moved to the interior. The plan increased the amount of office space, but it was second-class office space. Compounding the problem, if the building went too high, the court became a wind tunnel.

To avoid the problems associated with interior courts, exterior courts were developed by the 1890s by removing the part of the building facing the street. The majority of offices in a U-shaped plan looked out on the open-ended court and offered at least some view of the street. The U plan, with its variations such as the H plan that was used in the Equitable Building at 120 Broadway and tilted at 90 degrees to present a flat façade to the street in the Park Row Building, was less wasteful of corridor space and at the same time moderated the whirlwind effect.

With the arrival of freestanding towers such as the Singer Tower and the Woolworth Building and the later tower buildings erected under the 1916 zoning law, the whirlwind effect was cured. The major advantage to the city was that towers cast smaller shadows on the streets below, and provided better light and air to the tenants.

An efficient and healthful work space requires light, and with the development of the steel-framed building, windows of any size and frequency could be installed without weakening the walls. Windows could be enlarged to the point where walls as they were known could be declared redundant—they could consist entirely of glass. Before the advent of air-conditioning, however, windows had to open.

Bay windows that jutted out were popular in the 1890s. They had double-hung sashes on each slanting face, welcoming the sunshine and breezes from different directions. But they also created problems. Bay windows required special steel framing that projected from the frame of the building, which increased the cost. They also produced irregularly shaped interior spaces that were awkward to use, and difficult to rent.

The Chicago window, as Louis Sullivan installed at the Carson, Pirie, Scott Store, consisted of a central, immobile horizontal window flanked by narrow, vertical windows that opened. This configuration reflected the skeleton of the building and provided a large expanse of glass with a means of ventilation.[8] But there were drawbacks with the Chicago window too. The bay was frequently so big that the space behind could not be used advantageously for offices, and replacements for the central panes frequently required a derrick to hoist them into place, an expensive operation.

The window that proved enduring was the standard double-hung window in any multiple of sets. Windows were ordinarily separated vertically from the ones above and below by brick, terra-cotta, or stone spandrels the width of the windows, and they were separated horizontally by the same facing material or by other materials that served as a foil. This configuration, with variations on its theme, remained the standard for the first half of the twentieth century, and is found in the Empire State Building.

Just as the configuration for windows in skyscrapers was fairly well established by the turn of the century, so was the design of office buildings. Again, the honor goes to a Chicagoan for laying down the law. Owen F. Aldis, a Yale-educated lawyer, arrived in Chicago in 1875. Within twenty-five years, said Earle Shultz and Walter Simmons in their book *Offices in the Sky*, Aldis had built and was managing almost one-fifth of Chicago's office space. His fundamentals of office-building design became a primer for office planning, as pertinent at the turn of the century as it would be thirty years later when the Empire State Building was designed.

---

[8]The Chicago window was elegantly updated by Skidmore, Owings & Merrill in the Marine Midland Building in 1967.

Among his tenets:

- Build no deep spaces, only shallow ones. Ill-lit spaces are second-
class space; they cost as much to build and operate as first-class
space, but the returns are smaller. The office building that gives
up the most for light and air is the best investment.
- Make no interior space permanent. Build interior space that can
be easily modified, and lay it out for intensive use. A large number of tenants occupying small spaces is far more desirable than
a few tenants occupying large spaces. Smaller offices can command a higher rate, and if one tenant moves, the owner is not
stuck with a large vacant space.
- Build only first-class public space for public areas. To simplify
maintenance, use only proper materials and details. Operating
expenses can make the difference between success and failure,
and the upkeep of an office building is as important as its construction.

Many New York builders in the first decade of the twentieth century
ignored some of Aldis's more commonsensical rules. The pace of new construction in Lower Manhattan at the time was hectic, and buildings were
being thrown together without much thought beyond a fast return on the
dollar. In the spring of 1906 alone, plans were consummated for the construction of fifteen tall office buildings, adding about 2.5 million square
feet to the real estate market.

This spirit of tearing down and building had been abroad in the land
as long before as the mid–nineteenth century, as Mayor Philip Hone
noted in his diary, but by the beginning of the twentieth century the face
of the city was changing at such a rapid pace that architectural critic
Montgomery Schuyler said that the visitor who remained out of town—
or even uptown—for a single year found downtown transformed in that
brief interval and threatening still stranger transformations.

By 1913, the city had set three more records for building heights. In
1908, the Singer Building, at 41 stories, or 612 feet, was built on Broadway between Liberty and Cortlandt Streets. A year later, the Metropolitan Life Tower, at 52 stories, or 700 feet, was built on Madison Avenue at
Twenty-fourth Street. Then, in 1913, the Woolworth Building, on Broadway between Barclay Street and Park Place, was built. The Woolworth
Building was 55 stories, or 787 feet high, and it would be the reigning
champion until the great building boom of the 1920s and the appearance
of the 1,048-foot-high Chrysler Building.

It wasn't just the size of skyscrapers that attracted attention; it was also their number. Drawing an arbitrary height of ten floors as qualification for skyscraperdom, by 1925 New York City had 1,686 skyscrapers. By 1929, it had 2,479. One hundred eighty-eight of them were twenty-one or more stories high.[9]

The Underwriters Laboratories in Chicago, a child of the National Board of Fire Underwriters, regularly tested products so that architects and builders could obtain information on just about every material or item of equipment that might be specified for these buildings. In the 1920s, the labs were the scene of conflagrations, boiler-room accidents, and tank explosions, all of which took place in a "bombproof, shockproof" building. To simulate the intensity of a building fire, the labs might shoot gas flames at a steel door until the temperature of the door reached 1,700 degrees, and the door was red-hot. A fire hose would then play on it with full pressure at close range. Every inch of the door would feel the force and shock of the water, and after it had let out a scream of hissing steam and groaning steel, the buckled steel would slowly return to something resembling its original shape, though hardly its appearance. Building columns would likewise be tested, but because they have to stand weight and heat together, hydraulic jacks would push them while the flames played on them.

In construction, small units were beginning to be replaced by large units by the late 1920s. Sheets of aluminum were being used for finished brick, large wallboards for plaster, light hollow plaster blocks for brick or tile, and reinforced concrete in great slabs for terra-cotta blocks. The skyscrapers of 1930 bore no resemblance to the skyscrapers of only a few years before, and the skyscrapers of only a few years in the future were not expected to bear any resemblance to the skyscrapers of 1930.

Through the 1920s, wide piers at the corners of buildings had usually been used to give the appearance of solidity. This stylistic hangover from presteel construction meant that the best space in a building—the corner office with expansive views—was compromised. By 1931, Starrett & Van Vleck had designed 21 West Street, where they eliminated corner piers completely, the result of some elementary deductive reasoning: In a steel-framed building where columns extend to the corners, the corner columns

---

[9]According to a survey taken by the Thompson-Starrett Company in 1929, six cities reported more than one hundred buildings ten or more stories high: New York, with 2,479; Chicago, with 449; Los Angeles, with 135; Detroit, with 121; Philadelphia, with 120; and Boston, with 104. Philadelphia had 22 buildings 21 or more stories in height, Chicago had 65, and New York had 188.

support a quarter as much weight as the interior columns.[10] You can eliminate the corner columns and cantilever the beams, which, in the case of 21 West Street, permitted the maximum utilization of the corner space, while at the same time making it "probably the first commercial building in America to be so designed," as *Architectural Forum* described it. The extent to which steel had liberated architecture from the burdens of past building techniques was not limited to skyscrapers. By the 1920s, it was the accepted method of construction in practically every type of structure, even in buildings as small as taxpayers—walls could be made thinner without sacrificing strength, and it was estimated that construction could go forward faster and at half the price of more traditional techniques.

Once the technical questions of skyscraper construction had been answered, the question of height arose. Frank Lloyd Wright might have said a mile, but a quarter of that was about as high as anyone could imagine in any reality in the 1920s, and elevators were one of the reasons.

A building two hundred stories high, for instance, would require elevators to travel at a speed exceeding 1,500 feet per minute to attain any efficiency, and nobody was certain whether the human eardrum could withstand the vibration in an elevator cab traveling at that speed, not to mention the pressure on knees. If the rate of acceleration upward is too great, knees will buckle as gravity's pull abruptly increases the weight. The elevators in the World Trade Tower that rise to the observation deck, 1,350 feet up, average about 900 feet per minute. They make the trip in ninety seconds. The elevators in the Empire State Building attain a speed of 1,200 feet per minute.

Elevators are space intensive. In a traditional skyscraper, where all elevators start at the lobby floor, the elevator banks occupy the lion's share of the lower floors, and valuable space is sacrificed that could otherwise be rented. The higher a tower goes, the more space is sacrificed, to the point where too high a tower runs the risk of profligacy.

Success in renting depends upon direct elevator service. If a series of transfers is required, the top floors become too inconvenient, hence of little value. William F. Lamb, one of the architects of the Empire State Building, said in 1928 that a number of ingenious elevator arrangements had already been designed to free the skyscraper of its limitations, but that the most radical ideas had not been put into operation, in part because they had not yet been fully tested. A possible solution was a shuttle elevator service that was considered in the proposed 110-story Larkin

---

[10]The Starrett in the firm of Starrett & Van Vleck was Goldwin Starrett, a brother of the two Starrett brothers who built the Empire State Building.

Tower, an idea later borrowed in the Empire State Building and perfected in the World Trade Towers. The distance an elevator can travel is limited by the length of the cable. If the cable is too long, it will become so heavy it can't support its own weight, and it will snap. Two of the elevators in the Larkin Tower would have traveled nonstop to the eighty-second floor, where shuttle cabs would have continued to the top floor. By a repetition of such a system, any desired height could theoretically be reached.

Plans for running two elevator cars—a local and an express—in the same shaft were being developed by Otis engineers in 1929. The express car would serve the upper floors, and would make no stops until it was well above the portion of the building served by the lower car, which would operate local and go only partway up the shaft. The two would never meet. They would take on and discharge passengers on two separate floors at the bottom. Another plan provided express elevators, like express subway trains, stopping, for example, at every tenth floor, with local elevators operating in shafts parallel to them.

Architects Dan Everett Waid and Harvey Wiley Corbett maintained that escalators had proved to be the most efficient vertical transportation system within a 150-foot height. Escalators substituted continuous flow for the intermittent method used for elevators. Waid & Corbett's plan for the hundred-story tower proposed in 1929 by Metropolitan Life for a site on Madison Square was to have escalators provide local service for the first thirteen floors, with express elevator service from the main floor to the thirteenth, where full service would begin.

Some architects and engineers were not sure that these ideas were realistic solutions. As far as Lamb was concerned, the elevator was the primary factor inhibiting skyscrapers from soaring to new heights, and until the problem was solved, further height, he believed, was out of the question.

Another obstacle to skyscraper construction in New York City was the conservative building code. In effect since the turn of the century, the code required buildings taller than 150 feet to resist wind pressure of 30 pounds per square foot. According to the United States Bureau of Standards, in order to exert pressure of 22 pounds a square foot, the wind must blow steadily at 76 miles per hour. It is rare enough that winds reach hurricane force, and when they do, winds come in gusts, seldom exerting the pressure for any length of time.

The steel framework of the 1920s had a greater elasticity by far than any other form of construction, yielding and bending to a relatively high degree without injury. The framework vibrated to the wind, and may have actually varied from the exact perpendicular under high wind stresses.

The vibration was no indication of weakness, but was a normal action by which the building adjusted itself to unusual conditions. The structural steel framework acts as a unit, with every subset being connected to the whole and assisting it. Together they work in harmony to distribute the strains and to resist them. The rigidity of the heavy steel beams and girders affords great, and, in some cases, excessive resistance to actual wind stresses. Add to the strength of the structural steel the immense stiffening provided by the walls, partitions, and floors, to say nothing of the thousands of tons of the building's contents, and there is an enormous inertia that has to be overcome before the structure can be harmed by wind.

If a building is unlikely to be blown over, the basic question of how high it can rise depends on how much the steel frame, with all its tensile strength, can in fact bear. Builder Colonel William A. Starrett said in 1929 that with sufficient ground area and the freedom to use as many columns as necessary, buildings 150 stories high, even two hundred stories high, could be seriously discussed. Other, less-bullish builders maintained that you could stretch the envelope only so far. A one-hundred-story skyscraper—roughly twelve hundred feet high—was feasible with the available materials and methods. After the last usable story was reached it was always possible to erect a peaked roof, tower, minaret, dome, even a spire, as would be seen in the Chrysler Building. It could be anything decorative, but nothing functional.

It was economic factors, not engineering possibilities, that limited the skyscraper's height in the late twenties. To secure the necessary rigidity in a very tall building, more and more steel and heavier and heavier construction are required. Furthermore, the amount of steel and the heavy construction required increases at a greater rate than the height. The distance from floor to floor has to be increased in order to get headroom under the necessary heavy cross girders. Braces have to be placed at all column heads. The owner soon finds that a height is reached beyond which it does not pay to build, regardless of how much rent he might get for his space. Taller skyscrapers would simply become masses of steel, with most of the space inside dedicated to the necessary girders, pillars, and bracing. Elevators would require practically all the rest of the space for their structure and machinery. At that point, the development of the skyscraper was confronted with the obstacle that stopped the upward growth of the purely masonry building: The volume of rentable space on the lower floors becomes diminished to the point of being negligible, the very problem that the skyscraper was thought to have solved.

A developer can consider a shorter, squatter building instead of a tall building, but it requires an arithmetical juggling act to determine the worth of the project. Buildings filling large plots are inefficient in terms of light, but not in terms of construction. Exterior walls are among the costliest elements of any major structure. The larger the area of a building's floor, the less exterior wall is required to enclose it. If a plan is 50 feet square, it contains 2,500 square feet of space, and its exterior wall is four times 50, or 200 linear feet. There are 12.5 square feet for every foot of wall. But if the floor is 100 feet square, it contains 10,000 square feet of space, and the exterior wall is 400 linear feet, or 25 square feet for every foot of wall. The 100-foot-square building takes only half as much exterior wall per square foot of rentable area as the 50-foot-square building.

One of the ironies of skyscrapers is that because they are efficient and increase the value of the site upon which they are built, they tend to sow the seeds of their own destruction. If a ten-story building can generate profits, then, theoretically, a building twice as high should generate twice as much, a building three times as high, three times as much, and so on until the mind boggles at the opportunities for profit. The untimely tearing down of perfectly good buildings became a regular twentieth-century phenomenon. A dramatic example took place in 1903 at Times Square. In order to make way for the coming of the twenty-seven-story Times Tower, the eight-story, steel-framed Pabst Hotel, which had only been standing since 1898, was torn down. Wreckers were familiar with tearing down structures with load-bearing walls, but here was a first—the demolition of a true skyscraper. At first blush, the George A. Fuller construction firm believed that the building could be taken apart and its parts numbered, then reerected elsewhere. The idea, it turned out, was impractical. Both the idea and the building were scrapped.

In the 1920s, the site at 1 Wall Street was about to have its third building in as many decades, with each successive building progressively bigger. And the $2 million, twelve-story Pictorial Review Building, erected at 530 Seventh Avenue on the southwest corner of Thirty-ninth Street in 1919, was demolished only nine years later to make way for the thirty-story Adler Building. The cost of the Pictorial Review Building was simply written off because the building no longer used its site with the efficiency demanded. Built for the printing crafts, it found itself within the decade in the midst of the Garment District. Its dozen stories, designed for presses and other heavy machinery, was about the same height as the average sixteen-story Garment District building. For a building with twenty-foot-high ceilings to flourish in a neighborhood where twelve-foot-high ceilings were adequate was unrealistic.

There was nothing economically unsound in demolishing relatively new buildings in favorable locations to make way for larger, more up-to-date buildings. Developer Abraham E. Lefcourt, who *The Times* said was "making canyon country out of midtown and downtown Manhattan," maintained that no building, regardless of its dimensions, could hope to survive if it failed to justify its existence from an economic standpoint. Architectural splendor and original cost mean little or nothing if the building fails to afford a profitable return on the investment required to carry it. Buildings were built not for posterity but for investment; when they outlived their utility, they were replaced. As architectural historian John Gloag described the phenomenon, "office blocks have an economic life, calculated by actuaries; so much floor space, so much rent, so many years of earning power as premises, and then demolition."

This constant tearing down and building up, this reinvention of the city every generation, was the single greatest hallmark of modern society to spring up with the coming of the Industrial Revolution. Before then, major buildings, at least, had been built for posterity, and permanence in buildings had been taken for granted. Suddenly, as Karl Marx discovered, all that was solid was melting into air.[11]

The phenomenon appalled engineers, who in the 1920s were learning that fifty-year-old buildings with adequately protected iron frames and supports were perfectly sound. Buildings built in the first throes of skyscrapers in the 1890s were even sounder. The life expectancy for the average skyscraper was at least seventy-five years. When the Gillender Building at the northwest corner of Wall and Nassau Streets was razed in 1910, its steel beams, which had been encased in concrete or cement, were entirely free of rust, the same phenomenon the wreckers discovered in Stanford White's Madison Square Garden. These early steel-framed buildings were already metallurgically sound. The designers had taken reasonable precautions against moisture, and the buildings were structurally as good the day they were torn down as the day they were built.[12] With prudent management, engineers say, a skyscraper could theoretically stand forever.

But engineers were not developers. Although the life span of the mod-

---

[11]This phenomenon is part of the modernism that Marshall Berman investigates in *All That Is Solid Melts into Air*. Berman notes that in the mid-nineteenth century, Friedrich Engels was "appalled to find that workers' housing, built by speculators for fast profits, was constructed to last for only forty years. He little suspected that this would become the archetypal pattern of construction in bourgeois society."

[12]This destructive bent was hardly unique to New York. Chicago's fourteen-story Tacoma Building, which had introduced the riveted skeleton and had been a showplace during the Columbia Exposition in 1893, was demolished in 1929 to make way for a skyscraper of forty-nine stories.

ern building was many times longer than its estimated utility, developers acted only upon economics. The average speculator would replace a twelve-story building with a thirty- or forty-story building because he would get a better return on the value of his property. But the same return on investment that influenced the speculator was wasted on corporate builders such as Singer, Metropolitan Life, and Woolworth, who were in the race for the "world's tallest" laurels.

Frank W. Woolworth publicly proclaimed that he was only interested in real estate as an investment. Privately, however, it was a different matter. Louis J. Horowitz, who headed the contracting firm on the Woolworth job, tried to convince Woolworth that the project was not fiscally sound, that by every test of economics the venture was a poor investment. The corporate headquarters needed only a few floors, and the rest was one big speculative gamble that was probably not worth taking. Woolworth told Horowitz that he had something up his sleeve: The intangible profits in publicity and brand-name recognition that his firm would receive for erecting the world's tallest building far outweighed any real losses he might suffer from the venture. Woolworth realized that all successful entrants in the biggest or highest of something, from the time when pharaoh vied with pharaoh and matched tomb against tomb, were essentially in the same race and reaped the same benefits. The day after the world's tallest building opened in 1913, Woolworth knew, practically every newspaper in the world would cover the story. The building would be pointed out to every tourist visiting the city, it would be written up in every guidebook to the city, and entered in every almanac and encyclopedia. Whatever the medium, the corporate name would be forever attached to the building.

The world's tallest building would serve as a giant billboard for its corporate sponsor, publicizing, in Woolworth's case, his chain of five-and-ten-cent stores that was spreading around the world. The original cost and maintenance could be fairly written off on the advertising budget. On that basis alone, a corporate name on a record-holding building was a sound investment as a corporate undertaking. Whether it is a sound investment as a purely speculative venture is another question.

The average New Yorker liked skyscrapers, regardless. He did not care if they were essentially huge billboards, nor how overcrowded, dark, and noisy the city was becoming as a result of them. He was not terribly concerned about working by artificial light instead of natural light, even whether he was breathing dust and gas instead of clean air. New Yorkers took a perverse pride in the very structures that were so largely responsible for those conditions.

By the 1920s, the skyline had replaced the Statue of Liberty as the symbol of the city. New Yorkers pointed to the skyline as their pride and joy, and they smiled with satisfaction as visitors related the excitement at witnessing the view of this forest of skyscrapers as their ship sailed into the harbor and up the Hudson River, or as they caught glimpses of it from outlying areas. No other city had such a skyline, and no other citizen could puff up his chest the same way a New Yorker could. H. G. Wells described the New York skyline as "the strangest crown that ever a city wore," and architect William F. Lamb, one of the architects of the Empire State Building, declared that "New York's beauty lies in the amazing grouping of its towers."

Journalist Clair Price, an expatriate of twenty years, returned to New York in 1941 to find the city changed in many ways, but the drama of the skyline as he sailed into the harbor remained the same. "The skyline of Manhattan soars into view, its towers and citadels shooting skyward in anarchic and bewildering profusion, overwhelming in their sense of power and their gargantuan beauty, looking more than ever like some unearthly fantasia out of a fairy tale. It is the one urban view in all of the world which sings at a journey's end like a public triumph."

With the coming of the Empire State Building, the biggest and arguably the best of all the skyscrapers, the vision of the towers of New York would be synthesized in one glistening tower. New Yorkers would walk a little taller.

# 3

# ZONING THE CITY

**U**ntil the end of the nineteenth century, man had lived and worked close to the ground. Only in his temples of worship did he lift domes and spires to dizzying heights in the skies. By the turn of the twentieth century, all that changed. Engineering and architecture teamed up to make skyscrapers so practicable, so feasible that they were popping up like mushrooms on a damp forest floor. Suddenly, working ten or twenty stories up in the air was not such an exceptional thing.

There is the movie myth that if you build a baseball field, the players will come. The truth is that if you build a skyscraper, workers will come if the economy is healthy, and New York City at the turn of the twentieth century was experiencing one of its periodic booms. The city was so expansive that by 1902 Manhattan already counted 181 buildings that were ten to nineteen stories high and three that were taller than twenty stories, and workers were coming by the drove.

City planners had given little thought to the far-reaching effect of skyscrapers, and were caught off-guard. The new city was just breaking out of its "brownstone shell," as architect Grosvenor Atterbury described it, and few planners or architects foresaw the kind of monster this hatching would produce. Until the arrival of the skyscraper, city planners had dealt in only two dimensions. With the skyscraper, their work became three dimensional, and problems multiplied exponentially.

Streets that had once been bathed in midday sun were becoming dark and narrow canyons, and the Financial District came to be described as the "canyons of Wall Street." It might be a cliché today, but it would not be a cliché unless the truth of the phrase had stood the test of time. The canyons appeared, canyons where sunlight seldom reached the sidewalks below, canyons that rose straight up for two hundred, three hundred feet or more, canyons created not by erosion but by economics.

At the foot of the canyons, Manhattan's streets were filled to bursting. Elevated railroads operating in part or in whole along Second, Third, Sixth, and Ninth Avenues complemented streetcars and horse trolleys serving major avenues and primary crosstown streets at the turn of the century. Beginning in 1904, a subway operated on the East Side from City Hall to Grand Central Station, where it zigged west along Forty-second Street to Times Square, then zagged north along Broadway on the West Side to 145th Street. These rapid-transit lines were dumping tens of thousands of riders onto the narrow streets and sidewalks of Lower Manhattan every workday morning.

The streets of Lower Manhattan that served the ever-increasing population working in skyscrapers had been laid out in the seventeenth century. The streets had adequately served the needs of a small city perched on the edge of a wilderness, but as streets designed to serve a twentieth-century city bent on erecting skyscrapers ever greater in number and scale, they were inadequate at best. At worst, the streets had the potential of strangling the city, and skyscrapers were the cause.

The "new" streets that appeared north of First Street as a result of the city street plan of 1811 might present a certain Cartesian regularity, but they were almost as useless as the city's earliest streets in terms of easing the plight of future growth. The plan did not call for a city of broad boulevards and wide vistas. New York was a commercial city, not a capital city. Its official street plan had rectangular blocks and straight streets that intersected each other at right angles. The street commissioners agreed with developers—the street plan, they said, should reflect the most economical way to build houses, and that meant straight-sided and right-angled. They saw the gridiron plan as the only solution.

The street commissioners intentionally made east-west streets more numerous than north-south avenues. The average block fronting on an avenue is two hundred feet long, whereas the blocks separating the avenues can be as long as 920 feet. The reason for the greater number of crosstown streets than up- and downtown avenues was self-evident to planners of the early nineteenth century but might not be so obvious to us today—intra-Manhattan commerce flowed east and west. In the days before railroads, dirigibles, and airplanes, the preeminent form of long-distance transportation and hauling was by water, and the piers and wharves along the East River had to link up with those along the Hudson if commerce was to flourish. Crosstown streets were designed to provide the way. The average crosstown streets were sixty feet wide, and major crosstown streets such as Thirty-fourth Street were one hundred feet wide; avenues, including Fifth Avenue, were also one hundred feet wide.[1]

By mid-century the ebb and flow of traffic was already on a north-south axis. The streets were often riotous affairs, with horse-drawn delivery wagons and omnibuses fighting each other over turf, with the problem becoming so exacerbated by the beginning of the twentieth century that the city experienced nascent forms of gridlock. There were simply not enough avenues to handle the traffic, nor were they wide enough. Nevertheless, the buildings continued to pile up.

Renaissance designers such as Leonardo da Vinci and Christopher Wren, imperial designers such as Baron Haussmann, and federal planners such as Major Pierre L'Enfant all knew better than to allow overbuilding. They realized that the height of a building should be regulated according to the width of the street on which it was erected. A building as high as the width of the street was desirable; one and a half times the street width was acceptable for major buildings placed judiciously, especially to provide scale and a sense of perspective; buildings twice the height of the width of the street, however, were to be avoided, and to consider such a scale as the norm for block after block was anathema. In addition to blocking light to the streets on which the buildings front, the bulk of large buildings causes physical discomfort for the beholder. Buildings can be most comfortably viewed at an angle no greater than 30 degrees. Buildings much over six stories are out of scale on most hundred-foot-wide streets. To see above the sixth floor from the perspective of the average avenue in Manhattan requires you to crane your neck. Skyscrapers are not much fun to look at up close. The only comfortable way to view them is from a distance.

Long shadows cast by skyscrapers create another problem. The longest

---

[1]Lexington and Madison Avenues were afterthoughts; they are seventy-five feet wide south of Forty-second Street.

shadow cast by a building is measured at 3 P.M. on the winter solstice, December 21.[2] At that time, the shadow is 4.4 times the height of the building on the latitude of New York City. The shadow cast by a building as high as the 1,250-foot-high Empire State Building is longer than a mile.

Light on the streets as well as within offices was an issue that ultimately proved more important economically than the utilization of every square foot of real estate. Although the city passed a law in 1885 regulating the height of residences to seventy feet on streets as wide as sixty feet, and to eighty feet on streets sixty feet or wider,[3] there was no law governing the height of commercial buildings. It wasn't until commercial buildings began to encroach upon one another's light and air that the idea of limiting the height of all buildings, commercial and residential alike, began to take root. It was an uphill battle in the days of laissez-faire, when many entrepreneurs regarded legislation that limited the bulk or height of buildings as a usurpation of private property. Reformers feared that only under a dictator or the imperial authority of a Napoleon III could buildings be made to conform to a standard height.

By the early twentieth century, however, the movement to limit the height of buildings gathered momentum, and not just in New York City. By the teens, Houston had limited buildings in business districts to 125 feet, and those in residential districts, to 80 feet. Baltimore restricted buildings to 175 feet, Portland and Denver, to 12 stories, or about 150 feet, and Los Angeles, with the exception of its public buildings, likewise restricted buildings to 150 feet.

By 1908, a municipal building commission in New York City urged a limit on the bulk of buildings in proportion to the size of the lot, which they felt was more important than limiting the height of buildings. The principle was that a building's size should not exceed in volume a certain number of times the area of the lot. The plan was comparable to giving each owner of the same-sized lot the same set of blocks and saying that he could build as much of a building on that plot as his set would allow. Some owners might want a building that covered the lot as solidly as the city's regulations for light courts would permit; others might set one block on top of another, making a tower as many blocks high as there were blocks in the set.

---

[2]The hour is not arrived at arbitrarily by the Zoning and Urban Design Division of the City Planning Department—at precisely sunrise or sunset, all buildings, whatever their height, cast infinite shadows.

[3]The law was later modified to allow residential buildings to rise to one and a half times the width of the street they faced.

A tall building should be set in the center of the plot, with space between the tall building and the building line to assure sufficient light and
air for the building's occupants and its neighbors, according to the commission.[4] If a builder erected a tall building on the adjoining plot, he
would have to do the same thing. The tenement-house law said that tenement houses that filled an entire block front were required to have a
twelve-foot break through the middle of the block to ensure light and air;
skyscrapers appropriated larger slices of the real estate pie than tenements, and should be made to adhere to the same minimum standards.

Architect Ernest Flagg, the designer of the now-demolished Singer
Tower on Broadway at Liberty Street, recognized that New York land values were becoming ever more fixed on the basis of high buildings. Flagg
argued that setting an artificially low limit on height would not only reduce the available area of floor space for the future—interfering with the
city's growth—it would also bring about a potential shrinkage of values.
It would discriminate unjustly against property owners who had not fully
developed their site's potential in favor of those who had. He maintained
that a developer should not be allowed to construct a building taller than
one and a half times the width of the street it faced. But, he said, the developer should be allowed to build a tower as high as he wanted on 25 percent of the plot, with no limit, provided the tower was set back from the
building line and all sides treated architecturally. Neighboring property
owners could sell their rights to adjoining towers, so natural light and air
were protected or compensated. As a bonus, said Flagg, "our street
façade would assume the appearance of order and sobriety which comes
of a uniform height and a continuous cornice line" with setbacks that
were one and a half times the width of the street.

Flagg pointed with pride to his design for the Singer Tower. Despite its
enormous height, he maintained that it did not usurp the rights of others. "The high part of the building occupies only about one-sixth of the
area of the plot on which it stands," he said. "It depends on its own land
for its light. It casts a shadow, to be sure, but it seriously interferes with
the light of no surrounding property. It presents a finished face to all
points of view. It adds to the picturesqueness of the skyline of the city, and
its bulk rises well back of the street façade." In short, the Singer Building did all the things that Flagg believed a skyscraper should do, and it
set the standard around which the city should rally. "It is certain," said
Flagg, "that the city cannot be built up solidly with high buildings of the
kind we now have unless we are to live in darkness."

[4]The building line defines the lot; a building may not project beyond it.

City agencies supported Flagg's idea. The health department was fearful that the city's health was suffering because of the loss of bacteria-killing sunlight in high buildings on narrow streets, fearful too that epidemics could spread because of overcrowding. The fire department had been arguing that the capacity of sidewalks was a critical factor in relation to tall buildings. Sidewalks, they maintained, should be able to hold all, or a large percentage, of the occupants of a building in an emergency. The fire department was worried that hundreds might be killed in a panic in the streets if the occupants of vacated buildings stampeded in an emergency. Some planners advised that if a sidewalk in front of a building could accommodate no more than two hundred people, then the building should house no more than two hundred people. Period. Nothing came of this plan, and by the mid-1920s, a former fire commissioner said that if all the buildings south of Chambers Street were emptied at once, the people on the streets would pile up five deep, one above the other, from wall to wall.

While discussions on limiting the height and bulk of buildings continued, ever bigger, ever bulkier buildings continued to be built. The building that finally forced the city's hand was the Equitable Building at 120 Broadway, which relentlessly rose up forty-two stories without a setback and blocked the sun from the streets below. In its shadow the city finally drew up a zoning law.

The zoning law of 1916—the nation's first—regulated the bulk of buildings, their height, and their uses. It divided the city into three zones—residential, business, and unrestricted—and empowered the Board of Estimate to regulate the use, height, and bulk of every building on every street in the city, depending on the zone the block was in.

Before 1916, almost any block in the city could have had a glue factory built next door to a private home, a stable next to a church, a gin mill next to a school. If the concomitant noise, smoke, fumes, heavy trucking, and general ambiance blighted the surrounding area, there wasn't much that anybody could, or would, do about it. Those professionally concerned with the city, from planners to realtors, had been urging the city to pass a law aimed at stabilizing values and preserving certain sections from objectionable intrusions. The history of the city showed one good residential neighborhood after another falling victim to industrial and commercial encroachments, which led many displaced home-owners to leave the city entirely. As far as they were concerned, the city had abdicated its responsibility by not properly protecting their home, the object that represented the major investment both financially and psychologically for the average home-owner. The zoning law would rationalize land use and might stem the flow of those fleeing the city.

The zoning law would halt residential districts from being inundated by factories and businesses, and it would check the invasion of retail districts by factories. Homes, schools, and churches would be on residential streets, offices and stores on business streets, and factories would be in manufacturing areas. It would prevent an increase in the congestion of streets, and temper growth where the population was already too great for the sidewalks and transit facilities.

Residential zones were set aside to be exclusively residential, with a mix of institutions such as churches, libraries, and schools—the very essences of neighborhoods—permitted within the districts. Some residential strips were zoned for commercial uses, which we might call mixed-use zones today. By allowing a mix of retailing and service industries in residential areas, residents could attend to the necessities of life within specified areas of the neighborhood. Since people prefer to live in residential areas and do their marketing on streets with many stores to choose from, this requirement made business streets more attractive and commercial rentals better because the street was devoted to business at the street level. It made residential streets more attractive because there were no encroachments.

Business zones could incorporate residential areas within their borders, but the goal was to keep out industry and heavy manufacturing and to allow white-collar trades and major retail establishments to congregate in specific areas. Recognizing that the tailor needs his workshop, the jeweler his ring setters, and the dry goods store its milliners, the zoning law allowed one-quarter of the floor space in business districts to be used for light industry, providing it was inoffensive.

Unrestricted zones included any kind of commercial or industrial undertaking, inoffensive or otherwise. They were not zoned for residences.

Designations were not ironclad. The commission recognized that a healthy city is not preserved in aspic. It is more like a healthy organism, where old cells die and new ones are created to take their place. To allow for change, the law provided that 20 percent of the property owners within a district could appeal to the Board of Estimate to change the character of a block or a larger area.

For builders of all types of buildings, commercial or residential, the law affected the city's skyline more than anything for the next fifty years: Buildings could start at the building line, but once they reached a certain height they could only continue upward provided they were set back from the line. On 25 percent of the plot, buildings could rise as high as technology and the will of the developer were willing and able to take them.

The law further divided the city into zones that allowed buildings to rise a different multiple of the width of the street before requiring a setback. In areas zoned for the most intensive use, such as the Financial District and Lower Broadway, buildings could rise straight up from the building line two and a half times the width of the street before a setback was required. Midtown was less intensively zoned, with buildings being allowed to rise one and a half or twice the width of the street before setbacks were required. In some specially zoned retail districts buildings could rise only one and a quarter times the street width, but in most of Manhattan buildings could rise one and a half times the width of the street.

The formula for setbacks was to double in feet the height to which the building could rise for every foot the building was set back. In the one-time district, the building could rise two feet for every one foot the building was set back; in the one-and-a-half-times district, the building could rise three feet for every one foot it was set back, and so on.

The setback law essentially required an architect to draw the hypotenuse of a right triangle from across the street to the perpendicular of his building. So each designated zone had a predetermined angle of the hypotenuse, with the width of the street the building faced factored in to the calculation. At the height of the building where the hypotenuse hit, a setback was required. Further setbacks were required every time the hypotenuse hit the building, essentially creating a stair-step effect. The setbacks could stop at any time to allow a freestanding tower occupying 25 percent of the plot.

With a two-hundred-foot frontage facing a hundred-foot-wide avenue, a developer in a two-time zone could theoretically build a tower-free ninety-six-story building. Beginning on the twentieth floor there would be a five-foot setback ringing the building every twenty feet up, a pattern that would continue nineteen times, until the building was ten feet wide at the top. At that size, the floors would have been reduced to such playhouse dimensions that no developer would regard the space as practical except for an ornamental tower or flagpole. The building would also look like a pyramid, or a dunce cap, depending on your perspective.

The idea of freestanding towers on 25 percent of the property overcame the problem of having every building above a certain height terminate in a series of diminishing boxes that looked like every other. At the same time, it blunted criticism over the usurpation of private property. There were two provisos in addition to having the tower limited to 25 percent of the site: The tower had to be architecturally treated on all four walls, which meant no blank walls typical of the kind you find in the rear of buildings, and the tower walls could not be closer than twenty-five feet from the building line on buildings facing one-hundred-foot-wide streets.

If an owner did not want to bother with a base from which setbacks and a tower would rise but wanted to build a sheer tower from the ground up on 25 percent of the land, that was okay, too.

The provision for towers on 25 percent of the site placated the egos of developers who wanted to make a statement, it provided for increased light on city streets, and it cleverly limited the bulk of buildings without directly stating so. Elevators occupy an enormous percentage within the core of tall buildings. By allowing a developer to build a tower of any height on 25 percent of the plot, the zoning law automatically created a check on the height of buildings. To build a building too tall would be economic suicide, because too much rentable space on the lower floors would be sacrificed for elevator shafts.

The zoning law did not legislate aesthetics. It granted absolute freedom of design, providing the architect conformed to the guidelines. As the architectural renderer Hugh Ferriss said, the law provided the "crude clay." The architect's role was to model it. Ferriss realized that the traditionally accepted base, shaft, and capital approach to design would not be successful for setback architecture. In 1922, he discussed the matter with several architects, including Harvey Wiley Corbett, who was himself formulating practical ways to design buildings based on the allowable zoning envelopes. Ferriss went on to show the development and refinement of the possibilities in a series of renderings that served as guidelines for many students.

The first building erected under the new law was the Heckscher Building at Fifth Avenue and Fifty-seventh Street, a conservatively designed tower that could have been designed twenty years before, and that rose from a single setback. The second building designed under the zoning law was the Shelton Hotel (the Marriott East Side Hotel in 1995), which more clearly delineated the shape of things to come and won the gold medal for architecture from both the Architectural League and the American Institute of Architects.

One of the secrets to the Shelton's success was solving the problem of a façade with windows that reflected the same-sized hotel room, a problem encountered by architects designing office buildings where every office is basically the same size and essentially performs the same function. The Shelton's architect created a series of vertical recesses, one or two windows wide. The recesses broke up the monotony of one room after another on the horizontal plane while creating a third dimension vertically through the shadows created by the recesses. He used entasis in the tower, a slight bulge to overcome the optical illusion of sagging. And on the lower floors, he incorporated batter, a slight incline from the vertical to create an illusion of height.

Overall, it was the Shelton's basic form and massing that made the building work so well within the envelope of space. It was a building with scale. Its architect was Arthur Loomis Harmon, who, five years after the Shelton was built, was enlisted by architects Shreve and Lamb to help design the Empire State Building.

Almost all of Midtown was designated as a business zone where residential and commercial buildings with light manufacturing could coexist. Midtown was bounded by Twenty-third and Fifty-ninth Streets, by Second Avenue in the east and the block west of Broadway in the west. Major exceptions included Murray Hill, designated a residential neighborhood. A minor swath between Third and Second Avenues and another on Fifth Avenue between Twelfth and Twenty-third Streets were designated for unrestricted use, the latter an acknowledgment that the garment industry was already entrenched there. Then there was Fifth Avenue between Twenty-third and Fifty-ninth Streets.

Fifth Avenue from Madison Square to Central Park, which included the site of the future Empire State Building, was specially zoned in an effort to keep the garment industry out. By the 1900s, the garment industry, although still engaged in farming out piecework, had also become rationalized. Manufacturers operated factories in loft buildings in the areas around Washington and Union Squares, and on Fifth Avenue between Twelfth Street as far north as Twenty-third Street. But the garment industry was moving northward. By the early 1910s there were 220 cloak and suit manufacturers operating in the blocks east or west of Fifth Avenue north of Twenty-third Street.

Fifth Avenue was already said to have the heaviest vehicular traffic of any street in America, and, with the possible exception of a few streets in London, probably of any street in Europe. At least fifteen buildings on the avenue were over twelve stories high, and many of those on the lower stretch of the avenue were loft buildings. The continued erection of tall buildings, especially of loft buildings catering to the garment industry, it was said, would naturally increase this congestion.

Under the direction of J. Howes Burton, a Harvard-educated textile manufacturer, local realtors, retailers, and the recently formed Fifth Avenue Association started a group called the Save New York Movement in the early 1910s, which regarded the Fifth Avenue buildings south of Twenty-third Street and their attendant conditions as ruinous to the avenue. They decried the loft buildings as cheap in construction and appearance. They said the loft buildings were crowded with hundreds of garment workers and operators who clogged the sidewalks at the beginning and end of every working day, and who swarmed the avenue during the lunch hour. More reactionary realtors described the conditions in plaguelike terms. Let the blight remain endemic to Fifth Avenue south of Twenty-third Street. They did not want an epidemic spreading farther north.

The Save New Yorkers, realtors and retailers of American-born stock or those of more recently arrived German-Jewish stock, began a public relations blitz to put a stop to what they regarded as an invasion of objectionable trades that employed undesirable immigrant minorities, mostly Jews from Eastern Europe. The garment industry should be centralized, ghettoized, and the Fifth Avenue realtors and retailers did not care where, as long as it was not in their backyard. The story fabricated for the benefit of the press had out-of-town buyers finding it increasingly inconvenient to cover a territory that stretched from Bleecker Street to Fortieth Street. The Save New Yorkers managed to convince the normally tolerant *New York Times* to proclaim that the "invasion of unsuitable trades, bringing throngs of workers who would monopolize the sidewalks and repel fashionable shoppers, was undesirable."

At the same time, the Save New Yorkers used strong-arm tactics to persuade the cloak-and-suiters that another part of the city would be more desirable for their businesses. They told the garment manufacturers that concentrating in a definite locality would help the garment industry by reducing overhead charges. The threat was more than psychological extortion. The Save New Yorkers had convinced major lending institutions not to issue loans to developers of loft buildings in the Fifth Avenue district north of Twenty-third Street. And they let it be known that realtors were with the movement. With the expiration of present leases, rents just might skyrocket. The art of persuasion was not lost on the garment manufacturers, who were made an offer they couldn't refuse. In a rush, 202 manufacturers within the Fifth Avenue area— among them, Abramson & Cohen, Lipshitz & Adelson, Osheowitz & Schneider, Sharfstein & Cohn, Menczer & Nadler, and Eidenberg & Ornowitz—agreed to move elsewhere when their leases expired. By the late 1920s, the new garment center would be concentrated along Seventh Avenue from Thirtieth to Fortieth Streets.

To preserve Fifth Avenue, to keep the garment center from legally spreading north along the avenue, the Save New Yorkers then influenced the legislators to make Fifth Avenue north of Twenty-third Street a specially zoned business area by limiting the height of buildings on Fifth Avenue to one and a quarter times the width of the avenue, or about twelve stories, before a setback. Realtors didn't complain that the value of their properties was being reduced. Developers said nothing about not being able to develop their Fifth Avenue sites as fully as their neighbors, nor that their property was being wrongly singled out and discriminated against, that their property was being usurped by government edict. They simply did not want the spread of loft buildings to continue. By the 1920s, the Garment District was in place a comfortable distance from Fifth Avenue, which continued to breathe its refined air.

In the meantime, the city was feeling other effects of the zoning law. In 1926, ten years after the law went into effect, 63.5 percent of the entire city was built up at once the width of the street, 12.4 percent at one and a quarter times the width of the street, 19.6 percent at one and a half times, 4 percent at twice the width, and only .5 percent at two and a half times the width of the street. The bulk of the tall buildings was concentrated in Manhattan south of Fifty-ninth Street, with very few buildings over twenty stories high anywhere else except Downtown Brooklyn.

The irony of all this is that skyscrapers were becoming the villains of the piece. The New Yorker's pride in skyscrapers did not keep editorial writers, government officials, city planners, architects, and anyone else from criticizing them. Skyscrapers were hardly the panacea to our urban problems, the critics were saying in the 1920s. In fact, they claimed that skyscrapers were one of the primary reasons *for* our urban problems, if not *the* reason. Even in small cities with skyscrapers, developers had not set aside space between tall buildings. Americans chose to build skyscrapers cheek by jowl. According to Irwin Chanin, who helped change the city's skyline, this was the result of man's being a "social animal with a herding instinct. We veneer this primitive urge with such terms as 'need for centralization' or 'demand for accessibility,' but the basic motive remains. . . . Those with a community of interest must gather themselves into meeting places."

The herding instinct might have been served by the Chrysler Building going up across the street from the Chanin Building, but tall buildings so close to each other were losing the advantages of isolated skyscrapers—the advantages of natural light and expansive views. In 1926, an advertisement for the Farmers' Loan and Trust Building, on the southeast corner of Fifth Avenue and Forty-first Street, claimed the "added advantage of permanent natural light and air, for all time. It is directly opposite the library and Bryant Park, two city blocks of open space." In 1928, an advertisement for the Flatiron Building was headlined A TOWER OF DAYLIGHT, which the Chanin Building challenged with 56 FLOORS OF SUNLIGHT.

Light was a two-edged sword. Skyscrapers gave light to their tenants but took from their neighbors, and the problem was compounded by crowds, congestion, and inadequate transportation facilities.

Few public questions were debated locally with more heat and persistence in the twenties than the value of skyscrapers. At one extreme were the fans of skyscrapers, advocates who sometimes waxed lyrical in their praise of the skyscraper. They saw in the skyscraper a necessary result of American conditions and a characteristic product of American genius, and they protested against any attempt to restrict or regulate the development of skyscrapers in any form. To them, skyscrapers were heaven-sent. A doctrinaire group of critics at the other extreme found in skyscrapers the source of most evils in city life. They advocated a restriction of building height to a maximum of eight or ten stories, which would have had the added benefit of a uniform height or cornice line, something they viewed as certainly more interesting than the irregular hodgepodge that was so often the scene. They said that Manhattan looked like a baggage room on the day after Labor Day, strewn about as it was with upended trunks and boxes. They believed that some day the city would learn that a reasonable harmony of design in architecture was as important as harmony in music.

The reality is that harmony has little to do with development, which is more likely to be described in Napoleonic axioms or the writings of von Clausewitz than with the sounds of the celestial spheres. Bowing to this reality, the city decided that it had to do something. Major planning groups urging further reform included the City Club of New York, the Regional Plan of New York and Its Environs, and the Municipal Art Society, which had been a force for a more livable city since the 1890s and would go on to be instrumental in the creation of the Landmarks Preservation Commission. Even architects who had designed skyscrapers began to protest them. Thomas Hastings, the Ritz Tower's architect, wanted nothing more to do with them. And Ernest Flagg, one of the most ardent advocates of the zoning law of 1916 and the architect who had designed an exemplar of the socially correct skyscraper in the Singer Building, likewise wanted a check on them.

Lawrence Veiller, the great tenement-house reformer, chaired a mayoral committee in 1926 that was charged with developing new standards for skyscrapers. To Veiller, New York was becoming a "sunless city," the blight created by the object of his scrutiny. He wanted a citywide "one-time" zone, and although he would have allowed towers to rise from setbacks because they had proved a picturesque embellishment of the city, he would have further limited the height of towers. To go up ten feet, he said, you had to start back ten feet from both the front *and* back of the plot, and there had to be a minimum of a sixty-foot open space between buildings in the rear.

*Land use* is a phrase closely associated with city planning, but the zoning law of 1916 did not deal with the fact that not all types of buildings are created equal. Some buildings, like George Orwell's pigs, are created more equal than others, and will use the land more equally.

What goes on inside a building affects what goes on outside. A department store will generate twice the pedestrian traffic as an office building of comparable size, and an office building will generate nowhere near the street traffic created by an equally large loft building engaged in light industry. Industry needs trucks and loading bays, with raw materials coming in, finished products going out. It means curbside parking for deliveries, trucks and pushcarts and dollies in addition to the usual automobile and pedestrian traffic, and it all results in congestion. The intensity of use of buildings is as important as the cubic footage as far as street traffic is concerned.

No one had foreseen that automobile traffic would increase tenfold in the ten years after the 1916 zoning law, and the automobile was the chief villain. The automobile is space intensive. A walking man requires about ten square feet of surface. A standing automobile requires about one hundred square feet; moving slowly, an automobile requires about two hundred square feet; at 15 to 20 miles an hour, it requires three to four hundred square feet. Even the Ford Motor Company, in a 1926 advertisement, recognized the problems: "Narrow sidestreets—teeming with traffic—pedestrians darting out at unexpected moments—cars honking at your heels—crowding from the sides. How much easier if you drive a Ford! How much less worry, strain and responsibility! It slides into narrow driving lanes—stops firmly and surely—picks up easily as the procession moves forward—parks in spaces that could not accommodate a larger car." Although operating a car on the city's streets was difficult, visitors packed the National Auto Show at Grand Central Palace in 1926 to see what *The Times* called "more concrete evidences than ever before of the wonderful progress in the auto industry. . . . Never before in a single exhibition have so many types of cars been displayed so mechanically perfect, so completely equipped for every possible use and every conceivable comfort and—perhaps most important of all—at such reasonable prices." The problem was, the city was simply not equipped to deal with any more automobiles.

One of the failings of the street plan of 1811 is that service areas were not taken into account. Without service alleys, all deliveries had to be made directly from the street. With space for sidewalks and a row of parked vehicles at the curb, the city was lucky to have thirty feet of active street left on the average sixty-foot-wide crosstown street. To overcome this shortcoming, Veiller and others recommended that industrial buildings provide off-street loading, and that all large loft buildings, department stores, and office buildings provide two hundred square feet of loading space for every 100,000 square feet of floor area for trucks serving the buildings.

One solution to the traffic problem was the arcaded street of three levels—the lowest level for subways, the street level for motor cars, the elevated level for pedestrians. Public passageways, or arcades through buildings, were also encouraged. They provide alternative routes for pedestrians, hence increased space; they can house shops, and shops pay rent; and arcades are protected during inclement weather, so people can stroll in comfort.[5] Veiller said that new streets should be cut through Midtown Manhattan, that elevated express highways should be built for north-south traffic to avoid the "interference" caused by crosstown traffic, and he argued for a great loop highway around all centers of congestion.[6]

Almost everyone agreed that the zoning law's stand on garages in business areas, which permitted new garages to be built only on blocks that already housed a garage, had to be changed. There were very few modern garages in the city. Most had originally been stables, built with ramps for horses instead of with elevators for cars—and the chance for building more was severely restricted because of the zoning law.

Garages were clearly needed in large buildings, just as loading docks were needed, and if garages were housed in the basements of buildings instead of in separate buildings, so much the better. The average basement tenants in the twenties were rathskellers. Garages, said the planners, would pay more rent.

Hardly any of these plans of the 1920s materialized in that decade. Underground loading areas for trucks appeared in Rockefeller Center in the 1930s, and an amendment to the law in 1935 permitted a variance to the garage ban that resulted in the six-story garage in the Eastern Airlines Building in 1939. It took until 1961 and a revision of the zoning law for some of the ideas from the 1920s to appear. Others simply never came to pass.

---

[5] The author designed the "Undercover Maps" for *New York* magazine in 1972 and 1973 that showed passageways in Midtown and Lower Manhattan that could be used to stay dry in the wet and warm in the cold.

[6] Robert Moses and a whole generation of traffic engineers proved him wrong—no sooner is a highway built to relieve congestion than it is overflowing.

Developers were succeeding in taking advantage of the variances allowed in the zoning law. The Board of Estimate was hard pressed to deny petitioners, and feared that disappointed petitioners would charge the board with favoritism or discrimination. Within the first ten years of the zoning law, about twenty thousand minor variances were requested, of which about seventeen thousand were approved. This flexibility was regarded by politicians as a feather in the municipal cap. It did little to assuage widespread fear among reformers that pressure would be increased to alter residential districts into business districts, and business districts into unrestricted districts, to allow businesses to go where they did not belong and to erect buildings that were bigger and bulkier.

Concerns were well grounded. While the new Eighth Avenue Subway line was being built, the seeds for towering structures along the route were being planted. In 1928, the zoning law was amended to change Eighth Avenue between Thirty-third and Fifty-ninth Streets from a one-and-a-half-time zone to a two-time zone. In light of the increase in land values in the boom of the twenties, investors wanted an inflated return on their inflated dollars. To have the zoning law changed from a one-and-a-half-time zone to a two-time zone was a major accomplishment for developers. For the speculator, the cost of skyscrapers and the value returned was the only standard. Unlike Frank Woolworth, who could rationalize the cost of a skyscraper by the value of its publicity, speculators did not deal with intangibles.

Curiously, realtors and retailers along Fifth Avenue pushed for downsizing and downscaling. By 1927, Fifth Avenue between Twelfth and Twenty-third Streets was rezoned from an unrestricted district to a business-use district, which "grandfathered" whatever industry was already in the neighborhood but would preclude further industrial development. The move was described as eliminating "internal stagnation."

In 1928, the Fifth Avenue Association discovered a loophole in the 1916 zoning law big enough to drive an army of pushcarts through. Clothing manufacturers were using only 17 percent of the floor space in their loft buildings for manufacturing. They could legally return to Fifth Avenue north of Twenty-third Street and carry on as they had. To ensure that the garment industry did not return to the retail stretch of the avenue, and to legitimize, as the association couched it, "the protection which was intended for this section," the Board of Estimate created a fourth zone: a retail-use district, which went into effect April 18, 1929, and was specifically designed to protect the high-class department stores and specialty shops on Fifth Avenue from Thirty-second to Fifty-ninth Streets. Only 5 percent of the floor space could be used for manufacturing articles to be sold at wholesale, but 25 percent of the floor space could still be used for manufacturing if the manufactured articles were sold at retail on the premises. Any operation would be small scale, but it nevertheless allowed retail shops to do some of the manufacturing on the premises. It would succeed in keeping out the "undesirable element."

The association wanted to maintain the high quality of its mile-and-a-half demesne, to protect its assessed valuation of more than $2 billion, or two-ninths of the assessed valuation of all the property in Manhattan, and to keep Fifth Avenue in the role of the nation's high-class emporium. This unsullied district, this gold coast, would be the setting for the Empire State Building.

# 4
# THE BOOM
# OF THE TWENTIES

If the business of America was business, as Calvin Coolidge would have had you believe, then the business of New York in the twenties was real estate. Business was booming, and developers and realtors had every reason for continued optimism. Real estate values, they said, rested on the firm bedrock of population, and New York City—world metropolis, center of finance, industry, and art—had new people locating there all the time. With its limited supply of space and an ever-increasing demand, realtors believed that New York property values would always be rising.

Like other Americans, realtors were certain that the good times would continue indefinitely, that this bubble, unlike all former bubbles, was not about to burst. As late as January 1929, headlines proclaimed that major industries were seeking more space in Manhattan, that a study of office building tenants revealed a steady trend toward the metropolis. When asked in 1928 by a *Times* reporter when Manhattan would stop being rebuilt, Joseph P. Day, the highly respected real estate agent and auctioneer, answered: "Never." Day had been bullish on New York real estate for years. The year 1925, he said, would go down in history as the year in which more millions were invested in real estate and new construction than ever before, the year in which real estate would rise to assume its proper position as the preeminent and outstanding investment. "It would be difficult," he said, "for any man to put his finger on a single piece of real estate in the City of New York that is not worth more today than it was ten years ago, and that will not be worth more ten years hence than it is today."

Day was right about former performance, at least. If you took the years between 1900 and 1925, assessed values in New York had risen from $2.22 billion to $6.72 billion, an average increase of about 12.5 percent a year. The driving force behind this seemingly constant real estate boom was commerce. In addition to having the efficiency of proximity, the city had a wide range of industrial and service activities that was unparalleled. Boosters said that practically every new successfully marketed product was produced and distributed by a concern that maintained at least an office, if not its factory and headquarters, in New York. The city was ideally situated midway along the eastern seaboard, and it had the best natural deep-water port on the Atlantic coast, in part because it was a double harbor, the lower harbor protecting the upper from Atlantic storms. The port's terminal facilities, with long-haul rail service terminating at facilities along the waterways for transshipment, allowed it to handle the major portion of the European import-export trade.

Aside from being the financial center of the world, the city did not depend on any one or two single industries as the basis for its wealth. It was not Steel Town, it was not Tinsel Town. Nor, with the exception of its harbor, did the city depend on any single natural resource. The city was not a specialist; it had many specialties. It was the wellspring, it was the metropolis.

Major real estate ventures were not for the financially timid. They required enormous amounts of capital. Buildings that cost as much as $5 million were not unusual in New York City during the twenties. With twenty-two buildings valued at $10 million or more, New York had more buildings at that valuation than any other city.[1] The Equitable Building at 120 Broadway was assessed at $31 million. Few monumental structures had cost that much to build.[2]

---

[1]Chicago came in a distant second, with only six commercial buildings with a valuation of $10 million or more.

[2]St. Peter's in Rome, went the estimates, would have cost $50 million to build if erected in 1928.

In 1927, the national income stood at around $70 trillion. A third of it was produced by the big three industries: agriculture, with $12 trillion; construction, with $7 trillion; and the automotive industry, with about $4.5 trillion. Those in the construction industry felt that their role was unique. Thomas S. Holden of the New York Building Congress said that construction was essentially a process of manufacture, consisting of assembling many material commodities, applying labor to them, and producing something that did not exist before. Its product was not a commodity to be consumed, but a new form of capital goods, an addition to the permanent wealth of the country. "Not only is the product of this manufacturing process a form of wealth, but the money that is spent for construction is practically always capital, not income," Holden said in *The New York Times*. "Construction is practically always paid for out of saved or borrowed capital. Construction, then, transforms one kind of capital, money, into another form of capital—buildings, bridges, highways and the like. . . . About half of the total is spent directly for wages on building labor. A certain portion goes to compensate architects, contractors and engineers. . . . A very considerable portion goes into the purchase of materials, which in turn are produced largely by labor. The money that is put into circulation when such capital is transformed into construction passes through many hands and purchases every conceivable variety of goods. So the influence of construction activities is felt in practically every line of business in the country."

To Holden, these facts explained why it was so important to stabilize construction, to smooth out the peaks and valleys of booms and depressions. "When you stabilize construction you stabilize one of the most important disbursers of community payrolls."

News stories bearing the indelible imprint of press releases led the reader to the conclusion that the key to success was more of everything, that a bigger New York was indeed a better New York. According to the Merchants' Association of New York in 1928, a baby was born every four minutes and six seconds. Using a twelve-hour day, more than fourteen couples got married every hour. The city's population of 6,056,000 consumed 2,659,632 quarts of milk and 7,000,000 eggs a day, eating a total of 3,500,000 tons of food a year, or about 1,000 pounds per person. More than 190 persons picked up the telephone receiver every second, and each day the 1,700,000 telephones were used to make 8,233,000 calls. Normally, there were 23,628 taxicabs in daily service, and on every business day, more than 500,000 persons arrived by train. There were 252 theaters where "spoken drama" was played, and 548 theaters exhibiting movies (they were silents, of course). In all, 850,993 persons could be accommodated at once in the theaters. There were 11,575 practicing physicians and surgeons, with one doctor to every 524 persons. The city had 138 hospitals, 927 elementary and high schools, 13 colleges and universities, and 1,584 churches. To show the importance attached to real estate in all these numbing numbers, the worth of the city's churches was couched not in their parish work or in how many wretches were saved from alcoholic dependency on the Bowery, but in real estate terms—the churches were worth more than $286 million.

About 1 million people lived in Manhattan south of Fifty-ninth Street in the mid-1920s, and about 2 million people arrived and departed daily. The bulk of the commuters did not come from what have come to be considered the suburbs, but from the city itself, with about 859,300 from Upper Manhattan and The Bronx, and 745,900 from Brooklyn and Queens. About 299,300 came from New Jersey, with the remaining 100,000 or so from the northern suburbs, Long Island, and Staten Island. Commuters had become a critical force; commuting had become a fact of life, and it was due in large measure to the enormous concentration of skyscrapers in Lower Manhattan.

The significant factor concerning the expansion of cities in the 1920s was not the rapidity with which people piled upon one another in closely packed residential quarters, as businesses were doing in commercial areas, but the manner in which cities were spilling their resident populations over vast surrounding areas. Between 1920 and 1927, Manhattan lost more than a sixth of its population, declining from 2.3 million in 1920 to about 1.9 million in 1926. Not only were there fewer families in Midtown between Thirtieth and Sixtieth Streets, but they were also becoming smaller—down from 4.5 persons per family in 1910 to 4.02 in 1927, when the average for Manhattan was 4.4. But the drop in the Midtown population was even more dramatic, as residents were displaced by workers. Between 1910 and 1927 the resident population dropped from 310,000 to 200,000. Only in two areas did the numbers rise: in Murray Hill, where apartment houses were replacing private homes, and Thirty-fourth to Thirty-eighth Streets between Tenth and Eleventh Avenues, where the erection of a large printing plant attracted working-class residents. At the same time, the population of Queens increased by 62 percent, from 469,000 to 764,000.

It was as if the cores of the cities, having been centripetal in the nineteenth century, had become centrifugal in the twentieth. Regional New York was enormous. In 1927 it held 9 million people, it included 5,528 square miles of territory, 60,000 manufacturing plants, 868 piers, 13 railroads, 1,800 miles of waterfront, 9,000 miles of streets, and 900,000 automobiles.

As residential areas spread horizontally, commercial areas grew vertically. The case was not unique to New York. Even small American cities that had ample room to expand horizontally showed a keen desire to expand vertically in downtown areas. Every American city that aspired to metropolitan importance wanted at least one skyscraper as evidence of its modernity, of having the "go ahead spirit" of George F. Babbitt. They wanted a "there" there.

New York already had a "there," and by the end of the twenties the city had embarked on major municipal undertakings to increase its "thereness." To accommodate more automobiles, the Holland Tunnel was built, streets were widened at the expense of sidewalks to accommodate ever more cars, and the completion of the "elevated circumferential plaza" at Grand Central Terminal heralded new automobile movement above the crowds, and around and through buildings. Under construction were the George Washington Bridge and the Miller (West Side) Elevated Highway, the Catskill Water System, and the Eighth Avenue Subway.

Private money was changing the face of the city at a faster rate than municipal money, and it had the city on the rise at a rate heretofore unknown. Investors large and small jumped on the real estate bandwagon, with developers who were putting up twenty-, thirty-, even forty-story buildings becoming a dime a dozen. Most of the buildings would simply lift the overall height of the city another notch or two, but a few would become icons of their age, if not for their architectural style, then for their form (the second college edition of the *American Heritage Dictionary*, for instance, used a picture of the thirty-eight-story Fred F. French Building at 551 Fifth Avenue to illustrate *setback*).

Real estate was one of the great growth industries of the 1920s, but among all the projects that went forward were dozens that went nowhere. Proposed record-breakers were touted one day, only to be forgotten the next. Among the aborted schemes were plans for the world's tallest apartment house that Fred French announced as part of his Tudor City development, plans for the world's tallest hotel that would have ranked as the world's second largest building—a sixty-story behemoth—for Columbus Circle, the plan of William Fox of Fox Theaters for a fifty-two-story tower at Forty-seventh Street and Broadway that would house a theater with a capacity greater than the 6,200-seat Roxy, and plans for a 53-story, 575-foot-high hotel on Broadway between Fifty-fifth and Fifty-sixth Streets whose rooftop aviation beacon would have had "a greater range of visibility than any in the vicinity"!

In October 1929, only a month after the announcement of the Empire State Building and weeks before the bottom fell out of the stock market, Abraham E. Lefcourt announced a $30 million, 1,050-foot-high skyscraper for the northwest corner of Broadway and Forty-ninth Street.[3] The two-story building on the site was owned by the Brill Brothers, who ran a clothing store in the building. The Brills planned to occupy a store in the new building, but most of the structure would be occupied by an unnamed client for whom the skyscraper was to be built by Lefcourt, who had already erected some of the tallest buildings on Manhattan Island. Lefcourt's two highest until then had been the forty-two-story Lefcourt-National on the former site of Temple Emanu-El at Fifth Avenue and Forty-third Street, and the forty-five-story Lefcourt-Colonial, which was under construction at Madison Avenue and Forty-first Street.

The second tallest building projected for New York in the decade was the Larkin Tower, which was planned in 1927 for the fifty-thousand-square-foot site on Forty-second Street between Eighth and Ninth Avenues that was later used for Raymond Hood's McGraw-Hill Building. If the proposed 110-story building had been built, it would have stood knee-deep amid the neighboring roofs, a true Gulliver in Lilliput. The Larkin Tower would have had a gross total area of 1.45 million square feet, about a million feet of which would have been rentable, making it the fourth largest building in the world. It would have been served by sixty high-speed elevators, two of them expresses direct to the eighty-second story, where passengers would catch shuttle cars to the 110th floor. The top three floors were entirely devoted to sightseeing purposes, a gesture that tried to salvage their impracticality for any other use.

The biggest of the proposed big building projects of the twenties came hard on the heels of the announcement of Lefcourt's Times Square project. Charles F. Noyes, head of the realty firm bearing his name, said that property in Lower Manhattan had been acquired for Schulte Realty, which had established a holding company called the Broadway-Church

---

[3]*The Times* categorized the building as "New York's Mount Everest," and went on to say that "if the school children of New York are still taught that any hill 1,000 feet or more in height is officially a mountain, then Mr. Lefcourt's description of his new building in terms of feet rather than stories will impress them for the construction marvel it is. For to school children and grown-ups alike, a 1,050-foot building readily conveys the picture of something fifty feet higher than a mountain, . . . heights which thus far nature has touched only with her own constructions and from which the works of man have been excluded."

Corporation for this single undertaking.[4] The idea was to build on the greater part of the two blocks bounded by Broadway and Church Street, Worth and Duane Streets. The property had been the site of the original New York Hospital, which still owned the entire site. Thomas Street, which bisects the two blocks, had never been ceded by the hospital to the city. Although it was left unsaid, there was the very real possibility that either the street would be arcaded and the building would straddle it, or the street would simply be closed. The proposed building, which was not scheduled for construction until 1937, would have been 150 stories high.

Few developers had studied the field as an academic discipline, even as an extension course at the YMCA. Nor did many developers start life in the field that brought them their greatest fortune. They might have been clothing salesmen or gang foremen, milliners or minor retailers, who rose by unequal parts of luck and pluck in the classic Horatio Alger tradition, parlaying a small holding into a bigger one, and the bigger one into an even bigger one, until the small-time speculator had become a big-time developer and a major force in New York's real estate trade.

Abraham E. Lefcourt's career is a classic. He started life as a newsboy, saved his pennies from the newspaper stand he was operating, and opened a bootblack stand on Grand Street. He did not want to give up his newspaper sales, and since he could not be in two places at the same time, he hired others to operate not just the first operation but the second as well, and he went to work at a third—in a retail dry goods store. Soon he was not the employee in a dry goods and garment business; he was the employer. In 1923, by which time he had made about $10 million, he decided to develop properties for the garment industry. Lefcourt set out to snatch up as much property as he could between Broadway and Eighth Avenue from Thirty-sixth to Thirty-ninth Streets. His first sortie into the future Garment District was the Lefcourt Garment Center, and his career as a builder was soon well under way. Within six years he had twenty-four skyscrapers under his belt, his worth had grown by a multiple of ten, and he was on his way to fulfilling the second of his lifetime dreams. His first dream had been fulfilled by building a major tower on Fifth Avenue (this was 521 Fifth Avenue, for which Shreve & Lamb were the architects). His second was to start his own bank, which, true to his proclivity for naming things for himself, was called

---

[4]Some national institutions such as Schulte's and United Cigar Stores were making as much money, and perhaps even more, out of real estate investments than out of the business with which they were regularly identified. Like United, Schulte had found itself a major realtor, preferring to buy the corner sites where their cigar stands were found, instead of leasing.

the Lefcourt Normandie Bank, located in the Lefcourt Normandie Building on Broadway at Thirty-eighth Street, one of the many corners where he
said he had stood selling papers as a newsboy forty years before.

Abraham N. Edelson started his career in the garment industry, which
he never abandoned—in 1929 he was still active in the hat trade—despite
the fact that his first two major ventures in the real estate business were
so successful that by 1930 he could build the skyscraper at 2 Park Avenue, which occupied the block front between Thirty-second and Thirty-
third Streets and was designed by Buchman & Kahn.

Louis Adler started his professional career at sixteen selling ladies'
waists for a wholesale house. His first large building for the clothing
trades, which was the tallest of its kind when it went up in 1924, was the
twenty-four-story 550 Seventh Avenue, an undertaking that had many
veteran garment manufacturers shaking their heads in disbelief at his
temerity. However, like the twin he built for the millinery industry, it was
entirely rented before completion. It was Adler who tore down the nine-
year-old Pictorial Review Building to build the thirty-story 530 Seventh
Avenue.

Benjamin Winter, a nineteen-year-old Polish émigré, arrived in New
York in 1901. When asked by his uncle what he could do, he said he could
paint. Although Winter meant *fine* painting, his uncle said "good," and he
was put to work painting houses. Soon he was decorating interiors, and
with his new contacts with architects and builders, he branched out into
real estate. He wound up buying the Vanderbilt mansion on Fifth Avenue
at Fifty-second Street for more than $8 million, the Spanish Flats on Cen-
tral Park South for $7 million, and the Astor mansion on Fifth Avenue and
Sixty-fifth Street, which he later sold to Temple Emanu-El for $6.5 million.

Fred F. French, a poor boy from The Bronx, started life as a general
utility man in a truck company, and was later a foreman of a gang of
workers on a reservoir project near White Plains. In 1905 he became a
timekeeper at the Home Club at 11 East Forty-fifth Street. By 1929 he
headed the $100 million Fred French Company, which had built the
French Building and Tudor City, and he owned the Home Club. One of his
few forays into the residential market was the apartment house he built
at 1010 Fifth Avenue for speculative and personal reasons. He incorporated a fourteen-room penthouse apartment atop the building for himself
that was as much a garden in the sky as it was a mansion in the sky.

Not all the projects proposed by professionals such as French, Winter,
and Lefcourt came to fruition, but these and other developers had learned
real estate by the seat of their pants and had a practical understanding
of the field. Many projects announced in the 1920s were more the whims

of amateurs than the hard-nosed approach of professionals, less in the realm of reality and more in the camp of Mickey Rooney movies ("Hey gang, I've got a great idea. Let's put up a building here!"). In some cases the projects lacked the financing, the site, even, at times, a constituency.

The American University Club, created specifically for university alumni who were not members of other college clubs, proposed a forty-story clubhouse for which Thomas Hastings had prepared plans but for which there was no site and, apparently, less money. The membership list was based on very uncertain evidence.

Plans were under way to erect a seventy-five-story mixed-use building in memory of Benjamin Franklin. The International Benjamin Franklin Society had not yet selected a site, but a Midtown location was desired, and a committee was to be named to try to raise the requisite $18 million. Profits from the planned office space would be used to underwrite space for a museum, auditorium, and memorial offices. Pie-in-the-sky projects such as the Franklin Society Building often included commercial space to offset the costs of not-for-profit projects. Two of the biggest projects were religious undertakings on Upper Broadway. The Broadway Temple that was scheduled for Washington Heights would have been big enough at 725 feet high, but the other project, the sixty-five-story Christian-Missionary Building, which would have been built between 122nd and 123rd Streets, would have resulted in the world's tallest building in 1926 if completed. It would have been eight hundred feet tall, and would have housed a hotel, a church, a hospital, and a bank.

All these wishful-thinking projects pale in comparison to the one proposed by the Inter-Church World Movement's Convocation Center, which in 1921 had Bertrand Grosvenor Goodhue design an office tower reaching a thousand feet into the sky, with a great auditorium/church on the ground floor. Convocation Tower would have been 218 feet taller than the Woolworth Building, and would have laid claim to the world's tallest building.

New York was not alone in projecting record-breaking skyscrapers that were never realized. Detroit in 1926 was to host The Book Tower, which would have been 873 feet high, ninety-one feet taller than the Woolworth Building and twenty-three floors higher. Two years later a seventy-five-story building that would contain a "virtual city within itself" was scheduled for Chicago. Called the Garment Center, the skyscraper would have stood on two square blocks of property and would have used the air rights above the terminal of the Illinois Central Railroad. The building would have reached 845 feet above street level, sixty-three feet higher than the Woolworth Building, second in height only to the 986-foot Eiffel Tower in Paris. The mixed-use building—part office, part showroom, part hotel, part auditorium—would have been the tallest occupied structure in the world, and, with 4.65 million square feet, have the largest amount of floor space. In the spring of 1929, Chicago was again in the news, this time as the site for another building that would rank as the world's tallest, a seventy-five-story structure to house the general offices of the Illinois Central Railroad and the Crane Manufacturing Co. The building, to be known as the Crane Tower, would have risen 1,022 feet, 36 feet higher than the Eiffel Tower. In addition to being the tallest structure ever erected by man, it would have been the world's largest office building, containing 3.5 million square feet of floor space. Features would have included a thousand-automobile garage for tenants, a convention hall, several smaller conference halls, a coliseum, a tenants' club, restaurants, Turkish baths, a gymnasium, and forty-eight hotel rooms for tenants' guests. Financing would have involved issues of $26 million in leasehold bonds and stock.

Despite all the projects that died on the drafting boards, by 1929 an enormous amount of construction had nevertheless gone forward. Thirty-six cities in the United States could claim 377 skyscrapers that were more than twenty stories high. Philadelphia had 22, Chicago had 65, and New York, with 50 percent of the nation's skyscrapers, had 188.

Developers were not the only ones making money. Nondevelopers—property owners who agreed not to develop their property—were also making small fortunes. Realtors estimated that the worth of office space depreciated about 20 percent when offices faced blank walls, and tenants were deprived of firsthand contact with natural light and views. The best way to safeguard a thirty- or forty-story building from having a new sixty- or seventy-story neighbor go up next door was by acquiring the air rights, as Ernest Flagg had envisioned. Although Flagg's idea was not authorized by law, it was legitimized in practice. Buying or renting small structures to ensure natural illumination and ventilation became a cost of doing business. Along Madison Avenue, for example, there were several three- and four-story brownstone houses crouching humbly at the foot of giants. Some of the low-lying buildings had been bought outright by developers; others were leased for long periods at annual rentals that were not much less than the total value of the property. In 1929, a peak price was paid for open space. The owners of the thirty-eight-story Harriman Building at 39 Broadway rented the undeveloped space above the adjoining five-story building at 31 Broadway. The lease was for $22,500 a year for thirty-three years, for a total of $742,500, with an option for renewal. "Perhaps it may seem to the layman that $22,500 a year is a lot of money to pay for the use of a bit of emptiness," said Douglas Gibbons, who represented the Harriman Building in the transaction, "but the truth is that Manhattan's skyline is becoming so solid that breathing space is at a premium." The landlords had the best of both possible worlds. The owners of the Harriman Building avoided the necessity of managing the neighboring structure, while assuring light and air for their tenants. The landlord of the five-story building earned as much money on his property as if he had torn down the existing building and erected a taller one.

Reading about how much money could be made led many people to get in on the ground floor, to make it big, and to cash in their chips. From the perspective of some professionals, this was a major problem with the building boom—it had not been precipitated by careful realtors whose desire was to satisfy a genuine demand for space. It had been created by investors with a plethora of idle money, who were seeking investment in what was considered a safe and well-paying field, which described real estate when it was not overstimulated.

There is no doubt that money—lots of it—was there. In 1924, there were seventy-five taxpayers in the nation who reported incomes in excess of $1 million, thirty-nine of whom were from New York State. A year later, the number was up to 207 taxpayers declaring incomes in excess of $1 million, with ninety-six of them from New York State. These were not taxpayers who had merely acquired $1 million—what you might call the run-of-the-mill millionaire—these were taxpayers declaring *incomes* in excess of $1 million. They weren't alone in their newfound wealth. There had been an increase of 43 percent in the average income in the six years between 1921 and 1927, combined with an actual decrease in the cost of commodities. Enough people were clearly far enough ahead in the financial game to give the illusion that Americans were destined to become, if not plutocrats, at least comfortably well off. A large amount of surplus money had piled up—so much, in fact, that many property owners were either paying off their mortgages entirely or dramatically reducing them. Money that did not go to pay off mortgages was going into the investment pool, which was big enough to float traditional stocks and bonds—the "blue chips" and otherwise—as well as real estate issues. Unlike former boom periods, this time the funds for real estate investment were not concentrated in the hands of a few large holders but scattered among people of comparatively modest incomes.

The "little guy" invested his money in the real estate market the same way he invested in stocks and bonds. Real estate developers such as Benjamin Winter, A. E. Lefcourt, the Tishmans, and Fred French had set up real estate corporations to float stock issues. Investors could buy shares in them, just as they could buy shares in General Motors.

An advertisement for the French Plan asked, "Have you $1,000 to invest? You want to invest your dollars where they will be safe—where they will grow—will work steadily to earn a consistent and generous income for you. Consider, then, these facts: Land is the most permanent form of wealth known to man. The steady growth of population in your larger cities results in a constantly increasing demand and an inevitable increase in the value of well-located real estate. Large scale real-estate development in New York City has established a record for generous and consistent profits not equaled by any other type of investment. Certainly you should consider New York real estate with its inevitable increase in value as the first field in which your dollar should be put to work for you. . . . Invest in the French Plan, which enables you to make a temporary investment that gives you a permanent income."

Real estate had traditionally been a frozen asset, but suddenly it was defrosted as a liquid asset in the form of stock. The stock owner could sell his stock holdings at any time through the ordinary workings of a stock exchange. And as an investor in a corporation, he did not single-handedly need the vast sums required for the big operations that would otherwise have eluded him. He could buy just a few shares of a stock plan, which gave the investor of average means the opportunity to share in the profits of the biggest real estate operations in the city without having to put up a vast amount of money. Real estate had become marketable, a commodity that could be bought and sold as easily as a phone call to your broker.

A number of issues were traded on both the New York Stock Exchange and the curb market by the late 1920s, and trading in real estate securities became more popular. However, real estate was an arcane subject that few securities analysts had mastered. Traders had little authoritative information on the soundness of real estate stocks, and many investors were still reluctant to place their money in little-understood real estate securities. The New York Real Estate Securities Exchange, which was created in the fall of 1929, would solve that problem by providing information to prospective investors. Securities could be traded only after the offering corporation or individual had passed a litmus test that included appraisals of property values and financial status, past activities, and the character of the individuals offering securities. Given the expert counseling provided by the new securities exchange, someone interested in investing in real estate did not have to become an expert himself. He could let others concern themselves with the design and construction of a building, real estate law, and the terms of a lease. Real estate was becoming perceived as a business of opportunities. All you needed to cash in was a broker.

Real estate still had to compete with the more popular stock market for investors, but newspapers were doing their bit to educate readers to its value. At every turn, readers were inundated by upbeat stories. General-interest publications saw no reason for a cessation in building activity in the mid-1920s and ran stories on the new prosperity that, subliminally at least, encouraged people to invest in real estate. Stories might have made the front page or they might have been buried in the inside pages of local real estate sections, but they kept appearing on a regular basis, and they kept hammering the same theme: Another site was sold for another record high. In 1925, Fifth Avenue was attracting realtors more than any other thoroughfare, and the sale of the Delmonico site on the northeast corner of Forty-fourth Street for $312 a square foot set a record. A year later, Benjamin Winter bought the site of Temple Emanu-El, on the northeast corner of Fifth Avenue and Forty-third Street, for $6.5 million. He was the second investor to buy the site, and by the end of the year he had sold it for $7 million, earning a handsome profit and making the sale, at $370 a square foot, a new high for Fifth Avenue. A. E. Lefcourt, hardly new to real estate, was the speculator who bought the site. One of the biggest deals took place on the northwest corner of Fifth Avenue and Forty-second Street in July 1929, when Walter J. Salmon announced that he had ac-quired the lease on the 100-by-208-foot plot. The unimproved value of the property was $28,000 per foot of frontage, which was exceeded only by the $30,000 for the plot at 1 Wall Street, where the Irving Trust Building would rise. On the Forty-second Street site Salmon would erect 500 Fifth Avenue, a fifty-eight story, 625-foot building in the setback style, making it one of Fifth Avenue's tallest buildings. It would be designed by the firm of Shreve & Lamb, and for them it would serve as a practice run for things to come.

Fifth Avenue took on a new face in the twenties. In the one-mile stretch between Forty-first and Sixty-first Streets, the avenue was home to ten new office buildings.[5] They were a total of 352 stories high, they had 2,648,000 square feet of rentable area, and they housed 30,000 workers

[5]The new buildings on the avenue were the Farmers Loan and Trust Building on the south-east corner of Forty-first Street (1926); 500 Fifth Avenue on the northwest corner of Forty-second Street (1930); the Lefcourt National Building on the northeast corner of Forty-third Street (1928); 535 Fifth Avenue on the northeast corner of Forty-fourth Street (1926); the Fred F. French Building on the northeast corner of Forty-fifth Street (1927); the S. W. Straus Bank Building on the northeast corner of Forty-sixth Street (1921); the Empire Trust Building on the northwest corner of Forty-seventh Street (1928); the Heckscher Building on the southwest corner of Fifty-seventh Street (1922); the New York Trust Company on the northeast corner of Fifty-seventh Street (1930); and the Squibb Building on the southeast corner of Fifty-eighth Street (1930).

(or a population greater than Albuquerque, New Mexico, at the time). In addition to the office buildings, three new hotels went up—the Savoy Plaza, the Sherry-Netherland, and the Pierre.

The 1929–30 crop of skyscrapers in the Grand Central District resulted in a change of Brobdingnagian proportions. New York had fifteen buildings over five hundred feet tall in 1929, and two of them—the Chanin and the Chrysler Buildings—were diagonally across the street from each other on Lexington Avenue at Forty-second Street. The new buildings in the Grand Central neighborhood would have an aggregate of 469 stories. They would add 5 million square feet of office space to the Grand Central zone. The tallest, which would hardly stand alone in majesty but would be crowded by several other huge structures, was the Chrysler Building, which occupied the full block frontage on the east side of Lexington Avenue between Forty-second and Forty-third Streets. At seventy-seven stories, or 1,048 feet high, this was the first building taller than the Eiffel Tower, and it would be the building that the Empire State Building had to beat if it was to be the world's tallest.[6]

In June 1928, while the Chrysler Building was still on the drawing boards, Walter Chrysler assembled a group of experts that included Earle Shultz to advise him on several subjects, including the renting potential of such a mammoth building.[7] The conclusion of the experts was that although there were "millions of square feet of office space now vacant," the building would be a success because, they speculated, with all the new space, other operators would halt their plans until the available rentable area was practically absorbed. They were wrong. Things hardly slowed down.

In one day, February 7, 1929, the Metropolitan Life Insurance Company made construction loans that totaled more than $74 million, a record

---

[6]Among the Chrysler Building's new neighbors on Forty-second Street were the fifty-six-story Chanin Building on Lexington Avenue, which had 703,000 square feet of area; the fifty-three-story Lincoln Building at Vanderbilt Avenue, with 915,000 square feet of area; and the thirty-five-story Daily News Building at Second Avenue, with 550,000 square feet of area. It adds up to over 3 million feet of rentable office and retail space, on 221 floors. And those were just the new buildings on Forty-second Street. There were also the thirty-three-story Graybar Building at 420 Lexington Avenue, with 1,050,000 square feet; the forty-story New York Central Building at 230 Park Avenue, with 810,000 square feet; the Lefcourt building, the forty-story 295 Madison Avenue, with 325,000 square feet; and the twenty-four-story 366 Lexington Avenue, with 185,000 square feet.
[7]Earle Shultz was the manager of Chicago's Edison Building at the time and later teamed up with Walter Simmons to write *Offices in the Sky*, one of the standard works on office-building construction and management.

for one day's authorizations by Met Life. One of the loans, the biggest individual loan ever made by the notoriously conservative insurance company, was $24 million for a mammoth building called the Waldorf-Astoria Building that was planned for the west side of Fifth Avenue between Thirty-third and Thirty-fourth Streets.

In the first nine months of 1929, plans were filed for 709 new buildings in New York City, with a total cost of over $472 million, as against 760 buildings, costing over $258 million during the same period in 1928. Although there might have been fewer buildings planned, they were bigger, they were far more costly, and they were in direct competition with the likes of the Chrysler Building.

To those of us far removed from the twenties, the image of the decade is one of unparalleled growth, of a boom that just kept on booming. However, there were peaks and valleys, and the peaks were sometimes made low and the valleys rose up. With this shifting of geological proportions came tremors, and the walls supporting even realistic financial transactions in real estate were beginning to show cracks as early as 1926.

Walter Stalber, the comptroller of Metropolitan Life Insurance Company, which was and still is one of the biggest lenders in the nation, said that real estate was "always a safe and profitable asset, if there is not too much of it seeking tenants." A moderate surplus had been reached by the end of 1925, when Met Life and other lenders that had survived periods of overexpansion, only to suffer consequent periods of contraction, recognized the symptoms and withdrew from the new-construction market. Reports showed a great surplus of space under construction in the uptown office section around Forty-second Street and Fifth Avenue, space that would be ready for May 1, 1927, the traditional date for renewing commercial leases. Unless storm signals were heeded, "the great prosperity of New York real estate," said Stalber, "the greatest it has ever known, is certain to receive a serious setback."

S. W. Straus, president of the banking firm that specialized in real estate and whose studies of the field made him one of its great experts, issued a formal statement to the press in 1927 that there should be no more new construction for six months to a year. His firm was taking a breathing spell, and the industry, said Straus, should take one, too.

It wasn't just the big guys who were pulling out. Builders' supply dealers announced in 1926 that they were giving up the banking end of their business. Dealers had never considered themselves financiers, but they had found themselves playing that role in an effort to supply commodities for what they later termed "rainbow anticipation." They had accepted 50 percent in cash and 50 percent in notes totaling about $40 million in working capital toward local building projects. As a rule, money put into a speculative building project was paid back through the earnings of the project within a year from completion of the building. Anticipating the usual, the dealers expected to be reimbursed after the building had been on the market for a renting season, so they could plow their capital back into their own businesses. Projects were only partially rented, however, and to the dealers' dismay, payments were only being partially made. The only way to get their money out when they needed it was by taking a loss.

By the end of 1926, Ethelbert Stewart, the commissioner of Labor Statistics, said that construction had caught up with needs, that "a continuation of the high rate of building as in the last few years might result in over-production with a sequence of a depression." Cities nationwide reported to Calvin Coolidge that the country was overbuilt, a saturation point had been reached, and a cooling-off period was needed. In the nation's principal twenty-five cities, the decline in new-building construction had been 4 percent; in New York, 5 percent.

By 1927, the vacancy issue had become so dramatic that real estate practitioners said that it did not take an expert to see what the future held. Any layman could see the problem for himself by taking a stroll through Manhattan.

Although the standard for New York had been to rebuild itself every generation, the abnormally fast pace that was set led some realtors to view the condition warily. Others argued that the stories about overbuilding and a glut on the market were exaggerated. The stories were unnecessarily scaring off the buying and investing public. These realtors maintained that a surplus was beneficial, that the moment there was not enough space for the demand was the beginning of the end. A choice in location, size, and cost had to fit different needs.

Demand for buildings in good locations, especially those with light and accessibility, continued at the expense of older buildings. "Progressive businessmen are not going to remain indefinitely in antiquated and time-worn structures and pay high rents," said realtor Nathan L. Ottinger. "As they prosper and their business expands, they are going to keep pace with progress and move into more sanitary and better lighted, better situated and more modern and up-to-date buildings as they are erected."

Although hotel construction fell off 50 percent in 1927, and office-building construction fell 13 percent, the yea-sayers rejected the notion that flush times succeeded by hard times was a normal feature of the economic system, especially in real estate. The saturation point in building, they maintained, did not suggest the same phenomenon as "depression" in manufacturing and commerce. Buildings were permanent goods. People didn't buy an extra apartment or lease an extra loft just because it was cheap, the way they might buy another suit of clothes.

Developers had been desperate to develop, but by 1927 they were desperate to rent, to fill their vacancies, especially in apartment houses where the problem was critical. Their recourse was to offer rent concessions for as long as two months. Since a concession was usually in a separate letter of agreement and not in the lease itself, the face value of the lease would not reflect the actual amount of income derived from the building; instead, the total specified in the lease would have been far more than the sum actually received. It is easy to see how rent concessions might deceive a prospective buyer of the property, how rent concessions hold within them the seeds of fraud. When the purchase of an improved property is considered, the buyer is swayed chiefly by its potential for income. If a paper return is higher than the real return, the prospective buyer gets an exaggerated impression of the possible yield from his investment. By 1928 the practice was condemned by the Ethics and Commissions Committee of the Real Estate Board, which said that any concession from a stipulated rent between landlord and tenant ought to be specifically stated in the lease, and that any agreement entered into modifying the terms of the lease should also be part of the lease.

The National Association of Building Owners and Managers maintained that a vacancy rate of 10 percent was normal, but by February 1929, the association had found the national vacancy rate at 11.44 percent, a surplus that would be dramatically increased when the new developments dumped their rentable space on the market. The association could not expect business to expand 10 percent in the next year. In fact, its members anticipated contraction rather than expansion. Other realtors recognized that the profession could not view the extremely heavy construction program without apprehension of a glut on the market. Midtown property owners were told that they had to prepare for some growing pains within the next few years.

Construction hardly slowed down. In the fall of 1929, a German architect visiting New York called on architect Harvey Wiley Corbett and asked Corbett to show him a tall building in the course of construction. Looking out his window in the Bush Tower on West Forty-second Street, Corbett saw just such a building rising some forty stories skyward only a few blocks away on East Fortieth Street. The visitor asked what the building was, who had designed it, and whether Corbett could arrange a tour. To the German's surprise and Corbett's chagrin, the local architect had to admit that he knew nothing about the building, nor, it turned out, did anyone else in his drafting room. "Ten years ago such a building would have been the gossip of the architectural world," said Corbett. "Today it is a mere incident."

The wonder at the rate of office-building construction was not lost on all practitioners. They saw it was proceeding at a faster rate than the demand for space, and revised storm warnings on existing renting conditions were posted by July 1929. Between Thirty-fourth and Fifty-ninth Streets there was about 20 million square feet of office space. About 1.5 million square feet of it was idle, or about 13.3 percent. With about 6 million more square feet of space coming on the market upon the completion of buildings already under construction, there would be 7.5 million square feet to be rented, or a vacancy rate of 28.8 percent. Excessive office-building construction during the following two years, it was reasonably feared, would exacerbate the rental situation and create other problems as well.

The streets could barely accommodate the crowds as it was. Even the Forty-second Street Property Owners and Merchants Association, Inc., an organization of property owners and managers that ordinarily saw only the bright side of things, had to admit that congestion had become intolerable. Midafternoons, when congestion was below its peak, cab rides on Forty-second Street between Lexington and Eighth Avenues were clocked at twenty-eight minutes, and streetcar rides from Second Avenue to Eighth Avenue took twenty-five minutes. When asked how congested the Grand Central District would be with an additional 5 million feet of floor space in the new buildings, with tens of thousands of new occupants crowding in, the boosters sidestepped the answer. They said that the real issues included the elimination of streetcars and the substitution of buses, wider streets, new garages, underground or overhead pedestrian sidewalks, and possibly the construction of multideck roads from river to river. Nothing, according to the builders and realtors, indicated that the Grand Central zone was overbuilt, as some "cautious" people feared. The tall-building era had just begun, they claimed, and many more skyscrapers would be needed to keep pace with the growing demand. The vacancy rate in the Grand Central District stood at 9 percent, which was better than many other cities were doing, including Chicago, Detroit, Cleveland, Philadelphia, and Boston.

The trend was unquestionably toward larger and better-designed buildings in all sections of the city, and some realtors believed that enough wealthy firms existed to absorb all the present available space, and that the new space soon to be ready for occupancy in the best and most centrally located buildings would be readily rented. The difficulty was seen in finding tenants who would accept less desirable locations and less attractive buildings. "Great caution should be exercised in selecting sites for and in the designing and planning of new office buildings during the next few years, particularly in the midtown section," said realtor Loring M. Hewen.

Realtors by and large shrugged off the caveats. They were under the impression that they had sufficiently good sense not to become panicky, in part because the normal growth and prosperity of the country would do the rest. "The statement of the nineteenth-century capitalist who said that any one who sold the U.S. short was a fool still holds good," said William J. Demorest, a vice president at the brokerage house of Cushman & Wakefield. "And if it can be said of the U.S. it can be said of New York and New York real estate, for if the country is prosperous, New York prospers."

# 5

# THE ODD COUPLE

The man primarily responsible for the Empire State Building was not trained as an architect, city planner, or engineer. He was not in the construction business, nor in the real estate business. His only direct dealings in real estate were of a personal nature— a mansion here and an apartment or summer home there—until he made the momentous decision to build the world's tallest building. The man he chose to be his colleague in the venture, the man who would act as his front man, was not in the real estate business either. He was a politician.

John J. Raskob was the money man. Born in Lockport, New York, in 1879, when he was twenty-one he found himself working for Pierre S. du Pont as a bookkeeper. Raskob had a quick and agile mind, and soon became du Pont's secretary. When Eugene du Pont died and the three du Pont cousins took over E. I. du Pont de Nemours & Co. in 1902, Pierre became the treasurer and Raskob his official assistant. He began to advise du Pont on what shares to buy, when, and at what price, and soon he became more than a trusted adviser, more than a friend. He became a Svengali of sorts, and until the 1930s, no colleague was ever as close to Pierre S. du Pont as John J. Raskob.

A stock that Raskob liked was General Motors. Hearing in 1913 that GM founder William C. Durant found himself in financial difficulties that forced him to borrow $15 million from banks, Raskob decided that GM was a good buy. He soon became bullish on GM in particular and the automotive business in general, and he induced Pierre du Pont to invest heavily in GM stock.

By the end of World War I, du Pont de Nemours found itself with an enormous cash surplus. Raskob told the company's directors that the automotive industry promised a larger and quicker return on the company's capital than further investment in the chemical industry, and he convinced them to invest $50 million of du Pont profits in GM stock. Du Pont became a major shareholder, and, after a reorganization, Pierre du Pont became GM chairman, with Raskob his vice president and chairman of the finance committee. Raskob was convinced that employee ownership was good for any corporation, and he strong-armed eighty of his colleagues at GM to invest in company stock. He basically told them to put their money where their mouths were. Those mouths would soon be singing his praises. In four years, employees who had invested as little as $25,000 apiece had become millionaires.

Raskob made many people rich, although perhaps a few might have fallen by the wayside. He believed that a man who bought an automobile and paid for it out of his next year's wages obtained advance pleasure and benefit for his family. He also trained himself to meet an obligation and learn responsibility. In 1919, Raskob created the General Motors Acceptance Corporation, an innovation in the automobile industry that meant installment buying at both the wholesale and retail levels. With the creation of GMAC, Raskob created a revolution. In 1927, only eight years after he had introduced the concept to the auto world, about 60 percent of automobiles in the United States were bought on installment credit at retail, and Raskob predicted that the greatest prosperity the nation had ever known would come in 1928, in part, no doubt, because of installment credit. Inflation was low, credit was abundant, and prices were holding steady.

Raskob firmly believed that what was good for General Motors was good for the USA. It did no harm that it was equally good for his own fortunes and those of his confrères. Raskob's tone was always avuncular and prudent. If a good stock was selling at a high figure he would say that it was advantageous, both to the corporation and to the public, to split the shares and create a wider distribution of the stock. In that manner, more people could buy into the profits. As chairman of the finance committee of the General Motors Corporation and a man filled with the booster philosophy of his day, you would think that Raskob would have been a social conservative, a George F. Babbitt incarnate. Although Raskob was a card-carrying Republican who had voted for Coolidge and appreciated Coolidge prosperity, Raskob did not adhere to the Republican's belief in the "noble experiment" of Prohibition. Nor did Pierre du Pont. Both thought that the money spent on enforcing the Volstead Act could be better spent in other ways, that it was simply a waste of taxpayers' money to enforce the law while robbing the nation of tax revenues that the liquor industry had traditionally provided. Between revenues lost on tax revenues and revenues expended on enforcement, the nation might have been dissipating as much as $1 billion a year.

One of the things that riled Raskob most about Prohibition was its hypocrisy, "the attitude of many successful men who have come up from the ranks, men whom I have known for years, men who drink now and who always have drunk. . . . These men, many of whom at one time wore overalls—and in many cases they were more appropriate than the plus fours or dinner coats that they wear now—set themselves as arbiters of the poor man's actions, and with champagne glasses in their hands say 'Oh, we must vote for prohibition; it is good for the fellows in the shop.' It is all hogwash. I have never seen any workman the worse for a glass or two of beer, while now that he cannot get it he is discontented." Both Raskob and du Pont were members of the National Association Against Prohibition, and Raskob's letters to the editors on the subject of Prohibition made him the association's leading spokesman. One of his fears was that both parties would skirt the Prohibition question in the 1928 election, and he wanted to make sure they did not. His letters hammered at the same theme—a growing disrespect for law and order spreading like an incubus throughout the country. Prohibition did not work, in part because spiritual and mental appeal was much more effective than denial.

Raskob said that he was a responsible man, a director in corporations employing over 300,000 workers, that he had a family of twelve children, ranging in ages from five to twenty-one years, and that he was not a drinking man, which, he was quick to add, did not mean that he never took a drink. One of the things that was giving him great concern in rearing his children and in the future of the country was that citizens seemed to be developing a thorough lack of respect for the nation's laws and institutions, while it seemed that the only thing wrong in life was getting caught.

Raskob also disapproved of the way Prohibitionists had forced their will on a large body of people in matters where no moral wrong was involved and where liberty was curtailed. "The spirit underlying the framing of the Constitution was one of tolerance and not of prohibition," he said. "The majority in this country have no more right to bind the minority to abstinence from wines, beer or even spirits than they have to curtail their right to freedom of religious worship. The menace of prohibitory laws is the spirit of intolerance underlying their adoption, and this is bound to result in rebellion. . . ." For this he was labeled a lawbreaker by overzealous Prohibitionists.

A revolution was brewing, at least, in the Democratic Party. In 1928, the Democrats nominated New York's governor, Alfred Emanuel Smith, as the party's standard-bearer. As Raskob had hoped, at least one party wrote an anti-Prohibitionist plank. Raskob and Smith by then were friends, an odd couple to be sure, and as unlike each other as two men could be. Raskob was the plutocrat, Smith the Democrat.[1] Raskob had made millions; Smith's salary as the governor of the nation's largest state was $10,000 a year. Ten thousand dollars was chicken feed to Raskob, who would buy presents for his cronies at Christmas that cost more than that.[2] But they had both risen from humble origins—both had fathers who died when the boys were young, both had been forced by the exigencies of money to drop out of school and go to work to help support their families. Both were quick studies, adept at mastering the details so that the big picture naturally came into focus, and both were enormously successful in their own fields. They came to bear for each other the kind of esteem that comes with being philosophical comrades in arms, especially in their battles against hypocrisy.

Raskob, the son of an Irish mother and a cigar-maker father of Alsatian descent, was a Roman Catholic from a large family, and he would remain a devout Roman Catholic all his life. In 1928 he was a member of the Knights of Malta and a Knight of St. Gregory, and he was generous to the Church.

---

[1]Raskob was identified as one of the Fifty-nine Leaders who "ruled" the United States in 1930 by James W. Gerard, the former ambassador to Germany and a man not ordinarily given to paranoia and the creation of lists. He included capitalists and financiers, leaders of industry, entertainment, and journalism, but excluded those holding political office, because the "actual power behind the throne is wielded by men whose wealth and important industrial position in the nation gave them a permanent influence in American life, whereas statesmen, diplomats and politicians owe their influence to the offices which they hold and are usually shorn of most of their power when they retire." The leader of the pack was John D. Rockefeller, Jr., followed by Andrew W. Mellon, J. P. Morgan, and George F. Baker, with Raskob coming in twenty-fourth. He was followed by the du Pont family.
[2]In November 1930, well after the reality of the Crash had set in, Raskob could afford to buy thirty-seven sets of the *Oxford Dictionary* in full Levant binding at $1,500 apiece to give to his friends. The total cost: $55,000.

One of his benefactions was a gift of $500,000 for "the advancement and preservation of the Catholic faith in the diocese of Wilmington," to which he offered an additional $500,000 as a matching grant.

Smith's roots were similar, as was his devotion to the Church. Born in 1873 in a tenement in the shadow of the Brooklyn Bridge at 174 South Street, Smith was a first-generation American of Irish-Catholic parents at a time when shop windows still bore signs that said HELP WANTED, NINA. The "NINA" was short for "No Irish Need Apply." His father drove a team of horses six days a week, and his mother had been an umbrella maker. They lived humbly, at least until Al Smith's father died when Smith was just thirteen. Then they were flat-out poor. Smith's mother ran a little grocery and candy store on Dover Street, and young Smith became a "newsy." By the time he was fifteen, the future governor of the state of New York and nominee for the presidency on the Democratic ticket left St. James parochial school and went to work full-time.

Smith worked at odd jobs—as a truck driver's helper, as a fishmonger at the Fulton Fish Market, as a salesman of plumbing supplies—until, in 1895 at the age of twenty-two, he got a break that would do for him what bookkeeping had done for Raskob. The local Tammany political club appointed him as a subpoena server for the commissioner of jurors at the unheard-of salary of $800 a year. In 1903, he threw his hat in the political ring and was elected to the New York State Assembly. There, he got to know some of the state's luminaries, including Robert Wagner, and soon his own name would be up in political lights. As biographer Frank Graham said about Smith, although "he did not like to say it, even to himself, because the event itself was a great tragedy that took more than one hundred lives," the Triangle Shirtwaist Fire that took place in 1911 catapulted him to fame. After the fire Smith listened to the pleas of reformers, and was converted. By 1918, seven years after he took up the reformers' cudgels that would have him fight for social legislation that included workmen's compensation, limitation of working hours of women and children, and pensions for widows, Smith was elected governor of New York State. He had worn a brown derby by chance during the gubernatorial race. He decided that the headpiece had brought him luck, and it became his signature.

Smith had an astonishing memory, which he ascribed to his training as an amateur actor in the St. James parish house theatricals of his youth. Before making a speech, he often dictated the text of his remarks to a stenographer so that newspapers could have advance copies. Then, with only a few jottings of what he was planning to discuss to remind him, he would deliver the speech word for word. As the *Herald Tribune* pointed out, Smith could also put an issue in a nutshell and make it stick. One of his favorite ways to dismiss an issue, for instance, was to say, "It's still baloney, no matter how you slice it."

Despite his mastery of details, Smith frequently claimed ignorance of the fine print, or even of the larger picture when faced with a question he wanted to duck. When asked to comment on the various ways that the Empire State Building might have been financed, for instance, he answered that there were many ways of financing with which he was "unfamiliar due to being a newcomer in the real estate field." This from a politician whose grasp of the tiniest details never failed to amaze his colleagues.

Stories differ of how Raskob and Smith came to know each other, but both reflect how tightly knit the Irish-Catholic community was in New York City. One story had it that Raskob became acquainted with two of Smith's friends, William F. Kenny, a contractor and real estate operator, and Terence McManus, a New York lawyer. The three had sons at the Newman School in New Jersey, and they were all members of the Father's Club, which would unofficially meet in the penthouse atop one of Kenny's properties at 44 East Twenty-third Street, at Fourth Avenue, an office building now known as 304 Park Avenue South. Kenny was a staunch Tammany man, and his rooftop preserve, the Tiger Room, was decorated in all manner of Tammany's mascot as well as in genuine Tammany "tigers" themselves. The Tiger Room was equipped with a banquet hall, a full kitchen, and a card room. But most important for some, there was a full bar, which served as Smith's own smoke-filled room.[3] Some say it was the setting for the meeting between him and Raskob.

According to du Pont biographer William Carr, the story of how Raskob was initiated into New York City's Irish fraternity and how he and Smith met was not so innocent. Raskob and Smith were introduced to each other in 1926 by Eddie Dowling, the actor, said Carr. The next day James J. Riordan, head of the New York County Trust Company and a friend of both Dowling and Smith, told Dowling that Raskob had $3 million of du Pont money on deposit in New York City. Riordan wanted Raskob to switch banks and deposit the $3 million in the County Trust Company, more than doubling the bank's deposits, and he asked Dowling to intercede on his behalf. The County Trust had been established in the 1920s by Irish-Americans, just as Italian-Americans had set up the City

---

[3] A vigorous defender of civil liberties, at the dedication of the new Tammany Hall on Union Square in 1929, Smith warned against encroachments on civil rights. An inveterate cigar smoker, he cited a move to ban smoking in public.

Trust Company. These banks were little ethnic villages. Each was staffed by members of its own ethnic group, each solicited its own ethnic group, and each was situated in its ethnic neighborhood. The County Trust, at Fourteenth Street and Eighth Avenue, straddled two great concentrations of Irish—the Irish to the south, in Greenwich Village, and to the north, in Chelsea and Hell's Kitchen.

Raskob transferred not only the $3 million to the County Trust, but also some deposits of the General Motors Acceptance Corporation. The County Trust became a $10 million bank, and Raskob became a major force in the Irish-Catholic community in New York City.

Whatever the circumstances of their meeting, by the time Smith's derby was in the ring for the Democratic nomination, he and Raskob were such good friends that when Raskob returned from vacation in Europe, Smith was liable to sail out into the harbor on a crony's yacht and board Raskob's liner to welcome him home. Both protagonists were good for quotes, both were popular with the press, and reporters would be there to cover the story.

Smith enjoyed hobnobbing with the rich and famous, but Smith saw more in Raskob than simply another successful businessman. Raskob's wealth and reputation made him an especially welcome recruit to the Democratic Party. The Democrats were on the outs and about to launch an assault on the party that was in—the party of big business that was claiming the prosperity of the twenties as its own doing. Smith figured that he would enlist one of "theirs." Raskob's only experience in politics had been to register and vote Republican, but Smith asked Raskob to be his campaign manager and to chair the Democratic National Committee.

The Republicans had set a precedent by ushering Andrew W. Mellon and Herbert Hoover into the political field from the fields of finance and engineering. But financiers and engineers are seldom farther to the left than a centrist position, and can be comfortably accommodated under the wing of the Republican Party. Inveigling Raskob into the Democratic Party was different. Here was a leader of one of the most powerful manufacturing companies in the world—who should by all rights be a high-tariff Republican and a social conservative—being asked to lead the liberal Democratic forces.

At du Pont's urging, Raskob accepted, and he immediately set to work. Raskob's position at GM lent credence to his utterances on business matters, so people listened when he told the press, just before Smith's nomination at the convention in 1928, that "Alfred E. Smith as President would give the country a constructive business administration. Business, big or little, has nothing to fear from Governor Smith." *The Times* reported that Raskob's remarks had frequently stimulated buying enthusiasm in the stock market before, and this time was no different. After his remarks had been telegraphed from Houston to New York by a correspondent of Dow, Jones & Co., and printed on the company's news ticker shortly after two o'clock, the market, which had been firm, suddenly turned buoyant. General Motors showed a net gain of 3 ½ points within the hour.

Smith's assumption was that just as Raskob influenced the market, so he would influence his business brethren and attract major contributors to the cause. The irony is that Raskob turned out to be the biggest contributor himself (du Pont threw in a paltry $50,000). And big business did not swing over to the Democratic cause. At best, Raskob blunted some of big business's antipathy. Raskob's major success was to establish a well-oiled machine, and soon others saw in Raskob what du Pont and Smith had seen—managerial ability that amounted to a genius at organization. GM did not appreciate his efforts, and told him to resign. The corporation could not have one of its most prominent senior executives in such a high-profile political position. Raskob countered that GM should encourage, not discourage, political activity at every level, and held that a leave of absence wasn't enough. Raskob resigned.

Raskob was clearly not cut out to be the model organization man, and he was sometimes criticized for doing things by the seat of his pants. One reporter claimed that a meeting with him dispelled all notion of Raskob as a captain of industry or even a political manager. Before his resignation from GM, for instance, the reporter had found Raskob sitting in his office in the GM Building just off Columbus Circle in shirtsleeves. There were no frills or fads about the man, only a doggedness of purpose. Raskob compared running a campaign with running a business: "In both cases you have to sell something. It is up to us to sell the Democratic Party to the people of the country. Our platform is what we have to offer. Now, as I look at it, about half of our entire population is already sold. They have either bought our line or our competitor's, so no matter what we can do we cannot affect their vote. The other half are prospects. When you have a prospect and you feel convinced that you have the goods, the only thing to do is to send your salesman after it. On account of his honesty, his past record, his absolute sincerity, and his belief in what he is selling, I think we have a pretty good salesman in Governor Smith."

According to a news story in *The Times*, Smith's nomination was a comforting sign to the French. In France, "where one never sees a drunken man, unless he is an English or American tourist, the eighteenth amendment and its non-observance has always been regarded as the last word in inept hypocrisy. . . . Smith belongs to that section of humanity which is understandable to the Latin mind, that section which treats life as something to be enjoyed and used sanely and openly and not to be perverted by moral and physical restriction of every kind in the feverish pursuit of material gain. 'Smith is no hypocrite' is the usual classification here of the Democratic nominee, and being 'no hypocrite' he is reckoned here as more recommendable than being even the greatest of business organizers."

Despite Smith's and Raskob's best efforts, the electorate was ready for a businessman at the helm, not a reformer. Smith was a "wet" at a time when the electorate was willing to wink at the realities of Prohibition. The gangland rubouts and the near-universal flaunting of the law did not seem to concern them. Compounding the Democratic ticket's problem, Smith was a Roman Catholic at a time when the electorate was convinced that a Roman Catholic in the White House would have the pope dictating foreign policy from the Vatican. It did not help Smith's cause that adding to the average American's distrust of Catholicism was an even more deeply embedded distrust of New York. When the Board of Temperance, Prohibition and Public Morals of the Methodist Church assailed Raskob and other major donors to the anti-Prohibition movement in October 1929, for example, the board made sure that New York City was singled out as having the greatest proportion of major sponsors to the anti-Prohibition movement. Nine of the thirteen largest contributors were New York City residents. Smith was every inch a New Yorker. In fact, he might have had the funniest New York accent ever heard west of the Hudson. Every time he spoke on the radio—which he pronounced "rad-dio"—people would fall off their chairs in convulsive sniggers at the way he sounded.

The line between Democrats and Republicans was drawn along the same lines as those that divided anti-Prohibitionists and Prohibitionists, liberals and conservatives, big-city standards and small-town values. Smith stood on the wrong side of every issue so far as the electorate was concerned. He was every inch the city boy from that liberal bastion, Sodom on the Hudson.

Smith's good-luck charm in the form of his brown derby, which would dangle in miniature from many a Smith political button, could not pull out a victory. He did not even carry New York State. Times were good and few voters were willing to rock the political boat by throwing out the Republicans. Hoover was viewed as a decent man, the man who had headed the Belgian relief effort after World War I and the man who, as secretary of commerce, could claim responsibility for the nation's commercial and financial successes in the mid-twenties.

On election night, Smith went to the Roosevelt-for-Governor headquarters in the Hotel Biltmore, where, as Raskob's successor as chairman of the Democratic National Committee, James A. Farley, described it, "Al entered . . . with his family. His chin was up and his indomitable heart was high. At the sight of his jauntiness in defeat, men and women workers burst into tears. Deeply touched, Smith barked out a few words of thanks to hide his own mounting emotions, clasped loyal hands, and was gone. Perhaps never in political history was there so much distress among the rank and file of the party as there was over his defeat."

On New Year's Day 1929, Smith found himself unemployed after forty years in the workforce. In his mid-fifties, in the prime of his life, Smith had to find a way to supplement his $6,000-a-year pension. Although he told the press he would not discuss his plans until he knew what he was doing, he promised to keep reporters posted on any major developments. Smith was, after all, grist for the reportorial mill. He had just handed over the reins of state government to Franklin D. Roosevelt, and although he had not carried the state in the presidential election, he had carried the city by a wide margin, and he was a popular local personality.

In February 1929, Al Smith joined Raskob and William F. Kenny at the Breakers in Palm Beach for three weeks in the sun (people say that this was the first time in Smith's life that he had ever been away from New York City in the winter, except for his time in Albany). A directorship for Smith at the Metropolitan Life Insurance Company was already in the works, and there was talk that Smith would be offered the chairmanship of a new bank in which Raskob and Kenny would have an interest. The group of financiers and capitalists promoting the new bank was also said to be intending to organize an affiliated investment banking corporation, which Raskob was slated to head.

If reports were true, Raskob was not playing the stock market by October 1928, when he told the press that stock prices were too high and that a readjustment was needed before it could lure back the prudent investor. He considered the business outlook sound, but he could not "see anything in the future to warrant the belief that corporations can increase their dividend payments sufficiently to make the yield on present security prices compare favorably with the high cost of money. All securities held by me," said Raskob, "are owned outright for the reason that it seems imprudent to be substantially in debt with the stock market and money market in the present position."

In the meantime, rumors were flying about what the fifty-year-old Raskob would do next. Raskob was a director of the Emigrant Industrial Savings Bank, and in April 1929 came the rumor that he would be charged with the financial affairs of United States Rubber, a position similar to the one he had held at GM. There was one rumor that he might even work with Walter P. Chrysler. Feeling a little more buoyant about Wall Street, he started talking about setting up an investment plan aimed at the small-time investor who could buy into the stock market on the installment basis, much as Raskob had advocated that motorists buy their cars on time. One reason for the uneven distribution of wealth, he claimed, was the "lack of systematic investment and also the lack of even moderately sensible investment." Common stocks had increased enormously in value in the twenties because the business of the country had increased, and he was sure that wealth was bound to continue increasing rapidly. "Anyone not only can be rich but ought to be rich," he said. Raskob advocated saving $15 a month and investing in equity securities. No stocks bought on margin, no money borrowed, nor any stocks bought for a quick turn or resale. All stocks, with few exceptions, would be bought and held as permanent investments, the dividends kept in the trust and reinvested.

Like all seasoned politicians, Smith and Raskob were adept at the art of dissembling, and the stories about the bank jobs and corporate undertakings or even the creation of new investment houses might have been plants to throw people off the scent.

One member of the inner circle places the beginnings of the Empire State Building at the end of 1928. As recounted by Richard O'Connor in *The First Hurrah*, the actor Eddie Dowling and Al Smith were at a dinner at the Lotos Club in honor of Governor-Elect Roosevelt (this is the same Eddie Dowling who intervened on behalf of Riordan and got Raskob to deposit du Pont and GMAC money in the County Trust). During a break, Dowling and Smith went to the men's room, where, while at the urinals, Smith bemoaned his future. He would soon be out of office, off the state's payroll. He did not have any money saved, and he did not know how he was going to make ends meet. Raskob had slipped into the men's room on their heels and overheard Smith's recital of his personal troubles. Dowling recalled that Raskob said, "Don't worry, Al, I'm going to build a new skyscraper—biggest in the world—and you're going to be president of the company."

Dowling's is a great story, if only for its unlikely setting, but there is no indication anywhere, no intimation, that Raskob was thinking of the Empire State Building or anything like it as early as the fall of 1928. And

Raskob probably did not think it up anyway. The seed was more likely to have germinated in the head of Smith. He knew of the site's transactions by serving on the board of directors of the Metropolitan Life Insurance Company, which had been involved in the negotiations for the loan on the Waldorf-Astoria office building before and during Smith's time as a director.

In all likelihood Smith planted the seed of the Empire State Building in the head of Raskob sometime in the spring of 1929. If Raskob was going to build a skyscraper and if he was going to make a go of it, he could do worse than financing some of it himself and finding others to join in the venture, while having his friend Al Smith serve as the front man.

Smith was the ultimate New Yorker, the ideal candidate for the job of president of the building that would become the very icon of the city. The city was in his bones. He could point out every landmark in town and talk affectionately and knowledgeably about the city and its people. Will Rogers said that Smith was "without a doubt the most sentimental prominent man" he had ever met. He gloried in the past, and—in the twenties, at least—he reveled in the present. He would be the general factotum, the majordomo, the official greeter, and he would never forget to plug the building—to work in its attributes—whenever he uttered a statement within earshot of the press.

When the announcement of the coming of the Empire State Building was made on August 29, 1929, the front-page headline in *The Times* the following day hardly reflected excitement at the fact that the world's tallest building was about to be built; it was: SMITH TO HELP BUILD HIGHEST SKYSCRAPER. His was the glory, his was the majesty that brought recognition and power to the undertaking.

It should not be surprising that Raskob should have chosen real estate to attain a personal goal. As we saw in chapter 4, a surprising diversity of pursuits marked the early business lives of many of the city's major developers. Many, like Raskob, had started out penniless and were scrappers. Furthermore, many, like Raskob, were more interested in new ventures than in operational details, more interested in expansion than in administrative duties. But there the similarity ends. Raskob had been able to work within the carefully structured corporate world, he had headed one of the nation's two mainstream political parties, and he had been an unofficial spokesman for the anti-Prohibition movement and Wall Street. The average developer was a small-time wheeler-dealer.

Raskob's uncertainty over his own immediate future coupled with his distrust of a stock market where such a high percentage of securities was being bought on margin might have been two of the reasons that he would

find real estate alluring. Real estate wasn't glamorous—it was traditionally viewed as a safe, dependable investment that was inordinately boring—but Raskob hardly needed glamour. He did not need the money, and
was satisfied with his lot. He already had an enriching home and family
life. All that he needed was an interesting venture for himself and a valued colleague. Raskob might not make a lot of money on the deal, but,
then again, the odds were that he would not lose a lot either. With the
right architects, the glimmer of the Empire State Building would soon
become a gleam.

# 6
# THE FIRM

**C**areer decisions for architects are similar to career decisions for anyone entering corporate life. It's wise to join a young firm on its way up, not one that is already ossified. And, unless you are on the fast track for top management or partnership, don't work for the same firm very long. Otherwise you are liable to become one of the ossified yourself.

Unlike manufacturers whose start-up costs can be prohibitive, architects can strike out on their own or join in partnership to start their own firm with little more required than a sense of purpose, a drawing board, and a shingle. It helps to have enough money to live on for a while, or to have a client or two already lined up.

John M. Carrère and Thomas Hastings, whose firm spawned the firm that designed the Empire State Building, followed the classic course for architects of the late nineteenth century. They both studied in Paris at l'École des Beaux-Arts, and they went to work for McKim, Mead & White at the beginning of the firm's early glory years, 1883–84, when the Villard Houses were being built in the style of the Italian Renaissance, which would put McKim, Mead & White on the map. Carrère and Hastings saw the handwriting on the wall. They got out.

Carrère and Hastings did not have to take a flyer. They had already lined up a rich and powerful client, Standard Oil partner Henry Flagler, who just happened to be a member of the congregation of the church where Hastings's father preached. Flagler had the young partners design several hotels in Florida, including the Ponce de Leon in St. Augustine, for which they developed a Spanish Renaissance–like style, a Hispano-Byzantine look that was comfortable in the Florida climate. But Carrère & Hastings never deserted their French roots. Two of their most famous designs, the Main Branch of the New York Public Library on Fifth Avenue between Fortieth and Forty-second Streets, and the long-demolished New Theater (aka, the Century) on Central Park West between Sixty-second and Sixty-third Streets, were two of the city's greatest manifestations of the Beaux Arts. It was the style that gained popularity at the turn of the twentieth century, in part because so many of the nation's architects had returned from the Beaux Arts imbued with the spirit of French neoclassicism and a firm grasp on site planning. Richmond H. Shreve, William F. Lamb, and Arthur Loomis Harmon, who teamed up to design the Empire State Building, achieved success by various paths, but the three essentially followed the prescribed course.

Richmond H. Shreve, or "R. H.," received his degree from Cornell's College of Architecture in 1902, and promptly joined the faculty. He taught at Cornell for four years, during which time he supervised construction of Goldwin Smith Hall, which Carrère & Hastings had designed. An indication of the quality of the man's work and his nature was that thirty years after Shreve had studied at Cornell he returned to find his exercises in shades and shadows and one of his life drawings still in use as models for design classes. He had to chuckle.

Shreve's partner, William Lamb, received his undergraduate degree from Williams College. He went on to Columbia's School of Architecture, and then on to Paris to receive his degree from the Beaux Arts in 1911.

Shreve and Lamb both joined the firm of Carrère & Hastings. Shreve had already established a relationship with the firm because of the work he had done at Cornell, and he was hired in 1906, when Carrère & Hastings's plans were being implemented for New York's library. Lamb joined the firm in 1911, by which time the library was about finished. That same year Carrère was killed in an automobile accident—a trolley hit the cab he was riding in. With his partner gone, Hastings lost his momentum. In 1920, he retired as an active member of the firm.[1] The beneficiaries were

---

[1] In semiretirement, Hastings worked on the Ritz Tower with Emery Roth.

Shreve and Lamb. At the outset, they called the firm Carrère & Hastings, Shreve & Lamb, but in 1925 they cut the umbilical cord. They changed the name to Shreve & Lamb.

Their working arrangement was the ideal professional relationship, one with the qualities of yin and yang. Shreve's proclivities were organizational—his was the genius that solved the operational and administrative problems that had the Empire State Building completed in one year. Lamb's proclivities rested more naturally in the design field. Each assumed responsibility in his chosen field, but neither abdicated responsibility in the other. Both were pragmatists, and one of their hallmarks was constancy—there was always the same approach to work, the same analysis, the same concern for the bottom line, the same workmanlike attitude. They ran a tight ship and made sure that their office work was swift and accurate. They did not view architecture as exclusively an art, a science, or a business; architecture was all of these, an indivisible whole. They were, in short, businesslike.

Operations had become large and complex by the teens and twenties. Science in its applied form was breeding specialists, technology was becoming the dominant force, and teamwork was a necessity. The ivory tower in which American architecture had been dwelling was crumbling, and architects had to change the way they conceived their work. This was just the atmosphere in which Shreve and Lamb could flourish. "The day that an architect could sit before his drawing board and make pretty sketches of decidedly uneconomic monuments to himself has gone," said Lamb. "His scorn of things 'practical' has been replaced by an intense earnestness to make practical necessities the armature upon which he molds the form of his idea. Instead of being the intolerant aesthete, he is one of a group of experts upon whom he depends for the success of his work, for the modern large building with its complicated machinery is beyond the capacity of any one man to master, and yet he must, in order to control the disposition and arrangement of this machine, have a fairly accurate general knowledge of what it is all about. Added to this he must know how to plan his building so that it will 'work' economically and produce the revenue for which his clients have made their investment."

On the most rudimentary level, an architect must have a good general knowledge of construction in order to design a building successfully. He must know how thick walls must be, how strong steel posts and beams must be, what forms and how strong roof trusses should be. He must know the kinds of building materials and how to use them, and he must keep abreast of the new products that regularly flood the market. It is folly, however, to expect an architect to be expert in all fields. He has to delegate responsibility not only within his firm, but outside as well. He has to depend on the integrity of his colleagues, and he has to maintain collegial relationships with builders, engineers, and other experts so that he can trust them to provide services of the highest order at the lowest price. Most important, he is always ultimately responsible for the value of the work completed by the subcontractors.

Shreve and Lamb believed that every problem was unique and suggested its own solution, and they never tried to impose preconceived ideas. They did not see the architect as an overlord or an independent deity who could do no wrong. An architect "has a better chance of keeping out of trouble" said Shreve, "if he works with the other directors in his task." When the Empire State Building was announced, a reporter said to Shreve, "We understand that you are to boss the job." "No," Shreve replied, "our plan is to find the best available brains in the real estate field, in various branches of engineering, in architecture, building and labor. Then we will put all our ideas on the table. The best of the ideas we develop in this fashion are the ones we will use." Specialists worked *with* Shreve and Lamb, not *under* them. Their coworkers were treated as equals, their clients made to feel complicit, as if they were colleagues instead of clients. Everyone felt at ease in his role.

The firm of Shreve, Lamb & Harmon was conceived on a train ride that Shreve and Harmon shared. Harmon, a one-man architectural band in the twenties, was afraid that the day would come when he would bid on a job and not be able to clinch the contract because he had no organization to transform a plan into a building. Shreve thought a while and said, "Loomis, I think you'd better come in with Lamb and me. We can go a long way together."

Born in Chicago, Harmon studied at the Art Institute and graduated in 1901 from Columbia University's School of Architecture. He joined McKim, Mead & White as a designer the year after graduation, and remained there until 1911, during which time he advanced to supervise the construction work on the Fifth Avenue wings of the Metropolitan Museum of Art. An associate in the firm of Wallis & Goodwillie for the next two years, he then ran his own firm from 1913 to 1929, during which time he designed the award-winning Shelton Hotel. Often identified with the Empire State Building, Harmon was sometimes a little embarrassed by the honor. He joined Shreve and Lamb in 1929 when they were already roughing out the building's plans, and although some of the critical design decisions show his skillful hand and he shared in the honors, he never regarded the Empire State Building as his monument. He could make other claims to fame. In addition to the Shelton, he designed the extension of the Juilliard School of Music on Claremont Avenue (the building now houses the Manhattan School of Music), as well as buildings for the Kent School in Connecticut, and for Connecticut College.

The Empire State Building was designed at just the right moment in the lives of the architects. As *The Times* architecture critic Paul Goldberger said, a few years earlier and it would have been designed with classical gewgaws. A few years later it would have been a sleek box like Hunter College.

The division of labor was never formalized. As was their wont, Shreve worked out the production schedules, and Lamb and Harmon concentrated on the designs, either singly or in collaboration. But the three would regularly sit around a big table in the library at their 11 East Forty-fourth Street office, where they would hash out problems until they were solved. They never felt protective of their "specialty," never defensive over their turf. Their only goal was to harmonize a project, and have it flow smoothly.

The firm's probity came to symbolize the ethics of the profession, as codified by the three-thousand-strong American Institute of Architects in 1927. The code said that "the profession of architecture calls for men of the highest integrity, business capacity and artistic ability. The architect is entrusted with financial undertakings in which his honesty of purpose must be above suspicion; he acts as professional adviser to his client and his advice must be absolutely disinterested; he is charged with the exercise of judicial functions as between client and contractors and must act with entire impartiality; he has moral responsibilities to his professional associates and subordinates; finally he is engaged in a profession which carries with it grave responsibility to the public."

Professor William A. Boring, director of Columbia's School of Architecture in the 1920s, split with the AIA's position on the standard fee structure of 6 percent of the construction costs, which had been adopted at the turn of the century as the proper charge for the architect's complete service. He thought that in theory the artistic success of a design should be rewarded in proportion to its merit. "This seems impossible to evaluate on a business basis," said Boring, "but a great architect, like a great lawyer, surgeon or portrait painter, could properly charge more than good practitioners whose work does not carry distinction. If this discrimination were usually acknowledged, the beauty of architecture would increase, and the architect would get his just reward. . . . As I see it, the fee embraces in general two elements. One is a business function and one is artistic, the creation of beauty." The service end of architecture was more or less static in every well-regulated office. The cost for the aesthetics was more intangible, more difficult to determine.

Shreve, Lamb & Harmon likewise disagreed with the 6 percent scale. The firm would determine how much time a project would take to accomplish, and bill accordingly on a flat-fee basis. They considered the flat fee especially appropriate for work on large buildings, where the plan of a typical unit or floor was repeated to a considerable degree. They claimed that a fixed percentage for architectural work, regardless of the type of job, was short-sighted.

The architect who demanded a percentage contract before studying the possibilities inherent in a job frequently lost an opportunity to develop real business, according to Shreve, Lamb & Harmon. They far preferred meeting with a client to consider all the requirements and possibilities of a prospective job, and only then would they analyze drafting and overhead costs of similar jobs and arrive at a budget for the job at hand. They would then add the desired profit, which could include the value of their aesthetic contribution, all of which seemed aboveboard and perfectly palatable to clients. Their forthrightness was revealed in the simple contracts they wrote—no "second parties of the first part," no "first part of the second parties," not even "Sanity Clauses." A sample of Shreve, Lamb & Harmon's standard contract in the early 1930s, decades before contracts in simple English instead of legalese had become the desired goal, was published in *Architectural Record* the month the Empire State opened:

Dear Mr. ———:

We write to confirm statements previously made to you as to the nature of our services as architects and the terms of our employment in connection with your proposed ——— building to be erected at ———. We will render professional services in accordance with the enclosed memorandum and will do all of the work listed for a fee of $———, this amount to be paid to us in stated payments, as follows:

1. Upon approval of preliminary sketches and authorization to proceed with the working drawings, the sum of $———.

2. Monthly thereafter on the first day of each month the sum of $——— until we have received in such payments the sum of $———.

3. Upon approval of structural plans and specifications by the Bureau of Buildings, the sum of $——— (or enough to make the total amount paid us at this date equal to $——— or ———% of the total fee).

4. Monthly thereafter during the progress of the work on the first day of each month, the sum of $——— until these payments shall amount to $———. Thirty days after substantial completion of the building, the balance, to wit, the sum of $———.

Total: $———

The professional services of Shreve, Lamb & Harmon, architects for this work, will include:

1. Necessary conferences with the Owner or with the Builder (and Owner's Real Estate Agents).
2. Further study of preliminary sketches which have had preliminary approval.
3. Submission of sketches to Municipal Authorities for preliminary approval of project in relation to Zoning Ordinance.
4. Preparation of preliminary specifications.
5. Preparation of the working drawings, including plans, elevations and sections, large scale and full size detail drawings.
6. Preparation of complete specifications by trades.
7. Checking necessary shop drawings.
8. Cooperation with engineers engaged by (us) (Owner) for the design of the structural steel, heating and ventilating, plumbing and electric work, and elevators, and the incorporation in the structural plans and specifications of any features necessary to provide for mechanical equipment.
9. Cooperation with the Builder in preparing the schedule for the execution of the work and in the award of such subcontracts as may be let.
10. Preparation of drawings and applications for submission of work to the Municipal Authorities for their final approval.
11. Keeping contract records showing the cost of the work as reported to us through general contracts, subcontracts, or vouchers, on account of which cost we will from time to time certify to the amounts due the General Contractor.
12. Supervision as necessary to assure that the work is being executed generally in accordance with the plans and specifications. This supervision will mean continuous supervision or detailed inspection of materials or executed work.
13. The above services are related to the basic building and standard or typical subdivision of spaces, and do not include special work for tenants or non-typical tenants' layouts, or

special finish of spaces for which detailed drawings of wall, floor and ceiling treatment will be required.

14. If, after drawings have been approved, changes are made necessary by decision of the Owner or by any cause beyond our control, we are to be compensated for the work of making such changes and bringing the drawing up to the stage previously approved. Such compensation shall be not less than —————— times the cost of draughtsmen's time required to make the changes.

15. The furnishing of —————— sets of copies of all working drawings, specifications and details. Any additional copies are to be paid for by others, and any disbursements made by us on the Owner's account, such as traveling expenses, telephone toll charges, telegrams, etc., are to be repaid to us.

Shreve, Lamb & Harmon did not "sign" their buildings, a venerable tradition that was beginning to be viewed askance. William Orr Ludlow, vice president of the New York Building Congress, had started to encourage architects to sign their names so that some personality would be attached to architecturally worthy buildings. Ludlow said that it was one way to arouse interest in the art of good building, that it was no more unprofessional for an architect to sign his building than for a sculptor to place his name on the fold of the garment of his statue, or for an artist to place his signature on the corner of his canvas. "By signing buildings we help to educate the public to the idea that a really good building is a work of art, not merely a structure, and that its author is an artist as well as a master builder," said Ludlow.

Benjamin F. Betters, editor of *The American Architect*, argued that even an unknown name on a product tells the public that the maker thought well enough of the product to want to be identified with it. And Charles Hanson Towne, who wrote for the *Rochester Journal* in 1931, said that "it would have been convenient to know, as one passed Fifth Avenue and 34th Street, just who designed the Empire State Building, and, two blocks further uptown what architect conceived the Morgan Library." Towne was right about the Empire State—the architects' names are not to be found on the building. However, he was not quite so right about the Morgan Library. The custom among the ancients was not to sign their works, and Charles Follen McKim, as defender of the classical faith, would not have violated the ancient tradition and had his name chiseled in the stone of one of his neoclassical masterpieces. It's not such a well-kept secret, however, that he had his face sculpted in bas relief as the sphinx in the panel on stage left. It is such an idealized depiction that any resemblance between the character depicted there and any actual person living or dead was purely coincidental, but sign the building he did in his own idiosyncratic way.

With the Empire State, we are dealing with perhaps New York City's most famous building, but the odds are that even if the architects had signed it, the average person would not know the name of its architects, a problem endemic to architecture. You can flash *The Night Watch* on a screen and people will immediately say "Rembrandt." Show the Empire State Building and ask who designed it, and you will draw a blank.

To look at a building and see an architect's distinguishing hallmarks and say to yourself, "That's by So & So," and then to have your hunch confirmed by finding the name incised in the wall is an extraordinarily satisfying experience. Pity that more architects do not practice the custom of signing their buildings. If they did, more of an individual's work would be recognized, and people might begin to learn some names associated with the history of their city. It could be that architects believe with Christopher Wren that their buildings are their monuments, that the buildings should do the talking for them. Unfortunately, we cannot frequently hear their voices. Commonly known twentieth-century architects might number a half dozen—Frank Lloyd Wright, Mies van der Rohe, Philip Johnson, I. M. Pei, and, of course, Stanford White, as much for his colorful life and dramatic death as anything he designed. More people probably know the fictional Howard Rourke than Shreve, Lamb & Harmon.

The irony is that the firm helped carry forward the city's tradition of the tall building to a climax that was not surpassed for years. Unlike their design for the Empire State, noted for its graceful proportions and restrained joyousness as well as for its great height, however, Shreve & Lamb's average building was noted primarily for its size and bulk. Here were journeymen architects, highly respected, perfectly competent. They were safe, they were sure, and they met deadlines. Just as there was little in William Van Alen's past to indicate that he would design such an exciting piece of architecture as the Chrysler Building, so there was little in the past of these three architects to indicate that they would design such an exciting building as the Empire State.

One of Shreve & Lamb's earliest commissions was 41 East Forty-second Street, across Vanderbilt Avenue from Grand Central Terminal, which they designed in the faux Renaissance style of Warren & Wetmore's "Terminal City." It was completed in 1922. That same year they designed the Standard Oil Building at 26 Broadway. They were still working in the medium as practiced by Carrère & Hastings, and the building was encrusted with just about every neoclassical chotchke known to man. But it showed their concern for site planning—the body of the building was bowed to conform with the curve of Broadway just north of Bowling Green.

By the late twenties, Shreve & Lamb were hitting their stride, perfecting their talents, and doing solid work—nothing spectacular, but perfectly competent, and always workmanlike. The firm designed the eighteen-story 11 East Forty-fourth Street that was built in 1927, where they moved their office in 1930, and they designed the National Lefcourt Building at 521 Fifth Avenue, an also-ran setback office building with a boxy tower that was finished in 1929. The General Motors Building, erected the year before on the trapezoidal block bounded by Broadway and Eighth Avenue between Fifty-seventh and Fifty-eighth Streets, however, was an important commission for them, one that won them a secure place in architectural history. It was not that the building won fame for its style, although the *WPA Guide* said that it had a "directness of expression evident in few commercial buildings," it's because working with General Motors, Shreve and Lamb got to know John J. Raskob of General Motors, who would later call upon them to design the Empire State Building. The output of Shreve & Lamb consisted of perfectly serviceable office buildings whose massing was similar to just about every other post–zoning law office tower in New York City, with architectural detailing that could have been taken off one building and applied to another with neither building being particularly harmed nor benefited.

It was not until Harmon joined the firm in 1929 and 500 Fifth Avenue was completed that there was a hint of things to come in both the massing and the decorative refinements of their design. Although the plot for 500 Fifth was less than a quarter the size of the Empire State Building's, which prevented experimentation in massing on a huge scale, the design was nevertheless strong and bold, with a 625-foot tower that leapt skyward, as if to defy gravity, an approach that was perfected in the Empire State Building.

Shreve & Lamb had never designed anything as dramatic as the Empire State Building, and the threesome would never design anything nearly as dramatic after. It was not through any fault of their own, but a result of the Crash. With the exception of Rockefeller Center, there were no jobs of a similar magnitude in the 1930s, when Hooverville shacks became the new architectural standard, nor were there many jobs in the 1940s, when military bases were about the only things the nation was building. The firm managed to design a few buildings in the thirties, including the now-demolished Best & Co. at Fifth Avenue and Fifty-first

Street. For 99 John Street, built five years after the Empire State, the firm used the same vertical fenestration they had perfected for their most famous building, with prefabricated spandrels separating windows, and with mullions flanking and defining the whole. For the corner at John and Gold Streets, which is oblique rather than the standard 90 degrees you find uptown, Shreve, Lamb & Harmon took a page from Voorhees, Gmelin & Walker's book for the design of the award-winning Irving Trust at 1 Wall Street, and chamfered the corner. They designed the annex to Bankers Trust in Lower Manhattan, and a YMCA in Jerusalem for which they used the Byzantine style. In association with Harrison & Fouilhoux, they designed the new Hunter College building on Park Avenue between Sixty-eighth and Sixty-ninth Streets. And Harmon designed a War Memorial to the American Expeditionary Force for Tours, France.

All three architects were full-fledged members of the architectural establishment. All of them were members of the Architectural League of New York and the American Institute of Architects, and among the three of them, just about every position of honor was filled at one time or another. Shreve served as president of the American Institute of Architects, as chairman of the International Congress of Architects, as president of the New York Building Congress, and as three-term governor of the Real Estate Board of New York. Harmon was the president of both the New York Chapter of the AIA and the Architectural League of New York, and he was an academician at the National Academy of Design. Lamb was a member of the National Institute of Arts and Letters (now the American Academy of Arts and Letters), a fellow of the AIA, and, like Harmon, an academician at the National Academy. Lamb was appointed by Franklin Roosevelt to the Fine Arts Commission in Washington, and by La Guardia to the Municipal Art Commission of New York. Shreve was appointed by LaGuardia to be the director of the Slum Clearance Commission, which drafted the legislation that created the New York City Housing Commission. Harmon was a consultant for the Parkchester, Stuyvesant Town, and Peter Cooper Village housing projects.

Like Carrère & Hastings, Shreve & Lamb never abandoned their roots. Their style, rooted in the classical approach, developed ever more toward traditional modernism during the twenties, and it kept on developing in the thirties. However, they never again had a big enough platform from which to launch themselves after the Empire State Building. Which is not to say that they slipped into total anonymity. If they wanted to show off the best example of their work, Al Smith recommended that all they had to say was, "Take a little walk with me down to the corner of Thirty-fourth

Street and Fifth Avenue and give the Empire State Building the once over." And they had clearly enjoyed themselves in the process of its creation. Lamb was asked if he was in favor of limiting the height of buildings to prevent the construction of future skyscrapers. "I would not," he replied. "If anyone can have more fun building a structure taller than any in the city, I wouldn't deprive him of the fun."

# 7

# THE SITE

For the first half of the nineteenth century, the future site of the Empire State Building was on the edge of development. It has been in the limelight ever since, first as a center for New York society, then as a center for national and international society, and finally, from the 1930s forward, as a great commercial and tourist center. Its fate started to change in 1827, when William Backhouse Astor plunked down $20,500 and bought a nothing little farm on a parallelogram of land that roughly stretched from Madison Avenue at Thirty-second Street to Sixth Avenue at Thirty-sixth. Astor was simply following an old Astor tradition, one that his father, John Jacob Astor, had begun. The Astors seldom bought property that had already been developed. Believing that the population of New York City would grow, and the only way it could grow was northward up Manhattan Island, the Astors liked to buy relatively inexpensive property on the edge of development and let the burgeoning population catch up with it. By no inherent virtue of the land itself nor by much that the Astors did to improve it, the property would nevertheless increase in value by dint of the press of population. Following this formula, John Jacob Astor, who arrived in America the classic penniless immigrant in 1792, rose to become the "landlord of New York" and the richest man in America by the time he died in 1848.

By virtue of their social status, the Astors created the city's most exclusive neighborhoods wherever they settled. In the 1830s and 1840s, a family compound was established on Lafayette Place, but by the 1850s, Caroline Schermerhorn Astor, the daughter-in-law of William Backhouse Astor, had grown tired of the old neighborhood. She decided to leapfrog the recently developed section of Lower Fifth Avenue that was housing New York's social elite and move to the southwest corner of Fifth Avenue and Thirty-fourth Street, which was still farmland. There, she and husband William built a substantial, freestanding brownstone house on the northern half of the block front in 1856. Her cousin, John Jacob Astor III, took the southern half of the block front. For the next forty years, the site would be on the cutting edge of society.

Neither house was architecturally distinguished, but both were big. What made Caroline and William Astor's house particularly famous was its art gallery, not so much for its substantial collection but for the room that housed it. A few times a year the gallery would be metamorphosed into a ballroom. With a comfortable capacity of about four hundred; that number, give or take a few, was how many guests would be invited to Mrs. Astor's balls. There were about three hundred perennials, with the balance made up of people in town for the season—a British dowager, perhaps, or a visiting debutante from Charleston. When this list and its number had become fairly well known, Four Hundred became the magical number for New York society with a capital *S*. If you were on the list, you were in Society.

By the 1870s, the salubrious air on Fifth Avenue between Twenty-third and Thirty-fourth Streets was being sullied by clubs, hotels, and shops catering to the needs of Fifth Avenue residents. By the 1880s, the press of trade and commerce was relentless, and a mass exodus began to greener fields, to the newly fashionable stretch of Fifth Avenue from Forty-second Street to Fifty-ninth. Although New York City had the greatest concentration of wealth in the nation, there were not enough of the fabulously rich even in New York to line both sides of Fifth Avenue with palatial houses the two and a half miles from Washington Square to Central Park.

The recently departed south of Thirty-fourth Street could not find buyers for their homes, nor could they find residential tenants who wanted to rent them. The private homes were regularly taken over by small retailers who used the lower floors as showrooms, the upper floors for warehousing or light manufacturing. At the same time, mansions such as A. T. Stewart's on the northwest corner of Thirty-fourth Street and Fifth Avenue were taken over by men's clubs. The Herald Square district one block west had become the new rialto, and hotels were becoming more attracted to the neighborhood.

William Waldorf Astor inherited his father's house on Thirty-third Street in 1890, but, with the neighborhood losing its grip as a first-class residential district, he spurned it as a home. He moved instead to Fifth Avenue and Fifty-sixth Street. By then he had decided that American society was not good enough for him in general, and that New York society, in particular, was egregious. He decided to take his millions and move to England, where he would be more graciously received. His departure was rumored to have been precipitated during the 1890 Newport season, when his aunt and neighbor, Caroline Schermerhorn Astor, started being called *the* Mrs. Astor. William Waldorf Astor considered himself the head of the family, and if anybody was going to be known as *the* Mrs. Astor, it would be his wife, not his aunt. To spite her, the story goes, he contemplated a huge hotel on his Thirty-third Street property, which would get his aunt's goat. The wealthy like to know their neighbors, and a hotel by nature houses transient guests. Compounding her misery, guests would be coming and going twenty-four hours a day, with no letup, no peace. It was bad enough that the Manhattan Club was already housed across Thirty-fourth Street. Perhaps most galling for Mrs. Astor, a tall building south of her house would throw her property in the shade.

From William Waldorf Astor's perspective, the hotel had to be grand enough to attract the right clientele. It had to do justice to the site, and to the family name. The Astors were old hands at the hotel business. In 1836, John Jacob Astor had built the six-story, three-hundred-room Astor House on Broadway opposite City Hall Park. It was the city's most influential hotel of its time, with innovations that included public rooms, interior plumbing, and seventeen bathrooms. William Waldorf Astor would have to build something just as good for his time. Despite the obvious attractions of spiting his aunt, Astor feared that New York might already have had enough hotels, and although population continued to move northward, he thought that the Thirty-third Street site might still be too far uptown. Astor became sanguine that the idea was sound after he had discussed the subject with his estate agent and counsel, Abner Bartlett, whom Al Smith described as "a man of keen judgment and force of character, who never misadvised the Astors." Bartlett assured Astor that a first-class hotel on the site would pay, and to ensure its success, he suggested that its manager should be George C. Boldt, the pet of the rich and fastidious patrons of Philadelphia's Bellevue Hotel. Boldt took the job, and became not only the Waldorf Hotel's manager, he became its guiding light.

Within a few weeks, architect Henry J. Hardenbergh, who had designed the Dakota Apartments and would design the Plaza Hotel, was at work on preliminary plans for the thirteen-story hotel. By the summer of 1891, the steel framework of the new Waldorf began to show itself, and in the spring of 1893, the Waldorf opened. Just as the amenities of the Astor House had impressed travelers in the 1830s, so the amenities in the Waldorf—its 530 rooms and 350 private bathrooms, its vast public spaces and elegant dining rooms—impressed the sophisticated traveling public of *la belle époque*. The Waldorf had its peculiarities. The lobby level seemed higher than necessary, requiring guests to climb a few steps at the Thirty-third Street entrance. And all the corridors upstairs ended at a brick wall at the north end of the hotel, a profligate waste of otherwise perfectly usable space.

No sooner had the hotel opened than stories started being heard about Boldt's fear that a rival might soon appear in the neighborhood. The Thirty-fourth Street corner next door, still the residence of the dreaded Mrs. Astor, was his particular worry. Boldt was said to have heard disquieting rumors that an apartment house was planned for the site, that a department store would be built on it, and finally, and most off-putting, that a competing hotel would indeed appear. Boldt's goal was to have the Waldorf transcend a mere hotel to become a semipublic institution furnishing the luxuries of urban life. His dream demanded more space. He had to bring the warring houses of Astor to the peace table, so he did the impossible. He arranged for the feuding factions to face each other.

Never let it be said that the Astors let a good business deal get in the way of personal rancor. Mrs. Astor's estate agent, George F. Peabody, worked with William Waldorf Astor's representative, Abner Bartlett, and together they poured as much oil on the water as the Exxon *Valdez* spilled. The addition would be called the Astoria—the names joined by a hyphen—and the hotel would be operated jointly under Boldt's management. Should the truce be transitory, some proprietary rights were reserved. The Astoria was to be built entirely separate from the Waldorf and linked only by corridors, and Boldt was required to put up a bond that would provide funds for bricking up every opening if the occasion demanded. Agreed. Henry J. Hardenbergh was asked to prepare the plans for the sixteen-story addition. Only then was it learned that Boldt's yearning for a bigger hotel had already been set in concrete. At his direction, Hardenbergh had designed the main floor of the Waldorf high enough above the Thirty-third Street level to compensate for the rise of the hill on Fifth Avenue. When the lobby floor was extended it would come even with the pavement of Thirty-fourth Street, where the main entrance to the new Waldorf-Astoria Hotel would be. And those peculiarly long corridors upstairs that ended at the northern wall would be joined to the corridors in the hyphenated Astoria by a few whacks of a sledgehammer. Boldt had planned for the contingency of an extension from the outset. The stories of his fears were a smoke screen.

Mrs. Astor leapfrogged society again, settling in the nether reaches of Fifth Avenue at Sixty-fifth Street, and in the spring of 1895 the demolition of the house that had been home to the Four Hundred was begun. In November 1897, the new hotel opened as the Waldorf-Astoria. With 1,050 rooms, the Waldorf-Astoria was the largest hotel in the city. Its main dining rooms extended along the Fifth Avenue side of the lobby floor. The entire second floor was given over to public rooms that could be used for private "entertainments." The ballroom held more dancers than Mrs. Astor's ballroom ever saw at one time, and it could be turned into a theater where eleven hundred guests could sit in gilt chairs and still more could be accommodated in the double-tier boxes that ran around three sides of the room. The hotel's most famous feature was Peacock Alley, the marble-clad, palm-festooned lobby-floor corridor where the rich and powerful came to show off their plumage, the men in their tails, the women in their flowing gowns and diamond tiaras. Out-of-towners and New Yorkers alike were seldom as happy as when they were in Peacock Alley, either putting on a vain show or taking one in.

To New Yorkers, Boldt's hotel became the semipublic institution he had visualized. It was a center of social activity, the place for luncheons, suppers, dinners, and banquets, for benefits and balls. Its walls housed the unofficial headquarters for financiers, the meeting place for politicians, dignitaries, princes, and rajas, the proper ambience for high rollers and big spenders.

The Waldorf-Astoria inaugurated Monday-morning musicales, and made them the fad of society. Reform-minded socialites who wanted to demonstrate the health benefits of urban roofs for exercise while larding their guests with luscious treats found the Waldorf roof ideal. When table tennis became popular, Ping-Pong tables were installed for women. For the men, of course, there had always been billiards. Boldt inaugurated room telephones, pneumatic tubes for mail delivery to the upper floors, floor pantries for room service, the floor clerk, and other administrative innovations that a generation later were the norm for good hotel practice. As *Fortune* magazine said in 1930, the Waldorf was like a British consulate in a Chinese port. It enjoyed a kind of extraterritoriality on Fifth Avenue.

Paul Starrett, who would later oversee the demolition of the Waldorf-Astoria and erect the Empire State Building on the site, recalled the awe he experienced on his occasional visits to the Waldorf during the days when the "Waldorf crowd"—John W. Gates and his associates—dropped in for their afternoon cocktail. He remembered the stately dining room and the days when a nod from Oscar, the city's most famous maître d'hôtel, was equivalent to knighthood. Starrett never passed the corner without thinking of the gigantic transactions that took place there, or the stock-market tips given to waiters with a lavish hand by the big speculators.

Money attracts, and absolute money attracts absolutely. Just as retailers in the service business had followed the wealthy to Fifth Avenue, so the magnetic force of the Waldorf-Astoria attracted major retail establishments to it, and the demand for business and office space continued unabated. This sweep of trade up the avenue was irresistible, and it caused residence after residence to pass into the hands of the wreckers.

By the turn of the twentieth century, a Romanesque Revival loft building had been built across the avenue on the northeast corner of Thirty-third Street, and another loft building, this one in the style of the Beaux Arts, was erected midblock by 1910. Diagonally across Thirty-fourth Street from the Waldorf-Astoria was the Knoedler Art Gallery. Occupying the balance of the Fifth Avenue frontage to Thirty-fifth Street by 1906 was the B. Altman department store, designed by Trowbridge & Livingston in a style more in keeping for a palace than a department store. Farther up the avenue stood two McKim, Mead & White palaces: the Gorham silver shop on the southwest corner of Thirty-sixth Street, and Tiffany & Co. on the southeast corner of Thirty-seventh Street. The neighborhood was becoming a first-class retail section, the new Ladies' Mile.

George Boldt was dead by 1918, when Coleman du Pont, retired from his family company with a golden parachute of more than $20 million in cash and securities, entered the scene. Du Pont had set out to play the real estate game in New York. He built the Equitable Building at 120 Broadway, the forty-two-story behemoth that forced the adoption of the 1916 zoning law. He then acquired control of the twenty-five-story McAlpin Hotel on Broadway between Thirty-third and Thirty-fourth Streets, the Claridge Hotel on Times Square, and an interest in the Louis Sherry and Savarin Restaurants.

Du Pont bought the leases on the Waldorf-Astoria from the Boldt estate in 1918 and created the Waldorf-Astoria Realty Corporation to operate the hotel. As president, he installed Lucius M. Boomer, who had been managing the McAlpin for him, and with whom he had been acquiring hotels, including New York's Savoy-Plaza. With the Waldorf in his pocket, du Pont controlled both anchors of the block between Fifth Avenue and Broadway from Thirty-third to Thirty-fourth Streets. Du Pont was becoming a major player.

The McAlpin was viewed as a strong bulwark of stability for Thirty-fourth Street's commercial prosperity. Du Pont's acquisition of the Waldorf-Astoria, in what *The Times* described as "an old-fashioned realty and business section," showed that metropolitan real estate, under good management and well situated, was an investment of permanent value. Du Pont had acquired only the rights to the hotel; in 1925 he bought the property from the Astors and promptly replaced some non-revenue-producing spaces with seventeen shops configured so that their entrances fronted on Fifth Avenue or Thirty-fourth Street, their back entrances on Peacock Alley.

To mark the Waldorf's thirty-fifth anniversary in 1928, flags gaily flew from every one of the hotel's flagpoles, and baskets of flowers graced the lobby. But it wasn't like the old days when the Horse Show was an annual event at Madison Square Garden and the residences of fashionable New Yorkers were within a ten-minute stroll. In those days the biggest trade in the dining rooms was for dinner and supper. By the late twenties, luncheon was it.

With high-class development as far north as Ninety-sixth Street, evening business was off. The kind of people who might have casually dropped in for dinner did not live in the neighborhood anymore. And although the Metropolitan Opera House was still at Thirty-eighth Street, the theater district's move to Times Square meant that the neighborhood from Forty-second to Fifty-ninth Streets was the place to go for dinner, especially if you wanted a drink. With Prohibition, there was no bar at the Waldorf, and it was no speakeasy.

It could have been that Americans just were not eating as grandly as they had been. Gone were the lobster palaces and the ten-course meals of only twenty years before. Oscar, the maître d'hôtel, attributed the change to the absence of wine. Prohibition sounded the death knell for grand dining, and, consequently, for many hotels, since a hotel's profits are often based on the success of its dining rooms. Revenue generated by any other means, including the creation of space for new shops at the expense of dining rooms, was critical.

Not only had dining styles changed, but styles in decoration had changed, too. Interior decorators like Elsie de Wolfe had started dusting out the Victorian cobwebs in the early 1900s, and interiors were lighter in tone. Within ten years of its construction, the Waldorf's Victorian velvet and plush seemed outdated next to the Edwardian styles at the St.

Regis and Plaza Hotels. By the late twenties, hotels like the Panhellenic (the Beekman Tower Hotel by 1939) were becoming daringly moderne. The Waldorf's wide corridors and heavily decorated public rooms were démodé. Worse, they used up valuable space without a return. The Waldorf-Astoria found itself an anachronism—it was out of time, out of place, and plumb out of luck.

In April 1928, the Waldorf-Astoria fervently denied the rumor that Lucius Boomer had received an offer for the hotel as a site for the Palace of France, which would house French government agencies as well an art and musical institute where Americans might learn about French culture. Within eight months, in December 1928, the site had been sold to the Bethlehem Engineering Corporation. The property, bordered by the two-hundred-foot frontage on Fifth Avenue between Thirty-third and Thirty-fourth Streets, and 425 feet along the side streets, included, besides the hotel itself, Astor Court, the private driveway between Thirty-third and Thirty-fourth Streets, and the Astor Court Office Building, an eight-story structure to the west of Astor Court.

The sale of the Waldorf-Astoria, estimated at $14 to $16 million, was the largest and most important real estate transaction of the year. The property was scheduled to be delivered in the summer of 1929, at which time the venerable hotel and its neighboring office building would be torn down, to be replaced by a fifty-story office building. Change and decay and rebirth was an old story in New York. Most hotels died of old age or the changing tides of residence and commerce. While some magnificent new hostelry was going up, an old one around the corner, perhaps just as magnificent in its day, was more than likely being altered into an office building or being torn down.

Some of the grandest hotels of the Waldorf's vintage had already given up the ghost. The Manhattan on Madison Avenue at Forty-second Street and the Knickerbocker on Broadway at Forty-second Street had both been metamorphosed into office buildings, and the Belmont, on Park Avenue between Forty-first and Forty-second, was tottering on the brink. There was a clear movement uptown for hotels that coincided with the movement of the social life of the city. In 1927, almost two-thirds of Manhattan's first-class hotels were above Forty-second Street.[1] It came as no great surprise that although the Waldorf-Astoria would retain all rights

---

[1] Between Twenty-third and Thirtieth Streets there were twenty-two first-class hotels, fifty-five between Thirtieth and Forty-second Streets, one hundred between Forty-second and Fifty-fourth Streets, and more than sixty between Fifty-fourth and Sixty-third Streets.

to its name, it was closing its doors on Thirty-fourth Street. Louis J. Horowitz, the president of Thompson-Starrett, believed that the Waldorf-Astoria stood for something that deserved to live. Late in December 1928, he sent a telegram to Lucius M. Boomer informing him that some of the banking firms represented on the Thompson-Starrett board would sell the necessary securities to the public to fund a new Waldorf-Astoria. And so the seed was planted for a new hotel on Park Avenue between Fiftieth and Fifty-first Streets.

Tearing down a big, unremunerative hotel made perfect sense to realtors, especially if the sale allowed the purchase of a block front on a prestigious avenue with the single swipe of the pen. Assembling a full block site had become difficult if not downright impossible as early as the turn of the twentieth century. Rowland Hussey Macy had failed to assemble the full block frontage for his store on the Broadway side of Herald Square. William Martin likewise failed to assemble the full block frontage for an office building on the Sixth Avenue side of Herald Square. Benjamin Altman tried to assemble the Fifth Avenue block between Thirty-fourth and Thirty-fifth Streets for his store, but could not wrest the Thirty-fourth Street corner from the Knoedler art gallery until 1911. By the teens, Frank Woolworth was regarded as either a very skilled negotiator or a very lucky man when, within two years, he had assembled the Broadway frontage for his tower.

According to developer Irwin Chanin, assembling large plots in 1930 was becoming increasingly more difficult in the active building centers, where it was either impossible or was accomplished only at great expense. "It is seldom, except when some old and large holding comes onto the market," said Chanin, "that an operation involving an entire block of property is at all possible. This is due mainly to the fact that the last property owner always holds out for the ultimate dollar, for which he cannot be blamed under the present system—or he flatly refuses to be drawn into negotiation of any kind."

The president of Bethlehem Engineering Company, Floyd de L. Brown, knew a good thing when he saw it. Floyd Brown was an architect by training—l'École des Beaux-Arts and Columbia University—and an assembler and developer by proclivity. His first structure was the Sutherland Apartments on Riverside Drive at 158th Street. By the teens he had installed himself as president of the Bethlehem Engineering Corporation. In 1923, Bethlehem built 1650 Broadway, which straddles the south side of Fifty-first Street to Seventh Avenue, and in 1925, Bethlehem built 1560 Broadway (165 West Forty-sixth Street). By 1927 he had won the Fifth Avenue Association's award for architecture for the seventeen-story

711 Fifth Avenue on the northeast corner of Fifty-fifth Street (known as the Columbia Pictures Building or Coca-Cola Building).

Like others in the field, Brown had been stung by holdouts. He had been forced to build an L-shaped building to wrap itself around a holdout on the northeast corner of Broadway at Forty-sixth Street when he built 1560 Broadway. The Waldorf property was his chance to do something big without having to deal with niggling problems associated with the site.

The sale was financed by the Chatham Phenix National Bank and Trust Company under the name Chatham Phenix Corporation, and concluded in the offices of Louis G. Kaufman, Chatham Phenix's president.[2] Brown said that he would begin demolition as soon as he could obtain possession, which would probably be June 1, 1929. Then he could go forward with what he called the Waldorf-Astoria Office Building, a combination loft-and-office structure. The basic distinction between an office building and a loft building is that an office building is designed for white-collar workers, where light and convenience are of paramount importance; a loft building is blue collar. It has relatively large areas and deep spaces that are suitable for light or heavy manufacturing, warehousing, storage, and related activities. Brown hired architects for the job who knew how to design a building efficiently because they looked at a project from all sides—none of that Jamesian business with the squirrel in a tree could fool them. They were pragmatists. They were Shreve & Lamb.

The new building would rise fifty stories from a two-hundred-by-four-hundred-foot base, leaving open a twenty-five-by-one-hundred-foot swath at the west end, so light would be accessible from all four sides all the way up. The building was planned to accommodate offices and showrooms on the relatively brighter upper floors. The lower floors, which would occupy more of the ground plan, might accommodate the full complement of light manufacturing allowed under the zoning law, with storage and warehousing in the deeper recesses. Shreve & Lamb's plans provided 2 million square feet of rentable space, the largest rentable area in the city—the Equitable Building on Lower Broadway had over 1.2 million square feet, the Graybar, 1 million.

If Brown had managed to pull it off, the Waldorf-Astoria Office Building would have had a feature that would have credited him with progressive thinking. Brown planned an off-street truck delivery system similar to the one that would later be built under Rockefeller Center. Ramps from Thirty-third and Thirty-fourth Streets would lead to the basement, where loading bays would allow deliveries to be made direct to the elevators. In

[2]This Phenix is without the *o*.

addition, the basement would contain what Brown termed "a complete automobile terminal," an idea *The Times* praised for "mitigating the congestion bred of his lofty spire." Within six weeks the plans for the building were revised. The height of the proposed building was now up to fifty-five stories, or 670 feet, and the $10 million price tag had swollen to $18 million. With those plans in his hip pocket, Brown secured a $24 million loan from the Metropolitan Life Insurance Company in February 1929, the largest amount ever advanced on a single holding by the ordinarily conservative Met Life. He was onto something. He was hitting pay dirt.

The contract with Phenix had Brown making three payments before the sale was final—$1.5 million upon signing, $2 million on May 1, 1929, and $1 million more on June 1. Brown made the first two payments, but in May he started describing the Met Life loan as primary financing. He needed secondary financing to the tune of $10 or $12 million, which he said might take a little time, but he had no doubt he would carry out the project as planned.

Brown could not make the third payment to Chatham Phenix, and it all slipped away from his grasp. Attempts at secondary financing had failed, and he sold his claim to the bank two days after his deadline.[3] Chatham Phenix retained the services of Shreve & Lamb, and organized a syndicate headed by Edgar S. Bloom, president of the Western Electric Company, to erect what they described as a monumental office and showroom building. Louis G. Kaufman, Chatham Phenix's president, and Robert C. Brown, the bank's first vice president, were both part of the syndicate, which included Edward F. Hutton, chairman of Postum Cereal; Ellis P. Earle, president of Nipissing Mines; and Frank Phillips, president of Phillips Petroleum. They were some of the biggest names in business.

By the beginning of August, a rumor was flying that Chatham Phenix was not going to develop the site, as originally planned, but had found prospective developers who would. The link between the site and the developers was the Metropolitan Life Insurance Company, which had made the loan to Brown. As a Met Life board member, Al Smith had been intimate with the details of the loan to Brown and recognized the desirability of the property, but he could not capitalize on the knowledge without help. Smith had a $6,000-a-year pension, and he had no private source of

---

[3]The failure seemed to do little damage to Brown's psyche. While the plan for the Waldorf was unraveling in May, he took an eighty-eight-year lease on the American Theater at 260 Eighth Avenue at Forty-second Street, where he planned a thirty-story office building.

income. He was serving on the boards of the insurance company and a bank, and he was writing the requisite autobiography that would be serialized in the *Saturday Evening Post*, for which he would be paid 90 cents a word. But he needed something to do that was more permanent, more lasting, something like the presidency of a big building. Smith knew that as a former governor he could stroll the corridors of power and exert his influence to fill even the largest office building with tenants. A deal like that could be his salvation.

John J. Raskob was likewise floundering. Although he had enough money to do nothing more than laze about in the Palm Beach sun, he was not happy unless his time was fully occupied. He was not returning to GM, other job possibilities had not materialized, and his role as chairman of the National Democratic Party occupied only some of his energies. He had to refinance the party and attack the incumbent administration, but Raskob wasn't really a politician. He wasn't by nature a backslapper, he wasn't fascinated by Machiavelli or obsessed by Byzantium. He was a businessman, a wheeler-dealer on the grand stage. Real estate was always a good venture for someone with capital, and his friend Al Smith needed a job. The marriage might work. Raskob had the money, and what he did not have he could readily raise. Smith, although not a realtor by trade, knew his way around New York.

Raskob decided to enter the world of New York real estate and give his pal a job as the head of the undertaking. Raskob convinced some of his wealthy friends, including Pierre S. du Pont, to join him in a syndicate, and they negotiated with Chatham Phenix for the Waldorf-Astoria site. They were the mysterious prospective buyers whose interest in the site had been floated. By all accounts, they got the property for a song—$16 or $17 million.

On August 29, 1929, the same day the city announced that Second Avenue would be the site for the next subway line, former governor Al Smith lived up to a promise made months before to newspaper reporters to announce his business plans. From his suite in the Hotel Biltmore, surrounded by trappings of his former office, Smith announced the creation of a company that would build a thousand-foot-high eighty-story office building—the tallest building in the world. It would occupy more than two acres of land, filling a 197.5-by-425-foot site. As president of the company, Smith would be in full executive control of the construction and day-to-day management. But he would play an even more critical role. He would be the front man.

The job was a dream. He would put in regular hours without the nuisance of citizen activists or reporters nipping at his heels and carping at his every utterance. Even nicer for the poor boy from the Lower East Side, his salary was $50,000 a year, more than he had ever made in politics. As Tammany man George Washington Plunkett might have said in this case, "He seen his opportunities and he took 'em."

Brown had dubbed his building the Waldorf-Astoria Office Building in honor of the distinguished site. The new project was soon given several unofficial names—the Smith Building, the Governor's Building, even Al's Building—which attested to Smith's public relations value. The official name likewise rammed home the association between the building and the man who would be president, the man who had been governor of the Empire State.

Its setting, said Smith, was ideal. The building would rise over the intersection of Fifth Avenue and Thirty-fourth Street, one of the busiest intersections in the world. There was crosstown bus service on Thirty-fourth Street, and the Fifth Avenue Motor Coach Company operated buses up and down Fifth Avenue. Bus service at its front door could take visitors downtown to Greenwich Village or uptown to the Frick Collection and the Metropolitan Museum of Art, even all the way uptown to the Cloisters.

Diagonally across the street was B. Altman, one of the city's grandest stores. Within a five-block stretch north of the building on Fifth Avenue were Best & Co., Gorham silversmiths, Tiffany & Co., Lord & Taylor, and Arnold Constable. West on Thirty-fourth Street were McCreery's and Oppenheim-Collins, both great dry goods stores. Macy's, the world's largest department store, was a block away on Herald Square, and between Thirty-second and Thirty-fourth Streets on the west side of Sixth Avenue were Gimbel's and Saks Thirty-fourth Street. Herald Square was the nexus, the heart and soul, of middle-class shopping in New York. And one of the reasons was public transportation.

Judging by the number of people who traversed it, the intersection of Broadway and Sixth Avenue at Thirty-fourth Street was perhaps the busiest spot in the whole world. No fewer than six sets of tracks crossed the intersection, running on three different levels—two underground, three on the street level, and one elevated. The BMT Broadway Subway (the N and R lines in the 1990s), served Brooklyn and Queens; the Hudson and Manhattan Tubes (PATH) went downtown on Sixth Avenue from Thirty-third Street to Ninth Street, and west to Christopher Street and New Jersey. At street level there were streetcars, and above was the Sixth Avenue Elevated Railway, which served Lower and Upper Manhattan and The Bronx.

On Seventh Avenue was the West Side IRT Subway (the 1, 2, 3, and 9

Lines), and on Park Avenue at Thirty-third Street was the East Side IRT Subway (the 6 train). The Eighth Avenue Subway Line (the A, C, and E) would open in 1932. Pennsylvania Station was two crosstown blocks to the west, and Grand Central Terminal was only a ten-minute walk away. The whole world was within walking distance.

Smith was convinced that the northward wash of building development had a counteractive wave southward. He claimed that the site of the Empire State Building stood as the "great apex of office occupancy, as a structure so high that its sheer personality brings an influx of office population to a district that was changing to an office status. . . . Thirty-fourth Street is the midway thoroughfare of the region between Madison Square and Forty-second Street. As the Waldorf-Astoria emphasized a great trade and hotel center, so, now, under the changed condition, does the Empire State emphasize the growing prestige of the region along office lines."

The site was said to be immune from contact with the garment center on the west and the loft-building region to the south. Smith pointed to the Columbia Trust Building at the northwest corner of Fifth Avenue at Thirty-fourth Street as an example of progress—it had recently had twelve stories added to it. Madison Avenue had witnessed the erection of office buildings just north of Thirty-fourth Street.

Other retail streets in the city might have been prominent, but when it came to a long stretch of exclusive shopping, with rentals to match, Fifth Avenue stood unchallenged. Just a year before, Best & Co. and Arnold Constable had expanded, which was seen as recognition that the avenue was destined to retain its supremacy as an emporium. The percentage of vacancies in retail shops was far lower than on any other major retail street. Of the 225 stores and shops available for occupancy along this gold coast in the beginning of 1930, only twelve were vacant. The booster spirit seemed perfectly appropriate for Fifth Avenue in general, and for the Waldorf site, as its southern anchor, in particular.

The last major residential building on the avenue between Thirty-fourth and Forty-second Streets by 1930 was the brick and brownstone home of Ella Wendel, which had stood on the northwest corner of Thirty-ninth Street since 1856. An eighty-year-old recluse and heir to a fortune estimated at $100 million, Miss Wendel was the last of the neighborhood Astors as well. If the generational count is right, her grandmother Elizabeth was the half sister of John Jacob Astor. Elizabeth, with Astor's blessing, married John Gottlieb Wendel, who, at the time, was employed by Astor as a porter. Astor helped Wendel set himself up in the fur business, and Wendel promptly followed his brother-in-law into real estate.

The senior Wendel laid upon his descendants the duty of buying the choicest of New York property and, following the example of the Astor family, never letting go of it.

There were eight sisters and one brother in the third generation of Wendels. In the tradition of Dr. Sloper in Henry James's *Washington Square*, the brother, John Gottlieb II, was fearful that any suitor for the hand of one of his sisters would be interested only in her money. He encouraged them to reject amorous overtures and to remain maidens. The brother died in 1914, and one by one the sisters died, their virtue unsullied, leaving Miss Ella alone. As Astor biographer Harvey O'Connor said, she was "cheated of life, paralyzed by Midas." She lived in the old house, which by 1930 was called "the house of mystery." It had never been wired for electricity, and it was lighted only by sputtering gas jets and candles. Not in twenty-five years had the front door been unbolted, and in later years Miss Ella never appeared in public. Only after dark was she spied venturing forth for a few moments to give her poodle, Toby, an airing in the high-walled garden behind the house. By 1930 Toby was dead, and the garden was bare. By 1935, Ella Wendel was dead, and on the site of her family home would rise one of the grandest five-and-ten-cent stores in the nation, the granite-faced S. H. Kress.

Mighty forces were already at work on the area's infrastructure, some of which came to pass. The Eighth Avenue Subway Line would open in 1932; its partner, the Sixth Avenue Subway, was scheduled for later in the decade; and a new subway line for Second Avenue was proposed. Construction of the elevated highway along the Hudson River (the Miller Highway, or the West Side Highway) promised to remove automobile traffic from local streets, and the East River Drive (the FDR Drive), the shorefront highway on the East Side, was expected to result in genuine real estate enhancements. The industrial plants—the coal yards and abattoirs—that blighted the East River shoreline would go. A vehicular tunnel from Thirty-eighth Street in Manhattan to Queens under the East River was planned (the Queens-Midtown Tunnel), and there was the idea of linking the Queens-Midtown Tunnel with the Holland Tunnel via a Thirty-eighth Street tunnel that would have passed under the hearts of Murray Hill and the Garment District.

With the arrival of the Queens-Midtown Tunnel, the Long Island Rail Road ferry to Long Island that operated at the foot of Thirty-fourth Street was declared superfluous. With its discontinuation, the "El" spur on Thirty-fourth Street that served as a link from the Third and Second Avenue Elevated Lines was razed. In the opinion of real estate experts, the El's departure and the arrival of the East River Drive would be the keys to rejuvenating the neighborhood. Realtors believed that a new Tudor City would be developed in the area, a new "walk to work" apartment house colony.

The growth of the suburbs was creating a noticeable shift in demographics in the thirties that played into the hands of the developers of the Empire State site. There had been streetcar and railroad suburbs, now there was the coming of automobile suburbs. Autos already used ferries and bridges into the city. With the coming of vehicular tunnels under the rivers to New Jersey to the west and Long Island to the east, an increasingly lateral pull on Midtown in the not-so-distant future would be exerted.

The historic northward drift of Manhattan population was being counteracted, as the metropolitan area became a city of concentric rings like London and Paris. Factory workers began to live on the fringes of Midtown, in the outer boroughs, even the suburbs. Displacing them and living in refurbished or new quarters in the old lower-class neighborhoods were white-collar workers. They were the ones walking to work.

The immediate area around the Empire State site was commercial, but Thirty-fourth Street had a clutch of sixteen-story apartment houses between Ninth and Tenth Avenues. Tudor City, the largest residential development of the twenties, was clustered around Forty-second Street between Second and First Avenues. Murray Hill, between Lexington and Madison Avenues from Thirty-fifth to Fortieth Streets, which had been an upper-class enclave, had seen the growth of an upper-middle-class population in the twenties, with the displacement of private homes and the coming of apartment houses. Residential hotels such as the Dryden, Tuscany, and Allerton House, all on Thirty-ninth Street, were a stone's throw away, and large transient hotels such as the McAlpin, Vanderbilt, and the new New Yorker, at thirty-nine stories the city's tallest transient hotel, were right there on Thirty-fourth Street.

The Fifth Avenue Association was convinced that relief from traffic congestion and the establishment of the retail zone were the source of great confidence in the Empire State area. Merchants who found the cost of doing business farther uptown too rich for their blood could find affordable rents around Thirty-fourth Street, and several who had deserted Lower Fifth Avenue for locations farther north were returning.

In September 1929, the Empire State Building Corporation rented space for its executive offices at 200 Madison Avenue. The building, on the west side of Madison Avenue between Thirty-fifth and Thirty-sixth Streets, meant a two-minute walk to or from the construction site. And the vista from Smith's tower office in the southwest corner of the twelfth floor provided an unobstructed view of the Empire State Building from about the tenth floor up. Smith kept a pair of high-powered binoculars in easy reach of his desk, and he would encourage visitors to view progress on the building through them.

True to the spirit of keeping things in the Democratic family, 200 Madison Avenue had been built and was operated by Jesse H. Jones, whose Houston Properties Corporation had also built 10 East Fortieth Street. The Texas carpenter-turned-developer was rich enough by 1924 to allow him to contribute $25,000 to the Democratic Party, tying him with Bernard Baruch as the second largest contributor to the party. Between 1924 and 1928, he chaired the Finance Committee of the Democratic National Committee, and in 1928, he contributed $60,000 toward the $400,000 debt that had been left from 1924.[4] Most important for Smith personally, Jones had been responsible for the Democrats' going to Houston in 1928 for the Smith convention. Renting space at 200 Madison was a small price to pay in partial repayment of the debt that Smith felt he owed Jones.[5]

The firm of Shreve & Lamb had been retained as the architects of the Empire State on September 9, 1929, by a vote of the board, which was not surprising. Raskob knew the work of the firm well. Raskob had been in on the plans for the General Motors Buildings at Columbus Circle, and he had maintained his New York office in the building during his GM days.

The design for the fifty-five-story Waldorf-Astoria Building that Shreve & Lamb had designed for Bethlehem and that Raskob had inherited would have to be reconsidered. Its massing would not meet the revised regulations of the special-retail-use zoning ordinance. Even if it did, the building's great depth and dark interiors would not attract likely tenants, certainly not the kind of clientele that the prestigious Fifth Avenue site deserved. Instead of contributing to the quality of the Fifth Avenue retail section and enhancing the commercial district, a loft building would diminish it. That was not the goal of Raskob and company. The original plans had to go. Raskob wanted a building of power.

Scrapping the original plans entirely would remove a major drawback to renting potential. More than half of all office space in New York was used by small- and medium-sized companies that needed shallow office space that was flexible and easy to subdivide. The lightbulb went on over the heads of the designers. For the enormous floor areas on the lower

[4]William F. Kenny gave $25,000 to the Democrats.
[5]By the time Jones died in 1956, people said he had been responsible for building just about every major postwar office building in Houston.

floors of the original plan, the architects would substitute smaller but better lighted space on upper floors. Preliminary plans called for a slim sixty-five-story building, but the consensus was that the building had to be larger still. How much larger was the question. There was a delicate juggling act required to balance the nature of the site in relation to the size of a building. Many tall buildings turned out to be in competition with themselves by providing more floor space than their locations warranted. A site that produced abundant returns from a twenty-story building might cause the owner "substantial loss on the excess investment" with a forty-story building on it. A large size and prominent location do not equal a building's prosperity.

But the reverse was also true. Months of study had determined that the Paramount Building on Times Square required a tower if the building was to pay, but at a great price. The higher the building, the greater the need to secure the necessary rigidity; the greater the rigidity, the steeper the price. The Paramount tower would cost 50 percent more to build than the body of the building.

Tall buildings require proportionately more steel and heavier construction, with some interesting side effects—posts and beams on the lower floors are increased in size, bracing is used where columns meet beams, and, because the necessary heavy cross girders take up so much room, the distance between floors is increased to create the required headroom.

It does not pay to build higher than a certain height no matter how much rent the developer thinks he can get for the space. A building reaches a break-even point and starts to become less remunerative, an economic fact reported by the American Institute of Steel Construction the very month the protagonists started to grapple with the basic plan of the Empire State Building. Among the experts who were consulted were Stephen F. Voorhees, of Voorhees, Gmelin & Walker; David Linquist, chief engineer of the Otis Elevator Company; and none other than Richmond H. Shreve.

The block the American Institute of Steel Construction used as its model was bounded by Forty-first and Forty-second Streets between Madison and Park Avenues. The plot was 200 by 405 feet, which was just a tad smaller than the 200-by-425-foot site for the Empire State Building. The valuation, at $200 a square foot, was slightly higher than the Empire State Building's site cost of about $185 a square foot. Plans were drawn for the test in strict accordance with the zoning law for eight buildings of varying heights. Planners calculated the construction costs, operating expenses, and income for each. A building sixty-three stories high reached the point of maximum economic return, at 10.25 percent.[6] Anything higher than sixty-three stories, and the return began to decline. On a seventy-five-story building, the return was down to 10.06 percent. At 131 stories, it was zero. A building as high as seventy-five stories would succeed only if the land cost as much as $400 a square foot. With its $185-a-square-foot valuation, there was hardly any economic justification for going much higher than the originally planned fifty-five or sixty-five stories on the Empire State site. And Shreve knew that.

Raskob, however, wanted something taller still. A proposed building of seventy, even eighty stories would make news and bring his project publicity, so when the building was introduced at the end of August 1929, eighty stories, or one thousand feet, was its announced height. It would be the world's tallest building. Shreve dutifully said that the height and number of stories had been determined entirely upon the economic basis of rentable space. The building as planned would occupy more than two acres of land, 197.5 feet on the avenue and 425 feet on the side streets. It would contain 34 million cubic feet of space, and 3 million square feet of floor space. It would house more than sixty thousand persons at one time, more people than were to be found in more than half the counties of the state.

The special Fifth Avenue zoning was ignored in the first groping toward a design—the early plan had the building rise fifteen stories before a setback—but the idea of attaining the great height of eighty stories by a freestanding tower was already established, and Smith started pounding home the advantages that came with such a tower. The upper fifty floors of the building would always have plenty of light and air for its tenants, and that part of the building would not be obtrusive to its neighbors.

The design's greatest contribution, even in its earliest incarnation, was far more immediate. The form of the Empire State Building would follow the function of providing rentable space that was well lit. Lamb knew they were dealing with an exceptionally large plot. He reasoned that the interior spaces could be used for extra elevator shafts, and the building could be taken even higher "so that the additional rentals, even though proportionately less, may be applied to increase the return on the total investment, including construction and ground costs."

John J. Raskob had a score to settle. During Raskob's hiatus from GM and before his decision to build the Empire State Building, there had been a flurry of speculation that he would go to work with Walter P.

---

[6]The net return on a fifteen-story building was 6.43 percent; on a twenty-two-story building, 7.75 percent; on a thirty-story building, 8.5 percent; on a thirty-seven-story building, 9.07 percent; on a sixty-three-story building, 10.25 percent.

Chrysler. The deal fell through, but what emerged was Raskob's desire to outdo Chrysler in his new real estate venture. Raskob wanted a building that would literally and figuratively put Walter Chrysler's building in the shade. But nobody at the time could say with any certainty how high the Chrysler Building would be.

The Chrysler Building and the Bank of Manhattan Building at 40 Wall Street were ostensibly in a race with each other. In April 1929, the announced height for 40 Wall was 68 stories, or 840 feet, but those plans were revised to take the building up to a height of 925 feet, or 71 stories, which would have made it the world's tallest. Walter Chrysler had decided not only to top 40 Wall Street, but ultimately to top the Empire State Building. By October 1929, the Chrysler Building had risen to a height of 68 stories, or 808 feet, surpassing the Woolworth Building by 16 feet, and it was still going.

A building taller than eighty floors was still more alluring to Raskob, who was fearful that Chrysler had an ace up his sleeve. By October 1929, Chrysler used his ace—his fourth—to win the race with the Bank of Manhattan Building and the Empire State Building as it would have stood at the announced height of one thousand feet. The height of the Chrysler Building was seventy-seven stories, or 1,048 feet, with the erection of Chrysler's secret weapon, a stainless steel spire. According to architect Kenneth M. Murchison, Raskob brought it upon himself. When Walter Chrysler heard that the Empire State Building was going to be a thousand feet high, he decided that Raskob had unilaterally ended a truce in the height competition. Who had agreed to this truce is a mystery, but Chrysler had architect William Van Alen change the top of the Chrysler Building from the originally designed Romanesque-style dome similar to the top of Brooklyn's Willamsburg Savings Bank to a stainless steel spire. The Chrysler Building as it stood was taller by forty-eight feet than the then-announced height of the Empire State Building. Van Alen accomplished the feat when he "examined his plans," said Murchison. "Right in the center of the tower he found a fire tower which, to the untutored mind, is nothing more or less than a large hole in a building. And there he went secretly to work. He . . . and [his engineer] evolved a modernistic flagpole of latticed steel. . . . They named the thing a 'vertix,' because the name hadn't been used before, and they had it made in three pieces. They hoisted it up in the fire tower and there riveted it together." That was the ace that Raskob had feared. But Raskob was holding a royal flush.

It was clear that Chrysler could not add any more height to the building once his building's spire was in place—a propitious time for Raskob to go to work and best him, to hoist Chrysler by his own petard. Arthur

Loomis Harmon had joined Shreve & Lamb by that juncture, and Raskob told them to go back to the drawing boards and design a building bigger than Chrysler's. The first thing was to have experts establish the technical problems that had to be solved before any serious work could begin, so consultants on heating and ventilating, plumbing, steel framing, and elevators were summoned immediately. They all recognized that if a building is to be practical, the supporting posts have to be far enough apart to permit the intervening space to be put to reasonable use. Fifteen feet from post to post is the minimum practical distance; twenty feet is better; twenty-five, better still.

To satisfy Raskob's desire to have the building taller than one thousand feet, and armed only with rough plans for the floors, the builders and the consulting engineers for the elevators were asked to estimate how high the building might go. "It was a coincidence," said Lamb, that "both arrived at a limit of 80 stories," plus five stories for what would be dubbed a "penthouse." That would make it eighty-five stories, five stories higher than originally planned.

If buildings were subjected to no force except gravity, erecting a tall building would not be difficult. But a skyscraper is subject to wind pressure, and for every foot the building rises, the pressure increases. On this the architects were willing to gamble—they bet that the problem of wind pressure could be solved by the existing state of technology.

The Empire State Corporation bought the six-story building at 27–31 West Thirty-third Street from the Astor Estate in November 1929, which gave the developers another 750 square feet of property. They had no immediate plans for the property, but it enabled them to claim the envelope of space for their own. A day later Smith announced at a luncheon of the Fifth Avenue Association in the Hotel McAlpin that the Empire State Building would not, after all, be only eighty stories high. It would be eighty-five stories, or 1,050 feet, two feet taller than the tip of the useless spire adorning the Chrysler Building.[7] The Empire State's observation

---

[7]Sources in the 1930s put the height of the Chrysler Building at 1, 046 feet. Some sources said the Empire State at this juncture was not really 1,050 feet but 1, 048 feet, giving credence to its claim of being two feet taller than the Chrysler Building. One thousand and fifty feet was a far more memorable number, however, so someone—maybe even Col. William Starrett, acting on the notion that nobody would actually go out and measure the building—cavalierly said that 1,050 feet would be the official height. With the Empire State at 1,050 feet and still publicized as two feet higher than the Chrysler Building, simple math would indicate that the Chrysler Building was 1,048 feet, which is the height according to more recent sources. For simplicity, 1,048 feet for the Chrysler Building and 1,050 for the Empire State are the heights used here.

deck would be on the roof of the eighty-fifth floor, the equivalent of the eighty-sixth floor. It would provide an unobstructed view, with the sky above, the city below. The Chrysler Building's observatory, on the other hand, would be from an enclosed space on the seventy-first floor, more than 150 feet lower. Most alluring, all floors leading up to the observation deck in the Empire State Building could be utilized to the fullest, unlike the Chrysler Building, whose topmost floors were practically useless except for the observation gallery, and perhaps a small duplex apartment and a club. The height of 1,050 feet would rightfully earn the Empire State Building the title of world's tallest building without resorting to any gimmicks.[8] The building's height would bring the building immediate celebrity status. But it would not come cheap.

Construction costs were based on a very rough rule of thumb. A run-of-the-mill skyscraper might cost 50 cents a cubic foot to build. But the higher the building, the more expensive. A tall building could easily cost 85 cents a cubic foot; an extraordinarily tall building might cost 95 cents a cubic foot. Raskob was talking about an extraordinarily tall building, one that would have about 36 million cubic feet, and he was conservative in his estimates of $35 million.

The construction estimates included recent financial developments in the labor field. By 1927, painters, plasterers, and plumbers were already working a five-day week, with the other trades still working a five-and-a-half-day week. The different workweeks complicated scheduling, and created tension among the trades. By the time the idea for the Empire State Building was perking along, all the building trades had been given the five-day week, plus pay raises. Bricklayers, for instance, had won an increase from $14 a day to $15.40 a day by the time construction on the Empire State Building began. The five-day week and a 10 percent pay increase would cause an increase of about 5 percent in construction costs, since approximately 50 percent of the cost of constructing a building went to labor, with the remainder spent on materials. Not only was the cost of labor rising, prices were rising for some building materials as well. Although steel doors could be installed in the twenties for the price of cheap

[8]Critics tried to deflate the PR balloons launched in 1930. The legitimate height of skyscrapers, they claimed, should have been defined by the building code—that is, by the building itself—and should not include the flagpole or the radio needle. This would have meant that the Eiffel Tower still reigned supreme as the world's tallest structure in 1930, since its observatory was 906 feet above ground; the Bank of Manhattan's tower, with its observatory 856 feet up, would have ranked second; and third would have come the Chrysler Building, with its observatory 783 feet up.

wooden doors twenty years before, the prices of glass and bricks were on the rise.

Raskob & Co. forged ahead. There were three holdovers from the Phenix syndicate—Kaufman and Brown, and Ellis P. Earle. Robert C. Brown, Chatham Phenix's vice president, took on the duties of vice president of the building corporation. Its directors were John J. Raskob; Louis G. Kaufman, president of Chatham Phenix; Ellis P. Earle; Pierre S. du Pont, who had followed Coleman as chairman of the board of the E. I. du Pont de Nemours Company; Colonel Michael Friedsam, Benjamin Altman's partner and then-president of B. Altman; and August Heckscher, financier, real estate operator, and philanthropist.

Smith had great respect for August Heckscher, who had come forward during Smith's governorship with a check for $262,000 to save one of the park deals on Long Island's North Shore that was being fought by some wealthy and powerful local residents, and Smith had always remembered Heckscher fondly for his act. Heckscher and Friedsam were there to smooth the way locally, to schmooze with fellow retailers and realtors, and to assure them that the building would be a good thing for the neighborhood. It would not be a loft building as had been originally planned; it would be a first-class office structure that would be the crown jewel in the diadem of Fifth Avenue's buildings. Friedsam even wrote a column about the building and its effect on the neighborhood in the real estate section of *The Times*.

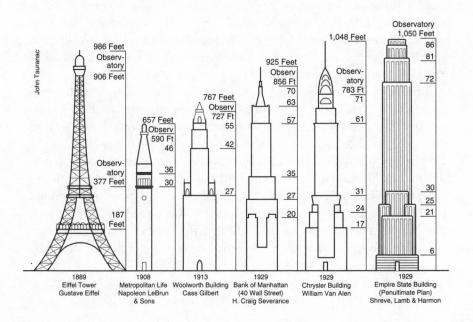

Four of the directors were there to perform more mundane tasks. Kaufman, Earle, Raskob, and du Pont would supply the requisite start-up funds, but not even those millionaires were willing to put up the cost of the entire undertaking. The issuance of stock was not deemed suitable. They needed a $27.5 million loan. They applied to Metropolitan Life, the same company that had made the $24 million loan to Floyd Brown, and the same company for which Smith still served as a director. Smith, however, recognized the impossibility of sitting on both sides of the fiscal fence, and confessed that he did not think it ethical to be simultaneously a director of Met Life and the head of a real estate company applying for a loan. Smith said that it was purely a question of business ethics that he resign, but New York State insurance law forbade a director or an officer of an insurance company from being financially interested in sales or loans made by the company.[9] Just as accepting the Democratic nomination for the presidency had Smith resign his governorship, so accepting the presidency of the Empire State Building would cost him another job. In November 1929, he resigned his directorship, and the loan was granted.

In January 1930, Al Smith twisted a few political arms in the tax department. The buildings on the site had been valued at $2 million by the Board of Taxes and Assessments, and the taxes had been set accordingly. Of course the valuation had been placed while the hotel and office building were still in operation, but since September 1929, the buildings had been vacant and were then in the process of being demolished. Smith argued that the site without the buildings could no longer be considered the same value, and that taxes should be reduced accordingly. Not only should the taxes be lowered, he told the board, but the taxes already paid should be reimbursed. The board agreed, and saved the corporation about $60,000. Smith more than earned his pay for the year.

Ultimately penny wise and pound foolish? Who knows, in the crap game that is New York real estate? The developers might be dead on target, or off by a few blocks. If they were off, very little would have any positive effect on leasing, and there were bad omens for the opening of the Empire State Building. In June 1929, the Regional Plan Association predicted that Thirty-fourth Street and Fifth Avenue would be too far downtown by 1965. The place where "metropolitan activity was brisk" would be Forty-second Street and Fifth, a shift that was already well under way. *The Times* reported in February 1929 that the peak of Manhattan's skyline, which from the time there was a skyline had been in Lower Manhat-

---

[9]In all fairness to Smith, he resigned from all other boards in November 1929 to devote himself exclusively to the needs of the Empire State Building.

tan, was shifting to Forty-second Street. By the time 500 Fifth Avenue
was finished in 1930, *The Building Record and Guide* was calling Forty-
second Street and Fifth Avenue "the best known corner in the world,"
where only shops representing a national advertiser or a firm doing an
enormous business could afford to locate. The action was not taking place
between Madison Square and Forty-second Street, as Smith claimed. It
was taking place between Fortieth and Fifty-ninth.

Something else should have clued in Smith and Raskob that, at the
outset at least, their hopes might be in vain and their efforts at renting
futile. In the spring of 1929, the Building Managers and Owners Association divided Manhattan into five districts to survey the vacancy rates in
office buildings. The districts were Downtown, Grand Central, the Plaza,
Columbus Circle, and the Garment Center, which extended from Twenty-
third to Forty-second Streets, from Sixth to Ninth Avenues.[10] There was
no office district worth surveying in the area of the proposed Empire
State Building. Specialty shops and middle-class stores were abundant in
the neighborhood, but there weren't enough office buildings to qualify as
an office district in the eyes of the building managers and owners.

The coming of such a huge building to the site raised some eyebrows.
As *Fortune* magazine said, they had "chosen a lot where no large office
building had ever grown before, a section which the Forty-second Street
development and the general march northward had overlooked. If they
were right they might succeed in domesticating the migratory real estate
operators of Manhattan within the present uptown frontiers. They might
fix the center of the metropolis." The conditional tense implied that the
opposite just might be equally true.

As late as the 1990s, the Empire State Building stands alone in majestic splendor, a towering peak in a valley bounded by Midtown's Grand
Central District a half mile to the north and Lower Manhattan a few
miles to the south. If the building was to succeed, if it was to carve its own
niche and fulfill its destiny, it had to be awfully good.

---

[10]The "Downtown" district extended south of Chambers Street to the Battery and from
river to river; the "Grand Central" district was between Thirty-eighth and Fiftieth
Streets, from Second to Sixth Avenues; the "Plaza" district was between Fiftieth and
Sixty-second Streets, from Second Avenue to midway between Sixth and Seventh Av-
enues; the "Columbus Circle" district was between Fiftieth and Sixty-second Streets,
from midway between Sixth and Seventh Avenues to Ninth or Columbus Avenues; the
"Garment Center" district was between Twenty-third and Forty-second Streets, from
Sixth to Ninth Avenues.

# 8

# THE STYLE

The romantic image of a 1920s architect is a Raymond Massey character standing atop a hill with the wind blowing in his tousled hair. He gazes out over the fruits of his labor, a dream city where freestanding towers shoot a thousand feet and more into the clouds. Lighter-than-air craft cast off from the tops of buildings, and double- and triple-decked streets serve as high-speed motorways where sleek cars glide efficiently and silently along. Pedestrians ride elevated moving sidewalks that connect one skyscraper with another, and sidewalks built of glass permit light to penetrate the lower levels. These megastructures house both residences and work spaces, with the residential areas in the upper reaches, because that's where the air is cleaner, more salubrious. Gardened terraces on setbacks offer the residents and workers the chance to live out their entire lives without setting foot on terra firma, the roof gardens saving them the effort of descending to wander in the grassy parks that fill the ground areas between the buildings. These city dwellers could exist entirely in the environment of their own making. It was ordered, it was "modern," and, in its purest forms, it never came to pass.

Modernism was soon successful, however, in one respect. It replaced the old order of historicism which incorporated the form and substance of historical objects by an architecture based on function, technology, and abstract design. Modernism had already become a reality in Europe at the turn of the twentieth century with such movements as the Secessionists, so-called because they wanted to secede from the academic approach to design. By the 1920s, the teachings at the Bauhaus School in Germany had architects moving toward a design ethic that was spare and lean, a philosophy ultimately synthesized in Mies van der Rohe's aphorism, "less is more."[1] Bauhaus designers wanted volume instead of mass. They sought strict regularity, minimal decoration—if any at all—and no ornamentation. They were purists, abstractionists—theirs was the starkest, most rigid geometry, where all angles were either 90 or 180 degrees. They wanted building façades on a grid.

The preachers and acolytes at the Bauhaus did not have an easy time converting clients. At the outset, their designs were seldom metamorphosed into brick and mortar (or, more precisely in some cases, into steel and glass). To make ends meet, many designed furniture, which was to architecture what off-Broadway productions are to Broadway extravaganzas—furniture is less expensive to construct than buildings, and experimentation is affordable.

The teachings at the Bauhaus came to be dubbed the "International Style." There are two stories about how the term developed. One is that because steel and concrete were used in buildings all over the world, if they were not produced locally, the materials could still be delivered to the site since they were distributed internationally. The other story is that Alfred Barr, the curator of architecture at the Museum of Modern Art, coined the phrase. With Henry-Russell Hitchcock and Philip Johnson, Barr curated the first museum-quality show in the United States on the new modernism as taught at the Bauhaus. Recalling how the Gothic style knew no European borders and was hence "international" and claiming that the new modernism would be to twentieth-century style what the Gothic was to the Middle Ages, Barr suggested in 1930 that the new modernism should be called the International Style. Propagandists of the style set out to replace the label "Modern" (which connoted nothing permanent) with that of "International," which might also have been chosen because it implied that every other style was local and suffered from parochialism.

Well into the 1920s, architecture in the United States was basically conservative, still under the sway of turn-of-the-century eastern archi-

---

[1] "Less is more" is in contradistinction to the Beaux Arts philosophy that "more was not enough."

tects McKim, Mead & White; Richard Morris Hunt; Daniel Burnham; and other neoclassicists. These leaders of the Beaux Arts movement in America borrowed heavily from the past. Their influence, like their designs, seemed eternal, especially after the impact they made on American society at Chicago's Exposition of 1893: every dinky cow town seemed to sport at least one overblown building that smacked of the Medici of Florence or the pope of Rome.

American architects found themselves between the devil of one type of architecture and the deep blue sea of another in the twenties. Ornament was still the preferred coin of the realm, but proselytizers for the Bauhaus style of modernism tried to sweep away what they regarded as meaningless ornament, to be replaced by flat, bare façades. The new look could hardly be called beautiful by those for whom a building's charm lay in the play of light and shadow over richly varied surfaces.

To the man in the street—indeed, to the average architect—"modern" was a label for something else. International Style buildings were hardly a source of admiration or inspiration, and by the 1950s—at which time they started to multiply in the United States—the buildings were ordinarily described as shoeboxes set on end. The buildings were bland at best, hard-edged, standoffish, and overtly hostile at worst. As Columbia's Professor William A. Boring said about them in 1930, before the land was inundated by them, buildings that bore the stamp of a machine culture lacked the personal element of craftsmanship, the soul of architecture.

American architects were reluctant to jump on the modernist bandwagon, especially one leading the European parade. While saying that modernism was the key to the architect's leadership in the arts of design, J. Monroe Hewlett, the chairman of the Committee on Allied Arts of the AIA, warned his colleagues in 1928 to beware entangling alliances with new fads. The great majority of American architects were neither extreme modernists nor were they old fogies. They wanted to be modern in thought and performance, but they did not wish to throw over the traditions of the past until they were sure they had found something better. And what was better, according to Hewlett, just might be a reaffirmation of the old truths.

Architects in the United States circled modernism warily, and even the self-proclaimed modernists were not as radical as some of their European confrères. American architects did not share a philosophy that demanded affordable workers' housing be designed.[2] They were not interested in using architecture as an element of social change. Nor would they go any-

---

[2]An unexpected development of the designs for workers' housing was that in the 1950s

where near the European glorification of the machine in all its nakedness. The machine did not have to be glorified to the average American. It was already an integral part of his life, one that would come to be mocked in popular culture by the mid-thirties in Charlie Chaplin's *Modern Times.*

American architects wearing the "modernist" label in the 1920s should really have worn ones that read "traditionalist." Well into the 1930s, Harmon said that the "present cult for harsh plainness is obviously a temporary one," referring to the International Style, whose philosophy was "based, no doubt, on a revulsion to a period of undue ornateness. It will pass. Those buildings which mirror most fully the present bleakness of outlook will be most violently rejected by a more normal, reasonable generation. Because one generation has gilded lilies is no reason why the next should strip them bare."

Real estate advertisements for homes reveal just how conservative America's architectural tastes were in the 1920s. Houses, perhaps the most important manifestations of personality, ranged in style from neo-Gothic to mock Tudor to neo-hacienda. Regardless of these anachronistic styles in twentieth-century America, architects happily designed them, and prospective buyers just as happily snatched them up. Americans did not jump on modernism as a dog jumps on a bone. A "modern" house meant it had central heating and indoor plumbing, with a new electric refrigerator and a gas stove in the kitchen. An American house in the 1920s was hardly, as the architect Le Corbusier said it should have been, a machine for living in.

Architects not only designed conservative homes for others, but even designed them for themselves. Three of the leading progressive American architects—Raymond Hood, Ralph T. Walker, and Ely Jacques Kahn—all lived in conservative houses set amidst conservative landscaping in 1931. When Ralph Walker, who had designed his own house, was reminded of his advocacy of modernism, he explained that he had not actually designed the house for himself. He had designed it for a client—his wife.

Commercial clients were just as conservative. Building contracts ordinarily went to conservative designs. Since designs that don't win contracts don't get built, the honors went to conservative designs. For 1928, the Fifth Avenue Association awarded its gold medal to Cass Gilbert's New York Life Insurance Building, a strange pastiche of the Renaissance and Gothic just north of Madison Square. In the same year, the Down-

---

they were foisted off on the unwary bourgeoisie.

town League's award for the finest commercial building in the Financial District went to the Royal Globe Insurance Company Building. Described as late English Renaissance in style, it was a series of diminishing boxes rising from setbacks decorated with neoclassical baubles with a pedimented temple on top. No lean, mean machines here.

In 1932, *The Federal Architect,* an architectural journal, asked the leading fifty architecture offices in the country to name the ten buildings whose architectural design was most satisfactory and appealing to them, with the condition that the firm include one building that it had designed. This last requirement ensured a certain contemporary quality to the list. About twenty-five firms responded (Shreve, Lamb & Harmon were not among them). The buildings:

1. Lincoln Memorial, Washington, D. C.
2. Empire State Building, New York City
3. Nebraska State Capitol, Lincoln, Nebraska
4. Morgan Library, New York City
5. St. Thomas Church, New York City
6. Chicago Daily News Building, Chicago
7. Temple of the Scottish Rite, Washington, D. C.
8. Low Library, Columbia University, New York City
9. Harkness Memorial Building, Yale University, New Haven, Connecticut
10. Folger Shakespeare Library, Washington, D. C.

Five of these ten buildings are neoclassical, and three are neo-Gothic. Only two buildings—the Empire State Building and the Nebraska State Capitol—would fit into what would become the conservative, or traditional, American notion of modernism in the twenties and thirties. Frank Lloyd Wright, the idiosyncratic radical who created pure, geometric solids and voids but still believed in decoration for its own sake, did not make the Top Ten in 1932.

Sixteen years later, in 1948, the *Journal of the American Institute of Architects* polled AIA members and compiled a list of buildings "that, whatever their spirit, possess an ageless, timeless quality of perfect architectural diction; which may therefore be said to be Architecture." Nominees were not restricted to the United States, but could include buildings anywhere in the world and from any period. In short, the list represented the finest buildings from the whole history of architecture in the eyes of the architectural profession in the United States at mid-century:

1. Folger Shakespeare Library, Washington, D. C.
2. Lincoln Memorial, Washington, D.C.
3. Rockefeller Center, New York City
4. Nebraska State Capitol, Lincoln, Nebraska
5. Federal Reserve Board Building, Washington, D. C.
6. Parthenon, Athens, Greece
7. Philadelphia Savings Fund Society, Philadelphia
8. National Gallery of Art, Washington, D. C.
9. Cranbook Academy of Art, Bloomfield Hills, Michigan
10. Chartres Cathedral, Chartres, France

Architectural historians would be hard pressed to improve upon the inclusion of the Parthenon and Chartres, but coming in sixth and tenth to the Folger Library's first-place showing might raise a few eyebrows. Paul Cret, a name hardly recognized today, emerged as the most-admired American architect, with buildings in first, fifth, and fourteenth places, all well ahead of Frank Lloyd Wright and his sole entry, Falling Water, which ranked seventeenth. Only the Philadelphia Savings Fund Society building might be classified as an example of the International Style. America's more usual conservative response to modernism was manifested in Rockefeller Center and the Nebraska State Capitol (the Empire State Building ranked thirteenth).

With the introduction of the steel-framed skyscraper by the 1890s, architecture had suddenly been given a new dimension, and although there was almost unlimited verticality to be taken into account, the potential had hardly affected the average architect. Architects continued to treat skyscrapers as horizontal objects instead of great vertical things. They cribbed styles from history and designed twenty- and thirty-story buildings with great ponderous walls, with rows of nonfunctioning columns, heavy projecting cornices, and everything slathered in neo-Quelquechose. It got so bad that some buildings had full-blown imitations of Greek temples at their rooflines. These travesties of Old World styles produced debates over the form an office building should take—whether it should be an extended Italian Renaissance palazzo, whether the varying classical orders should be piled atop one another, or whether the façade of a tall building should take on the principles of a column, with base, shaft, and capital.[3]

[3]It could well be that Adolf Loos's entry in the architectural competition for the Chicago Tribune Building was a parody of this debate—his submission was a building in the form of a Doric column.

As the honor for perfecting the skyscraper fell to midwesterners in the late nineteenth century, so the honor falls to a midwesterner for setting down the principles of modern American skyscraper design. Architect Louis Sullivan, who studied at M.I.T. and the Beaux Arts, and who early broke with the neoclassicists, believed that predetermined ideas should not be borrowed from one form and applied to another. The effect of sticking decoration on a building willy-nilly was disorienting—the building seems restless, the eye cannot focus, the brain becomes disturbed. Sullivan sought natural resolutions. He thought a tall building should be a soaring thing, its natural upward thrust reflecting the frame of steel upon which the walls are hung to reveal the offices, all of which are about the same size and essentially perform the same role. He said that an office building's form should follow its function, which is, after all, to house offices. Lower floors should be set aside as service areas for banks, stores, restaurants—whatever might serve tenants' needs and those of passing pedestrians. The building should then rise as a shaft, with openings for windows set between the framework and occurring at the necessary places. The top should house machinery required for the building's operation. Not only did his solution have common sense, it had the added virtues of being aesthetically satisfying and fitting the Aristotelian standards for a work of art—there was a beginning, middle, and end.

Sullivan's was a voice in the wilderness at the turn of the twentieth century, but by the 1920s his vision that steel construction involved entirely new architectural principles and had to be treated accordingly began to be influential. Since the curtain wall was of no structural significance in the construction of a skyscraper, the wall could take any form. It could be a sheer, unencumbered cliff, its facing of virtually any material—terracotta, limestone, marble, metal, even glass. It could look like something, or nothing.

Instead of translating the design of a skyscraper into the terms of a formulaic palazzo, or using a style that restricted the design to a prescribed number of windows of specific size, architects began to move toward new forms that allowed them to determine the size and number of windows per floor based on the structural design. Architect Raymond Hood said that this perspective allowed the architect to create an exterior design that satisfied the needs of the interior.

Only gradually did the notion come to be accepted by American architects that the skyscraper had to shed its old skin and be independent of old models, that the skyscraper style should not be derivative but should forge its own identity. It had to be forthright and display its own originality. It had to reflect the necessities that governed the interiors. This change in philosophy led to the belief among some architects that to achieve beauty in their designs, they had to eliminate gimcracks on their buildings, just as Raymond Hood maintained when he discussed the role of sculpture in contemporary architecture. The architects themselves had to be the sculptors. They had to concern themselves with the skillful distribution of masses for their decoration. They had to depend upon a strong unity of design and the power of the bulk of the building. They had to plan organically.

Defining architecture as the "art of building beautifully" begged the question, what *is* beautiful? Where some architects saw beauty, others saw only ugliness, and these became iconoclasts. The old-fashioned skyscraper, the attenuated Italian palace, the piling of one classic temple on another would no longer pass muster. Slavishly copying ideas of the past did not fit into modern lives. They wanted to build honestly and logically. They might hang on to the tenets of classicism, but they wanted it without the sham or pretense of neo-classicism. Practicality and convenience, the American modernists believed, determined the elements of the modern building.

The result, visible by the late twenties, was a more conservative modernism that came into being not as a result of revolutionary fervor but of evolutionary thought, one where speculators and developers, not some mythic need, were the driving force.

There was a growing appreciation for rationalism, for expressing the functional nature of the building and not masking it. Rational designers, or "functionalists," such as Raymond Hood and his colleagues, were held in low esteem by the International Style aestheticians, who accused them of building merely for maximum use at minimum cost. In the eyes of the extreme modernists, functionalists were concerned with neither beauty in the abstract, nor with the aesthetics of the thing. If pushed to extremes, the modernists even claimed that functionalists did not care whether what they turned out was "architecture." If it was, it was by accident.

Raymond Hood said that the radical modernists were wrong for claiming that those in the functionalist camp did not give a fig for aesthetics, but he said that archconservatives were equally wrong with their useless palaver about the collaboration of architect, painter, and sculptor. At issue, said Hood in 1931, was the collaboration of the architect, the engineer, and the plumber. Arthur Loomis Harmon similarly responded to being caught between the conservatives and the modernists. He and William Lamb certainly did not believe that function was the only thing.

They'd rather "try to make the building useful and efficient and still have the exterior handsome," said Harmon, but they had to strike a balance between larding the design with meaningless statuary and having no relief from a grid.

If the aestheticians said that as a first step toward modern architecture, classic cornices with their overhanging projections had to go, the functionalists very well would have consented, not necessarily out of a sense of a higher aesthetic, but out of practicality. Cornices were expensive to construct and killed the light of floors beneath them. If the radicals said that pilasters had to go, the functionalists would happily have sacrificed them, because it might have meant another row of windows for light and air. The functionalists were simply practical, but they were still committed to decoration and ornamentation.

The influence of the American version of the modernist movement— one without social overtones—began to take hold by the end of the 1920s. Raymond Hood pointed out that in 1925 perhaps only 30 percent of the exhibits at the first Architectural Allied Arts Exposition showed modern tendencies in art and architecture. That percentage was doubled at the second exposition in 1927, and at the third exposition in 1929 probably 90 percent of the exhibits were modern.

Perhaps the most influential "modern" design for a commercial building of the early 1920s was Finnish architect Eliel Saarinen's entry in an American architectural competition. The *Chicago Tribune* had invited ten architects to submit plans, all of whom would be awarded $2,000 for their efforts. Unlike the average competition, the *Chicago Tribune* competition was also open to any qualified architects from around the world who wanted to submit their plans, with no compensation unless the entry placed.[4] The goal was simple: The *Chicago Tribune* wanted the most beautiful and distinctive office building in the world. The award went to John Mead Howells and Raymond Hood for their neo-Gothic design, which neatly synthesized the ambivalence of the early 1920s: The building's engineering and technical know-how were among the most sophisticated of the period, while its façade was couched in historicism.

Second place went to Saarinen, whose vaguely Gothic design was strongly vertical, but it was a verticality without the hard edges that be-

[4]This approach was attempted in 1888 for the design of Grant's Tomb, with one difference—anybody, from crackpot to the most prestigious architectural firm, could enter. Three thousand entries were the result, and *commonplace* was the word used to describe the design of the grand-prize winner, in part because professionals eschewed the offer.

came a hallmark of the Bauhaus/International Style. The setbacks were not at 90 degrees—they gently sloped—and he used ornament and sculpture in a supporting role to further soften the effect. Saarinen's building adhered to Chicago's zoning regulations, comparable to New York City's at the time, and his design could have served as the prototype for several New York buildings, including Raymond Hood's later work on the American Radiator Building and Rockefeller Center, and Shreve, Lamb & Harmon's designs for 500 Fifth Avenue and the Empire State Building.

Harvey Wiley Corbett claimed in 1928 that with the exception of architecture, America had not yet acquired enough tradition to create art that was fluent and rich, that it was still in an age of stocktaking. He maintained that the nation was in transition culturally, and was unable to find its intellectual footing. Architecture, he claimed, was the only art in which America was accorded "first place by the rest of the civilized world, and in which she is suspected of having created radically new forms."

Even Ralph Adams Cram, an architect who had a lingering admiration for stylistic eclecticism, said in 1928 that although he regarded music, painting, and sculpture to be in general decline, American architecture was not. He was theoretically opposed to skyscrapers, but they were the perfect outward form of the new architecture. American architecture—that is, skyscrapers—led the world. Cram's grudging admiration of skyscrapers might well have said more than he intended: As much as he disliked them, skyscrapers were becoming synonymous with architecture. Seeing these buildings lifting their terraced bulk against the sky made it difficult not to feel something of the austere splendor of the spectacle.

Modernism in a variety of guises was coming to be recognized for skyscraper design, and one of the great influences for American skyscraper design—one that has been called the defining style for a whole generation of American skyscrapers—occurred in Paris. In 1925, a highly stylized form of modernism whose eclectic decoration was molded into new forms and set into a sleek, streamlined spareness that made Machine Age architecture palatable, was popularized by l'Exposition Internationale des Arts Décoratifs et Industriels Modernes. That tongue twister of an exposition was the eponymous root of perhaps the chicest architectural movement of our time, Art Deco, the name and style that came to define a period.

Unlike its image, the modern movement in 1920s Europe was hardly monolithic. There wasn't just Bauhaus, there were various manifestations of modernism traveling under different names, including Jazz Modern, Zigzag Modern, Streamlined Modern, Constructionist, Cubist,

Expressionist, Paris 1925, Art Moderne, Moderne, or just plain Modern.[5]

Just as New York's Armory Show synthesized modern art in 1913, the Paris show on decorative arts in 1925 synthesized another kind of modernity and influenced commercial and decorative art, popularizing it to the point where industrial designers became household names. Art Deco, like many movements in the design field, began as a movement in furniture and decorative arts, but its influence in one form or another extended beyond interiors and magazine covers and the figures of Erté, to the design of automobiles and even locomotives. American representatives of the design field could only witness the Art Deco exposition in Paris. No American displayed anything, because Commerce Secretary Herbert Hoover would not sponsor any U.S. representatives as entrants in the show. It appears he did not believe that an American could adhere to the exposition's two critical criteria of submitting designs that were both new and original. But the Americans who went as observers returned with raves. If this spectacular new form of modern architecture took root anywhere in the nation, they said, it would be New York—as the nation's communications center, it would spread the word on the style.

It wasn't New York's earliest touch with modernism. As early as 1919, Joseph Urban had opened a display room on Fifth Avenue that represented the work of Josef Hoffmann of the Wiener Werkstätte, the Viennese workshop that set out to design a new aesthetic, particularly one that combined all the arts (Hoffmann felt that the Viennese Secessionists had not gone far enough, so he seceded from the secessionists).

In 1928, New York saw three blockbuster shows on modern design: Macy's displayed modernist furniture; Lord & Taylor mounted a show on French furniture organized by Ely Jacques Kahn; and the Metropolitan Museum of Art exhibited furniture designed by American architects including Raymond Hood, Ralph T. Walker, Joseph Urban, and Ely Jacques Kahn.

Academic terms did not concern them. American architects never called their style Art Deco at the time, nor did the reviewers.[6] This was simply the *new* architecture, a style oxymoronically described as "avant-garde traditional" or "evolutionary" or just plain "modern American skyscraper." The style that is now dubbed Art Deco had a joyous urban vitality to it, a sophisticated Fred Astaire–like dance in stone and stain-

---

[5]None of these was the modernism preached at the Bauhaus, which was too avant-garde, too dramatic a break with the past. It would take another twenty years until that modernism, divested of its cultural overtones, would catch on among American architects.
[6]*Art Deco* was not popularized until the 1960s.

less steel. The philosophy of its practitioners was hardly that of the Teutonic Modernists at the Bauhaus, where you could imagine asking where to find *la joie de vivre*. Art Deco was more Gallic; its philosophy, as became the Jazz Age, somewhere to the left of whoopee.

American architects played with the rich, decorative materials of Art Deco, while managing to remain faithful to the otherwise basic and traditional plan for buildings as laid down by Louis Sullivan. They stamped the urban scene with a traditionalist's view of modernity, and they did it with a panache seldom witnessed since Napoleon III said he wanted a new Paris to rise from the old. When lured to excess, the Art Deco architects designed buildings that were seemingly drunk on bathtub gin. Like a tootsie out for a night on the town, their buildings wore gaudy jewelry and were daubed with makeup in the form of polychromatic terra-cotta or slick brickwork that changed color as it climbed higher. The practitioners would laugh in the face of the academic modernists. They liked decoration, and they flaunted it.

Advocates of the International Style, who claimed their style was more chaste and beautiful, more elegant and sincere, held Art Deco in contempt. Worse, at least to the aesthetes who believed that true art had to rise above popular taste, the people liked it; Art Deco's very popularity became its undoing so far as the elite was concerned.

Art Deco architects in America took the squares, circles, and triangles of plane geometry and merged them with the cone, cube, and sphere of solid geometry to create their own sacred geometry. The architects updated Gothic tracery, and metamorphosed it into metal panels that were installed as spandrels to provide a great vertical sweep to buildings. They created a bizarre new iconography that ran the gamut from Egyptian and Greek to Assyrian, Aztec, and Mayan, complete with ziggurat pyramids and wild jungle plants. They created cubistic birds that never flew and stylized lightning bolts that no Zeus ever threw. They intensified these architectural details with curves, diagonals, and geometric forms to such a degree that the vertical and horizontal lines of the structures themselves were often transmogrified.

Some Art Deco patterns are clearly a rebellion against the more strident modernists' contention that any angle not at 90 degrees was crooked, and that any decoration was beyond the pale.[7] In Art Deco, decoration is an appreciation of the natural forms that are the hallmarks of

---

[7]Emery Roth had an explanation for the differences in architectural tastes that existed between the turn of the century and the thirties. He said that the curvilinear architecture of

classical decoration—natural forms such as acanthus leaves or palm leaves, anthemions, papyrus capitals, even egg-and-dart motifs, but always in updated forms.

A Central American influence in the American Art Deco movement might have had its roots in architect Francisco Mujica, a professor at the National University of Mexico. He used elements of primitive America, the art and architecture of the pre-Columbian civilizations of Central America, to create what he dubbed the neo-American style. In 1919, Mujica drew a perspective of a thirty-four-story skyscraper inspired by the Pyramid of Huatusco, Mexico, and he later published it facing an elevation of the Fisk Rubber Company Building, a 1919 building designed by Carrère & Hastings for the south side of Fifty-seventh Street between Broadway and Eighth Avenue. Mujica wanted to show the similarity of form in the massing. Perhaps he accomplished something more.

Mujica had made careful renderings of sculptural elements from the Museum of Mexico, and he had drawn speculative restorations of ruins. He incorporated these pre-Columbian icons in the façade of his hypothetical building, which might go far in explaining how Aztec and Mayan motifs started showing up in the work of the traditional modernists in American Art Deco. The movement in America used neoclassical motives happily interwoven with designs indigenous to the Americas, creating a uniquely American style that was hardly the same as the Art Deco movement in France.

The American style is a study in motion, almost a synthesis of modernism. Windows, with their spandrels set vertically into an eye-lifting framework, add to the soaring nature of its skyscrapers. Setbacks are architecturally hunched, ready to spring. Rooflines aren't always flattops, as the pure modernists advocated, but domes and spires and pyramids, some of which look more like the nose cone on a Buck Rogers rocket ship than a proper terminal element for a building. Building tops aren't just decorated, they are frequently outfitted with elaborate lighting to call attention to themselves while enhancing the nighttime skyline with the play of light. Indeed, the top of a building is often its most significant architectural detail, its own idiosyncratic characteristic, its calling card.

The decoration was more than cosmetic, of course. It put the buildings

---

1900 reflected the fact that "our ideal of beauty in 1900 was Anna Held and Lillian Russell of large curves, and the architects went for curved lines, while the 'modernistic' is going in for long straight lines. Our ideal now is for the long and slim, and our architecture follows our taste in ladies."

into perspective by providing scale—there wasn't the same old module stamped out by a machine and repeated on a grid, International Style, ad nauseam. There were dips and curves, innies and outies, there was the stuff of dreams.

No single material was used exclusively for façades.[8] Stone was popular, especially Indiana limestone, which was used in three of the city's biggest projects: the Irving Trust Building at 1 Wall Street, the buildings of Rockefeller Center, and the Empire State Building. Stone in the form of white Rockwood was used as a foil for the black Swedish granite in Walker & Gillette's Fuller Building on Fifty-seventh Street, the same granite that was used to frame the entrances to the Empire State Building.

Terra-cotta was also a favorite building material. It had the virtue of being stamped out of a mold, so motifs were easy to replicate, especially important in the decoration you find on buildings like the Chanin Building. Perhaps more satisfying to the designer was that terra-cotta did not have to be the usual terra-cotta brown. Terra-cotta could be polychromatic, which added a whole new dimension to the cityscape.

Glazed terra-cotta was best for fighting fading. It was used in the biggest and boldest manner in the roofline of the Fred French Building, but it was usually used as an accent. Ely Jacques Kahn used it with intriguing results on the setbacks at 2 Park Avenue, and several doorways in brick buildings were given grand entranceways with it. Churchill & Lippman achieved it at the Lowell at 28 East Sixty-third Street, as did Godwin, Thompson & Patterson at 240 East Seventy-ninth Street.

Of all the materials, unadorned brick was the most popular facing in New York buildings, in part because it provided a color palette, and a depth to the façade. Above the glazed terra-cotta at the Lowell, for instance, is an elaborate variation on English Bond in red brick that provides a rich facing for the building. Brickwork allowed the variegated spandrels of Raymond Hood's News Building on Forty-second Street, it created the intensity of color in the walls in Cross & Cross's RCA (GE) Building on Lexington Avenue and Fifty-first Street, and it allowed Schwartz & Gross to design walls that are flamelike—flamboyant, if you will—for 55 Central Park West, where the colors are lighter the higher the brick. It was brickwork that created the contrasting colors of the horizontal striping you find in the rear of the Century Apartments on Central Park West at Sixty-third Street, and the elaborate geometric patterns in William Van Alen's Chrysler Building.

---

[8]One material that was not frequently used in New York, unlike Paris, was tile, large or small, glittering or flat, set in geometric bands or mosaic-style swirls.

Aluminum, a fairly recent development on the building scene, was relatively inexpensive, light, and easy to mold, attributes that led to its frequent use as panels. Raymond Hood, who designed a geometric pattern for the aluminum spandrels in his 1928 apartment house at 3 East Eighty-fourth Street, probably blazed the trail.

And then there was stainless or nickel-chrome steel. Stainless steel might have seemed an extravagantly expensive material for architectural decoration at first glance, but it was touted as being durable and worth the expense, which it proved to be. It has a tensile quality, which was ideal for covering large expanses, and it could be easily worked at the factory and welded at the site. Since it is alloyed with chromium, it resists abrasion and corrosion, and, when combined with nickel, it achieves an even shinier finish. Its use in the Empire State Building for the mullions that race up the sides is one of the great secrets of the building's subtlety and aesthetic satisfaction. Perhaps its most famous use in New York is the crown of the Chrysler Building.

Not everyone was pleased with the new style of architecture these materials afforded, especially those who were accustomed to a less glitzy, more sedate style. The *Los Angeles Express* said simply that a "freakish tendency to break with tradition" was everywhere apparent.

Architect William Pope Barney said that the post–World War I period, which demanded of architects a more logical and scientific approach, was a mixed blessing. They responded with buildings functionally perfect and economical, structurally more scientific and aesthetically more sincerely expressive, but buildings in which a cultured appreciation of the beauties of the past was missing.

J. Monroe Hewlett, chairman of the AIA's Committee on Allied Arts, said that "the present vogue for new character of detail and ornament will wax and wane without leaving any permanent and valuable contribution to our freedom in design. Suggestions of natural form where used are not so much conventionalized as brutalized. Oddity seems to be a distinct aim. The results are highly manneristic. Mannerisms are the easiest things to copy, and we shall, therefore, probably be subjected to a severe and country-wide epidemic of this particular disorder. It is, however, essentially a skin disease. We may hope that it will leave the vitals unimpaired, and that its brevity will equal its violence."

Architect Emery Roth, who was hardly on the cutting edge of the Bauhaus style, did not think that any of the Sturm und Drang was worth fretting about. He pointed out that the Eastlake School had taught that the thistle, rose, and cabbage were more suitable for English architecture than the acanthus or honeysuckle. It would make no difference twenty-five years in the future, he claimed, whether a building erected in 1931 was in-spired by any one of the historic periods of architecture or whether it was planned with a conscious search for originality. Whether a building was de-signed along "moderne" lines or with the use of historic precedent, each building could be equally good and each would equally represent the spirit of the times. All, he predicted, would be referred to as 1930 buildings.

The Chrysler Building, which most people regard in the 1990s as the most stylish of the class of 1930, was hardly the cynosure of the critics at the time. In fact, it was probably the most vilified. One newspaper said that its spire gave the effect of an uplifted swordfish. It was called "the height of commercial swank." "A stunt design," said *The New Yorker*, which went on to say that it had "no significance as serious design."

The Empire State Building was the major exception to all these railings.

When the building opened in 1931, architect Philip N. Youtz said the Empire State was "a milestone marking the beginning of modernism, [with] no attempt at novelty, no tendency to welcome the bizarre." William Orr Ludlow, chairman of the committee on industrial relations of the AIA, said that nobody should "be misled by the lot of worthless stuff recently put on the architectural market. It has not been done by real ar-chitects, but by men who mistook novelty for beauty, who, scorning every-thing traditional, have used lightning strokes, acute angles and bizarre geometric patterns ad nauseam. All this has been copied and duplicated because it is supposed to express modern art. Modern expression in ar-chitecture that has real and enduring artistic value is exemplified in the Empire State."

Even *The Times* joined in the flaying of the Chrysler Building and the praising of the Empire State Building. "Such a union of beauty and strength in a great building makes of it a valuable possession for the whole community," said *The Times*. "Men and women, boys and girls who have occasion to gaze daily at the splendid lines and massive structure of the Empire State Building will not easily reconcile themselves to archi-tecture that is cheap or mean or even extravagantly whimsical."

There was nothing whimsical about the architects of the Empire State Building. They were stolidly serious, classic functionalists. They never described themselves in Polonius-like terms, nor did they describe the building in them. Historians today generally describe the building as "Art Moderne" with "Art Deco" touches, as seen in the spandrels. The archi-tects never called the building "Modern," "Moderne," or "Art Deco." In fact, Lamb's opinion of the more flamboyant Moderne, according to An-thony Robins of the Landmarks Preservation Commission, "was rather low—he referred to it once as the 'Little Nemo school of architecture,' meaning fancy and fantastic, like the comic strip." And whether others called it "Avant-garde Traditional," "American Evolution," "Shrevian," or even "Al Smithian," it was the logical and simple answer to the problems set by the economic and technical demands, and that was all the architects cared about. To that extent it was "modernistic."

The styles that came of age in the boom of the late twenties were, alas, brief, snuffed out by the bust of the thirties. During their short reign, the exuberant structures grabbed you by the lapels and let you know that you were not dealing with anonymous slouches. These buildings—big and brassy—were objects of self-congratulation that allowed big business to serve notice of its achievements on us mere mortals. They stood as the architectural capstone for the twenties in America, and they still fill us with a sense of awe.

# 9

# THE DESIGN

If it is true that architecture is a guide
to the study of civilization, then Empire
State is an index to our present-day civilization.

—Al Smith

**W**ho made the first graphic depic-
tion of the Empire State Building depends on who's telling the story, but
either Raskob or Lamb pulled out a big pencil and held it skyward. That,
it was decided, was the way the Empire State Building should look. To accomplish the task was daunting. Nobody had ever successfully navigated
the uncharted and treacherous shoals of completing an eighty-five-story
building, but architects Shreve, Lamb & Harmon did not hit a reef, they
did not run aground, they did not founder.

In his Joe Friday–like recitation of the facts behind the design of the
Empire State Building, William Lamb's modesty had him play down the
critical element of time. The less time between the purchase of the site
and the opening of the building, the better for the owner—the moment
the building opens, income stops going out and starts coming in. Management wanted the building open on one of the two traditional days for
the beginning of annual commercial leases, May 1 or October 1.[1] In Sep-

[1]The traditional moving dates of May 1 and October 1 created confusion, congestion, and
a certain mass hysteria. In the summer of 1929, New York landlords were moving to end

tember 1929, just as the architects were getting down to work on this un-precedented building program, management set a date that seemed un-realistically early—May 1, 1931.

That date gave the architects a year and nine months in which to design the building and to oversee its construction. They had twenty-one months from the beginning of sketches to the completion of the job, or about 630 calendar days from the beginning of the demolition of the Waldorf-Astoria to the opening of the Empire State Building. As late as summer 1930, then-Governor Franklin D. Roosevelt asked former governor Smith when the building would open. Smith said "next May 1st," to which Roosevelt replied that he supposed that meant the following October. "No," said Smith. "You put it down on your calendar."

Although May 1, 1931, was at their throats, Shreve, Lamb & Harmon remained calm. The special retail zoning plan that had gone into effect the former spring ruled out the loft building of the original plan, so they had to devise, build, and equip an entirely different structure. They worked closely with the board of directors, the real estate agent, and the building manager, the group that would sit as a building committee. Their goal was to design a building that would provide space that was bright enough to justify pre-mium rentals. Once they had determined the basic floor plan, the architects felt that the mass of the building would take care of itself. The speed re-quired for the construction would determine the characteristics of the de-sign, including a simple cladding. They were dealing with an exceptionally large plot. If interior spaces were used for extra elevator shafts, the build-ing could be taken high enough "so that the additional rentals, even though proportionately less, may be applied to increase the return on the total in-vestment, including construction and ground costs," said Shreve.

There had been nothing originally determined about how the building should look except that it should resemble a pencil, nothing said about the building's style. Indeed, style was secondary. According to Lamb, the style would be determined by simple, logical answers to the problems set by the economic and technical demands of the program. No caryatids would be straining for effect, no buttresses would be running up the cor-ners of the tower, no oversized heads would be staring blankly into space.[2]

---

the moving-day rush by distributing the lease expirations more evenly throughout the year. Suggestions for a "four-season" year, even a "twelve-season" year, in which leases would begin at the beginning of any month, had been endorsed by the National Associa-tion of Real Estate Boards, which recognized the economic loss involved in a system un-der which just about everybody moved on the same day.

[2]The giant heads at the setbacks of Cross & Cross's City Bank Farmers Trust Company

There would be no cornices to cast shadows, no entablatures, architraves, or other conventional ornamental devices to break the soaring lines. The design would be strictly functional, determined by the notion that the function of the object should determine its design and materials. It was Louis Sullivan's "form follows function" redux.

Architect Raymond Hood, whose work Lamb greatly admired and who was a close friend, said that the demands of tenants probably more than the desire of avant-garde architects was responsible for the popularity of the modern style, of this functionalism. Tenants wanted the light and space that modern buildings afforded, and were willing to accept modern design to achieve their needs. Suddenly designs that only a few years before might have seemed radical had won a more secure place. It wasn't that ornament cost so much more, but even if the syndicate had been willing to pay the little extra for it, there were more fingers in the fiscal pie than those of the four primary underwriters. The Metropolitan Life Insurance Company was a conservative investor whose goal, naturally enough, was to secure the greatest possible return upon invested capital. Underwriters were willing to tie up their investment over a period of many years, but less willing to pay for what was deemed redundant decoration. Hood told of one banker who rejected a design that was all gussied up. When the architect returned with something more practical, the revised plan was financed. Hood said that architects and developers were catching on to the fact that mortgage money would more readily go to office buildings in the modern, functionalist style than those designed in a more traditional style, a trend that would continue, since the two building styles were for one building type performing the same function.

Underwriters also saw a correlation between the financial return on a building and the efficiency of its plan. They insisted on flexibility, and they wanted buildings that could easily be converted from one type of occupancy to another. As James B. Newman of the firm of Ely Jacques Kahn put it, "this, in common parlance, means safety of investment through diversification."

Lamb was considering the financing, as well as the operation. He had always listened to people who had to deal with the nitty-gritty of building management. Building managers, like bankers, are ordinarily regarded as Philistines by Romantics, but they know what makes a building work efficiently, what makes a building tick, and Lamb was no Romantic. The average building manager did not give a fig for fancy decoration—an office

---

Building on William Street were cleverly masked air vents.

building should be strictly a structure of utility, and the nearer the design of an office building came to fulfilling its purpose, the more beautiful it was, according to Clarence Coley, who was managing the Equitable Building. The only good investments made in office buildings were those that contributed to their use and comfort. Every cubic foot had to be constructed for intensive use and wear; every piece of material used in construction had to have a purpose to warrant its existence. The investment was strictly a cold-blooded proposition, and owners whose office buildings showed individualism were fools soon parted from their money. The Empire State would be standardized, made up of approved and tested units, and all sentiment would be eliminated from the design.

With the building's extraordinary height, wind bracing would become extremely important, requiring a complete gridiron of in-line steel posts and beams both vertically and horizontally. Only when the steel skeleton was roughed out could the general size and location of ventilation and pipe shafts be taken into account, and only then could the building contractors estimate how much the general construction would cost. The idea that finally turned the tide for the architects, the notion that made everything fall in place, was to set the elevators in a central core, which would allow the Empire State Building to provide rentable space that was well lit. From that point forward, they were home free—the solutions were at hand. The architects had already recognized that the maximum floor space was not always the most desirable, so they substituted small but well-lighted floors on the upper stories for large, unbroken floor areas on the lower stories. The sixty-four elevators, together with mail chutes, staircases, and other equipment, would be centered in space tapering upward to a cone, instead of being distributed throughout the wings of the building. "The logic of the plan was very simple," said Lamb in 1931 in *The Architectural Forum*. "A certain amount of space in the center, arranged as compactly as possible, contains the vertical circulation, mail chutes, toilets, shafts, and corridors. Surrounding this is a perimeter of office space 28 feet deep. The sizes of the floors diminish as the elevators decrease in number. In essence there is a pyramid of non-rentable space surrounded by a greater pyramid of rentable space, a principle modified of course by practical consideration of construction and elevator operation." The core of the building would be used to house the requisite utilities; the rentable office space, assured of light, would surround the core.

A freestanding tower with services in the central well was nothing new. John Mead Howells's Panhellenic Tower, Raymond Hood's American Radiator Building, Cass Gilbert's Woolworth Tower, and Ernest Flagg's Singer Tower all incorporated the idea. It was a building plan that made eminently good sense, and it reflected what Shreve described as the most important element in the economic design of an office building. It established the basic office unit, the cell whose multiplication around the central group of building utilities set the standard for the typical floor plan and so produced the total structure. Proper floor planning was essential to the successful design of an office building if the structure was to earn income in excess of expenses. Little else was of importance.

Tower floors, as opposed to loft floors, would meet the requirements for the greatest number of employers who sought to increase the efficiency of their workers. The offices would be better lit and ventilated, and they would be quieter, since offices in a tower are set back from the street and its concomitant noise. Although the tower floors had smaller floor space, the working conditions would be better, and the space could be rented at a premium. If the solution meant less floor space per floor in a tower versus more floor space per floor in a squatter, more traditional building, less was definitely more.

What happened then was topsy-turvy. Ordinarily, a building is planned from the ground up, piling floor upon floor and breaking the vertical rise where setbacks are required, until the desired height is reached. In the case of the Empire State Building, however, the interiors set the standard. Instead of designing the floor plan at the bottom and working up, Shreve, Lamb & Harmon set a standard for light and designed the building from the top down.

The architects must have known they were onto something when the builders, engineers, and subcontractors gave their approval to the plan in two hours. The "parti," or the marriage among them, said Lamb, was set. The basic plan of the building was reached in four weeks. The night before the presentation a charette produced a series of five or six of the essential plans, an elevation, a perspective, and a fairly accurate tabulation of rentable areas.

When the presentation was made to the building committee the next day, whoever had said he wanted a building that looked like a big pencil got his wish, and more. Raskob, Smith, and their colleagues saw a plan with massing that was bold and daring, a building whose design had become refined over a series of iterations to be one of the most elegant of skyscraper profiles. As the *Federal Architect* later said, it was "transcendentally well designed as to mass, ornament, relation of its parts."

Instead of the lower floors covering the entire ground site and climbing ten or eleven stories on Fifth Avenue before having a setback, which would have been allowed under the special Fifth Avenue zoning law, or instead of the usual series of setbacks stacked upon each other within the confines of the zoning law, a five-story base covered the plot. At the sixth floor was a major setback—sixty feet from the Fifth Avenue building line, and twenty and thirty feet from the building lines of Thirty-third and Thirty-fourth Streets.

From this low base there rose a tower that in diminishing jetés soared majestically to the eighty-fifth floor. The lower part of the tower was set back from the street lines well within the limits of the zoning envelope, and extended upward about 350 feet, or twenty-nine stories, above the street level. The east and west faces of the shaft were about 135 feet long, the north and south faces, 185. The tower's rectangular floor plan was set on an east-west axis, rising with a minimum of setbacks from the low base. As the building shed itself of the lower floors, it stepped back from the long dimension of the property to approach the square form of the shaft. By the thirtieth floor, the building only occupied 25 percent of the entire site, satisfying the zoning law that permitted a building to go as high as the developer wished on one-quarter the plot. There the major set-backs ended, and the seven-hundred-foot-high tower rose unbroken to the eightieth floor. Its sheer walls created a dramatic vertical thrust above the attenuated trunk, and terminated with the five topmost floors slightly re-cessed, their corners chamfered and acting as the capstone, 1,050 feet above the sidewalk. The building was almost all tower.

From a vantage point almost a quarter of a mile above the heart of Manhattan, the vast panorama of the metropolitan region would unfold to the view of sightseers from the world's highest observation deck, or promenade, as it was frequently called. The entire 80-by-130-foot roof of the building would be given over to tourism, with several thousand square feet of space dedicated to the promenade. It would be about 150 feet higher than the observation platform of the Eiffel Tower, and over 250 feet above the observatory in the Chrysler Building. The fact that the building was clearly so much taller than the Chrysler Building made it particularly attractive to the developers, who knew that people measure a building by the number of its stories, which is the true measure of the height of a building, and theirs would be a full eighty-five stories of us-able space.

Most important, perhaps, was the overall design of the building itself. It was big, it was bold, it was beautiful.

There is a clarity of design that contributes mightily to the building's satisfaction. The harmony of design, with all the elements balanced in true classical form, is sheer elegance. At every stage horizontally and ver-tically there is a beginning, middle, and end, an introduction to the theme, a development of the theme, a recapitulation of the theme.

The classical truths of the building are self-evident. The subtler attributes are not. On the base and up to the second setback is stone that has been cut into sets of vertical, convex bands, rather like a three-dimensional scallop motif. These bands make the lower part of the building appear stouter, and although they are the same limestone as the rest of the building they nevertheless add coloration by virtue of the shadows they cast. All but the outside bands rise to the setbacks, the outside bands falling short to act as shoulders and to provide balance. The midsection seems firmer, more solid, yet ever so graceful. From it, the upper tower rises unencumbered.

The massive bays provided a depth to the building. Light and shadow played and added to the building's satisfaction, much as the recesses in Harmon's Shelton Hotel had created light and shadow. And the bays, most of which were six windows wide, had the added benefit of creating a floor plan with more desirable corner offices than a simple four-cornered box tower.

Walls at the setbacks were gently tapered—almost but not quite the entasis as practiced by the Greeks, who tried to counteract the curvature of the human eye by giving a slight bulge outward in vertical elements and upward in horizontal ones, an attempt at fooling the eye into seeing things straight instead of sagging. The top five floors were chamfered, their corners cut away and softened so that the building reached a logical denouement.

Great ribbons of windows and spandrels reached for the sky, their soaring quality enhanced by vertical strips of stainless steel that flanked them. Topping these great vertical bands were fanlike motifs, Art Deco responses to terminating features that some critics interpreted as sunbursts, others as anthemions. Whatever their root, they serve as perfect capstones.

The theatricality of most buildings of the period was confined to the street level and to the rooflines, for the obvious reason that those are the places where they can best be seen and appreciated—you can see the lower part of the building up close, the upper part from afar. The Empire State Building in its penultimate form was different. The shaft took on a life of its own. The 1,050-foot building was tall, but with the building gently sloping toward its summit, it appeared even taller and more magnificent. What registers in our eye, in following the building upward, and what is perceived in our mind, which is aware that the size of anything decreases with distance, combine to create an even greater impression of height, the illusion created by the building's shape.

Perhaps the major design flaw was the roofline's flattop approach, which seemed earthbound, flat-footed, and static compared with the rest of the building. Nevertheless, it was a dramatic design. The critic Lewis Mumford thought that the dignity of the unbroken shaft gave it the same effect as the Washington Monument. Hugh Ferriss said that there was no escaping a strong emotion in the presence of its vast steps and sheer ascending planes, that in its forthright structural simplicity, its scale, and its power, the Empire State Building announced the coming of a new order.

The elevator system was one of the keys to both the general arrangement of the plan and the height to which the building could rise. Eighty floors had already been established as the practical limit of the single-deck high-speed car running to the street level. The weight of the extraordinarily long hoisting ropes in the high-rise banks, coupled with the weight of the car and its load, imposed duties never before attained in passenger elevators, but the designers' goal was to work with already existing technology, modifying only if necessary. The team did not have the luxury of time to allow engineers to experiment. They rejected Otis's plans for running express and local cars in the same shaft, they rejected the "skylobby" or plaza floor like that found in later buildings such as the World Trade Center (1973), and they rejected the double-decked elevators found in the Citicorp Building (1979). To the greatest extent possible, they opted for the tried and true.

The elevator banks were placed parallel to the main axis of the building, with the four groups of high-rise elevators—capable of a speed of 700 feet a minute, the maximum permitted under the city code—in the center of the building, with the low-rise groups flanking them on the east and west sides. As the building rose and fell away, the flanking elevators fell away.

Rentals are directly affected by elevator service. Floors with nonstop service are the easiest to rent, and can demand premium figures. They have the fastest service, with the added benefit of being transfer floors. The elevator schedule took into account not just express service but local travel, allowing tenants and visitors to take short trips in the same bank or to transfer easily from one bank to another, and it apportioned elevator service equally among the floors as follows:

Bank A, four cars, third to seventh floors
Bank B, ten cars, seventh to eighteenth floors
Bank C, eight cars, eighteenth to twenty-fifth floors
Bank D, ten cars, twenty-fifth to forty-first floors
Bank E, eight cars, forty-first to fifty-fifth floors
Bank F, eight cars, fifty-fifth to sixty-seventh floors
Bank G, ten cars, sixty-seventh to eightieth floors

Above the eightieth floor, two transfer elevators would provide service to the eighty-sixth floor.

The plot that the Empire State Building would occupy was enormous. The building filled 197.5 feet on Fifth Avenue, and 425 feet on Thirty-third and Thirty-fourth Streets, or about 84,000 square feet. The frontages on Fifth Avenue and on Thirty-fourth Street faced one-hundred-foot-wide streets, which was about as wide as you could hope for in Mid-town without overlooking a park or a break in the right-angled street pattern. The Thirty-third Street frontage overlooked a standard sixty-foot-wide side street. The site provided Shreve, Lamb & Harmon with three exposures. Small, full-block sites with four exposures produced the finest spaces, because the interiors stood the greatest chance of receiving adequate light. The architects knew that anything adversely affecting the amount of light in an office equally affected its value. The architects had to deal with the bad features associated with a large plot, the negative of a positive.

The seed had already been planted, of course. If the building was to resemble a pencil, then the whole building would essentially be a slim, free-standing tower. From the sixth floor up, the building would have four exposures, not just three, and light would enter from all sides and fill the shallow office spaces.

Smith immediately took advantage of the public relations opportunities the plan presented, which he heralded as a model for others to emulate. Although some developers still objected to "the waste" of space that resulted from setbacks, the developers of the Empire State Building were willing to sacrifice rentable space to achieve their goal of providing sunlight and air, as well as freedom from street noises. That was why a setback was provided on all sides at the sixth floor. Although the building would contain about 3 million square feet of rental space, the developers were taking about 300,000 square feet less than the amount permitted under the zoning laws for a building plot of its size. And although the skyscraper would be eighty-five stories high, light and air for neighboring buildings and for the building's own tenants would be protected through the setback and floor arrangement that Smith called the "Empire State Formula," as though it were a patent medicine that could be sold over the counter to any developer.

The elegance of the façade was the brainchild of Shreve, who devised a method of treating the building's sixty-four hundred windows to express solidity of mass while avoiding "the impression of a perforated shell, of adding dignity to utility while escaping the inherently monotonous grid-iron of oft-repeated floors crossed by the slotted vertical bands of uniformly spaced windows." The lateral theme composed for the façade was a module of limestone, mullion, window/spandrel, mullion, limestone, etc. Shreve took to heart the maxim to keep things simple.

Windows on the lower five floors were installed in the conventional manner. Above, however, they were different. Shreve said that the great breakthrough came when the decision was made to "eliminate the customary reveals of soffits and jambs,[3] and their attendant assertive shadows." It didn't matter that the walls of a skyscraper had nothing to do with supporting the building; people still believed that the thickness of a wall conveyed the strength of the structure. Windows were usually placed within deep openings, but Shreve was not sure that even an eight-inch-deep reveal would be terribly convincing or reassuring in a masonry wall a thousand feet high. He thought the mass of the tower would seem sturdier if its outer shell were treated not as a load-bearing structural element but as a wrapping, that its appearance would be more satisfying if the windows were placed flush with the façade. The walls would appear seamless, one of the guiding precepts of modernism.[4]

Typical of Shreve, the plan was not purely aesthetic. The window frames were set into the openings so that the frames covered the edges of the flanking stone and were flush with the spandrels. Since the window frames covered the joins, the stone did not have to be finished, which greatly reduced the cost of the stonework, and simplified installation. A method of window support that did not involve experimentation or custom manufacture would assure the greatest speed and continuity of execution, so Shreve ordered off-the-shelf steel window frames, "a standard type without special features of design." The windows were painted a deep tomato-soup red for protection against corrosion, which incidentally provided a foil for the silver and varying tones of gray of the rest of the building.

The logic behind using stone for the facing of the Empire State Building seemed irrefutable, the choice of Bedford Indiana limestone unarguable. Limestone is not as durable as granite, but neither is it as dense or as dif-

[3]The soffits that Shreve was referring to in this case are the undersides of the window frames, the jambs the inside frames of the windows.

[4]Placing windows flush with the wall seemed to be in vogue—in December 1930, architect Kenneth Franzheim announced that the building he was designing for 22 East Fortieth Street would have windows installed flush with the exterior walls, and Harvey Wiley Corbett said that the entire surface between the steel supports of the proposed Met Life Building would be made of metal and glass, would be flush with the spandrels of the floors, and would run unbroken from the base to the top.

ficult to cut. Marble, although it might glisten in the rain and create a soft glow in light, was soft and malleable, and although it might have been easy to cut, even relatively easy to carve, it does not weather well in New York's climate and increasingly polluted air—what experts refer to as a "sulfurous atmosphere." The city's largest marble building, the Main Branch of the New York Public Library, was already beginning to turn to dust, and other marble buildings such as St. Patrick's Cathedral and Grace Church would require the replacement of great swaths of stone.

Limestone incorporated some of the best attributes of both marble and granite. It was easy to turn into ashlar at the quarry at no great cost, and it could be finished locally. Limestone, although gray, was hardly mono-chromatic. Its coloration had a striking depth, with flashes of silver in it. And it was durable, said to last at least five hundred years if protected from moisture building up between it and the frame. Another virtue of the stone is that it possesses a thermal inertia that amounts to heat storage, a virtue shown when the energy consumption of limestone buildings is compared with the profligacy of more modern glass-walled buildings. Washington's Pentagon and Chicago's Merchandise Mart are each roughly equal in size to the towers of New York's World Trade Center, yet neither consumes half as much energy.

Shreve's plan had the merits of good sense and utility. Above all else, as far as he was concerned, construction could be streamlined. He de-signed the outer walls so that they were carried directly on the structural steel of spandrel beams. The stone was not set into the wall as much as set on the spandrel beams, which allowed the installation of thinner stone. It was easier to install, and less of it was required.

The façades were designed without cornices and other architectural features. Only bands of cut stone, some of which would rise uninterrupted for hundreds of feet, would be visible. The simplicity of the stonework, and the fact that the stone piers were independent of one another and free from troublesome intersections, meant that cutting and fitting the stone at the site was abrogated, saving further time and money.

A unifying vertical element critical to the building's efficient construc-tion was the use of cast-aluminum spandrels, the same material and Art Deco style that were first seen in Raymond Hood's design for the 1928 apartment house at 3 East Eighty-fourth Street. True to the style, the spandrels for the Empire State were decorated with facing pairs of stylized lightning bolts that were set in a chevronlike pattern that almost met at midstroke.

The average spandrel was 4 feet, 6 inches high by 5 feet wide, and weighed only 130 pounds. The spandrels were placed in front of common brick, with their flanks designed to fit between the chrome-nickel steel mullions that ran up the face of the building. Their upper edges fit under the sills of the windows, their lower edges set into the tops of the window frames. The spandrels were angle-braced for rigidity (a bar was fixed to their backs) and attached to the structure's ribs by steel straps. The faces of the spandrels were sandblasted to produce a dull gray surface to contrast with the metal trim on their flanks.

Chrome-nickel steel the color and texture of silver was used for the mullions that would run from the sixth to the eighty-fifth stories. An alloy steel containing approximately 18 percent chromium and 8 percent nickel, chrome-nickel steel is rustless, stainless, impermeable to weather, and can be washed with plain soap and water.[5] Rolled in sheets half an inch thick, the mullions generally came in one length—the height of one story—and, depending on their placement, in one of two widths, ten or twenty-two inches. In addition to contributing to the upward sweep of the façade, the mullions were a critical element in the ease of construction. Like the window frames, they too covered the joins.

The building was the first to employ polished metal facing for architectural as well as ornamental purposes, and it resulted in a very low ratio of stone volume to building volume, an innovation regarded by architects as a revolutionary departure that foreshadowed major changes in architectural and building practice. Other stone buildings designed for similar use had one cubic foot of stone for every forty-five to fifty cubic feet of building; the Empire State Building had only one cubic foot of stone to every two hundred cubic feet of building. That alone was a considerable saving, since aluminum and chrome-nickel steel were relatively inexpensive, but Shreve maintained that the saving was even greater. On a one-to-one basis, the limestone used in the Empire State Building cost less than comparable stone on any job of similar character in recent building history in New York City, primarily because of the way it was cut and delivered as ashlar.

Great expanses of floor area also contribute to savings in the construction and operation of a building. Exterior walls are among the most costly parts of any major structure. The larger the area of a building's

---

[5]This alloy was developed during World War I to provide the greatest possible resistance to both corrosion and erosion for gun linings. Within a decade it was being used for the bright metal parts of automobiles, for equipment in handling milk, fruit juices, and other food products, for gasoline refining equipment, for hotel kitchens and hospital clinics. In the America of the 1950s, chrome would probably be most famous as the material of the Dagmar bumpers.

floor, the less exterior wall is required to enclose it. If a plan is 50 feet square, it contains 2,500 square feet of space. Its exterior wall is four times 50, or 200 linear feet. It thus contains 12.5 square feet for each foot of wall. But if the floor is 100 feet square, it contains 10,000 square feet of space, and the exterior wall is 400 linear feet, or 25 square feet for each foot of wall. The 100-foot-square building takes only half as much exterior wall per square foot of area as the 50-foot-square building.

Each floor was designed with as few obstructions as possible to allow flexible layouts and maximum use. In fact, Shreve, Lamb & Harmon decided that they would not even bother finishing the floors. Tenants could then tailor them to their needs, allowing office units in the tower that could expand from six hundred square feet to complete floor areas of thirty-six thousand square feet. Under a local law passed in the spring of 1929, showroom offices could be divided and subdivided by partitions of wood, or of wood and glass, if the building was fireproof and equipped with automatic sprinklers. It meant that jerry-built partitions could be erected easily and disassembled just as easily, anticipating the open plan that became increasingly popular in office design in the 1960s.

Shreve, Lamb & Harmon were well aware of the pecking order of office life. Usually the boss took the prestigious corner office, or at least a window office, with the reception area housing secretarial and clerical help relegated to the space between the private office and the corridor wall. For maximum light to enter the reception area, the partition dividing the private office from the reception area was often glass. The glass was frequently opaque, which prevented people in the more public outer office from seeing into the workings of the more private inner office. The most valuable space was by a window, and the values were readily translated into what tenants were willing to pay.

North light is the most desirable because it is steady and indirect. East light is the second most desirable, because it is indirect most of the time. It is only direct and glaring very early in the morning, usually before office workers are on the job. But even direct sunlight coming through an office window does not penetrate very deep except when the sun is low in the sky. Artificial light is usually required to supplement daylight ten feet away from a window, and artificial light must be used in deeper offices at all times. The plan that produced a building with all rentable space no farther than twenty feet from windows could demand top dollar, or $2.80 a square foot in 1923 dollars. If the space cost $15 a square foot to build, the return would be 18.65 percent on the investment. However, the value of space that was thirty feet from a window fell to $2.40 a square foot and kept falling until, at fifty feet from a window, the space was worth only $1.65 and the return on investment was 11 percent.

A floor plan that commanded the highest rate per square foot was not necessarily the one that provided the largest amount of space; it was the one that produced the largest amount of well-lighted space. Tenants wanted shallow space and were willing to pay for it. The twenty-eight feet that Shreve, Lamb & Harmon decided should be between the window and corridor wall became the engine that drove the design.

A distance of about twenty feet separated the center points of the columns along the exterior walls, making the average office unit about nineteen feet wide. With partitions down the middle, the interior could be comfortably divided to form two nine-foot-wide offices, each with its own window, and an anteroom. Harmon said nine-foot-wide offices were considered the most desirable by the greatest number of tenants—there was room for a desk and a passage, as well as a few chairs and cabinets—so the resulting offices would be ideal. Whatever the configuration, the space would be bright, since each unit would have two windows.

Something that was missing in the design of the offices was radiators, which were cleverly hidden under the window sills in space made available by the use of the thin aluminum spandrels. This innovation not only cleaned up the appearance of the offices and improved the general ambience, it also provided more rentable space.

Thirty-six stores with entrances from both the sidewalks and either the lobby or the circulating corridors were planned for the main floor. The shop fronts were virtually all glass, accented by a cornice of aluminum and black granite above and a black granite base. To mask the columns, the windows were flanked with narrow aluminum mullions that terminate in updated and very elegant volutes. Not obvious at first is that the wall of shop windows projects and provides its own miniroofline, avoiding what Lamb regarded as "the seeming lack of support which is inherent in the 'all-glass' show window." Another subtlety was the window awnings, which could be tucked right into the wall, with only the awnings' supporting arms visible when stored away.

Shreve, Lamb & Harmon planned five entrances to the building. The two on each of the side streets were strictly functional, giving onto low-ceilinged corridors that led directly to the elevator banks. Although the lower five stories were missing the stainless-steel mullions, the same metal was used to frame the entrances, which were also marked by marquees that were more like decorative cornices than canopies—three parallel bands of stainless steel inlaid with bronze strike a strictly regulated rhythm whose regularity is softened by rounded corners. There was nothing angular or sharp-edged about the canopies.

The main entrance, which is smack in the middle of the block on Fifth Avenue, is a thirty-foot-high portal. Defined by a diamond-shaped grille framing the glass, it is solid, substantial, and dignified.[6] Colossal engaged columns[7] flank the entrance. Instead of concave grooves, you find the convex fluting that reflects the motif running up the building, and instead of terminating in the usual capital, you find eagles, perched and ready to soar. Mixing their metaphors, the architects ran vaguely Egyptoid pilasters up the façade to the fourth floor, with a variation on a lotus worked into their capitals.

Incised above the entrance in a V-cut are the words EMPIRE STATE in a clean, serif typeface. The architects recognized the illegibility of some of the more avant-garde Art Deco typefaces, and were more sensible in their choice than some of their more daring colleagues. Since legibility is the whole point of a typeface, those that are difficult to read generally prove to be evanescent, as ephemeral as any product that fails to work well. Shreve, Lamb & Harmon imprinted the building with a message that would prove legible over the long haul.

The glory of the five-story base is that it holds the building line and is designed at a human scale. From it rose the tallest building in the world, but the ambience is not in the least oppressive. The base is blessedly set at a height that allows us to look at it from across Fifth Avenue without craning our necks, and it sets the perfect foil for the tower that rises from it. The architects did not have the luxury of a full block, the luxury of space that Raymond Hood enjoyed at Rockefeller Center, so the setting lacks the grand approach via the Channel Gardens to a soaring tower (the RCA, now GE, Building), but they nevertheless worked well within the tight confines. The tall main entrance hall substitutes for the grand approach. It provides the excitement, the romance of being taken by the hand and ushered into the building. It contributes to your sense of place.

The lobby of the Empire State Building was reserved, with a more serious, more stolid demeanor than many of its peers. Although it might have been far less showy, its materials were certainly no less rich. It

---

[6]Some office building entrances of the time drew criticism for lacking a certain dignity. Critics thought that the seahorses and ships depicting the evolution of transportation in the Maritime Exchange Building at 80 Broad Street were a bit too playful, while Sloan & Robertson's framing for the doorway at 29 Broadway was simply too daringly modern.

[7]Columns are graded somewhat like olives: Those taller than two stories are called "colossal." Columns that are "engaged" are almost married to the wall; they are part of it. To extend the metaphor of togetherness, a column in order to be a column is single, not attached to anything.

looked nothing like the lobby of the Chrysler Building, whose marble walls featured lighting set behind strips of stainless-steel ziggurats, whose signage was set in a modern typeface and fabricated in stainless steel. Nor was it anything like the Daily News Building, which had a spinning globe half sunk into the lobby floor, and weather charts and clocks showing the time around the world.

The marble walls inside the Empire State Building lobby were devoid of ornamentation and carving except a subtle repetition of the convex grooving from the façade, and featherlike capitals that hinted at the age of flight. The designers theorized that by diminishing the decoration and by having great expanses of glass for the arcade's vitrines, the beauty of the marble's natural color and veining would stand out. Probably without a thought of plagiarizing from the Daily News Building, the lobby was slightly meteorological—a discreet wind indicator that was hooked up to a rooftop anemometer informed the public of wind speed and direction at the observatory.

The wind indicator looked for all the world like a clock (and a clock, in fact, has since replaced it). Close inspection revealed compass points, with an *N* at the top instead of a *12*, an *E* instead of a *3*, etc. Smaller figures reported the wind, from *0* at noon's place, around the dial twenty-five miles each quarter circle, so that the hand would go all the way around to noon again for a hurricane force of 100 miles an hour. The wind indicator was discreet, hardly an object that called attention to itself, although it did face visitors who entered the building from the Fifth Avenue entrance.

The wind indicator was set within a larger and far more dominating whole—a mural that depicted the Empire State Building against an outline map of its namesake state. The bordering states and provinces of Canada put the Empire State in perspective, and New York City and Albany—the state's two capital cities, as it were—were highlighted. Beams emanated from the top of the building, shedding rays across the state and all the way to Canada. In the lower left-hand corner was a plaque that gave the names of the owners, architects, and builders, all of which was placed against a background of highly polished German marble of a mulberry color set into a frame of Belgian black marble.

Several contemporary buildings celebrated themselves in an art form, including the Citgo Building, which had a model of itself at the Pine Street entrance; 500 Fifth Avenue, which had a relief statue holding a model of the building at its Fifth Avenue entrance; and the Chrysler Building, which had a portrait of itself in the ceiling that pointed, compasslike, westerly. People were used to murals in many forms—mosaic, fresco, paintings on canvas firmly affixed to ceiling or wall—they were even accustomed to sgraffito. But this mural had the Empire State Building represented in aluminum, with the state's chief two cities represented by starbursts of gold.

The mural took a little getting used to. One reviewer wondered if a purist in the ancient craft of metalwork, such as Samuel Yellin of Philadelphia, would consider it a correct use of metal. Even the architects might have had second thoughts. Less than a year after the building opened, Arthur Loomis Harmon was the guest architect at the Mural Painting Atelier of the Beaux Arts Institute of Design, where students were regularly given problems from the guest architect's own current or past work. Harmon, perhaps curious about what young designers might conceive, gave the students the task of designing a panel for the end of the lobby in the Empire State Building. The subject matter was left to the student designer, but it had to be "vigorous in scale and should symbolize the vast and varied activities" for which the building had been created. One student employed a construction theme, rather startlingly providing some of the mechanics with halos fashioned from cogwheels.[8]

Unlike the McGraw-Hill Building lobby, lined with moderne chandeliers dramatically suspended from the ceiling, the source of the lighting in the Empire State's lobby could barely be distinguished. The Fifth Avenue lobby received light from the window overlooking Fifth Avenue, but artificial illumination was provided by 150-watt lightbulbs set into a shelflike cornice. The light was aimed upward and outward upon the ceiling, from which it bounced downward into the room, but not before highlighting the ceiling, which was decorated with gold, platinum, and aluminum leaf in a design of circles and stars. The decoration and lighting were designed by the Rambusch Studios, who had decorated over eight hundred of the great movie palaces of the 1920s, including one of the grandest, the Roxy Theater, and who would go on to decorate the building's observation deck and the lobbies of the new Waldorf-Astoria and Radio City Music Hall.[9]

The two-story-high lobbies continued a similar lighting pattern on a smaller scale, using 60-watt bulbs. To link the mezzanine, which is divided by the two-story-high halls in the north and south sides of the building, pairs of chrome-steel bridges were installed with horizontal banding.

---

[8]Maybe the bizarre was becoming all the rage—who could figure, for instance, the anachronism of Abraham Lincoln in the mural over the information desk in the RCA Building lobby that depicted the construction of Rockefeller Center?

[9]The Rambusch Studios is in its fourth generation in the 1990s, and is still going strong.

The ceilings above the bridges were stepped up, and chandeliers hung from them, and the undersides of the bridges were boldly corrugated aluminum. The lighting again was indirect. The lights were set on reflectors in chromium troughs that were suspended, so the light bounced off the reflectors onto the ceiling, which diffused it downward.

The lighting scheme was different in the elevator lobbies and the one-story lobbies that connected them. There the lights were installed in fixtures where wall met ceiling. These fixtures had chromium tops and dead black backs, so when the light shone upon them a part of the light struck the bright metal surface and was reflected downward and outward. All of this indirect lighting was set behind intaglio glass by the Corning Glass Works. The purpose of the black back, which did not reflect light, was to serve as a background for the etched glass, so the fixtures glowed. As the *London Architect* said, a "feeling for restrained modern design permeated the treatment of the public spaces."[10]

The big question was whether the work on the Empire State Building could indeed be finished within the allotted time and within the estimated budget. That was an important question, with carrying charges accumulating during construction at the rate of $10,000 a day. A capable builder could take the preliminary plans and prepare a scope of work, a time study covering every subdivision of the building that would provide a pretty good indication of how long the entire project would take. Most important perhaps, the builder had to determine whether the project was feasible at the desired cost. If the estimates erred on the side of caution, so much the better. If the estimates were overly optimistic, everyone could lose.

[10]These were all changed in the 1950s.

# 10

# THE CONTRACTORS

The developers of the Empire State Building were hardly sleazy speculators whose goal was to build a schlock building with the intent of unloading it on some gullible buyer at the first opportunity. They wanted a first-class building that they would hold on to, a building that they would care for as stewards. They had entered the construction and real estate business for the long haul. They had made no little plans.

The developers needed a first-class builder, a general contractor who could successfully carry out the plans of their architects and their structural engineer, H. G. Balcom. They had to beware the low bidder. They could not afford an unscrupulous contractor who takes a job at or below cost and then finds himself in a fiscal pickle, the contractor who will salvage what he can by skimping, substituting inferior materials for what had been specified. Nobody wanted to be faced with the problems that John Roebling had encountered in the construction of the Brooklyn Bridge. They needed contractors whose reputations were unsullied, builders who were honest and could get the job done as promised.

The directors asked five builders to appear before them in Smith's office in the Biltmore Hotel to discuss the job and to make proposals. One firm went into the meeting an odds-on favorite. It was Starrett Bros. & Eken, arguably the standard-bearer for the industry. Originally there were five Starrett brothers, each of whom was talented at building. One became an architect; the other four went into the construction field, often in competition with each other for the same job. Two of the brothers— Paul and William—formed Starrett Bros. & Eken in the early 1920s.

The boys had grown up in Kansas, sons of a preacher who built his own church and house, a house that the youngest brother, William, returned to after World War I to find a ruin. He saw that the transom over the front door still held the original glass, inscribed, he said, "in beautiful but simple lettering" by his father's hand: "Into whatsoever house ye enter, first say, Peace be to this house." He made arrangements to secure the window, and took it home with him.

Colonel William A. Starrett, who held the corporate position of vice president in Starrett Bros. & Eken, was one of the greatest building contractors of his day. He had started out professionally with only two years of study in civil engineering from the University of Michigan (he later went back to school for his B.S., and still later was awarded an honorary doctorate). Unlike his brothers, all of whom served an apprenticeship in Daniel Burnham's office, William first worked in a wholesale grocery house. At twenty-one, he joined brother Theodore, and went to work for the George A. Fuller Company in 1898. He graduated from office boy to timekeeper for the Flatiron Building job, where he learned an invaluable lesson—how long a task should take. A few years later, the not-yet-thirty-year-old William was superintending the construction of Daniel Burnham's Union Station in Washington, D.C. The superintendent heads the field organization and is responsible for the completion of the contract on schedule. It is his task to oversee the various departments in his organization—auditing, purchasing, inspection, the traffic department, hosts of timekeepers, engineers, surveyors, foremen, and laborers—and to coordinate their activities with those of the subcontractors on the job.

During World War I, William Starrett served as head of the Emergency Construction Section of the War Industries Board, which made him the nation's largest builder. The housing constructed under Starrett's guidance had a capacity of 1.8 million soldiers (that was more than the population of Philadelphia at the time), and it was said to be the largest contracting business ever handled in one office. It wasn't just housing, as temporary as it might have been, but sewers and electricity, roads and communication, everything that constituted a small town a dozen times over. One hundred and fifty million dollars was spent between the middle of June 1917, when the first contract was let, and September, when the first contingent of the army was called. The marvel of William Starrett's direction in the war effort was the speed with which he finished projects. Each of the cantonments, for instance, was completed in about ninety days, which meant the draft army could begin training before the winter of 1917 to be prepared for the critical summer of 1918. By the time Starrett was demobilized, he held the rank of colonel.

Just as Shreve, Lamb, and Harmon were all leaders in their professional societies and served the commonweal, so William Starrett served as a member of President Hoover's organization on unemployment relief. He was a member of the American Society of Engineers, the American Society of Mechanical Engineers, and, in 1932, as evidence of his standing within the engineering community, he was the president of the Associated General Contractors of America.

Paul Starrett was no slouch as a builder either. Apprenticed to Chicago's Burnham & Root, he soon learned as a draftsman's helper that he had very little originality as an architect. Although he was a "lousy designer" (his words), he had a great aptitude for the engineering phases of architecture. After working as a construction superintendent at the 1893 World's Fair, for which Burnham designed the general plan, he went to work for Fuller & Company, and wound up in charge of Fuller's New York office. Both brothers worked on Fuller's Flatiron Building on Fifth Avenue at Twenty-third Street, which Burnham had designed. Charles Follen McKim, whose office at 160 Fifth Avenue commanded a fine view of the building's progress, marveled at the rate of construction on the steelwork—one floor a day, a hint of how the Starretts got things gone. During World War I, Paul Starrett formed Starrett & Goss, which built steamships for the government. By the time Starrett Bros. & Eken was formed in 1922, Paul had already built Macy's to the designs of De Lemos & Cordes; Pennsylvania Station and the Main Post Office to the designs of McKim, Mead & White; and Warren & Wetmore's Biltmore Hotel, where the meeting with the Empire State's directors would decide their fate.

Paul and William Starrett teamed up with Andrew J. Eken, with whom they had worked at Fuller, to form Starrett Bros. & Eken. Eken had risen to the vice president's office at the George A. Fuller Company, and to the presidency of Fuller in Canada. He became known as the "dean of the American skyline builders," and, like his partners, he too was involved in professional organizations. After World War II, for instance, he served as chairman of the Building Officers Foundation, which sought to unify and modernize building codes throughout the country.

The offices of Starrett Bros. & Eken in the 1920s were on the thirteenth floor of the Architects Building, which stood at 101 Park Avenue on the northeast corner of Fortieth Street until the early 1980s. The building was filled with showrooms for the trade; you could roam from showroom to showroom as if it were the biggest architectural trade show ever mounted. The offices of Starrett Bros. & Eken were not, however, designed for show. Their furnishings were bare, with old-fashioned upright desks, the walls decorated not with original paintings and etchings but with photographs of friends and family.

Paul Starrett, a genius at negotiations and management, was installed as president to free his brother and Eken for the role of managing day-to-day affairs at construction sites, which was their particular forte. This was the team that would erect the seventy-story Bank of Manhattan Building at 40 Wall Street, and Cincinnati's Carew Tower, the tallest building in the Ohio Valley, and they could lay claim to a series of speed records along the way. On September 20, 1928, they placed the first upright at 111 John Street, and fastened the last crosspiece to the twenty-seven-story building on November 10—a total of six and a half weeks. Demolition of the buildings on the site of 63 Wall Street started in May 1928, and the new thirty-five-story building was enclosed by November 9. Although these buildings were relatively tall, they were also relatively small—111 John Street had only about 246,000 square feet, and 63 Wall, about 339,000.

In 1929 the firm received their largest project to date, the one that might have won the day for them on the Empire State project—they built the Bank of Manhattan Building at 40 Wall Street, which was pitted against Chrysler in the race for the world's tallest. The foundations were started in May 1928, before the site was entirely cleared; less than a year later, the bank moved in. The seventy-story, 927-foot-high building was completed in eleven months. Its total rentable area was about 903,500 square feet.

Raskob appreciated speed—was in a hurry himself—and he and the architects knew that it was wise to have a general contractor with whom to consult as early as possible. There were several ways of building any structure, and a wide choice of building materials with which to do it. A good contractor would show the way. A great one would do it quickly and efficiently.

Paul Starrett was already on good terms with two of the principals at Chatham Phenix. Before Robert C. Brown became a banker with a specialty in the construction business, he had been a building supplier, and Starrett had been a customer. After Brown joined Chatham Phenix, his boss, Louis G. Kaufman, wanted to build an apartment house as an investment, and Brown had been fruitlessly seeking a site. Starrett did Brown a favor—he found the site for him. As Paul Starrett described the situation, "relations of confidence with the group" were established. The relationship meant that when a Starrett competitor told Brown that the Starretts had "spent money like drunken sailors down there on overtime [on the construction of the Bank of Manhattan Building]," Brown could call Starrett on the q.t. and ask him to set the record straight. Starrett admitted that there had been overtime, but even with overtime, the building had still been brought in under the original estimate, not to mention the fact that it opened on time. Having the building ready for May renting was worth $2 million to the owners. To be criticized for the investment in a little overtime seemed picayune. Soon after this conversation, three politicians called on Paul Starrett. They told him they had an "inside" with the governor, and they offered to act as go-betweens to procure the contract for a cash payment of $50,000. Starrett picked up the phone and called Brown to inform him of the offer. Brown went straight to Smith, called Starrett back, and told him that Smith had said to tell "those guys to go straight to hell."

Brown in turn did Paul Starrett one big favor. He asked Starrett where he wanted to be in the order of presentations to the board while making his pitch for the construction job—first, middle, or last. "Naturally," said Starrett, "I said last." Paul and William Starrett went to the meeting more than hoping that they would be successful in their bid. So far as Paul Starrett was concerned, this was the job he had been working toward all his life, the climax of his career.

The Starrett brothers sat outside Smith's office and nervously watched their rivals go in and come out. On their turn, the ever-blunt Al Smith asked, "Well, what have you got to say for yourselves?" Paul Starrett, equally bluntly, told Smith that he and his brother had come to prove that they were simply the best builders for the job. Fudging the truth somewhat, he told Smith they were the only leading contractors in New York whose members had been educated as architects before going into the building business. Despite this peccadillo, their track record was as glorious as Man-o'-War's. They had just built the New York Life Building, for which they had been chosen by one of the most exacting owners in existence. They had done important work for Metropolitan Life, an insurance company that Smith knew well because he still served on its board, and the company had already made an enormous loan on the property to the site's former developer. For the builder to be on good terms with the lender would be another feather in the promoters' collective cap should they go to the insurance company, befeathered cap in hand, to ask for a loan. And Starrett Bros. & Eken had just shattered all speed records on their work on the Bank of Manhattan, a job that Brown, at least, knew had come in on time and under estimate.

When Smith asked the critical question of how much equipment the Starretts had on hand, Starrett was sure that the other builders had told the committee that they already had "a wonderful lot of equipment" to handle the job, and what they did not already have they would rent. Starrett said they had none. "Not a blankety blank thing," he said. "Not even a pick and shovel."

"Gentlemen," Starrett told the startled committee, "this building of yours is going to present unusual problems. Ordinary building equipment won't be worth a damn on it. We'll buy new stuff, fitted for the job, and at the end sell it and credit you with the difference. That's what we do on every big job. It costs less than renting secondhand stuff, and it's more efficient."

When asked what proportion of the work they would do themselves, Starrett again told them he was sure that other builders had said that they would do a great deal themselves. Starrett shot back that they would not do anything that they could sublet to advantage. When asked how long they thought the Empire State job would take to build, Paul Starrett said that they could tear down the Waldorf-Astoria Hotel and finish the new building in eighteen months. He also said that their fee for all this would be insignificant compared with the amount of money the corporation would save by having the construction completed in such a short time.

Smith asked how much their fee would be. "Six hundred thousand," said Starrett.

"That's your asking price," said Smith.

"No, that's our real price!" Starrett replied.

Smith considered the fee a little pricey, and he told the Starretts that they would get a lot of free publicity out of the job, the kind of advertising that he provided Dobbs hats every time he made a speech and held up his hat so that people could see the name inside the crown. "Think of it," said Smith, "the biggest building in the world, and your name down there on the fence!" Starrett told him that the firm did not need that kind of advertising.

Hardly had the brothers returned to their office than a call came from Smith's secretary to say that Smith and Shreve were on their way over. Apparently without a second thought to the wisdom of their choice, the directors had chosen Starrett Bros. & Eken. All that remained was some

hondeling.[1] Smith seated himself, told Paul Starrett that they had decided to have him build the building, clapped him hard on the knee, and
said that they were going to pay the firm $500,000 for the job. Starrett
demurred, but, not wanting to lose sight of the higher goal, he struck a
bargain. "Well, Governor," he said, "I feel pretty sure that in six hundred
thousand dollars you are only paying me a fair fee, but I suppose as a
good businessman you have to pare something off. I'll tell you what I will
do. If you will make some minor changes in the contract, allow us to carry
our own liability insurance, and provide the money as we require it, I'll
say yes." Smith agreed.

Less than two weeks after the selection of the architects had been
made, the directors awarded the building contract to Starrett Bros. &
Eken.[2] The directors did not award on price alone, although that was
clearly a consideration. Their primary concern was the ability of the contractor to finish the job in as short a time as possible.

Starrett Bros. & Eken took the kind of approach to management that
Raskob admired. Raskob said that the three governing factors in industrial production were capital, labor, and management, each of which was
essential to the successful conduct of a manufacturing business, and construction was, after all, simply another form of manufacturing. He
stressed, however, that the three parts were not equal. The integral part
was management, the brains necessary to direct production, and the only
way to measure managerial ability was by performance. At that, Starrett
had no equal.

A policy committee on design and construction was established
straightaway. It was understood that Smith, Raskob, and Kaufman would
always be available for consultations and would attend some policy committee meetings, but they would not necessarily attend every meeting.
Robert C. Brown and John McInerney, the general superintendent, would
represent the owners. Richmond H. Shreve, as the business head of
Shreve, Lamb & Harmon, would attend, as would William F. Lamb, the designer of record. Also from the architects' office would be H. R. Dowswell,
the firm's specifications expert, and Irwin Clavan, the job captain. Andrew
J. Eken would represent the builders, and R. H. Hunter would be in

---

[1]"Hondeling" is a transliteration of the Yiddish word for "to haggle over price."
[2]Paul Starrett said that when the time came to dot the *i*'s and cross the *t*'s on the contract,
there were times when he was forced to say that what was in the draft was not what had
been agreed. Smith would turn to his lawyer and say that indeed the wording had been altered, and, to Starrett's astonishment at Smith's facility, he would dictate to his secretary
in the "briefest language the modifying clauses, some of which were highly technical."

charge of construction. Joining them on an ad hoc basis would be the consulting engineers. They held meetings as frequently as several times a week. Some basic and fairly critical decisions had to be made early on.

One tentative plan that had been floated was to have a department store occupy some of the lower areas of the building, but Eken pointed out that a department store needs great, open spaces. In all probability, it would require the elimination of some columns. The necessary construction required to compensate for them would cost too much and take too long. It would also destroy the glorious strength provided by all of the posts rising from the base right up through the building to their various terminals. He won his point.

At one of the earliest conferences, with Raskob in attendance, discussion turned to the façade. The use of terra-cotta, which was still popular, had been rejected. Terra-cotta had its drawbacks. Paul Starrett, who had been one of the bidders on the Woolworth Building job, had urged Frank Woolworth to use stone. He told Woolworth that stone could be cut so that there would be little if any chance of the weather having a deleterious effect on the building, certainly not to the point of disintegration. In undiplomatic terms, Starrett told Woolworth that if his building were built of terra-cotta it would look like a five-and-ten-cent-store proposition, but in stone it would be magnificent. Paul Starrett did not get the job, the Woolworth Building was given a facing of terra-cotta, and if Starrett could have seen in the 1950s the spectacle of the upper part of the Woolworth Building wired up with metal mesh to catch the falling terra-cotta, he might have felt that although his politesse had left something to be desired, his judgment on construction methods, at least, had been vindicated.

Early designs called for a limestone facing for only the lower five floors, then brick with limestone trimming above. Finished brickwork was one of the most expensive aspects of any construction job. A few years before construction of the Empire State Building, bricks cost $21 per thousand, and bricklayers in 1930 were receiving $15.40 a day. A good day's work meant setting six hundred bricks, which came to $28.10 per thousand. More than 1.5 million face bricks were used in the exterior wall of Cross & Cross's General Electric Building, an expensive proposition. As Sam Rayburn might have said, you talk about a million bricks here and a million there and pretty soon you're talking real money.

The decision to use stone instead of bricks for the façade of the Empire State Building seemed eminently sensible. Facing a building in brick was relatively slow and inefficient, and it was becoming increasingly more expensive.

If limestone was used for the entire building, said Paul Starrett, it would add immeasurably to its beauty, and he did not think it would be much more expensive. Raskob asked Starrett how much more he thought it would cost to use limestone all the way up. Starrett had the figures at the ready. Raskob thought the difference in cost was reasonable enough, and moved that limestone be used for the entire façade, no doubt to Shreve, Lamb & Harmon's delight.

Paul Starrett had nothing but praise for the fairly radical ways the architects devised to save time in the construction of the building. He said that the innumerable simplicities and economies in detail were the underlying factors behind the design, which the architects sometimes worked out unilaterally, sometimes with the contractors.

The contractors would take the working drawings and specifications, and prepare an itemized list of materials, equipment, and supplies with subcontractors. They priced each item and estimated the labor required to assemble the material. They prepared detailed schedules for every step involved in the construction process, and they arranged to have the materials fabricated and installed. Then they orchestrated the process of construction. As much was to be prefabricated at the factory as possible, so that when the material arrived at the building site it had only to be assembled or installed. The less work done at the site, the better.

There were few firms comparable to Starrett Bros. & Eken within the industry. Small-time contractors were the rule, and carpenters were the dominant trade in the labor force. Since domestic construction was the greatest part of the industry, and the average house was built of wood, a good carpenter could do almost the entire job himself.

Things were different on the level of construction carried on by Starrett. Just as no single trade could have built a cathedral in the Middle Ages, so no single trade could undertake to build a skyscraper in the twentieth century. Specialization was the norm, and delegation was the rule. One firm might wreck the building that was already on the site, another might dig the foundation for the new building, ironworking firms would erect the frame, masons and bricklayers would put on the facing, plumbers and steamfitters would install the water and heat, elevator companies would install the vertical transportation, and glaziers would install the windows. There was specialist after specialist—sixty in all at work on the Empire State Building—each to his own task. The industry had left its cottage-industry roots behind and had reached the stage of big business and mass production. They used machine methods and a corporate hierarchy.

Given the design of the Empire State, said Paul Starrett, their job was one of repetition—the purchase, preparation, transport to the site, and placing of the same materials in the same relationship, over and over. It was, as Shreve had said, like an assembly line—the assembly of standard parts. Unlike the usual manufacturing plant, however, the temporary nature of the construction business made it impossible to maintain the same staff from one job to the next. The organization on almost every big job had to be built from the ground up, which gives some idea of the problem facing every superintendent. It was his job to forge the multifarious disciplines from nothing into a harmonious whole for every job.

William Starrett said that the builder of a skyscraper could be compared to the general of an army. For the builder must lead and inspire the thousands of men whose united labor results in a mighty structure; he must control his source of supply; and he must see that his "supply trains" keep pace with his need for them.

Perhaps the most important job of the general contractor—perhaps even more important than coordinating all the various activities and getting the job finished—came before any of his on-site activities. The contractor had to familiarize himself with the engineering problems presented by each site. He had to estimate the labor required to assemble the material, and he had to receive realistic estimates from the subcontractors on the costs of machinery, equipment, and labor. Armed with the estimates from subcontractors and costs that he knew from past operations (one of the secrets of a competent builder was good record keeping), he could create detailed estimates of future costs. If he did his job well, it spelled the difference between success and failure.

Starrett Bros. & Eken knew that they had been chosen because they had the reputation of getting things done quickly and well, that they had the spirit and the will to do the job. The completion of a skyscraper even a day late meant a loss of hundreds of thousands of dollars in revenue for the owner, and severe inconvenience to tenants who had contracted for space. It was a matter of considerable pride to the Starretts that a large number of their buildings were finished not only on time, but ahead of time. The question facing them before they started was whether to manage this job by decentralization or centralization.

If centralized, the contractor used a large staff of expediters who dogged every step of the production process. They would frequently dispatch expediters and tracers to a factory or steel mill to watch the fabrication of an order, not particularly to inspect the quality or workmanship, but more to ensure that the order was not delayed. They would maintain close contact with the car- and truck-tracing departments of the railroads and truckers that served the job, and, since their mission was to speed up the work, they would frequently even "ride it through," which entailed traveling in the caboose with the train crews, or being at the transfer points along the route to see that the material was switched in time to make necessary connections. The expertise and initiative of the subcontractors was subordinated to that of the general contractor's organization.

The decentralized method provided autonomy to the subcontractors. It gave the subcontractors the freedom to put their specialized knowledge and skill to work in getting the job done, in coordinating their own work with the work of the other subcontractors, and with the operation in general. It meant finding responsible subcontractors who would meet their part of the schedule and share the philosophy of working in a spirit of mutual cooperation.

Starrett opted for the decentralized route, and they did it with remarkable results. Everyone on the job knew that in order to get the job done—a job that Eken called "the greatest building operation in history"—required friendly relations among those engaged in the work. They needed a forum in which to encourage open dialogue among the subcontractors, a forum that would explore the coordination of the various tasks and to thresh out any problems that might be encountered. The Empire State Building Club was formed to promote just that.

These meetings would not be middle management's status report meetings where employees have to stand up and give an accounting of the week's activities. These meetings would take place once a month over lunch at places like the Hotel Vanderbilt, where representatives of all those engaged in the construction of the building would discuss the progress in an open dialogue. John McInerney, Starrett's construction manager at the site, later said that few people could comprehend the stupendous task of planning and constructing an office building on the scale of the Empire State. The building presented problems to architects and engineers for which no precedents existed. They had no bases upon which to find solutions. However, the architects, contractors, and engineers united in reducing every question to mathematics, ascertaining to a pound or an inch the complete accuracy of their plans. The building was planned and built, down to the smallest detail, on paper before the first step was taken.

Starrett had told Smith and Raskob that his firm might choose to do some phases of the work themselves and not to contract the work out, but they would only do that if they could perform the task for less money than anyone else was asking. Their work would be close to cost. They wound up demolishing the Walforf-Astoria, laying the floor arches, roof, and fireproofing, and setting the exterior stone and backup.

To erect the approximately fifty thousand tons of steel, which con-

stituted the largest order ever placed for the erection of a single building, they chose Post & McCord, fellow tenants in the Architects Building, and the firm that had supplied the twenty-one thousand tons of
steel for the Chrysler Building. Because of the exigencies of the schedule and the danger of overwhelming a supplier, Post & McCord split the
steel-fabricating contract between the American Bridge Company and
the McClintock-Marshall Company.

Starrett chose the Otis Elevator Company for the $2.9 million contract
to design, manufacture, and install the elevators. They chose the Indiana
Limestone Company to provide the limestone, and they gave a $500,000
contract to the Allegheny Steel Company, a subsidiary of the Carnegie
Steel Company, to produce the stainless steel for the mullions. Each sub-
contractor and supplier, like Starrett Bros. & Eken, set the standard in
its field.

The sequence of events that Starrett followed was perfectly logical.
First, the site had to be cleared and the foundations laid. Then came what
the contractors dubbed the four "pacemakers," the divisions of construction that set the pace for the other trades: the erection of steel, the setting of the concrete floor arch construction, and the installation of the
enclosing walls, which was divided into two parts—the limestone construction, and the exterior metal trim and aluminum spandrels. When
those jobs were accomplished could come the "roughing in" of plumbing,
heating, wiring, and other facilities that had to be covered up, the installation of machinery such as heating and elevators, and, finally, the flooring, plastering, painting, and decorating. Some of these operations had to
be done serially, some could be done concurrently. One of the secrets to
success was which ones could be juggled.

Once the starting and completion dates had been set, the question of
feasibility arose—the reality of whether each of the trade groups could indeed work quickly enough and coordinate its operation to meet the requirements of its own schedule and make way for the operations of others.
Wrecking the Waldorf-Astoria was scheduled to start September 24,
1929. The general excavation was scheduled to start on January 22,
1930, which allowed only four months for demolition. The excavating
work was to be finished on March 17. Then the actual construction could
begin.

A progress chart was ruled off according to months from February
1930 to April 1931. Closely following the structural work came the line
for the exterior walls, which began to appear in the middle of May and had
to be completed by the end of November. Interior partitioning was scheduled to start in June and be finished by the end of January. The metal

window frames began to appear in May and were all to be in place by the end of December. The elevator enclosures were under way from the middle of May to the end of March. Painting and decorating were to begin in March and were to continue until the building was ready for occupancy. The various plumbing and electrical fixtures progressed from the rough work to the installation of the final fixtures. Even the installation of mail chutes was on the chart (they paralleled the installation of the elevators), as were the revolving doors, which were scheduled to be finished just as the first tenants were ready to use them.

An example of the speed required was that the fifty thousand tons of steel had to be fabricated, shipped, hoisted into place, and secured by October 4, 1930, so that the floors and fireproofing could be finished by October 10, to allow the cladding to be installed by December 1, so that the interior work could be finished by April 1, so that everything could be in readiness for opening day, May 1, 1931. The controlling dates for sixty trades were tied to this schedule.

The most critical schedules were the four pacemakers. If those schedules were not met, all other schedules would be thrown out of kilter. A virtue of the timing, however, was that the building would be enclosed during the spring, summer, and fall, so the builders could beat the bad weather. Ironworkers and construction workers in general will not go up when it is raining or snowing, nor in high winds, which combine to make outside work hazardous. The winter months of 1930–31, when weather would have otherwise played havoc with schedules, would be occupied by activities that by then would be protected from the elements.

Before work could begin, however, there was a wrinkle that had to be ironed out. According to one story, Smith thought that the building needed something to top it off, something as distinctive as his own brown derby. The story is probably apocryphal, but it's as good a reason as any for what came next.

# 11

# THE MOORING MAST

On December 11, 1929, Al Smith announced the news that the Empire State Building would not be the tallest building in the world by a mere two feet. It would be the world's tallest building by 202 feet, rising to the astonishing height of 1,250 feet. The difference in height between it and its nearest competitor was so dramatic that one comic said, "If it was bein' put up by just a regular politician and not Al Smith, wouldn't any of us believe it. We would demand a recount."

What so satisfied Raskob and his colleagues was that they could still feel supercilious about the top that had been added to Walter Chrysler's building. On an aesthetic level, their top would be as distinctive as any in the city. More important, theirs would be more than ornamental, more than a spire or a dome or a pyramid put there to add a desired few feet to the height of the building or to mask something as mundane as a water tank. Their top, they said, would serve a higher calling. The Empire State Building would be equipped for an age of transportation that was then only a dream of aviation pioneers.

"Building with an eye to the future," said Smith, the building would be topped by a dirigible mooring mast that could accommodate passengers for the already existing transatlantic routes, and for routes planned to South America, the West Coast, and across the Pacific. It was a proposal akin to a fantasy of Jules Verne, something like the dream of guidebook publisher Moses King at the turn of the century, who depicted great balloons casting off from the rooftops of skyscrapers. The dirigible mooring mast atop the Empire State Building would make the dream a reality.

By the 1920s, steel-framed dirigibles, or zeppelins, were being touted as the aircraft of the future for long-range hauls. With a top speed of 80 miles an hour, they could cruise at 70 miles an hour for thousands of miles without refueling. Some dirigibles were as long as a thousand feet, or about the length of four north–south New York City blocks including the side streets that separate them. Helium and hydrogen, which are lighter than air, filled their cavities and compensated for the weight of the dirigible and its load. The gas provided the lift.

One operational drawback to dirigibles had been a lack of adequate terminal facilities, a neglect regarded as having retarded airship progress perhaps more than any other factor. Colonel John Reed Kirkpatrick, a vice president of the George Fuller Construction Company, had thought in 1926 that perhaps several blocks of buildings would have to be razed and a towering dirigible landing stage erected high above the housetops to provide convenient terminals. Smith's plan did not involve knocking down blocks' worth of buildings and dedicating a massive amount of real estate and construction to the project. His plan would allow a dirigible to anchor atop the city's tallest building for a period of three or four hours, during which time arriving passengers would disembark, the airship would be serviced, departing passengers would climb aboard, and the dirigible would cast off for distant ports of call. Docking the dirigibles would require warping them to the mast—a line from the dirigible would be hauled in by an electrical winch—much as an ocean liner is warped to its pier. An airship once fast in its swivel, said Smith at the unveiling of the plan, could swing in the breeze and yet be controlled enough to allow the passengers to walk down a gangplank to an open observation platform. From there to the corner of Fifth Avenue and Thirty-fourth Street, it was estimated, would take seven minutes flat.[1]

The addition of the dirigible mooring mast meant reconfiguring the top of the building. No longer would the roof of the eighty-fifth floor be the top. It would become the eighty-sixth floor. Glass-walled observation

---

[1] There seemed to be no accounting of having to pass through passport control or customs in these computations by the backers of the Empire State Building.

galleries raised above the parapet walls would provide spectacular views while protecting sightseers from the elements, and roof terraces would provide unobstructed views, as originally planned.

A thirty-five-foot-square shaft of metal and faceted glass would rise 158 feet from the eighty-sixth floor to the conical roof atop the structure for the dirigible mooring mast. The winches and control machinery would be installed at the base of the mooring mast; the cables, elevators, and stairs would be in the shaft; and the mooring arm would be housed under the conical roof.

A bonus was that two observation levels were planned for the top of the tower. An elevator would travel the 167 feet from the observation deck on the eighty-sixth floor to the totally glassed-in observation level on the 101st floor, a circular room thirty-three feet in diameter, where windows would provide unobstructed views. Above this room and reached by a stairway would be the 102nd-floor observatory, this one twenty-five feet in diameter and ringed by a platform protected by a low wall. The cylindrical structure was surmounted by a conical dome whose tip was 1,250 feet above the sidewalk. On a clear day and with a powerful pair of field glasses, said the boosters, spectators on the 102nd-floor platform would see all the way to the Delaware Water Gap in the west and Storm King Mountain in the north. The primary purpose of the platform, however, was not so much to wow visitors with the view but to serve as the boarding area for the anticipated dirigible passengers.

Arriving passengers were expected to walk down a plank extended from the dirigible to the platform on the 102nd floor. From the platform, the passengers would take the stairs down to the observation floor on the 101st floor, thence by elevator to the eighty-sixth floor, where lounges and baggage rooms, ticket offices and customs officers would await them.

The mooring mast was "on the level, all right," said Smith. "No kidding. We're working on the thing now. One set of engineers here in New York is trying to dope out a practical, workable arrangement and the Government people in Washington are figuring on some safe way of mooring airships to this mast." Shreve, Lamb & Harmon had taken inspection tours of the equipment and mooring operations at the Naval Air Station at Lakehurst, New Jersey, and at the St. Hubert Air Field at Montreal. They had consulted with dirigible experts, including Commander Jerome C. Hunsaker, vice president of the Goodyear Zeppelin Company and president of the recently formed airship transport company that planned a transpacific service. Smith said that Hunsaker considered the mooring mast perfectly feasible. Smith visited Secretary of the Navy Adams, who assured him of the cooperation of the Navy Department, the leader in the field of dirigible research and development in the United States. The navy might even allow its great dirigible, the *Los Angeles*, to be used in testing the mast.

Smith conceded that the stresses of a thousand-foot airship swinging in the wind and held to the top of a 1,250-foot building by a single connection presented technical problems that required revisions to the structural plans. The mooring mast had to have strength enough to withstand a horizontal pull of fifty tons at its head; it had to be constructed so that stresses resulting from that load and from wind pressures would be transmitted through the building to its foundations nearly eleven hundred feet below the base of the mooring mast. This required engineering changes to the entire frame. Such problems, Smith blandly acknowledged, were no greater than might have been expected under such a novel plan. Tentative sketches had been made, but the work of calculating the stresses and strains, and determining the materials necessary to withstand them, remained to be done. Undaunted, Smith maintained that the steel frame of the structure could be strengthened sufficiently to withstand the pull of the greatest dirigible in anything less than a 50-mile-per-hour gale.

Unlike the average corporate decision, where a project is researched and the bottom line invariably determines whether a project is go or no-go, no estimate of the additional cost of the project had been made at the time of the announcement, nor had feasibility studies been made or any market research done to determine whether people were actually willing to walk a gangplank from a dirigible to a mooring mast suspended almost 1,250 feet in the air. Nevertheless, Raskob had told Smith to proceed, and the board had already authorized the roughly $60,000 worth of revisions to the steel specifications to allow the framework to bear the added burden of the mast. The whole job was estimated at about $750,000, a paltry 3 percent addition to the final costs. It was a small price to pay to ensure the building its title.[2]

Early renderings of the mooring mast, including one by Hugh Ferriss, depicted a slim, functional structure without decoration. Who among the three architects came up with the idea of the four great wings flanking the mooring mast and serving as buttresses is guesswork, but the architects let nothing escape their eyes. In February 1930, Rochester's Genessee Valley Trust Building[3] was one of about a dozen skyscrapers featured at the an-

---

[2]Lewis Mumford hated the mooring mast—he said the only reason for its being was to assure the building the title as world's tallest. Although he might have been right about the title, he was just about alone in his criticism of the mooring mast in general.

[3]Today the building is called the Times Square Building.

nual Architectural League show in New York City. Ralph Walker, of Voorhees, Gmelin & Walker, crowned the building with an Art Deco tower with perforated stone carving, behind which floodlights played. Protruding from the top of the tower and sticking straight up in the air were four great aluminum wings—the "Wings of Progress"—set in at a 45-degree angle from the building, their feathers facing outward. The wings were no part of the structure of the building, no part of the design of the building intended to house offices or even to mask a water tower. They were freestanding. All three principals of Shreve, Lamb & Harmon probably read *The New York Times*, which wrote about the building's unique roofline at the time of the show. All three were members of the Architectural League at the time of the show. And the odds are pretty good that all three attended the show and saw Ralph Walker's rendering of the building.

Eureka.

The Empire State Building too would have a tower that was lighted from within, but instead of having wings perched precariously atop the tower, the wings would flank the tower and be an integral part of it. Without having to come out and say as much, the wings were the perfect symbol for the mooring mast—the age of aviation.

The tower meant farewell to the static, flattopped roofline that had originally been proposed. It would be sheathed in chrome-nickel steel from the stepped-back, windowed base, up the shaft to the conical top, with the winged buttresses in cast aluminum. The rocket-shaped mooring mast would provide a directional element to the verticality of the window bays. It would present a gleaming surface to the sky, visually freeing the building from the gravitational constrictions of the lower stories. The tower would act as the capstone of the building, and bring it to a conclusion with an exclamation point. It would make the building soar.

What's more, the building would join ranks with others of its age. Its roofline would be lit. By the 1920s, the practice of lighting buildings from within and by floodlighting was becoming more and more popular. New York had buildings that flashed light—both the Metropolitan Life tower on Madison Square and the Con Edison Building on Fourteenth Street flashed the hours in white, and the quarter hours in red. Lighting was also being installed for less informative reasons and more for the pure fun of it. The city's first building to be floodlighted was probably the Heckscher Building on Fifty-seventh Street. A soft flood of light was thrown up indirectly at the tower, burnishing the wing tips of the gold cock, who took on the look of a barnyard fowl taking a stroll in the moonlight, said *The New Yorker*. An appropriate image for a building, considering the product for which the building was named, was found atop

Raymond Hood's American Radiator Building in 1924, which Hood described as a "pile of coal, glowing at the top." Behind filigree work on its roof, Cross & Cross's RCA (GE) Building on Lexington Avenue and Fifty-first Street flashed now white, now red, with the regularity of a Broadway marquee. The illuminated top of the Chanin Building was described as a "red-hot grate." The dome of the Williamsburg Savings Bank had light streaming through louvers set within its dome. The huge lantern atop the New York Central Building on Park Avenue housed bulbs of more than 6,000 watts that were amplified and projected by lighthouse reflectors, and several banks of floodlighting illuminated the tower from all sides. The lights had a total of 100,000 candlepower. The original plan for the Chrysler Building called for a dome made of steel and crystal that would have been lighted from the interior, giving a night effect of a great jeweled sphere. When William Van Alen changed his plans to include the spire and the distinctive triangular windows, he had lighting fixtures installed to enframe the windows, a feature that was not implemented until the early 1980s.

With the dirigible mooring mast, the Empire State would arguably have the best of the crop. It would have a vertical strip of illumination, "pencils of light," that would shine from within each of the four faceted faces to light up the night sky, while directional beacon lights would play above, giving the building an unmistakable character and adding to the drama of the nighttime skyline. Lighting engineer Clifford Spencer pointed out in 1930 that when a large portion of a building presents an unobstructed view of itself, light of lower intensity could be used, in part because of the psychologically cumulative effect of lighting large areas. True to this notion, lighting the four 160-foot-high "sawtooth" windows successfully took less than you might think. The engineers had no models to follow, so they built a full-sized simulacrum and set it up in position on the building itself to test lamps of different wattage. Lights of comparatively high wattage resulted in a blur that obliterated the outline of the windows and made them appear as a "shapeless nebula," as electrical engineer Eugene Clute described the effect. Lamps of somewhat lower wattage cured this trouble, but brought another difficulty—they created bright spots on the glass. Lights of only 5 watts that were comparable to Christmas tree ornaments created no blur of light, nor bright spots, and the illumination was powerful enough to be seen at a great distance.

Keeping the classical balance, the illumination from the windows of the observation rooms on the eighty-sixth floor created a horizontal band of light at the base of the tower and provided a secure footing, and another horizontal band of light shone out from the 101st-floor observation floor.

The result was lighting that was horizontal, vertical, horizontal.

A reporter for the *Montreal Star* commented to a friend in February 1931 that he thought a pretty fine sight on a summer evening would be a dirigible moored to the top of the Empire State Building. His friend, of a more practical nature, said that what bothered him was "how on earth the passengers could get down." Neither had the slightest idea, but they agreed that Al Smith had probably had the foresight to make some arrangements in that connection, so they stopped worrying. They shouldn't have.

The scheme had hardly been given the careful forethought the reporter and his friend assumed, and the dirigible mooring mast would be the folly of follies, perhaps the looniest building scheme since the Tower of Babel. Nobody knew with any degree of certainty whether it would work, and when Smith returned from Washington, where he had discussed the feasibility of the mooring mast with the secretary of the navy and the military's leading dirigible expert, Rear Admiral William A. Moffett, chief of the navy's Bureau of Aeronautics, Smith should have had an inkling that it would not. Moffett had faith in the future of dirigibles in the United States, but he had enumerated several serious drawbacks to the plan.

For starters, only airships based in the United States could conceivably be accommodated atop the Empire State Building. The United States had a monopoly on helium, and only U.S. dirigibles used helium. Dirigibles of other nations such as Germany used hydrogen. The buoyancy, or "lift," of pure hydrogen is much greater than helium,[4] which, the admiral acknowledged, was a disadvantage for airships using helium, but not when you took into account that hydrogen-filled dirigibles faced a very serious risk of fire. Hydrogen will explode.

We have the advantage of hindsight, but imagine if the *Hindenburg* had used the top of the Empire State Building as its terminus instead of Lakehurst. Docked, the zeppelin would have been tied up midblock between Thirty-third and Thirty-fourth Streets and stretched north between Fifth and Sixth Avenues to the blocks between Thirty-seventh and Thirty-eighth Streets. Instead of bursting into flames in the middle of a sparsely settled area, it would have exploded over one of the densest.

Unlike hot-air balloons, dirigibles at least were propeller driven and could be steered,[5] but at their best they were less than stable, considerably more at the mercy of the winds than heavier-than-air craft, and

[4] In a cubic meter, air weighs 1.293 kilograms, helium weighs .178, while hydrogen weighs only .090.
[5] The root of the word is from the French *diriger*, to direct.

crashes were not uncommon. The dirigible *Shenandoah*, the pride and joy of the U.S. navy airships when it was built in 1923, was destroyed in a storm only two years later.

Although the navy had acquiesced to Smith's request for research, Smith implied that it was tantamount to approval. The plan might not even have been seriously considered by the navy. It was certainly never endorsed. Doubts were voiced within the service about the plan's feasibility the first time experts heard about it. The problem was having a thousand-foot-long steel-framed airship hover at the top of a building, where air currents can turn into swirling whirlpools. Wind has to go somewhere when it hits a building. It goes up, it goes down, it goes sideways. It bounces off other buildings, it ricochets, it creates constantly shifting patterns to the point where things atop the Empire State Building get topsy-turvy, where snow is often seen going up instead of coming down.

At the slow speed required for a safe docking maneuver, dirigibles are at the mercy of the gentlest zephyr. Officers at the Lakehurst Naval Air Station said that the air currents set up by high buildings would require continual trimming to keep on anything like an even keel. Trimming a ship might necessitate throwing out ballast, which in dirigible terms would mean dumping tons of water on the streets below.

No less an authority than Dr. Hugo Eckener, commander of the *Graf Zeppelin* and the chief operating officer of the Zeppelin Company of Germany, considered the proposal of the mooring mast impractical the first time he heard of the possibility. "The difficulties of mooring a great airship to a mast over New York City would be very great," Dr. Eckener said, smiling at the idea. "The violent air currents up and down caused by your high buildings would, I think, make such a project almost impossible at this time." Once Eckener had actually inspected the mast, he was even more skeptical. He pointed out that problems would arise in mooring the craft through lack of a ground crew, and that only under favorable weather conditions would it be possible to moor a ship to the tower. Before any attempt could possibly be made, investigations had to include "much study" of the characteristics of air currents over an area studded with skyscrapers before it would be safe to attempt to moor an airship to the top of the building. Asked if he would undertake to moor an airship to the mast, he laughed and said, "I have always been very careful. There would have to be many, many experiments."

Eckener was right about the lack of an adequate ground crew. The conventional practice in mooring an airship called for the use of port and starboard yaw lines that ground crews ordinarily handled, and the usual mooring anchored a dirigible's tail as well as its nose. At most fields, the ships were held at the rear by a cable attached to a revolving disk. The plan at the Empire State Building called for dirigibles to be tied up only by their noses. The dirigibles would swing in the breeze.

Smith had been sanguine that it could be done. "Some pretty smart fellows in the Navy Aviation outfit" believed a workable method could be devised, but even Smith had to admit after the first blush of the announcement that there were problems. He started changing his tune. "You can hitch one of those babies all right, but they won't stand hitched like a horse," said the revisionist Smith. "If there's a wind blowing—and there always is up here where we are—the dirigible would be whirled around like a top, and that wouldn't be so good. Elsewhere when the airships are moored to masts they are weighted down at the stern, with enormous lead weights, so that they will stand hitched even against a stiff wind. But I don't believe they would stand for that here. Half the population of Manhattan Island would get the heeby-jeebies at the thought of forty or fifty tons of lead swinging over their heads. But there must be some way to work the thing out, and if there is our engineers will find it."

The developers had to concern themselves with other problems. There were laws against airships flying too low over urban areas. If it was illegal to fly to and from the mast, it was equally illegal to erect a mast, because it would encourage, as lawyers at Chadbourne, Stanchfield & Levy phrased it, "such possibly illegal flying." The lawyers' fifty-five-page brief did contend, however, that the mooring mast did not offer a menace to air navigation, nor did it threaten either trespass or nuisance to the owners of private property affected by its use. The lawyers ended on a note of caution, saying that "on the whole, . . . the courts will probably hold that erection and use of the mast will be legal, but this opinion is an enlightened guess and not a prediction made with assurance. The answer is too speculative to be given positively."

Only once did a navy dirigible come close to the mooring mast, and then the captain never intended to couple—the flight was made in 1930 at the request of a motion picture newsreel company that had no official connection with either the Empire State Building or the naval air service. "Slowly and with its command on the alert lest the delicate fabric of its envelope be staked on the sharp spires of the tall buildings in the Pennsylvania zone," reported *The Times*, "the semirigid dirigible J-4, auxiliary of the *Los Angeles* of the Lakehurst Naval Air Station, reconnoitered about the dirigible mooring mast at 3:15 Tuesday, December 17th, while thousands watched from the streets below. . . . A stiff wind was blowing as the dirigible hovered with throttled engines and approached the tower. In the cabin of the airship Lieutenant S. M. Bailey, the commander, kept his hands on the controls and ballast releases in case a gust threw him too close to the near-by buildings. Bailey . . . declined to comment on the feasibility of attempting to tie up to the mast and added that he was kept so busy at the controls while the ship oscillated in the treacherous air currents over the city that he had little time to notice the details of the mast."

Only once did a dirigible actually make contact with the Empire State Building. It was brief, and marginal at best. In September 1931, the pilot of a small, privately owned dirigible that was outfitted with a long rope flew as near to the top of the building as the captain was willing to dare. The pilot jockeyed for position for about a half hour, or until the airship's ground crew of three could catch the rope. They hung on to it for dear life, and the dirigible was made fast atop the mooring mast for three minutes, a maneuver that brought Fifth Avenue traffic to a halt. All the while a steeplejack was armed with a sharp knife, poised to cut the rope should it become fouled. The dirigible did not use the mooring mast as it had been originally intended, nor was permanent contact made with the building. The pilot later maintained that he thought the mast could be used for landing mail and express packages.

Two weeks later, in a publicity stunt that was part of a larger promotion for the twenty-fifth anniversary of the *New York Evening Journal*, the Goodyear blimp *Columbia* dropped a hundred-foot-long rope to the roof of the newspaper building at 210 South Street, where, on the second attempt, a bundle of newspapers was hooked to it. The blimp then flew to Thirty-fourth Street, where it finally maneuvered close enough to the Empire State Building. A steeplejack atop the mast would catch one rope to secure the blimp while the ground crew's chief rigger on the 102nd floor hoped that the bundle of newspapers would come close enough for him to catch that rope. A handful of dignitaries, including Raskob and Smith, looked on. "Hold my legs, somebody, in case I get pulled," the rigger said quietly, and Raskob held him fast. From the gondola hung the line with the bundle of newspapers dangling at the end of it. On the third attempt, with the blimp's motors at idle, the rigger leaned over the parapet with penknife in hand, grabbed the bundle, pulled it to safety, and cut the bundle loose. The blimp's ground man handed the papers to Smith, who said "very well done," and proceeded to the eighty-sixth floor to make a short speech for newsreels celebrating the first roof-to-roof airship delivery of newspapers. Hundreds of people had watched the delivery from the eighty-sixth-floor observation platform, and thousands more gathered in the streets below, creating yet one more traffic jam.

As far as the building's publicist, Josef Israels II, was concerned, the whole thing—not just the publicity for the *Journal* but the mooring mast itself—was one huge publicity stunt. Israels proudly told the *Daily News*'s Inquiring Photographer that the biggest publicity stunt he had ever arranged was when he "suggested and participated in the exploitation and building of the mooring mast on top of the Empire State Building, making it the highest building in the world. The resulting publicity, with pictures of dirigibles moored to the mast, was printed in every city in the world."

One man's publicity stunt was a terrifying experience for Mrs. Margery Lewis, whose husband had been the steeplejack atop the building when the blimp tried to tie up.[6] Mrs. Lewis wrote a story for the *New York Mirror* as part of a series by wives of men who had dangerous jobs. Margery Lewis's story:

> Ellis once did a particularly hazardous job atop the Empire State Building. There was actually no repair work on this job, it was just a stunt for the edification of the public and newspaper photographers.
>
> The plan was to moor a Goodyear blimp to the top of the Empire State Building. You go and stand on the ground some day and look up there and see how far it is; how far that skyscraper goes into the air and what a distance it would be to fall if ever a man did fall from the dizzy heights, then you will realize that a steeplejack needs agility, iron nerve, and considerable spunk. . . .
>
> On the very pinnacle of that lofty tower Ellis stood there in the afternoon sunlight, waiting for the blimp, which had been maneuvering about for an hour or so, with its mooring line hanging down, swaying in the wind.
>
> Again and again that blimp swept by the tower, each time coming closer in an attempt to have my husband grasp that steel rope and moor it to the mast.
>
> Twice he almost fell from his lofty perch.
>
> Then the blimp came closer and closer. You couldn't even see Ellis from the ground where I stood. Even the photographers were nonplussed, for they had no higher structure from which to take their "shots" of the scene.
>
> As I stood there, I felt a queer heaviness in my heart. I wanted to dash into the building, take one of those fast-moving elevators to the

---

[6]The specifics of Margery Lewis's story—not the hows but the whens—are a little vague, but it seems that steeplejack Ellis Lewis was on the top of the building for the drop of the bundle of *Journals*, if based only on the statement that the attempted landing was a specific publicity stunt.

top tower and shout to my husband not to go through with it. I wanted
him to come down to the ground with me, where he would be safe. But
I didn't do that. You just can't, you know; you would only ruin his
nerves if you interfered and I've long ago learned that if I remain cool
and collected it helps Ellis to do his job thoroughly and efficiently.

So I watched from the ground, not, as I have said, that I could really do anything.

That blimp was never moored to that tower.

They simply couldn't do it. The wind was too strong. On the third
try Ellis caught the mooring rope and tried to bring the blimp in. But
a sudden gust of wind tore the blimp away and lifted Ellis two feet from
his post. Frantic signaling from the control room of the blimp told him
of his danger—he let go, and quite disappointed, came down from the
tower.

The next day the blimp *Columbia* tried to reverse the maneuver and pick
up bags of mail from the top of the Empire State Building. The indicator
on the tower registered a wind velocity of less than the 5 miles an hour required to bring the blimp to a standstill with its two 110-horsepower engines throttled to the proper speed. After maneuvering for more than an
hour, the pilot and his rigger gave up. For contact to have only been made
in the blind hope that a rope flung over the side of a dirigible would be
caught by a rigger who would then hang on to the dangling rope for dear
life was a seemingly odd and unnecessarily dangerous maneuver to attempt
when the mast was theoretically equipped with high-tech rigging.

Never ones to let a bad fact get in the way of a good story, nobody in
the management of the Empire State had confessed that the rigging had
not been completely installed. The promoters of the building had quietly
decided to postpone the final installation. As late as February 1931, according to Irwin Clavan of the architects' office, "the as yet unsolved
problems of mooring air ships to a fixed mast at such a height made it desirable to postpone to a later date the final installation of the landing
gear." R. H. Hunter, a vice president of the Starrett Construction Company, told the New York Building Congress in April 1931 that the mooring mast was strong enough to hold any airship then in existence with an
ease and safety equal to the mooring masts at Lakehurst and Montreal.
When asked when the test would come, Hunter's reply was a vague
"When the conditions are favorable."

The same month, Smith announced that he and his colleagues had "enjoyed the quips and jokes about the Empire State mooring mast, on the same
principle as the individual in high public office enjoys the slings and arrows

embodied in cartoons of him. It is all in a lifetime. The Empire State Building was built to stand all kinds of wind pressure as well as hot air. We of the management feel flattered to know that Empire State has attracted the attention of the universe." Smith still did not let on that the equipment had not been installed and the mooring mast was not to be used as originally planned, although the decision had already been made. He continued the charade in speeches and in newsreels, and his public affairs staff continued to send out releases showing illustrations of dirigibles tying up to the mooring mast. The illustrations were still running as late as March 1932.

According to building vice president Robert C. Brown, the mechanism to moor dirigibles was complicated, and the technology was changing rapidly. As the situation stood in October 1931, the Empire State mast was permanent up to the top, where the cone, which was carried by some light temporary trusses in eight sectors, could be lifted off. When a mooring mast was perfected, which was expected to be two or three years in the future, the completed mechanism would be set in place.

In 1930, when work was still progressing in earnest on the dirigible mooring mast, the handwriting was on the wall for the future of dirigibles in the United States. In the first six months of the year, scheduled domestic airplane flights carried 208,357 passengers. Only a handful of dirigibles was in operation at the time, and only the hydrogen-filled *Graf Zeppelin* was carrying passengers. Its capacity: twenty. By 1931, Great Britain had abandoned its dirigible program in favor of flying boats. In December 1930, columnist Walter Trumbull suggested that instead of a dirigible mooring mast, Raskob and Smith should consider a landing pad for the autogiro that Juan de la Cierva had invented. This type of aircraft was "the most outstanding thing in its line since the Wrights' first flight. The ability of the 'windmill' plane to descend vertically means that no great space is necessary for a safe landing."[7]

In February 1931, while the publicity mill was still churning out stories on the mooring mast, came the first substantial hint that the mooring mast would not be used as originally planned. The hint did not come from the building's management, and the story did not run in a major news medium. The prediction that the mooring mast would soon be used for a totally different reason came couched in a release from Merlin H. Aylesworth, NBC's president, and it ran in the *Film Daily*. The story said that the mooring mast would be used to broadcast "sound pictures"— what we call television.

[7]A variation on that theme would suit the Pan Am Building in the 1960s, until a helicopter crashed and one of its rotors went flying over the edge.

The machinery needed to complete the operation of docking dirigibles never was installed, except for what *The New Yorker* called a few "pathetic mementos" a reporter found in 1939. By the time the building opened and months before the news leaked out from Aylesworth's office, management had very quietly dropped the facilities for dirigible passengers and substituted amenities for sightseers. Into the space on the eighty-sixth floor that would have been used for the baggage rooms, customs inspection offices, and ticket desks for dirigible passengers went the "world's highest soda fountain and tea garden."

The architects overlooked a spectacular use for the mooring mast that was not considered until 1979, when two students from Cooper Union contributed ideas on how to redesign the observatories. Michael Hallasy and Richard Hoyan said that clear glass should be installed in the "pencil lights" and the space within the mooring mast should be opened to visitors. The visitors could walk down a spiral staircase from the 101st floor to the eighty-sixth, a walk that would put to shame the climb to the crown of the Statue of Liberty or to the peepholes in the Washington Monument. As *Times* critic Paul Goldberger said, these student architects correctly realized "that the chance to descend down a glass-enclosed stair 100 stories above the street could be an architectural experience of profound drama." Amen.

# 12

# BUILDING THE BUILDING

Never before in the history of building
had there been . . . . an architectural
design so magnificently adapted to speed
in construction.

—Paul Starrett, Builder

**B**efore Starrett Bros. & Eken could
start work on what would be the world's tallest building, they had to tear
down what had been the city's largest hotel, and everyone agreed it would
be no easy task. The wrecking business had changed in the twenties.
Wreckers had formerly either paid for the privilege of removing a building or they had done it free of charge, which they could afford for the
value of the materials they salvaged. By the twenties, however, some
wreckers started charging as much as $200,000 to do a job.

Buildings built in the previous thirty years were built of firmer stuff
and had become more difficult to demolish, and the cost of reconditioning
salvage had risen. Wreckers had been able to take the "precious" metals
such as lead, brass, and zinc and have them recycled for industrial uses,
and junkmen had taken plumbing fixtures, but in the boom of the twenties there was less and less demand for secondhand hardware. Likewise,
most of the old granite that had been recut and used for tombstones or
foundations was declared redundant in the twenties and had to be hauled
away and dumped, the cost of which swelled construction costs. The same
held for lumber. Wreckers could no longer use timber or boards for

shoring or bridgework to protect sidewalks or expect to sell it for others to reuse if it meant that a carpenter earning $14 a day found his saw encountering nails. Wreckers had even lost the sale of small and otherwise useless pieces of wood to the "wood merchants," who had previously paid as much as $10 a load. These entrepreneurs had hauled the discarded wood to their basement workshops where "woodchucks" cut it up into kindling sizes and sold the recycled wood by the bag to tenement dwellers to burn in their woodstoves. With that outlet dried up in the twenties, wreckers and builders frequently disposed of the wood by hauling it at $15 a load to swamplands, where, in what seems the making of an ecological mistake, it was burned.

When construction was under way and there was lumber to be disposed of, Smith, or one of his publicity directors, had a better idea. In November 1930, when the hardship of winter was beginning to be felt by the down and out, Smith announced the establishment of a free woodpile in a vacant lot on West Thirtieth Street. The pile would be replenished every day with about six truckloads of wood no longer required on the site. The "woodchucks" who had vanished in the boom of the twenties had resurfaced in another form in the bust of the thirties, and for Smith it was a good deal—he saved money on trucking the wood out of town, while performing a public service. The bulk of the other detritus was carted to an East River dock, where it was loaded onto barges and dumped in the Atlantic Ocean fifteen miles off Sandy Hook. As Smith said, it was cheaper to send the bulk of the Waldorf-Astoria to the bottom of the Atlantic than to try to salvage it.

Called the morticians of the building trade, wreckers were hardly a lugubrious lot. From their perspective they cleared the site for something new, for progress, and they came with pneumatic drill and crowbar, dynamite, pick, and shovel to do it. Their fans, who pooh-poohed the steelworkers on their aerie perches, said the wreckers were the real heroes at construction sites, and the greatest hero of them all was the barman. The barman's tool was a pinch bar, which was fashioned of tempered steel. He was the one worker who was madcap enough yet cool-headed and skillful enough to drive the toe of his pinch bar into a wall that he might have been standing atop and loosen the timber or bricks below him without causing the wall or himself to fall down. There weren't many barmen in the city in the mid-twenties—perhaps three hundred—and they were primarily Russian or Polish. Their pay, at about a dollar an hour, was pretty decent.

The greatest number of workers at a site were the common laborers who cleaned and sorted debris and did other odd jobs, but in addition to trades that you would expect in the mass of steel, concrete, brick, and stone, were wood sawyers, who played an important role in the many activities of demolition and rebuilding. Wood of all sorts, sizes, and shapes had to be pulled from the old structure, cut apart, and trucked away, and beams and boardings for temporary shanties and sections of sidewalks had to be prepared with fresh wood.

After the stone and masonry were removed, structural-steel workers disassembled the exposed metal beams, having already erected steel canopies that remained in place for the duration of the construction work to protect passing pedestrians from the danger of falling objects (the canopies were called "sidewalks" in the trade). Electricians strung temporary lights under the canopy, and carpenters built offices and shanties atop the "sidewalk," and—in the case of the Empire State site—a first-aid station.

Sidewalk canopies until the mid-twenties had been wood, but several recently averted calamities showed the wisdom of all-steel canopies. Perhaps the most dramatic had occurred at the Chase National Bank Building, which was then under construction at Pine and Nassau Streets. The street was crowded when a derrick spilled its three-ton load of steel beams onto the steel canopy from about twenty stories up. The impact of the beams was absorbed by the steel, and although the posts were severely distorted, not a person was injured. Had the canopy been made of wood there would have been no telling the carnage.[1]

Before demolition could begin, a scaffold had to be built around the Waldorf-Astoria to provide a platform for demolition workers, and to catch any material that might fall. The introduction of tubular-steel scaffolding and fire-retardant planking was an important development, and was found at many sites at the time of the famous Sherry-Netherlands fire. The hotel's builder had chosen to save money and use the less expensive all-wood scaffold. It was only after the fire that the builder decided to use the new tubular scaffolding with noncombustible flooring, with treated wood that was fire-retardant. As the fire chief at the time

[1]There was no guarantee, of course. The builders of City Bank Farmers Trust Company Building at Exchange Place and William Street were described as "not unmindful of their obligation to safeguard the public." However, the protection was deemed inadequate. The sidewalks surrounding the construction site were equipped with canopies, but during most of the job the protected sidewalks had been closed to the public, forcing everybody out into the open. None of the four streets surrounding the building averaged more than twenty-five feet from curb to curb, and the sidewalks across the street had no protection. Prudent pedestrians took detours.

said, it was "absolutely asinine to put up a forty- or fifty-story fireproof building and then surround it with a frame structure."[2]

To build scaffolds, the workers used a venerable method of passing boards from one floor level to another. A man stood at the edge of each floor to receive a plank that was swung up to him in an arc by a coworker below. He took it and in turn swung the plank to the man above, until it reached the level where it was needed.

To minimize falling debris and to prevent accidents, Starrett built chutes down the center of the building. The wreckers then proceeded to rip down the outside walls and everything else they could find, dumping as much as possible down the inside chutes and directly into trucks that were accommodated within the site. This system, indicative of the thoughtfulness of Starrett's approach, minimized curbside activity, and made the streets safe for passing pedestrians and vehicles. Furthermore, the crews made "free use of water," as Paul Starrett said, hosing down the site regularly to minimize dust, thus appeasing local realtors.

With the goal of incorporating some of the old Waldorf in the new hotel, the owners had decided to preserve the Blashfield ceilings from the ballrooms and to keep pieces of statuary and bric-a-brac, including the clock that was originally at the 1893 World's Fair. Souvenir hunters made off with almost all the towels that were embroidered with the hyphenated name during the hotel's last months of existence, and over a thousand more-principled souvenir hunters made official requests for mementos. "A man in Keokuk, Iowa, wrote asking for the iron railing fence on the Fifth Avenue side," said Paul Starrett. "A Connecticut woman wanted another railing . . . (and) a man from Maine wanted a flagpole. Somebody in Washington pleaded for stained-glass windows. Other people asked for fireplaces, pieces of marble or brick, or lighting fixtures. One man and his wife were made happy by getting the key for the room they had occupied, many years before, on their honeymoon."

The management put up for auction whatever remaining articles they thought would be of interest, but the auction was not a great success, in part because the whereabouts of the Waldorf-Astoria's most sought-after souvenir, the brass-railed mahogany bar, was a mystery. According to one

[2]The public affairs office for the Sherry-Netherland tried to make a good thing out of the fire. The day after the fire, advertisements appeared in newspapers. AS PER SCHEDULE, proclaimed the headline. "The scaffold-fire of Tuesday night will not interfere with the completion of the schedule of the Sherry-Netherland. It simply proved, in a spectacular way, that the Sherry-Netherland is thoroughly fireproof." The renting office was open.

rumor, the bar had been put to use in the hotel as a theater ticket counter, but it was nowhere to be found. The hotel's chief engineer believed that part of the bar had gone to a speakeasy somewhere on Hester Street, and although he believed that both the bar and the speakeasy were still in existence, he could add nothing further to the solution of the mystery. Preservationists at the John Ringling Towers Hotel in Sarasota, Florida, might have tracked it down in the 1990s. They believe that a bar from the Waldorf, though not necessarily *the* bar, was installed in the hotel, which began life as El Verona.

The Starretts had hoped to save some of the Waldorf's fine mahogany woodwork, but union regulations required carpenters to do the work of salvage, making the cost prohibitive. They did succeed in salvaging over one thousand doors, and again John Ringling enters the scene. The doors were shipped to Ringling in Sarasota, where he planned to incorporate them in the Ritz Carlton Hotel he was building in Longboat Key. The hotel was never completed, and the doors, stored outdoors, rotted away.

The Waldorf-Astoria did not go gladly. The steel had to be cut apart, which required steelworkers with acetylene torches. The steelworker would take the torch with its fine blue tip, swing it like a wand over the beam he was going to cut, and turn up the oxygen. The flame would shoot out, and, as it ate into the steel, fiery particles would cascade down (when the torches were not being used to cut apart steel, some workers cavalierly used them to light their cigarettes). About thirteen thousand tons of structural steel, two thousand tons of scrap iron, and about forty tons of copper, brass, lead, and zinc were removed from the old building and sold for the benefit of the owners.

The steel frame and great thick walls proved so staunchly built that before the Waldorf-Astoria was finally razed and the last broken fragments of its wall had been removed, $900,000 had been spent.[3] Demolition was a risky business, not only for the workers but for passing pedestrians as well, and insurance on a job like the Waldorf-Astoria accounted for about 35 percent of the total cost.

It's a mystery that no prelate came to bless the great work that was

---

[3]It wasn't just steel-framed or reinforced buildings that caused problems. Some brick masonry buildings of an earlier day had been built for the ages, too. When the wreckers started to tear down the storage warehouse that stood on the site of the Chanin Building they found that they had to contend with walls built literally to withstand siege. Erected just after the time of the Civil War draft riots in New York, the warehouse was constructed to resist possible cannonading from gunboats on the East River.

then about to begin. The miracle is that the builders would pull it off. Even before the Waldorf's walls were completely down, six hundred men, working day and night in shifts of three hundred, started digging the excavations. Four steam shovels, three cranes, three derricks, and four air compressors were used. At the same time, two blacksmith shops were built and operated. Large excavation sites like the Empire State's were the biggest shows in town, a drama of the streets. Behind the high board fences surrounding the wrecking operation appeared a cavernous excavation, an open-pit mine. Although most of the work might have been mundane enough, the beehive of activity was constantly fascinating. And there was always the element of danger. You couldn't help but wonder whether the buildings that had been shored up to ward off collapse might not fall into the pit, or whether one of the trucks hauling away refuse might not actually tip over the side of the precariously angled ramp. The price of admission was right, especially after the stock market crash and the beginning of the Depression, and the curious, the "sidewalk superintendents," would peer down into the pit through cracks in the walls and from other vantage points to watch—fascinated and in awe—the digging and hauling.[4]

The most exciting event was the blasting. One workman drilled a hole in the stone. Another took the sticks of dynamite from small wooden boxes and, using a rod, pushed them one by one into the hole. With the explosives tightly packed, wires were attached. Everyone except the operator of a nearby steam shovel then backed off. The steam shovel operator covered the hole with a large steel mesh mat. Then, to make sure that no loosened rocks went flying, a second mat was dropped on top of the first. Once the steam shovel operator had retreated to a safe distance, a whistle blew warning workers to stay away and alerting everyone to brace themselves for the blast. A muffled *thunk* would be heard, the carpets would surge up, a cloud of smoke and dust would come from the hole, and the very ground beneath would shake. Then the workers would return to prepare for the next blast, and the cycle would continue.

Few engineers could learn from site surveys whether a long covered and forgotten stream had originally flowed through the site, and wise engineers would consult old maps and records before finding themselves

---

[4]Carol Krinsky tells us that the first formalization of sidewalk superintendents took place at Rockefeller Center. John D. Rockefeller was told by a supervisor to move along when he had paused to view the scene, which resulted in the "Sidewalk Superintendent's Club," with actual membership cards issued—a public relations coup.

knee-deep in water. The Empire State site had a stream that immediately required pumps to carry away the water and ultimately required accommodation.[5]

Engineers could be fairly certain that when they scratched Midtown Manhattan's surface they would encounter an igneous rock called Manhattan schist, the rock whose strength made for Manhattan's greatness.[6] The Empire State Building was lucky. They hit a solid stratum of rock at thirty-eight feet, and kept digging until they were at the forty-foot mark. By the first week in March 1930, an astonishing 28,529 truckloads of earth, rock, steel, and debris had been carted away.

With the clearing of the site came the challenge of construction. Shreve was noted for his hyperbole, but, as flowery as he could be, he nevertheless had a way of synthesizing the important aspects of a job. He said that "one may well believe that with its organized cooperation in the labor of men and the fabrication and placing of materials, its precision of performance to match the timing of a trunk-line railroad and connecting services, almost the powers of Aladdin's genii were harnessed for a building project. None of all the ancient world wonders in any way matched the amazing assembly of skilled craft and fashioned materials which with uncanny accuracy find their places in the daily wrought miracle of a modern skyscraper."

The logistics and assembly of the parts, as directed by Eken, were a testament to the way Starrett Bros. & Eken got things done. The components that made up the building came from factories, foundries, and quarries from far and wide—the limestone from Indiana, steel girders from Pittsburgh, cement and mortar from upper New York State, marble from Italy, France, and England, wood from northern and Pacific Coast forests, hardware from New England. Hundreds of other things from equally distant points of manufacture or origin were delivered to the building site and assembled into one great structure, each fitting into its proper place as detailed in the architect's plans. "When we were in full swing going up the main tower, things clicked with such precision that once we erected fourteen and a half floors in ten working days—steel, concrete, stone and all," said Shreve. "We always thought of it as a parade in which each marcher kept pace and the parade marched out of the top of the building, still in perfect step. Sometimes we thought of it as a great assembly line—only the assembly line did the moving; the finished product stayed in place."

[5]The apartment house at 2 Fifth Avenue has a fountain in its lobby that is fed by Minetta Brook, which still flows under the building.
[6]Columbus Circle is the major exception in midtown.

If a supplier could not perform on time, Starrett found another that could. The choice of facing marble for the entrance hall and public areas was originally to have been dark Hauteville marble, but the decision was revised when the quarry informed Starrett that it could not keep up with the pace of construction. The solution was to buy an entire quarry in Germany for the Rose Famosa marble. As Al Smith described it, they "took the stuff out by tons."

Lamb said that handwork was done away with as much as possible. In quantity production, with thousands of pieces of each material identical in shape and size, the delay would have been disastrous. Windows, spandrels, steel mullions, and stone were all designed so that they could be duplicated in tremendous quantity and with almost perfect accuracy, then brought to the building and put together. The limestone ashlar, much of which was alike and of simple form, was so easily fabricated that one-third of the total order was finished in seven weeks.

The ease of scheduling deliveries of the limestone explains a certain diabolical brilliance (or just plain business sense) on behalf of the contractors—the Indiana Limestone Company rough-cut the stone at the quarries, but Starrett had the milling done locally, and there the milled stone sat until it was required at the site. This eliminated storage problems—the local millers doubled as warehouses.

Driven by the exigencies of the schedule, the designers had the draftsmen make drawings from the bottom up. They did not worry about designing the eighth floor until the drawings for the third floor had been completed and sent to the fabricators. Erecting the building required a synchronization of infinitely varied activities that had scarcely ever been attempted before. The supervision entailed was enormous. The overseers, from job foreman to architect and engineer, were on the site constantly, watching, seeing that everything was proceeding according to both plan and schedule.

The plans for the steelwork were not given to the men at the site until the middle of January 1930. By then the foundation was almost ready. Contrary to public opinion, laying the foundation for the building did not require digging an enormous hole. Construction began forty feet down, where pier holes were dug so that concrete workers could begin to pour the massive footings on which the steel supports of the building would rest. The first steel construction would include the erection of the 210 steel columns that would constitute the building's vertical frame, twelve of which would run uninterrupted from the foundation to the top of the building, 1,050 feet up, there to join the steel columns for the mooring mast. Before half the footings were in place, the builders set the steel in place in the already completed footings. According to schedule, it was the second week in March.

Before the steelwork could begin to be set in place, however, some very delicate political maneuvering had to be accomplished. In 1928, the Merchants' Association of New York had proposed a revision to the building code that would have permitted an increase of the basic working stresses in structural steel from 16,000 to 18,000 pounds per square inch. It was a modest proposal, according to William Starrett, who said that the 18,000-pound standard was already in use in nearly all American cities at the time.

The local building code had not been revised since the turn of the century, when comparatively little was known about the behavior of steel under stress. By the mid-twenties, the quality of steel had greatly improved, and scientific testing had set more accurate standards than the more conservative, seat-of-the-pants estimates. The new standard of 18,000 pounds stress had been approved by a long line of authorities, including the American Institute of Steel Construction and the American Society of Civil Engineers, who all agreed that the new standard would not sacrifice safety. Passing the legislation would mean a 10 to 12.5 percent reduction in the total amount of steel needed to erect a building. Since steel represented 15 to 20 percent of the cost of a skyscraper, the savings to builders would be considerable.

Mayor Jimmy Walker vetoed the bill in 1928, claiming he did not want to make revisions to the building code piecemeal. The proposal sat until the beginning of 1930, when, in a lobbying effort couched in stimulating building construction and thus alleviating unemployment, the Board of Aldermen adopted an ordinance calling for seven changes in the building code. All seven revisions had been drawn up by a committee headed by the Merchants' Association, which had been asked by Mayor Walker to assist. Shreve served on the committee, and one of the revisions was the same one for steel that had been proposed two years before.

At the same time, the corporation was politicking—perhaps with more urgency—in private. If the code could be changed in time for the corporation to take advantage of the revision, the savings on the steel bill would be about $500,000. They had a talk with Jimmy Walker, and, mirabile dictu, despite his former refusal to revise the building code piecemeal, in March 1930 the mayor signed into law the revision on steel—and not a moment too soon. The corporation had already ordered tons of steel according to the proposed new standard, some of which, according to building vice president Robert C. Brown, was sitting on the New Jersey waterfront on the day the bill came up for final passage. If Walker had procrastinated by a few weeks and the corporation decided to wait on his assurances, construction would have been delayed; if Walker had not signed the measure, the corporation would have been stuck with that much worthless steel on its hands. The day after Walker signed the bill the steel began to be set, and within a week the giant framework was beginning to rise.

The columns had to support the collective weight of the building in addition to a pull of fifty tons from a dirigible that might be docked at the 102nd floor. The simplest and smallest rolled-steel I-beam column that was used was capable of carrying loads up to 4.5 million pounds. The next largest, a reinforced I-beam column, could support loads up to 5.7 million pounds. The largest columns, fabricated as the "master" link in the steel framework, were box columns with a core section of the heaviest rolled column, two plate webs, four angles, and cover plates as wide as forty-two inches. These columns, 693 square inches of steel in cross section, weighed a ton a foot, and were designed to support a weight of five thousand tons, or more than 10 million pounds. Shreve said that "nothing like it ever was constructed before for an operation of this kind."[7]

Work on the giant frame started March 17, and soon the steel framework, with the derricks in place in their strategic positions, had begun to fill the whole area. A continuous stream of girders flowed in from Pittsburgh, 440 miles away. The American Bridge and McClintock-Marshall supplied the steel for alternating sections that ranged from six to eight stories each. The steel was shipped first to a waterfront supply yard near Bayonne, New Jersey, from which the amount needed for two floors would be withdrawn in a single requisition and delivered to the site. A seemingly endless caravan of supply trucks loaded up in New Jersey, crossed under the Hudson River, and made its way through Midtown traffic to the site. The contractors and truckers carefully surveyed the routes over which heavy supplies were transported; below the surface of New York's streets is a mechanical maze of electrical, steam, water, gas, and telephone conduits channeled in a rootlike system, as well as larger tubes for the subway. The truckers had to travel the streets gingerly.

All deliveries were received within the building except the steel mem-

---

[7]The assumption is that Shreve was referring to construction of a strictly office building. Traffic was stopped one holiday morning at Times Square when Thompson-Starrett hoisted 115 feet in the air the steel beams that would act as trusses to bridge the auditorium in the Paramount Building in 1926. One truss weighing 144 tons was 122 feet long and 16 feet high. They used a derrick that resembled the kind of gantry cranes used in shipyards to set the trusses in place.

bers for the framework and the limestone facing for the first five floors—
those deliveries were made directly from the streets. Derricks lifted the
steel off the trucks and set it near where it would be installed. When the
building was up to the sixth floor, the sixty-foot setback could be used as
a staging area. Lifting steel more than thirty stories in one motion was
not practical, so a series of relay derricks were built on setbacks or on
platforms built out from the edge of the building. Depending on how high
the building had risen, the steel would be transferred directly to the erection derricks, or to the relay derricks and finally to the erection derricks.

The steel posts and beams arrived at the site marked with their place
in the framework and with the number of the derrick that would hoist
them so that with the aid of a blueprint they could be quickly and conveniently set in place. The great bundles of steel at the ends of cables would
be swung toward the working platform high above the street, where the
metal members of the structure were set in orderly rows. From the platforms of the highest relay derricks, the erection derricks would then lift
the beams from the platforms to the men who were waiting at the top. The
ironworkers would swing the steel into place and have it riveted as soon
as eighty hours after it had come out of the furnace, barely enough time,
it seems, for the steel to have cooled. Those steel members that seemed to
float so effortlessly in the air and fit so easily into the great jigsaw puzzle
in the sky had to be set perfectly plumb and absolutely level, their parts
so accurately fabricated that they could be assembled with no more tolerance for error than one-eighth of an inch.

In the wake of the cranes that hoisted the beams into place, the steelworkers swung higher and higher into the air. These men who put the
pieces together seemed quite unaware that they were actors in a metropolitan drama. Passersby stood three and four deep, taking deep breaths
in wonderment as they watched the steelworkers at their acrobatic work.
"Like little spiders they toiled, spinning a fabric of steel against the sky,"
said *The New Yorker*. "Crawling, climbing, swinging, swooping—weaving
a web that was to stretch farther heavenward than the ancient Tower of
Babel, or than all the older towers of the modern Babel." *Times* reporter
C. G. Poore said that ironworkers put on the best open-air show in town.
They rode into the air on top of a steel beam that they maneuvered into
place as a crosspiece by hanging to the cable rope and steering the beam
with their feet, then strolling on the thin edge of nothingness. Harold
Butcher, the New York correspondent for London's *Daily Herald*, was another fan. He said that you do not have to search musty libraries for stories of classical heroes. They were right there, "in the flesh, outwardly

prosaic, incredibly nonchalant, crawling, climbing, walking, swinging, swooping on gigantic steel frames." Many of the workers—"hairy-chested huskies, strapping youths, clean-limbed, and clear-eyed," as Butcher described them—were over the hill by the time they hit their forties, their bodies, so magnificent in youth, heading for the scrap heap in middle age. Some did not even make middle age. Some were killed, some had accidents or witnessed them, never to return, their nerves shot, their verve gone.

The girders and columns that the cranes and workers swung into place were permanently fastened together by the riveting gangs, who worked just below the topmost pieces of steel as they were set in place, shooting their red-hot rivets into the rows of holes at the junction points. They too filled their fans with admiration for the nonchalance with which they defied the law of gravity. The riveters' work might not have seemed as spectacular as that of the ironworkers fitting together the frame, and although their pay was not as high as the hoisting engineers, who made $2.31 an hour, their pay was higher than the ironworkers'. A riveter worked eight hours for $15.40, or a union scale of $1.92 an hour for ordinary weekdays, from 8:30 A.M. to 4:30 P.M., with a half hour for lunch and double pay for overtime and Saturdays.

A riveter never worked alone. He was part of a gang of four: the heater or passer, the catcher, the bucker-up, and the gunman. Riveters selected their own mates, and trained together as closely as a trapeze act. No "boss" would try to inflict a new member on a team. If one member of a team did not show up for work, the gang was laid off for the day. There were thirty-five to forty gangs of riveters at work on the Empire State Building at one time, and an expert gang could drive more than five hundred 1 ⅛-inch rivets in a seven-and-a-half-hour workday, or more than one a minute. Each man had his own specialty. The job of the heater was to put about ten large rivets into his forge of flaming coke. When the rivets, which resembled a bolt with a head on it, were red-hot, he would take a pair of three-foot tongs, pick out a rivet, and toss it with an easy underhand throw in the direction of the catcher, who would catch the rivet in a battered tin can.[8] Throws of fifty to seventy-five feet were common, and it was easier—a more natural arc—to throw rivets up a floor than to

---

[8]The cans that riveters used for their spectacular catches were at one time merely old paint cans, which some riveters, true to tradition and unimpressed by the newfangled notions of the gadget age, still used. But a patented conical catching can had come on the market, and many catchers had come to prefer it.

throw them to a catcher on the same level. The catcher too was armed with a pair of tongs, with which he would fish the rivet out of the can, tap it on the beam he was standing on to remove any cinders, and stick it into one of the holes in the steel plate, where the bucker-up would support it. The gunman would then take the yard-long riveting hammer with its trailing air hose and hit the head of the rivet, forcing the still red-hot bolt in and smashing the end of the rivet into a cap. Sparks would spit out, the metal would fuse together from the heat, whereupon another rivet was taken from the forge, tossed through the air, caught, and set in place. All of this took place while the riveters were balanced on little more than the horizontal bars that formed the skeleton for the future floor, with the forge perhaps precariously balanced on a plank between two girders.

The noise from riveting was ear-shattering, but engineers who had tried to silence the noise had failed. They claimed that there was simply no way of quieting the sound of hammer hitting rivet, let alone silencing it. The blows fell at the rate of two per second behind the driving force of 100 pounds of compressed air per square inch. In the average skyscraper, from 80,000 to 100,000 rivets were driven, and the higher the tower, the more rivets were needed as strengthening against wind stresses and heavier loads.

As recently as fifty years before, little tumult had accompanied building operations. Excavations were dug by hand and buildings were erected of brick and stone, put in place in comparative silence. But with the advent of the steam shovel for excavation and the riveting of steel skeleton construction, all that changed. Whenever a new skyscraper went up, said health department officials, the telephones on their desks began to ring. With the first rataplan came a few calls, but then, as the unceasing roar set in, the calls would come in by the dozen. "Can't something be done to stop it?" the health department would hear from frustrated neighbors. "We can't dictate! We can't telephone! We can't think!" To which the inevitable reply of the inspector was, "Sorry, the department can do nothing about it," and they would regularly cite Article 804 of the building code: "Beams resting on girders shall be securely riveted to the same."

As part of its attempt to overhaul the building code in 1928, the Merchants' Association had advocated the substitution of electric welding for riveting, which tests had shown was just as efficient while eliminating much of the cannonading of the pneumatic hammer, but Jimmy Walker refused to go along with that proposal, too. The code only countenanced riveting. One of the few examples of welding in the city was found in the Junior League Club House that was erected in 1929, but it was not the frame of a skyscraper that had been welded, it was the steel basin of the swimming pool.[9]

Riveting was a noisy business that affected people for blocks around, but it was allowed between 6 A.M. and 11 P.M. Working those hours would have cost overtime, but at least one contractor who erected an apartment house on Madison Avenue at Seventieth Street was willing to pay it and go for broke. He pushed it and his luck, until the residents of 837 Madison complained. The police came and arrested the offending workers at 2:45 A.M. and held them on $500 bail for breaking the curfew.

Riveters and ironworkers, however deafened they might have been by the racket, regarded weather as the most dangerous part of their work, and they read the weather forecast every day, whatever the season. Even a good forecast was not always a good enough guide to follow, however, since a gale could be blowing up top without being felt in the street below. When it rained, the danger was slipping. When it was cold, the danger was different—the workers' hands would sometimes get so stiff and numb that they could not hang on to anything. In rainy, bitterly cold, or windy weather they seldom went aloft. With all their seeming braggadocio, the workers were still inclined to self-preservation. No worker in his right mind was willing to risk his life, nor was Starrett willing to risk the lives of employees.

Once the steel was in place, it had to be protected from fire. William Starrett pointed out that the A. T. Stewart (Wanamaker) Building between Fourth Avenue and Broadway from Ninth to Tenth Streets had exterior walls of cast iron filled with masonry. This feature made the building "thoroughly fireproof according to the best traditions of the early 1870s."[10] The same pains in an updated version were taken with the framework of the Empire State Building. First the steel was protected by an iron oxide and linseed oil paint for the trip from the steel mill to the site, where it was given an asphaltic coat to resist alkali and to keep it from breaking down when brought in contact with cement. The lower story columns, where the hazard of fire is great during construction, were fireproofed with cinder concrete. The exterior columns above the street level were fireproofed with four inches of brickwork. All other columns were fireproofed with two-inch cinder blocks, and the floor construction steel was fireproofed with cinder concrete.

---

[9]About forty-five municipalities, mostly in the South and West, allowed welding in the work of steel-framed buildings in 1931. The biggest welding job had been for a twelve-story addition to the Homestead Hotel in Hot Springs, Virginia.

[10]This "fireproofing" might go far in explaining why the frame still stood after a ruinous fire had destroyed everything else in 1954.

The first small-scale architectural plans for the structural design were completed about the middle of November 1929. Two months later, by the middle of January 1930, the first plans, showing the framework for supporting the load and the lowest tier of columns, were turned over to the steel contractors. At the same time, the men who would be working on the site were told what they had to know about the concrete column foundations and walls. As the plans were completed—always working several floors at a time from the bottom up—the structural design drawings would be furnished to the steelmakers, allowing them to prepare detailed drawings and to fabricate steel. The design for the roof over the eighty-fifth floor was only completed by the middle of June. "There were days when the messenger reached Pittsburgh with drawings only an hour before the steel mills started rolling the I beams we would need a few days later," said Shreve. "Steel had gone up thirty stories before plans could be finished for some details of the ground floor. We had to keep ahead of the workmen no matter what happened. We had enough close shaves to make us all turn white."

The frame was erected during the best seasons, and the orchestration of the steelwork was at a brisk, legato tempo. By June it was clear that a record was in the offing. Three and a half stories per week had been the record for a comparably scaled building. Starrett determined to erect the Empire State at the rate of a story a day, or five stories a week, a rate they nearly accomplished. Four and a half floors of steelwork were added each week.[11] By June 20, twenty-six stories had been completed. On September 15, 1930, the steel was in place up to the eighty-sixth floor. A few days later, workmen standing 1,050 feet above the sidewalks of New York raised a large Stars and Stripes—the "flag of triumph," said *Times* man Poore—to celebrate the topping out of the steelwork a few days before. The workers had placed steel at the record rate of twenty-four hundred tons a week, they had completed their end of the contract in six months—twenty-three days ahead of the appointed date—and raising the flag atop the eighty-fifth floor was as powerful a symbol to them as the raising of the flag over Iwo Jima's Mount Surabachi would be to a later generation of marines. They had won a major battle, and a score of workers waved

[11]Charles Follen McKim had been amazed at the rate of construction of the Flatiron Building, whose steel went up at a floor a day. However, compared with the Empire State, the Flatiron Building is tiny. Its plot measures 8,460 square feet, it is only twenty stories high, and its total rentable area is 144,000 square feet. The Empire State's plot measures 83,980 square feet, the building is 102 stories high, and its total rentable area is about 2,175,000 square feet.

their hats from their slender perch on the roof beams to celebrate. As one newspaper said, "You should have heard those workmen cheer." Two months later, on November 21, workers raised the flag again. The dirigible mooring mast tower was topped out. Fifty-three thousand tons of steel had been set in place. Just as builders threw stones higher into the sky during the Gothic period than anybody had ever thought possible, so the builders of the Empire State Building threw steel into the sky not just higher but faster than anybody had ever dreamed possible.

Although the topping-out ceremonies belonged to the workers, the laying of the cornerstone and the symbolic driving of the last rivet fell into management's orbit. It was Al Smith who wielded the ceremonial silver trowel on September 9, 1930, cementing into place on stage right of the great Fifth Avenue entrance arch the forty-five-hundred-pound semicircular Swedish granite block measuring two and a half feet thick and six feet in diameter. Ever the politician, Smith played to the gallery, where half the crowd of five thousand were workers. He made it known that he was a member of the bricklayers union in good standing, that his dues were paid, and that his union card was sitting in his office at 200 Madison Avenue.

A copper box placed within the stone contained what Smith described with a perfectly straight face as "certain articles of value indicating the trend of the time. If this building is ever demolished to make way for a greater building the people of that day can read pretty accurately the history of this day." The "articles of value" consisted of a history of the building and the company erecting it, photographs of the architects, contractors, and officers of the building company, a copy of that day's *New York Times* on rag paper, and samples of the coinage and paper currency of 1930 in all denominations from one cent to a hundred-dollar bill. Al Smith, ever the publicist, knew a good thing when he posed for it. "Since the advent of the movie camera, the radio and other means of communicating sound," he said, "the laying of a cornerstone of a public building today becomes somewhat of a photographic gallery performance."[12]

It would be Smith, of course, who "shot" the last rivet in the steel to top off the structure on the 102nd floor. This was not the kind of rivet that had been shot into the steelwork by the thousand. It was solid gold.[13]

---

[12]A "photographic gallery performance" is certainly a more felicitous phrase than the "media event" and "photo op" of the 1980s and 1990s.

[13]Irwin S. and Henry I. Chanin, the builders and owners of the Chanin Building, clearly outshone Smith's efforts. Each of them drove a gold rivet into a column on the fifty-sixth floor to declare the Chanin Building's frame finished.

Before he went up to perform the act, he said to a few newspapermen that he would be glad when he had completed the ceremony. "I'm thinking of getting me a stout leather belt and tying myself by a chain," said Smith. "I marvel at these steelworkers—the way they move about almost as high as the sky with as little fear apparently as we walk the streets."

Steelworkers might get all the glory for their derring-do, and setting steel records was certainly satisfying, but the records would have been hollow accomplishments for Starrett Bros. & Eken if the other materials could not have kept pace and had not been set in place in a comparably short time. Miraculously, they were. When the steel frame was topped out on the eighty-fifth floor, the outer walls were already carried to the seventy-fifth, and work was progressing on all fronts. Ingenious methods of coordination were applied, and it wasn't as if they were working in the middle of nowhere. They were at the center of an important retail district. As Shultz and Simmons said in *Offices in the Sky*, "of all the places you might pick to build a skyscraper, the most desirable site for the developer is probably the most God-awful site for the contractor." There was hardly any room to turn around at the average construction site, and whole sections of streets were ordinarily cordoned off to serve as a temporary warehouse for materials.

The Fifth Avenue Association was ever vigilant in keeping roadways and sidewalks clear, and the association went further than the rules laid down by the borough president's office in maintaining standards of decorum. The association regarded the sacks of cement, gravel heaps, and mounds of brick as nuisances, and they requested builders and contractors to store as much material as possible on the site itself.[14] Like so many miracles, the miracle of construction that was the Empire State Building did not take place for all to see. It took place on the first floor and downstairs in the basement, where the builders did just what the Fifth Avenue Association wanted. All the building materials, except structural steel and the facing for the first five floors, were received and unloaded within the building and hoisted to the workers within the building. Nothing sat outside in piles to create eyesores, nothing was hoisted outside except the structural steel and stone facing for the lower five floors. Traffic was not blocked, and the ever-constant hazard of falling materials was minimized.

[14]The Fifth Avenue Association also made sure that signs on "sidewalks" did not project one inch beyond the temporary structure. These were the kind of signs that Smith thought Paul Starrett would like to see advertising his services.

Truck entrances on Thirty-third and Thirty-fourth Streets led to twenty-five-foot-wide driveways extending around the first floor. Drivers only had to drive through a gate to the appointed docking area, unload, and drive off. Eken said that they "ran trucks the way they run trains in and out of Grand Central. If a truck missed its place in the line on Tuesday, it had to wait until Wednesday to get back in." The building materials were all hoisted within the building in four shafts that would later accommodate passenger elevators. In the early stages, the hoists traveled at 80 feet a minute, but they were soon replaced by mine skips that zipped along at 1,300 feet a minute.

Almost all the work was performed during the normal workday. About all that took place after hours was the removal of construction debris. If the debris was heavy, it was taken down by hoists; if light, it was sent down metal chutes (wood chutes would not have been strong enough to withstand the weight and velocity of even light debris). The debris went into a hopper on the first floor, it was transferred to trucks, and out it went.

Just as Paul Starrett had told the corporation that all equipment would be new, it was also novel. An industrial railway system was used to distribute the material at the site—a first for an office-building construction job. It was not as if there were four-by-eight locomotives up there. The railway cars were handcars with no motive power other than human push power, but they rolled along at a merry clip, and each car was the equivalent of eight wheelbarrows. Narrow-gauge tracks that were designed to reach every work site were laid on the floors of every floor of the building and the hoists, with twenty-four double-side-rocker dump cars and twenty-four platform cars serving the building. Sheet iron, metal parts, bales of wire, coils of cable, sand and cinders and lumber and pipe would arrive; each would be unloaded in a special corner of the first floor, loaded onto a car, and sent shooting to the floor where it was needed. Mortar could be delivered at the rate of twenty-one cubic feet per trip in the cars, compared with seven cubic feet per trip in barrows. It saved labor by decreasing the number of handlers, hoists, and hoist men, and it saved time, and that meant money.

At the ordinary construction site, materials such as bricks were dumped in a pile in a cordoned-off area of the street, then delivered to the workers by wheelbarrow, an admittedly backbreaking, labor-intensive, and not terribly efficient method. Starrett did something different. The building required an enormous quantity of bricks—about 10 million—and the bricklayers had to keep pace with the stone setters who worked on a schedule of one story a day. The contractors constructed two brick hoppers, each with a capacity of twenty thousand bricks, in the first basement. They built chutes leading into the hoppers near the entrances on the main floor. Trucks only had to back up to the chutes, tip their bed, dump their bricks through the chute into the basement hopper, and move out. These hoppers, with inclined bottoms, allowed the bricks to slide through gates and drop into the dump cars. The cars were then taken "up hoist," and the bricks were deposited alongside the bricklayers, without having been handled from the time they came into the building until they were picked up and placed in the wall.

Cement was delivered in bags, unloaded, and was likewise dumped into a floor opening to a basement hopper, which fed a large mixer. A rather ingenious method of handling the bags that minimized back strain and hand injuries was devised by the superintendent and fashioned by the house blacksmith. It was a pair of tongs that was round on the end to prevent tearing the bags.

All the limestone from the sixth floor up was delivered in an equally brilliant fashion (the limestone for the first five stories was raised by stiff-leg derricks that operated from the sixth-floor setback). A truck drove into the building's loading area with the crated stone keyed for the appropriate section of the building. The stone was made in such dimensions that it could be handled on ordinary material hoists within the building, so electric hoists, which were like small cranes that operated from an overhead monorail, lifted the stone from the truck, swung the stone along the monorail, and deposited it on a platform car. The stone would be trundled by platform car to the perimeter of the floor where it was to be installed, and from there it was dropped by cable into its place in the wall between the steel jamb pieces already set. Two hoists handled all the stone for the building, not only eliminating a large number of hoisting derricks and engines but, since the hoisting was inside the building, doing away with a grave source of danger to the public.

An unexpected perquisite came with the site. The Waldorf's architect, Henry J. Hardenbergh, had taken advantage of the right to extend the basement to the curb line when he designed the hotel. Starrett, seeing the opportunity to add to his work space, made sure these vaults were shored up during demolition. He then installed storage and supply rooms in the vaults for subcontractors during construction, freeing that much more space in the interior of the building.

The masonry wall consisted of an eight-inch backing of brick faced with either limestone or aluminum spandrels. The bricklayers put on the walls with a precision of operation that allowed for the least possible wasted motion. Suspended on a covered scaffold, they picked up bricks from the piles that their helpers placed in easy reach, set them in place, spread the mortar, turned, and put in the next brick in a model of time-and-motion studies.[15]

When the framework was about six stories high, the lower floors became scenes of increasingly complex activity, with movement everywhere. The work was fully synchronized, all done in unison. While the skin was being set outside, plumbers and electricians started to install the building's veins, arteries, nerves, and alimentary systems—the ganglia—that fleshed in the skeleton. When the window frames were in place and glass had been installed, plastering and woodwork and painting could begin. All the finishing trades followed in such a rapidly moving but orderly parade, said Shreve, that the plasterer might appear in the lower floors even before the roof was made tight.

When the building was about twelve stories high, workers started to install the fifty-eight passenger elevators and eight service elevators that Otis had built. The Otis Elevator Company had used laboratories to simulate the conditions under which the elevators would operate, problems that they were sure could be solved. However, a seemingly insurmountable and intractable problem was not technology, it was the same old bugaboo: The building code had been written when the standard elevator was hydraulic, and the code restricted the speed of elevators to 700 feet a minute. For the giants among skyscrapers, that was too slow, and the Merchants' Association had been working at getting the elevator code revised as part of the entire overhaul of the code. The association's committee was chaired by Bassett Jones, who was blandly described in the press as a "well-known engineer." He was, in fact, the Jones of Meyer, Strong & Jones, Inc., the consulting engineers for mechanical and electrical equipment of the Empire State Building. Another Empire State representative on the committee was by then an old hand at having standards revised—it was Shreve. Jones wanted the cars to travel to the eightieth floor in slightly over a minute, which meant that the code had to be revised to allow elevators to travel as fast as 1,200 feet a minute. Any faster than that, the engineers admitted, might be uncomfortable.

The designers were caught in a bind with the old standards still in ef-

---

[15]This model of efficiency resulted in financial savings, since the cost of bricklaying had become one of construction's major labor expenses. In 1900, the price of bricks was $4.50 a thousand, and a bricklayer received $2.50 a day, for which he was expected to lay about two thousand bricks. By 1926, the cost of bricks had risen to $21 a thousand, bricklayers were earning $14 a day, and the placing of six hundred bricks was the standard for a day's work. The cost of bricks laid had risen from $5.75 a thousand to $37 a thousand.

fect. As Jones pointed out, large tower buildings increased the number of passengers that had to be handled in a given time, and the Empire State Building probably had the biggest headache of all—the estimate was that more than fifteen thousand workers and visitors would have to be taken up and down in less than a half hour at the beginning and end of each working day with the building at capacity. Numbers like that introduced new problems. If the elevator cars were made bigger to handle more passengers per car, the size of cars would mean larger shaftways, which would begin to impinge on the rentable area. The same problem existed if the size remained the same but the number of elevators was increased. The only solution was to increase the speed of elevators.

Jones and the architects knew that only with high-speed elevators and only with the design and construction of new equipment could the building be adequately served. The weight of the very long hoisting ropes in the high-rise banks, coupled with the weights of the car and other dependent parts, imposed duties never before reached in passenger elevators. They discovered, for instance, that to "pawl" the car, or to bring a car to a stop in case of overspeed, required two safeties, one below the car, the other above. They even had to figure out new depths for the pits, since the old standards did not apply. The $2.9 million elevator contract with Otis for sixty-six cars was the largest single-building contract ever let. The magnitude of the work was so great that Otis established a construction organization in the field.[16]

Owners of the newer, taller buildings, said *The Times* in 1931, had assumed—no doubt with good reason—that there would be a change in the old rules to permit the operation of faster elevators. Just as the Empire State's planners had bet that the standards for steel would be revised, so they gambled that the standards for elevators would be revised, and they went ahead and ordered the high-speed elevators. Granted, the gamble was not as great with the elevators as it had been with the steel. If the law had not been changed, the elevators would not have been a total waste—they were just as capable of operating at 700 feet a minute as they were of operating at 1,200, and for the first six weeks after the building opened, the elevators operated at the slower rate. By the second week of June, however, the gamble paid off—under the new elevator rules adopted by the Board of Standards and Appeals, elevators could whisk their passengers upward at the rate of 1,200 feet a minute.

---

[16]The statistics, as with so many in the Empire State Building, were so vast as to create a sense of numbness, but one statistic is telling and is worth retelling: The total number of elevator landings was 1,239.

The elevators were about as safe as any form of transportation. Working on a construction site was not, and the statistics surely created a certain reluctance to enter the profession. In 1929, the national death rate in the construction industry was second only to the mining industry. In New York State, the Department of Labor reported that deaths in the manufacturing industry had been decreasing at the rate of 26 percent for two years, whereas fatalities in construction had increased 61 percent. In 1931, the AIA said that the culprit was the speed at which old buildings were demolished and new ones erected. The demolition of one large but unnamed building in New York City had resulted in sixteen fractures, nine bad lacerations, three burns, two amputations, and two deaths.

New safety devices at the Chrysler and Irving Trust Building sites had been singled out for praise. Pedestrians were protected by an approved sidewalk shed that did not impede traffic. Material hoists were enclosed in metal, passageways were kept clean, material was always neatly piled, and all debris was promptly removed. To further ensure safety, ladders and temporary stairways were checked for safe construction, large floor openings were adequately guarded, planks were installed over small openings, and watchmen were posted at all entrances to keep out unauthorized persons. And the Chrysler Building had a full-time nurse in attendance.

As much out of self-interest as concern for the well-being of others, the Empire State corporation and their contractors bested even the Chrysler and Irving Trust Buildings on the safety issue, but even then there were problems. One stemmed from the lack of a foolproof gate at the openings of elevator shafts to prevent the curious mechanic from sticking his head in to see where the elevator was, and one worker was killed doing just that. Aside from that, however, the corporation was an exemplar.

The men who worked on the outside of the façade—the men who installed the stone, the stainless steel mullions, the aluminum spandrels, and the windows—worked from scaffolds, or "duck walks," suspended from the floor above. These scaffolds were equipped with solidly planked protection overhead and underfoot, with guardrails, and wire mesh between rail and platform. Beneath the scaffolds were two catchall scaffolds that were fairly widely separated from each other. The first was set under the stone and brick setters and was solidly planked in addition to being wired. The second scaffold consisted of rope net and wire mesh strung between supports. Set about fifteen floors below the stonesetters' catchall, it was designed to catch lighter objects that might fall within the intermediate floors. To show the worth of the catchalls, a foreman who escorted a reporter around the construction site asked the reporter if he had noticed a bolt that had dropped to the scaffolding. "That little chunk of iron is worth about $10,000. If it had dropped to the street, instead of right here, and if it had hit somebody, they—or their relatives—would have got the money."

On floors that did not yet have exterior walls, rope-net protection was installed. In addition to keeping people and things from toppling off into the void, the netting permitted more light and offered less resistance to wind pressure than a customary tarpaulin. All elevator shafts and hoists had wire-mesh panels and pivotal bars across the openings. Temporary stairs were avoided as much as possible, and those that were built were substantially constructed with midrails and handrails. Any ladders that were used (and their use was discouraged) had to be secured firmly at the bottom and had to extend well above the level they were to serve. All floor areas were kept as clean of debris as possible.

Fire-alarm boxes were installed on every floor from the second basement to the fifth floor, and on every other floor from the sixth to the top. Half-hourly tours were made by watchmen from 5 P.M. to 7 P.M., when there was the greatest risk of fire, and on hourly tours from 8 P.M. to 6 A.M. Each watchman was equipped with a small portable fire extinguisher, and large extinguishers were distributed on various floors, especially where there were subcontractors' shanties and on floors where formwork and decking were in progress. A twenty-four-hour service was maintained, with a pumpman always on hand to supply water, an electrician to supply light and power, and a hoisting engineer to operate an emergency hoist or elevator for firemen. Only one fire was reported during construction. It broke out in the lunch room of the forty-seventh floor at about 6 A.M. in November 1930. The building's fire alarm system sounded, the fire department arrived, and they were able to extinguish the fire with the equipment on hand.

Despite an extraordinarily good safety record, rumors on the number of deaths incurred in the demolition of the Waldorf-Astoria and the construction of the Empire State Building soon became rampant, and they started to grow beyond all credibility. One completely specious but quite memorable danger gauge was that one workman would be killed for every floor a large structure went up. The fatalism still persisted in 1930, when stories had the Empire State Building claiming one hundred lives. Edmund Wilson held that the Empire State Building claimed forty-eight lives. The socialist *New Masses* magazine, whose goal was to expose the evils associated with untrammeled capitalism, was more conservative. They ran a Hieronymus Bosch–like cartoon in June 1931, showing dozens of bodies in various stages of pain and discomfort crammed into the Empire State Building. The caption: 42 MEN KILLED CONSTRUCTING

THE NEW EMPIRE STATE BUILDING . . . "THE BUILDING WAS COMPLETED ON TIME." Starrett responded by going public with the figures: With an average of six hundred men employed in the demolition of the Waldorf-Astoria and with five thousand men employed on the construction of the building, five workers were killed. One worker was hit by a truck as he was sawing a plank; the second ran into a blast area; the third stepped off a scaffold; the fourth fell down an elevator shaft; and the fifth was struck by a hoist.

In addition to all the safety precautions, one reason for the low death toll was that a complete hospital was maintained with first aid administered by a trained nurse on full-time duty and a physician who made regular visits during the day and was on call for serious injuries. To keep serious injuries from becoming more serious, an entrance on Thirty-third Street was kept free at all times for ambulances.

For all the workers' serious commitment to getting the job done as well and as quickly as they could, these men were frequently still boys, and their puerile actions could be witnessed any workday when those same workers who seemed so blasé while hanging off a steel girder or wielding a trip-hammer at a dizzy height were observed in their leisure moments over lunch. They sat upon the sidewalk under the "sidewalk" that ringed the building, or they propped themselves on bits of wooden scaffolding. They stretched their legs far out into the sidewalk, staking out their turf. As one newspaper phrased it, "they looked at the attractive maidens who sauntered by, even as the gents in front of the country drug store at Spivvens Centers." Unlike the small-town johnnies, perhaps, these men made catcalls and emitted slow whistles when good examples of pulchritude passed by. One of the workers could imitate a yelping dog, a merriment he furnished for his coworkers. Seated far at the end of a long line, he would wait until an attractive young woman was passing, whereupon he would let out a yelp. As she and other startled pedestrians jumped, a loud howl of glee would erupt along the line.

An enormous difference in the work patterns for workers occurred late in 1929. The owner or contractor had to provide elevator facilities to take workmen to within fifteen stories of the point where the steel was to be set. Until then, steelworkers were sometimes forced to climb up and down a twenty-or-more-story building a couple of times a day with only ladders for their use, or, as the more adventuresome steelworkers preferred, by shinnying up or sliding down the posts. Even workers in great shape seldom had enough energy left to go to work immediately, much less to work out on the end of a girder dangling several hundred feet high in the breeze. Where there was fatigue, there were always accidents. On the most mundane level, it behooved the employer to get the workers to their workplaces more efficiently. The workers punched in at the bottom, so the employer was paying for the workers to climb to their workstations and to catch their breath.

Construction workers on the Empire State Building were saved climbing any great distances from workday one. Completely enclosed elevators with sliding doors had been salvaged from the Waldorf and set up temporarily to carry workmen until the usual hoists could be set in place. When work had progressed, permanent workers' elevators were installed in degrees to keep pace with construction, until finally they went all the way to the top.

Even with elevator service, it took time for the workers to get down to the sidewalk from their high perches to enjoy the passing scene, and it took time for them to get back up. At its peak, there were about 3,000 men at work on the job at one time, among them 225 carpenters, 290 bricklayers, 384 brick laborers, 107 derrick men, 285 steel men, 249 elevator installers, 105 electricians, 192 plumbers, 194 heating and ventilating men, trade specialists, inspectors, checkers, foremen, clerks, and water boys. There were even workers who did nothing more than settle the dust on the planked wooden floor with watering cans. Some workers would remain at their aerie perches to eat, but more ate out—or tried to. When worker after worker started reporting back late after the lunch break with the excuse that he had not been able find a place in which to eat on the outside, the builders realized that there might be some validity to the stories. They struck a deal with a local restaurateur. Starrett would build cafeterias if the restaurateur would operate them and feed the workers. As the building climbed, cafeterias were built to keep up with the height, until there were finally five floors with cafeterias—the third, ninth, twenty-fourth, forty-seventh, and sixty-fourth.

According to Paul Starrett, the custom of the trade underwent a bouleversement. Instead of the usual scurry to get out at noon, the men would walk to the nearest cafeteria, and five minutes after the noontime whistle had blown, lines of hungry workers would be crowding in. Starrett maintained that the restaurateur who operated the cafeterias made a fair profit, and the men were able to buy good food at cheaper prices than they could have found outside the building. Forty cents bought a good-size meal of hot meat, vegetables, and potatoes, or a couple of sandwiches, bread and butter, coffee, milk or cocoa, and the inevitable pie for desert. The men ate leisurely in the cafeterias, and would still get back to work on time. Except, said Starrett, the Italians who were on the job. They spurned the cafeteria cuisine, and brought home-prepared lunches.

Throughout the day, water boys would deliver beverages to the men on the job, and they peddled cigarettes at the same time. They did not have to travel great distances for water. A maze of temporary pipes laid over the concrete floors of the building pumped fresh drinking water to the work sites. Ten miles of piping, every piece of which would have to come out before the building could be completed, were laid. The cost to Starrett of allowing a workman to have a drink of water without leaving his job was estimated at $25,000, but it probably saved that much and more in downtime. Sixteen-year-old Joe Carbonell was one of the youths who carried a water bucket to the thirsty construction workers. "It was kind of a thrill working on the beams," Carbonell recalled on the building's sixtieth birthday. "I learned, don't look down, just look to the end of the beam."

Starrett's John P. Carmody, who was charged with the field organization, said that a date had been set for each division to begin and finish. Not a single contractor lagged behind the assigned period, and the average contract was completed ahead of schedule. Each of the four pacemakers—the trades that had to take the lead and set the pace for the trades that followed—was ahead of schedule:

| TRADE | SCHEDULED DATE | ACTUAL DATE | TIME SAVED |
|---|---|---|---|
| Structural Steel | October 4 | September 22 | 12 days |
| Floor Arches | October 10 | October 6 | 4 days |
| Exterior Metal | December 1 | October 17 | 35 days |
| Exterior Stone and Backup | December 1 | November 13 | 17 days |

The building, scheduled to open May 1, 1931, could have opened in April.

To commemorate the completion of the building, about sixty subcontractors tendered a dinner on April 16 "to celebrate the completion of an enduring monument, a towering milestone on the road of human progress."

"Far above the sidewalks of New York soars the Empire State," went the blurb on the menu. "To the public it is a mighty symbol: a supreme expression of Man the Builder. To those who have participated in its making, it has been a great adventure; an adventure made possible by the vision and scientific knowledge that can turn dreams into stone and steel. The makers of the Empire State are here tonight: the owners, whose faith was an inspiration; the architects, whose boldness and simplicity of design was the solution of unprecedented problems; the builders, who brought skill, speed and unselfish co-operation to their task. To each comes the thrill of participation. To each comes the pride in accomplishment."

The sixty-two guests included Pierre S. du Pont, Shreve, Lamb, and Harmon, August Heckscher, Timothy J. Mara, John McInerney, John J. Raskob, Alfred E. Smith, Alfred E. Smith, Jr., and three Starretts— Paul, R. W., and Colonel William. Not a Miss or a Mrs. among them.

MENU

American Beauty Cup

Clear Green Turtle Westmoreland

Celery    Salted Almonds    Olives

Boned Southern Shad and Roe Meunière
Pressed Cucumbers

Fresh California Asparagus
Sauce Hollandaise

Breast of English Pheasant Singapore
Potatoes Dauphine
Salad My Fancy

Fresh Pear Cardinal
Raspberry Sauce
Cakes

Demi Tasse

They could afford to celebrate themselves. One of the bedazzling feats behind the scheduling was that almost all the work was done in a regular five-day week. Only occasionally, as Andrew J. Eken acknowledged, did work have to be extended beyond quitting time. If, for instance, a cement floor was being poured, the operation could not be expected to stop precisely at the quitting whistle.

When the whistle blew at four-thirty, the sudden quiet, which bordered on silence, became more noticeable to the observer than all the noise of the day. Work ceased almost instantly. The rhythm of forge and hammer and trowel and torch and riveting gun wavered, then stopped. Tools were put away. Coats were found, lunch pails picked up. From their high stations the workers began to make the long descent to the street that had meant nothing to them during the day but a foreshortened picture.

The last day was different. For those workers who could proudly stand atop this masterful piece of work and gaze out over the city that many of them had helped build, there was little to look forward to. At the dinner commemorating the completion of the building, Al Smith was given a drawing showing a woman standing on the roof of a tenement with her son. Below them, at street level, are the mundane signs of everyday life—a laundry, a delicatessen, even a billiard parlor. Rising above the gritty scene, and seemingly reaching for the heavens, rises the Empire State Building. The caption read: TONY, YOUR OLD MAN'S BUILDIN' THAT. The irony is that the ironworkers laboring away on the steel cage of a skyscraper had no share in the ideals of their enterprise, whereas their ancestors, the stonemasons who had built the great Gothic cathedrals, at least had a part in their church. After they built their cathedral, there was a place—and it was not a negligible place—for them within.[17]

What was there for the workers on the Empire State Building, who had striven so hard, who had set practically every record in the books, and who had built a masterpiece? Granted, thirty-two of the best of the forty-two hundred were awarded Craftsmanship Awards and had their names inscribed in the lobby for posterity, the way a church might honor a choirboy and call him "optimus," and Smith was undoubtedly sincere when he said at the "consecration of the house" ceremony that he hoped the honored workers would come back and share the glory of the place with their grandchildren, the way he had shared the opening-day celebrations with his. But although stonemasons had a place within their cathedrals and honored choirboys have one within their church, workmen usually feel out of place in the lobbies of great office buildings. When construction workers revisit the scenes of their triumphs, they feel obliged to wear ill-fitting suits. They stand around awkwardly, shifting from one foot to another, not knowing where to put themselves. They don't feel as if they belong. They are fish out of water. Earl Sparling wrote a fictional monologue from one ironworker to another—"sky boys," he called them—for the *World-Telegram*. The narrator talked about the emptiness and depression that ensued when the big job was done and life held nothing but a vague thought of the next tower to be built. He tried to pick out the shaft where a carpenter had been killed and couldn't find it. "All the shafts look alike now, and the elevator operators are all dressed up in swell uniforms. . . ."[18]

---

[17]Allan Temko, who wrote the wonderful history of Paris's Notre Dame, said this first.
[18]A movie where the Empire State Building is the subject tangentially is the coming-of-age story *Breaking Away*. The father, played by Paul Dooley, was a cutter in the local lime

These workmen, many of them skilled artisans, had built the world's tallest building in record time. Instead of getting on line to sign up for the next job, they were in all likelihood going to stand on one line to sign up for relief, and then, when the benefits ran out, they would stand on another line—for bread. The rate of new construction in the metropolitan area in October 1930 had fallen off almost 15 percent from the month before, and a full 50 percent from October 1929. The workers stood half as much chance of finding a job as they would have the year before, and things were getting bleaker. Not only was there no place for them within, by 1931 there would be no place for them without. The workers had little to cheer about.

---

stone quarries around Indiana University, the same limestone quarries where the limestone for the Empire State came from. He says how out of place he feels on the campus, which had used some of the local product. "I cut the stone for this building," he says. "I was damned proud of my work. And the buildings went up. When they were finished, the damndest thing happened. It was like the buildings was too good for us. Nobody told us that. Just felt uncomfortable, that's all. Even now, I'd like to be able to stroll through the campus and look at the limestone, but I just feel out of place."

# 13

# THE OPENING

It's a great piece of work.

—Al Smith

Opening day, May 1, 1931, was a
cool day with a slight haze, but the chill and less-than-ideal visibility did
little to restrain Al Smith's exuberance for the consecration of the house.
There was a warmth manifested at the occasion, an almost small-town in-
timacy that the press ascribed in large measure to the fact that this was
"Al Smith's building," or, as the *Brooklyn Eagle* described it, "The House
That Smith Built."

True to his sentimental nature, Smith thought it only fitting that two
of his grandchildren should start the ceremonies by cutting the red ribbon at the Fifth Avenue entrance. Smith explained later that he had the
children cut the ribbon because the building had been built "for generations to come down through the ages, and the two small children, with
scarcely the proper understanding of just what was going on, were there
to symbolize for all time to come that this building is to be a monument
for generations to come."

After the ribbon-cutting ceremony, at precisely eleven-thirty, the lights
suddenly went on throughout the entire building, and Smith used an occasional silver key to open the doors. The magic act with the lights did not

yet qualify as a tradition but at least had a precedent. In 1913, Frank W. Woolworth had inveigled President Woodrow Wilson into pressing a button from the White House that would turn on the Woolworth Building's lights, and Smith had President Herbert Hoover do the same. On the stroke of the half hour, Hoover took a break from a cabinet meeting to flick the switch in Washington.

Al Smith posed in front of the doors with his wife and two grandchildren, then—while special details of patrolmen and mounted police held back the thousands of spectators who tried to rush through the police lines—he invited everyone who had an invitation into the Fifth Avenue lobby. Smith posed in the lobby in front of a crowd; he posed on the eighty-sixth-floor observatory with Governor Franklin D. Roosevelt; he posed with Mayor James J. Walker; he posed with any dignitary or luminary who was around. All those smiling photographs of Smith led one jokester to say that Smith could afford to smile—he had finished his great building while Herbert Hoover was still mending his fences.

The city's geography was changed by buildings like the Woolworth and Chrysler Buildings, but the Empire State Building had a singularly dramatic effect upon Manhattan's skyline. Its height and bulk together dwarfed the spires and towers that had pointed the way heavenward in the past, and Smith reveled in the hugeness of it all. He went about reminding the visitors on opening day that on a truly clear day they could see fifty miles out to sea and as far as Storm King Mountain, or Patchogue, Long Island, or Plainfield, New Jersey. "Being this high up sort of pulls the island together—constricts it—lays it out like a kid's map," he said. Few could do a better job of pointing out the city's landmarks and their history than Al Smith. The city was his hobby. It was in his heart. From the top of his Brobdingnagian building he ebulliently pointed out this seemingly Lilliputian building and that apparently insignificant monument, all the while extolling the virtues of the view, which made the city an open book, a vast panorama of information. It was a theme he would later develop with his publicists.

Governor Roosevelt, his usual punctiliously proper public self, hailed the building as an achievement for the state, and found its name most highly fitting because of the years of service that its leader had rendered to the state of New York. Off the record he was more his genial self, admitting that he was a "little awestruck." He thought it would take a while before he could get back his sense of proportion. "In looking out from this building, I have got an entirely new conception of things in the city of New York."

Mayor Walker hailed the building as an achievement for the city, and rolled his official remarks and his fun-loving self into one. He wished for its great success because the city would receive the revenues, then directing his remarks right at Smith, "but I have this consolation in that, and this satisfaction, that no matter what we tax you, you know that it is worth it." The Hotel McAlpin Band played "The Star-Spangled Banner," telegrams were read ("One day out at sea and I can still see the building," Lamb had wired to Smith), and national hookups on the Columbia Broadcasting System and the National Broadcasting Company carried the ceremonies. With the speech making over, Smith escorted his guests to a buffet lunch. Two hundred invitations had been sent out, and within two days there were two hundred acceptances, with requests for 160 more places. Cynics might have said they just wanted a free lunch, but for many of the invitees it was a matter of saving face—people were clamoring to see the building, and family and professional demands had to be met.[1]

With wholehearted enthusiasm, New York made the formal dedication and opening of the Empire State Building something of a general holiday that was perhaps more in keeping with the coming of a "grand emporium" to an upstate village than the opening of the world's tallest building in the nation's largest and, some might have said, most unneighborly city. The enthusiasm was not all generated by Smith. The building itself seemed to imbue the city with its great shining beauty, adding "one more splendor to Manhattan's enchanted isle," as the *Post* couched it.

BUILDING IN EXCELSIS trumpeted the editorial in *The Times* on opening day, wittingly or unwittingly making a play on words on the Empire State's motto "Excelsior." "The ceremonies marking completion of the Empire State Building are only a kind of climax to what has long been going on under the eyes of the people of this city," said the paper. "They have seen the audacious plan formed. They have watched the majestic design of the architect taking form in one upward flight after another toward the clouds."

McCreery's Department Store devoted all its windows on Thirty-fourth Street to the pageant of fifty years of styles and the growth of Midtown, culminating in the erection of the Empire State Building. Neil Petree, president of the store, hosted a luncheon in honor of the building the day before the opening. Smith, the guest of honor, arrived from the Empire State Building with an escort of one hundred of the "city's finest," staging a miniparade along Thirty-fourth Street and priming the publicity pump all along the way.

---

[1]There was one declination that made the news. Smith had sent Walter P. Chrysler a special invitation for a personal tour after the opening, but Chrysler spurned it.

Corporate friends and neighbors sponsored page after page of advertisements heralding the arrival of the building. The Hotel McAlpin welcomed the "world's greatest building to the center of convenience of the world's greatest city." The Hotel New Yorker extolled the virtues of Thirty-fourth Street, where, "in the center of everything that's going on—is the world's largest department store—New York's most popular hotel. And now—the world's tallest office building." Tudor City, which was within a half-hour walk of the building, ran an ad saying that the day marked "another great forward step in the development of our city."[2]

Some ads were thinly veiled attempts to cash in on the building's image of gigantism. Weber and Heilbroner showed its line of Manhattan Shirts neatly stacked in a pile as high as the Empire State Building, stretching the point that "The Empire State, towering high into the heavens, is the largest building in America. A like comparison: our Manhattan Shirts are the largest assortments in America." The Dutton publishing company cashed in on the story in an advertisement for Axel Munthe's *The Story of San Michele*. The visual depicted the top third of the Empire State Building, the headline said TOWER ABOVE THE REST, and the copy read, "As the Empire State is the giant among buildings—so is this amazing biography the giant among current books. 102 stories in one—as many in the other."

There was a carnival atmosphere on opening day, a celebration that lasted a few days. That first Sunday the curious flooded the neighborhood, and where there are crowds there are vendors to sell to them. Those who came to look stood gazing upward, some from two blocks away so they could better see the tower and mooring mast, some venturing close to the building as if to get a literal feel for it, and all the while the vendors worked the crowd, hawking carnations, candy, and "souvenirs." The visitor count to the top that first Sunday was 5,108, a record total that was a large portion of the seventeen thousand who visited the observation deck the first four days it was open. More than fifty uniformed attendants, a score of plainclothesmen, and special policemen were kept busy handling the crowd.

There had been plenty of publicity, plenty of advertising and peripher-

---

[2]The ad ended with an Al Smith quote that no self-respecting politician would make today. Smith said that the solution to one of the city's problems lay "in the building near the business centers of residential districts. This has been attempted in Tudor City. . . . It is better for health to walk five or ten blocks in the morning than to take a chance of life and limb in the subways."

als. Opening night, a heavily promoted radio show was broadcast from the eighty-sixth floor. An ad in *The Times* said:

Tune in Tonight
10:30 WEAF
And NBC Network
Regular Friday Evening
"RKO THEATER
OF THE AIR"
1,000 Ft above New York City
FORMAL OPENING
EMPIRE
STATE
WORLD'S TALLEST
BUILDING
Guest Stars
Floyd Gibbons
Weber & Fields
Harry Richman
Hon. ALFRED E. SMITH
GUEST SPEAKER

Two-column advertisements for the observatories were placed in newspapers the weekend the building opened. The view, with mooring mast and observatories in the foreground, was to the southwest, toward the harbor and the Statue of Liberty. The Chrysler, Woolworth, and Bank of Manhattan Buildings were conveniently outside the range of the view. Only the antediluvian record-holding Metropolitan Life Tower on Madison Square could be seen, and in 1931 it must have seemed pretty insignificant. The message was simple:

Look down on everything from the Top of New York
86th and 102nd Floors
Open 10 A.M. to Midnight

Even without all the advertising and hoopla, the building would have been a hit. The first thing the tourist saw upon entering the thirty-foot-high Fifth Avenue lobby was marble. The walls of the entrance halls were resplendent in ten thousand square feet of different foreign marbles of striking markings and alluring hues. "The marble you see on the upper part of the walls—the kind that looks like wonderful, pale, old Oriental rugs—is called pink Famosa," said Al Smith on one of his innumerable tours of the building, "and the marble on the lower walls, the deep-hued, richly red marble is Estralante." Someone found a tiger "couchant" in the texture of the marble, "an unmistakable Tammany tiger, grim and ferocious." It was upside down, and more like a Rorschach test than a real tiger, but it made the news because of Smith's association with Tammany.

At the observatory ticket office on the main floor at the westernmost entrance on Thirty-fourth Street, a visitor could buy tickets, redeem coupons, and check belongings. The observatory manager quickly found a standard for whether the day would be busy. If he could make out the Statue of Liberty from his office on the thirty-second floor, he knew the crowds would come.

For many visitors, the first real thrill of the building came when, armed with their tickets for the observatories, they rode in one of the elevators. Visitors were excited at the idea, even a little timorous, but they were generally amazed at the comfort. They felt hardly any sensation of speed on their way to the eighty-sixth floor, and the only common complaint was a tightening in the ears from the change of pressure, a problem easily relieved by swallowing (naturally the ride up or down became called a "flight of swallows"). At its most mundane, the ride was comparable to being enclosed in a small room for a minute with a bunch of total strangers.

A 1934 brochure published by the building's management said that "when you step out of the elevator on the 86th floor . . . you find yourself in comfortable and luxurious surroundings and just as SECURE and SAFE as you would be in your own home. Here you will find a Writing-room for your convenience, a . . . Ladies' Retiring Room and a Gentlemen's Retiring Room."

On the eastern side of the eighty-sixth floor, with a view overlooking the East River and Long Island, was "The World's Loftiest" tearoom and soda fountain. The tearoom, occupying the space that would have been the lounge and ticket area for dirigible passengers, was completely equipped as a refreshment bar, with sandwiches and other light foods served at the fountain for standees, while "soda tables," or café tables, were provided for those preferring to sit while they ate. The fountain, with its sleek, black Carrara-marble top, provided a feature that Smith liked—a brass rail.

The aluminum fountain was designed by Shreve, Lamb & Harmon. Its banding was familiarly horizontal and its corners rounded, echoing the metal striping of the marquees on the side streets and harmonizing with the architecture of the building. The fountain stood in front of a wall decorated with a color map of the northern half of Greater New York, which gave the distance in miles to numerous outlying towns and cities by way of concentric rings. The perspective of the map had the Empire State Building at ground zero, so it corresponded with the view from the tower. As soon as Repeal came in December 1933, the fountain underwent changes, and by the spring of 1934, part of the soda fountain was replaced by a bar. The brass rail that had been ascribed to Smith's longing for the good old days suddenly proclaimed his prescience, and the "world's highest fountain" became the "world's highest bar."[3]

"Enjoy all the pleasure of sipping a Cocktail in an Aeroplane, right at the top of this building without leaving Terra Firma!" the ads said. Dry martinis cost 25 cents and included orange bitters, an ingredient not usually found in martinis. The bartender would make Manhattans and Bronxes (gin, Italian and French vermouth, and orange juice), sidecars and daiquiris (40 and 35 cents, respectively), and one special at 35 cents, the Empire State, which consisted of Amstel bitters, orange bitters, French vermouth, Scotch whiskey, and dry gin, a drink that no doubt stemmed from the exigencies of Prohibition. Rupperts Beer, a good local product, was 20 cents. Budweiser was 25 (Anheuser-Busch had rented space in the building).

The Tea Room's selection might not have gone from soup all the way to nuts originally, but it had some interesting choices and it did start with soup. Hot bouillon was 15 cents, various sandwiches such as liverwurst or tongue were 20 cents, and a junior club cost 50 cents. Specials ranged from toasted English muffins, strawberry jam or orange marmalade, and tea, coffee, or milk for 30 cents, to the 75-cent special, which included fruit salad, assorted sandwiches, ice cream and cake, and choice of beverage. Sundaes, including the unexplained "Governor's Choice," were 25 cents.

The eighty-sixth floor had the obligatory souvenir counter where sightseers could buy postcards, paperweights, abalone shell knives—the usual chotchkes that are sold as mementos of tourist attractions. Almost all of the souvenirs bore either an image of the building or the magical words *Empire State Building*. (One visitor found metal paperweights in the form of elephants, the dreaded Republican symbol. "In Al Smith's building!") By 1938 the store was selling the classic miniature reproductions of the Empire State Building, as well as a lamp whose base was the building.

[3] In order to oblige the State Alcoholic Beverage Control Board's requirement for a photograph of the exterior of the premises before granting a license, management did the only reasonable thing—they hired a plane, put an aerial photographer onboard, and took the required photos.

According to the *London Daily Mail*, the souvenir shop did a land-office business from the day it opened. People sat down on the gaily upholstered red furniture to write postcards just as soon as they had bought them so that friends back home could know that "the thrill had been accomplished. Then they stepped to a slot in the wall and sent their messages dropping down, down, down to the ground floor, ready for the postman." The mail chutes were equipped to retard the speed of letters at the sixty-fifth and twenty-eighth floors so the envelopes and postcards wouldn't be scorched by the friction of a continuous fall.

Within a few months of the opening, exclusive postcard views of the building by the Unusual Photographs Corporation had already made their debut. The silver-and-black package design by Brooks & Porter, in keeping with the character of the building, was sleekly modern.

J. B. Black, the candy concessionaire, made a special souvenir line of chocolates for the opening. Black was certain that when the chocolates had been eaten, the boxes would be cherished as prized souvenirs, so each bore the image of the building and statistical data on its size, construction, and design. The more expensive line, "The Governor's Choice," was covered in brown sueded paper evocative of Smith's derby, and sold for $2; "The Empire State" sold for $1.50.

But few tourists would go to the souvenir stand or the fountain before taking in the view from the promenade. Just as visitors to the top of Trinity Church in the mid-nineteenth century had said that people looked like ants from that exalted height of 284 feet, so the clichés started from the first day forward to describe the view from the top of the Empire State Building. *The Times* reported that Smith's visitors "saw men and motor cars creeping like insects through the streets; they saw elevated trains that looked like toys." The *London Daily Mail* said that people saw "Lilliputian motor-cars halting or moving forward in groups appearing like a slow procession. They see trains gliding along like worms and people as ants scarcely moving, . . . neighboring buildings, monsters of steel and stone when viewed from below, dwarfed to insignificance."

Although clouds blanketed the metropolitan area and bad visibility set in soon after opening day, the crowds continued. At a dollar a head for adults, 25 cents for children five to fifteen, and children under five admitted free, people stood on line to buy tickets to the observatory as if the proverbial hotcakes were on sale. The number of visitors to the top for the first thirty-four-day period was 96,109, or more than 2,875 a day. On several occasions, visitors were forced to mill about in the corridors awaiting empty elevators. To accommodate the crowds, the hours for the observatories were extended from midnight to 1 A.M. One newspaper conservatively said that this was "evidence that the sightseers' space was turning out to be a profitable venture financially as well as an advertising medium for the corporation."

If you found yourself at the top without a camera, the building would arrange for an in-house photographer to take your picture. Because customers often requested a view of the city in their photographs, the photographer would stand on a ladder to get the best composition. Downstairs on the eighty-fourth floor was a complete studio where the negatives were developed and the photographs printed. Within twenty minutes the prints, but not the negatives, were delivered to the customer on the eighty-sixth floor. The negatives were filed, so repeat orders could be easily filled.

High-powered Bausch & Lomb telescopes were installed at each of the four corners of the eighty-sixth-floor observatory. Ten cents in the slot and a slight push of the plunger operated spring-driven timers releasing the shutter and permitting a minute and a half of viewing. In the first six months, the Empire State Building realized $3,000 in dimes and nickels from the telescopes.

When the sightseer was ready to rise to the next plateau, he could board a rather small elevator—it had a capacity of only about ten—to the topmost observatory, where he found a bit of deception endemic to the publicity surrounding the building. When you bought a ticket to the "observation tower" you were given two tickets. One said "Admit One to 86th Floor," the other said "Admit One to 102nd Floor." Although the second ticket clearly stipulated "102nd Floor," the 101st floor was where the elevator deposited you, and the 101st floor was where you stayed. There was a 102nd floor, and stairs led to it, but a single guard on the 101st floor and a locked gate kept sightseers on the level at which the elevator had deposited them. Despite all the hoopla about the 102nd floor and the endless publicity surrounding it, the 102nd floor was not open for sightseeing. The confusion over the floors might have stemmed from a decision that was forced on management and the publicists. The 102nd floor—the very top level—was originally planned to serve the double function of the dirigible landing platform and an open observation deck; the 101st floor was to be the enclosed observation area. Management no doubt realized that the platform on the 102nd floor was too dangerous for tourism and decided against opening it, thereby forcing the publicists to revise their publicity downward, something no publicist wants to do. The solution by management was to soft-pedal the situation—the odds were pretty good that nobody would be able to tell the difference in the view anyway, so they ignored the fact that visitors were relegated to the 101st floor, installed signs that were obfuscatory, and kept the publicity mill churning out the same old story about viewing the city from the 102nd story. With the exception of one reporter, they got away with it.[4]

"No one seemed to be staying long in the highest observatory," a *New York Sun* writer reported after visiting the tower the first week. "Nothing to see but mist, nowhere to sit, not a tremendous amount of room, and perhaps a rather odd feeling, being up so high" in what he described as "the dungeon of a medieval keep, painted silvery and raised among the clouds!"

Earl Sparling wrote in the *New York World-Telegram* that a tourist had told him opening week that the view from the Woolworth Building was, in fact, better. "It was down below the clouds and you could see something." Sparling admitted his tourist friend was correct—you could see more from the eighty-first floor of the Empire State Building than from the eighty-sixth, and more from the eighty-sixth than from the very top, but only because it was so overcast that first week. "Not being able to see very much," said Sparling, "the customers have started a habit of scratching their initials in the walls up in the tower room," a satisfaction that was short lived—the initials were sandpapered off once a week.

The maintenance was worth every penny. When Woolworth built his tower he would have been content if it had only paid for itself in advertising, but the observatory fooled him. Visitors paying 50 cents apiece to view the metropolitan panorama from the top contributed over $125,000 a year for seventeen years. The Woolworth Building attracted over five hundred visitors a day, the Statue of Liberty attracted more than a thousand, but the Empire State observatories outshone them all. The Empire State Building quickly became the sight-seeing goal of New York's millions of visitors. It was to New York what the Eiffel Tower was to Paris.

The gate for the ordinary, everyday view would have pleased a Scrooge. By the middle of November, the observatories were averaging 2,200 visitors a day, and had brought in $698,554. In the first year, a total of 775,000 visitors provided a gross income of $875,000 for the observatories, including the profits from ticket sales and the sale of souvenirs and refreshments to visitors. At that rate, the building was grossing about 2 percent of the building's construction costs every year. Maybe, said the critics, the idea of the mooring mast wasn't so loony after all.

[4]The deception continued in 1995. The 101st floor was still called the 102nd, and the elevator that shuttled between it and the eighty-sixth floor created a still worse misconception. It flashed the number of feet high the elevator was traveling, starting with 1,150 and going as high as 1,250 upon reaching the 101st floor. One thousand two-hundred fifty feet is the total height of the building. The 101st floor is 1,212 feet up.

Ninety percent of the daytime visitors were out-of-towners, but at night there were more New Yorkers than out-of-towners. It made sense. The out-of-towners did not work in the city; they were vacationing in New York and taking in the sights. New Yorkers were living and working here, which meant having to get to the dry cleaners and the market when there was a free moment between ballet class and music lessons for the kids, so they took in the Empire State Building when they had a chance. Even if they did not visit, they still liked the idea of the place, they were still proud of it. As Ed Sullivan said in the mid-1930s, "New Yorkers never visit the Statue of Liberty or the Empire State Building, but that doesn't stop us from bragging."

From the perspective of management and the publicity people, bragging was not good enough. They wanted more New Yorkers to visit the observation galleries, and in October 1934, a full-page ad ran in *The Times* "written" by Al Smith. The building's press agents continued to perpetuate the myth that the upper observatory was on the 102nd floor and was 1,250 feet up, and they had Smith saying that he had noticed from the building's registry that comparatively few residents of Greater New York had taken advantage of the opportunity to see their own city from "1,250 feet in the air." He thought they owed it to themselves to witness the great scene. The press agents also got their reportorial minions to work on the problem of getting New Yorkers to the top. Walter Winchell wrote a column in 1934 chastising New Yorkers for being blasé about their city. He said that "One of the better known New York girls returned from Paris last week and she gushed and gooed about her trip to the Eiffel Tower heights. 'Have you ever been to the top of Al Smith's Empire State Building?' one of us asked her. She hadn't. She never thought of seeing New York, New Jersey and the Sound that way, at all. And I suppose many of us here haven't gone to . . . Smith's tower—but were we in Paris—we'd certainly take in the Eiffel Tower, which is a midget by comparison." She went, she saw, and, according to Winchell, she was conquered.

Alice Liddell Hargreaves, the original Alice of Lewis Carroll's *Alice's Adventures in Wonderland*, was equally conquered. She arrived in New York in 1932 to view the city's wonders and to participate in the celebration of Carroll's centenary at Columbia University. When the Cunard liner *Berengaria* sailed up the Hudson and she saw the massed skyscrapers, she said they were an "extraordinary sight," but it was the massing of the buildings, not their mere height that impressed her, a comment perhaps elicited by her fictional self who needed only to drink from a mysterious bottle to grow tall. Nevertheless, when she left she singled out her visit to the building as one of her most interesting remembrances.

Perhaps the only celebrity who made a point of being leery of going to the top was Fay Wray, who had starred in *King Kong*. She thought she would like to go to the top of the real Empire State Building to see what it was like, but she was not sure she would enjoy the experience in real life, she said in an interview in the *New York World-Telegram* as she was passing through New York on her way to Europe in 1933. She never felt comfortable in high places. Her own acrophobia—whether real or the result of a public relations ploy—no doubt served to heighten her role in the movie and make the top that much more exciting to potential audiences.

Many New Yorkers who visited the top realized that the reward was beyond their wildest dreams, that they had lived in the city all their lives but had never really *seen* it—all of it—before. *The New York Journal*'s Johnston D. Kerkhoff admitted in 1936 that he had often scoffed at the Empire State Building, and felt superior to the tourists who could not wait to reach its observation tower, but he took it all back once he had been up there himself. "The sun was setting when we got there," he said. "Everywhere you turned, Manhattan was agleam; the Hudson was golden lava; cool winds that never whisper at street level brought relief to body and soul; and there stirred within me a long-dormant pride, almost a boastful pride, of THE CITY. Not pride exactly, but something tingling, that was yet peaceful and warming." Charles Hanson Towne, a New Yorker, admitted in October 1931 that he was glad that he had finally gone. "Here it was, at last, in all its iron and agate glory, and I viewed it as an eagle might have viewed it. . . . You cannot speak at first. You simply stand, like any automaton, waiting for the spectacle to sink into your consciousness. . . . I strove to locate all the other skyscrapers, the towers of which I had eagerly climbed, as each had outdone the other; and they looked like dwarfs, and I wondered why I ever had considered them anything at all."

Residents gravitated to the views that were most familiar to them. They genuinely enjoyed looking at places and things they already knew, and they would frequently pick out features that were prominent only to their eye and then try vainly to pinpoint them for others. The locals were far from omniscient, however. Five elderly New Yorkers who refused help in finding the sights, saying they knew all the places by heart, promptly pointed out New Jersey—in Brooklyn.

Pete McGuire, the captain of the Empire State observatory guards, frequently visited the top of the RCA Building on his day off, where he took relish in rattling his colleagues. When a big crowd gathered he would ask the guide to point out the Statue of Liberty, which he knew was blocked by "his" building. When the guide admitted that it could not be seen, McGuire would cheerfully add that it could be seen perfectly from the top of the Empire State.

Some local institutions, aware that visitors were looking down on them from on high, aimed to make themselves more recognizable. They had their names, and in some cases slogans, painted on their rooftops so that visitors could spot them more readily. Frank A. Duggan, managing director of the Hotel McAlpin, had a sign installed on the hotel roof with letters fourteen feet high, and Gimbels and the Pennsylvania Hotel followed suit. One building bore the legend BUY YOUR FURS FROM FOX. Macy's, not to be outdone, had its famous slogan painted on its roof: MACY'S—IT'S SMART TO BE THRIFTY.

Most tourists wanted to see the Flatiron Building, according to Pete McGuire. The building had never held any height records, nor was it the city's first skyscraper, but it had taken advantage of its dramatic site, it had probably appeared on more postcards than Little Egypt and Sally Rand combined, and people simply liked it. After the Flatiron Building, they wanted to see their own hotel.

Two Cleveland women who visited the city on a shoestring in 1937 were determined to see the view without paying. They saw in the building directory that the Board of Design for the World's Fair and the office of Pierre S. du Pont were both on the eightieth floor. As told by Helene Lasche in a story she entered in a contest in the *Plain Dealer*, for which she won second place and $5, the two women brazenly marched up to an elevator man, and her friend announced that they were there to see Mr. du Pont. "Oh, Mr. du Pont?" he echoed suspiciously. "No, no, it's the Board of Design," Lasche said hastily, and up they went. The elevator man watched them closely as they walked slowly toward the Board of Design. A man stood there. Lasche looked back at the elevator man, then courageously stepped forward. "Mister, can we please look out of your windows?" she trembled. "Sure," he answered with a friendly grin. "There's all New York below you."

What the two women from Cleveland saw from the windows probably did not make any sense to them, if you believe Pete McGuire. In a most undiplomatic manner, one that no doubt brought down the wrath of Smith and his PR people, McGuire was quoted in the *New York World-Telegram* in 1934 that out-of-towners didn't ordinarily have any idea what they were looking at half the time. "They look out there at the Chrysler Building and they say, 'That's a church.' Then one of them will say, 'It must be the steeple of Trinity Church.' You see, they have always heard about Trinity Church. In a small town the church steeple sticks up above everything else. . . . But imagine them thinking the Chrysler Building is a church."

Neither the Empire State Building nor the city could expect to attract out-of-towners with remarks like McGuire's. They had to be wooed, they had to be won over. They had to read stories like this dispatch from St. Paul, Minnesota, which catered to its readers' basic distrust and dislike of the city, denigrating the city while at the same time extolling its glories: "If you have never understood New York before—its complacency, its audacity, its feeling of being unique among the communities of the world—you will understand it as you stand on the balcony of the eighty-sixth floor of one of the most beautiful buildings ever built. There lies New York before you—spectacular, arrogant, and splendid."

The opening of the Empire State Building's observatories gave skyline lovers such a good look at this "arrogant" city that it sent the profits of Manhattan's other observatories plummeting. The Paramount Tower, once the pride and joy of the Paramount Building at 1501 Broadway, had, in theatrical terms, "gone dark." Its observation deck, only about 450 feet up, was said to provide a view of the entire city and the harbor, but with the opening of the Empire State Building, business had fallen off to such a degree that only the watchman was left atop the building, and he could doze undisturbed by any visitors anxious to get a glimpse from it.

The draw of the Woolworth Building had been steadily dwindling since the opening of the Chrysler Building, and the coming of the Empire State accelerated the pace of its decline. The Chrysler tower, considered a master point from which to view the skyline at the time of its completion, was feeling the pinch of its rival by the summer of 1931. The fee for a trip to the Chrysler tower was 50 cents for adults—half what the Empire State Building charged—and 25 cents for children. Although several hundred of the curious still took the ride up to the tower in a day, business was not what it had been. Even at half the price of a trip to the top of the Empire State Building, it just wasn't worth it.

Although the Empire State Building's direct competitors might have been suffering, the success of the Empire State Building's observatories encouraged others. There was talk of installing express elevators in the George Washington Bridge's steel towers to carry tourists 635 feet above the water to "twin pergolas of glass," where there would be sandwich and coffee shops, lounge chairs, and an open-air promenade, as well as the usual telescopes. The profits from the towers were expected to add about $200,000 yearly to the revenue of the Port Authority, but the proposal never got off the drawing board.

The observation deck atop the RCA Building at Rockefeller Center became a legitimate rival when it opened in 1933. With admission to the observation deck linked with the NBC studio tour, it attracted almost half a million sightseers in the first eleven months of 1936. The RCA Building's two-tiered, open-air deck was only 850 feet up, or two hundred feet lower than the open-air observatory on the eighty-sixth floor of the Empire State, but some viewers said that, like the Woolworth Building, it allowed a greater sense of the city because they were a little closer to it.

It might very well have been the great distance from the streets below, a sense of already floating above the city, that made the Empire State Building appear to be such an invitingly spectacular place to commit suicide. The first suicide, however, was not from the top. It was from the seventy-second story, and it occurred in April 1931, before the building was even finished. The news coverage was minimal. One story simply related that the suicide was "an unidentified Italian about 45, whose body crashed from a great height." Edmund Wilson was a little more specific in *American Earthquake*. He said that the man who killed himself had lost his job as a worker on the Empire State Building, and could not find work elsewhere. He had returned in the hope of being rehired, only to be turned away.

Observatory Manager Joe Bolton said in 1934 that the building was well organized to guard against "leapers" from the observatories. Ticket sellers refused admission to wild-eyed customers, and the observatory guards were trained to be on the qui vive. "We have men in our employ who can pick 'em off," said Bolton. "You would be surprised to learn how many persons intending to jump from the building indicate their purpose by their manner. Not only do we have men expert in this line of work, but we have complete machinery including ambulances to function in case someone jumps from the building." The design of the building was perhaps the single greatest frustration for would-be suicides. "Some bent on suicide come up here with the idea of making a pyrotechnic display of it by dropping in on the avenue," but what Bolton termed "the mighty terrace sixty feet broad which sweeps back to the foot of the tower" was the source of frustration. "The would-be suicide cannot drop down on Fifth Avenue. He would only light on hard girders. His dream is busted. How many suicides are deterred by this disappointment we can only guess, but we know it is a factor."

When suicides did occur, there seemed to be few second thoughts on the part of the leapers. It all seemed to happen at a coolly determined pace. The first attempted suicide from the eighty-sixth floor, in September 1933, was C. Cass Lawler, who calmly removed his topcoat, put it and a note on the tower floor, climbed out on a parapet, and jumped off, all in the twinkling of an eye and without a moment's hesitation. Two women who witnessed the deed could only gasp. The would-be suicide fell only to the eighty-fourth-floor ledge and suffered two broken bones. His note said that he had been suffering from bad rheumatism.

The first successful suicide from the observatory, in February 1935, was written up by *Time* magazine, which implied that the victim was famous for her melancholia:

Died. Irma P. Eberhardt, 22, moody Manhattanite; by jumping from the 86th floor of the Empire State Building; in Manhattan. . . . She set a record for distance, landing on a marquee 1,029 ft. below with the violence of a loud explosion.

The *Mirror*'s story, under the headline LEAPED—FOR LOVE! FROM THE WORLD'S HIGHEST BUILDING, was slightly more sympathetic. Irma Eberhardt had thought her boyfriend was seeing other women and was not paying enough attention to her. It was a "cold, blustery night and the wind screamed around the 86th floor observatory," where there were only four or five people atop the tower. She asked the guide questions and seemed interested in his answers, but she also nodded absentmindedly. The guard turned away to tend other business, and the next thing he knew she was "atop the parapet, swaying in the howling wind, and leaped, sailing out into space like a huge bird. The wind was howling, and she cleared the 48-foot horizontal ledge two stories below her."

Irma Eberhardt's suicide occurred almost four years after the building opened, so either the allure was not so great or management was indeed doing a good job guarding against suicides, yet it and other phenomena were often blown out of proportion. Contrary to public opinion, visitors to the observatories who suffered from nosebleeds did not suffer unduly at the top, nor had anyone suffering from heart trouble found his condition aggravated, at least not within the first year. Timid people, however, were sometimes in for a shock. One woman made it to the top, but after she saw how far away she was from the street she became fearful of taking the trip down in the elevator. A nurse responded with the ever-ready aromatic spirits of ammonia, and some words of good cheer, neither of which availed. The visitor decided the only safe way down was by foot, and she insisted that the nurse accompany her. The nurse demurred, and the visitor finally tested her mettle to discover that the trip down wasn't so bad after all.

Grossly exaggerated stories about how much skyscrapers swayed in high winds were rampant in the 1920s and the building was used as a model to determine the extent of sway in tall buildings. David C. Coyle, a civil engineer, said that the only conclusion that could be drawn was that either skyscrapers were unsafe or witchcraft had staged a major comeback. There were stories of clocks that simply stopped, of pictures that slid to and fro along a wall, of a hanging lamp that swung six inches in northwest breezes. There was an enchanted rocking chair, and an unruly bathtub that threw water clear up to the ceiling. Such fearful stories circulated about the swaying of the spire of the Ritz Tower when it opened in 1925 that top-floor apartments went unrented. Arthur Brisbane, who owned the building, moved into the topmost suite to demonstrate that there was no danger.

Tall buildings do vibrate, or sway, infinitesimally. Their tops are like the tops of tuning forks, an elastic cantilever, held by the earth at one end and free to vibrate at the other. Like a tuning fork, a building has a particular frequency of its own at which it always vibrates, and it would give off a musical note if the vibrations were only a little faster. A steady wind might make a building lean, and gusts will push or pull it and cause it to vibrate. If a strong gust hits the building going forward, it increases the swing; if it hits the building on the rebound, it will stop the vibration dead.

Readings were taken by the American Society of Engineers in most of the tall buildings in New York during an eight-month period in 1928–29, and even in a gale no vibrations of more than an inch were observed. That means half an inch off the vertical either way. The frequency of vibration was the cause of the gossip, said David Coyle. If any object had a harmonic motion of its own, like a pendulum, and if it were given a series of slight pushes timed to its own frequency, it would swing violently. Hence the trouble. Nearly all the wild tales of skyscraper movements seemed to deal not with sensations of motion or with the movement of the building itself but with the movement of objects within the building, and if the stories had any truth to them it was because of the characteristic of swinging bodies to respond to anything that tunes in on their own wavelength.

The discomfort was caused by seeing objects swaying within the building, not motion, claimed Ohio State professor Clyde R. Morris, and the movement of objects caused "skysickness." A hanging light, for instance, will swing several feet when the building itself is moving only a fraction of an inch. The solution was to change the offending lamp for a stiff fixture or to hang it by shorter cords.

There was hardly a well-built skyscraper that did not sway, but the sway in the Empire State Building was so slight that measurements seldom had the building a half inch off center. The week the Empire State Building opened, a *New York Sun* reporter witnessed someone trying to balance a pencil upright on a windowsill on the 101st floor. The wind was blowing, and the reporter was convinced that the building was swaying, but the pencil stood without trembling. After the story ran, the Empire State Corporation wrote a letter to the newspaper saying that it was the "firm belief of the architects and engineers who built Empire State that the possible swaying of the building in a 220 mile wind would be absolutely negligible. The highest measurement made so far indicates a sway of less than one-tenth of one inch."

Scientists measured the sway of a building with a "vertical collimator," an instrument especially designed and built for the United States Geodetic Survey. The American Institute of Steel Construction installed one in a fire stairway of the Empire State Building in April 1931.[5] The building was an ideal guinea pig, "almost made to order for the proper study," said *The Times*. It was "symmetrical in design and unusually tall. Hence the interest in it." The measuring device was a camera set in place at the sixth floor that was aimed at an illuminated target at the eighty-fifth floor. Any sway greater than a quarter of an inch would show on film, and the taller the building the more accurately the device could read the sway, thanks to the greater distance between camera and target. An engineer waited for a high wind to set the sight at the sixth floor, and let the photographs do the rest. Other instruments were attached to columns and beams and set in walls to measure the direction and velocity of the wind, stresses associated with bending and turning, as well as the pull of the partial vacuum created on the leeward side.

While the vertical collimator was in operation at the Empire State, the Bureau of Standards in Washington used models to study the resistance of modern skyscrapers to windstorms. They built a five-foot-high model of the Empire State Building based on the architects' blueprints, which they tested in isolation as well as in a miniature neighborhood they built to scale of the six blocks around the Empire State Building—about eighty models in wood. They set the whole thing in a wind tunnel where sixty-mile-an-hour gales could blow away. Working with the American Institute of Steel Construction, the bureau could make comparisons be-

[5]The first building measured by a vertical collimator was Columbus, Ohio's, forty-story American Insurance Union Building in 1928. It swayed less than one-tenth of an inch in a thirty-mile wind.

tween a model of a building and the full-scale structure itself. They discovered that although the neighboring buildings surrounding the Empire State Building were considerably lower, they shielded it from wind buffeting, and the Empire State Building in turn shielded them.

No building has ever been erected that is perfectly rigid, although the Empire State Building has achieved what engineers call "maximum stability." Its elastic steel skeleton, which the *Real Estate Record* described as "more permanently elastic than rubber," enabled the building to "give" in high winds and yet minimize their effect. Under normal wind pressure, the Empire State Building's movement off center was never greater than a quarter inch at any time. The ultimate test came with the hurricane of 1938. With top winds of 110—120 miles an hour atop the building, this was the most violent hurricane within memory. The structure was said to sway a "little more than four inches" in a period of seven and a half seconds, which means two inches off the vertical either way, a sway that was imperceptible. But it was the first official word that the building might sway more than a half inch.

The building also served as a phenomenological laboratory to disprove the notion that lightning never strikes the same place twice. It has been known since Franklin's time that lightning picks out the tallest point presented to it, and the Empire State Building fit the bill—it seems that every time there's an electrical storm anywhere near the building, it gets hit.

The first major lightning bolts to hit the building were reported in August 1931. One particularly fierce bolt that was accompanied by "detonations" produced a great flash of fire seen as far as a mile away. Telephone operators on the eighty-sixth floor saw a sheet of flame shoot down the sides of the building, a report corroborated by a policeman on Fifth Avenue, who described the electricity as a "stream of electric fire" that sped down the building's side and disappeared when it hit the sidewalk. Within the building, nothing was disturbed. The Empire State Building was perhaps the safest place to be during an electrical storm. It was Manhattan's lightning rod, the tallest, most elaborate, and most successful lightning rod ever erected by man at the time. Time and time again the mast has been struck by flashes with a potential of 10 million volts, only to be dissipated by the intricate steel structure into the ground. But the best of all safeguards is not merely a rod, it is a cage, and the Empire State Building is essentially an enormous set of steel cages. The energy is divided and subdivided.

Dr. Karl B. McEachron of General Electric, who had been studying lightning since 1924, started taking photographs of the building in the mid-1930s. He mounted a battery of cameras on the twenty-sixth floor of the Daily News Building on Forty-second Street. During the summer, the peak of activity for lightning, forty-eight bolts were recorded.

The American Institute of Electrical Engineers used the Empire State Building to record the speed of lightning, and set up a motion picture camera atop a skyscraper a half a mile from the building that filmed every flash between 1934 and 1937. The speed of lightning: 10,000 miles a second. They also settled a long controversy by discovering that some lightning flashes move from cloud to earth, others from earth to cloud. A tall building such as the Empire State Building uses a tongue of fire to wheedle lightning down. Frequently before lightning hits the Empire State a spiraling flame leaps upward from the top of the tower. The flame does not go all the way to the clouds, but guides the lightning that always follows.

In 1951, the American Physical Society reported that New York City is so supercharged that the phenomenon first noticed at the Empire State is a citywide phenomenon. Eighty percent of the city's lightning travels up, and when lightning travels up from Manhattan's streets to the sky, it frequently discharges clouds without building up a current "peak." There are plenty of colorful lightning flashes but comparatively few thunderclaps.

Not long after the Empire State Building was opened, St. Elmo's fire—a luminous electrical discharge that is generally seen on ships at sea or on high mountains, and named for the patron saint of Mediterranean mariners[6]—could be seen on the eighty-sixth floor. All the outer metalwork glowed with what engineers call a brush discharge. It makes a hissing sound and, although it is not dangerous, it might create a tingling sensation if you're around it.

Another kind of phenomenological experiment was held at the Empire State Building in 1937. Lieutenants Albert J. Hoskinson and Carl I. Aslaskson of the U.S. Coast and Geodetic Survey, and Dr. Maurice Ewing, professor of physics and geophysics at Lehigh University, concluded a series of tests at the Empire State Building to determine how much the force of gravity changes in relation to the height above the surface of the earth. Among other things, they found that a man who weighs two hundred pounds at street level weighs only 199.8 at the top of the observation tower. The weight of a body is the force with which it is attracted to the earth. Weight, therefore, depends upon two factors—the amount of mat-

[6]The name is a corruption of *Sant' Ermo,* or St. Erasmus.

ter it contains, and its position in respect to the earth. The nearer a body is to the center of the earth, as long as it remains upon the surface, the greater its weight. Thus, a body of a given mass will weigh more at the base of a tall building than at the top.

There was also a Stonehenge-like lesson to be learned at the Empire State Building. The Everett, Washington, *News* had a column called "Factographs." On October 24, 1931, they ran this story: "Sunrise at the top of the Empire State Building . . . occurs on an average of about half an hour earlier, and sunset about half an hour later than on street level. The actual difference in time varies with the seasons."

Wherever the sun was in the sky, the view had a mystical quality. "The city flung out like a handful of jewels over black canyons of stone and shadow, laced with slow-moving black-and-silver rivers," said *Vogue* magazine about the nighttime view in 1936. "A veritable fairy land of lighted towers and mysterious bridges, with its sound and fury too far below you to mean anything."

"What a monstrous maelstrom, on which the individual is like a tiny wavelet on a lonely sea," said newspaperman Joseph Fort Newton in the Greensboro, North Carolina, *Record*. "What streams of people, eager, busy, hurried, harried, or happy, behind each face a romance or a tragedy; each life a blend of iron, agony, faith, fear and fleeting gayety; all winning or failing, all serving or adding to the burden of the world."

Perhaps the most remarkable reportage was by the blind Helen Keller, who went to the top with her secretary, Polly Thomson. As Keller's sensitive fingers lightly touched the glass windows on the observation tower, a *Times* photographer took a picture that appeared in the paper the following day. City College President Dr. John Finley saw the photograph, and wrote to her asking what she had really "seen." The remarkable letter that Helen Keller wrote to Dr. Finley was first published in *The New York Times Magazine* and later published in booklet form in 1933 by the Empire State Building under the title *The New York That Helen Keller Sees*. Her response, roughly one thousand words, contains perhaps the most dramatic language ever used to describe the view:

As I stood there 'twixt earth and sky, I saw a romantic structure wrought by human brains and hands that is to the burning eye of the sun a rival luminary. I saw it stand erect and serene in the midst of storm and the tumult of elemental commotion. I heard the hammer of Thor ring when the shaft began to rise upward. I saw the unconquerable steel, the flash of testing flames, the sword-like rivets. I heard the steam drills in pandemonium. I saw countless skilled workers welding together that mighty symmetry. I looked upon the marvel of frail, yet indomitable hands that lifted the tower to its dominating height.

Until the coming of the Empire State Building, Manhattan had boasted many skyscrapers. Suddenly there was only one.

# 14

# THE STAFF AND TENANTS

The day-to-day running of the Empire State Building fell to the building's manager, Chapin L. Brown, who operated as if he were the mayor of a small town. Brown supervised about 350 service employees (full tenancy would have called for one thousand), including fire and sanitation departments and a police force, as well as elevator operators and mechanics, engineers, plumbers and pipe fitters, electricians, painters, cabinetmakers, a house smith, and a staff for the general welfare of the workers, which included a nurse.

Brown laid out schedules for his department heads that he expected to be followed to the letter, and he prepared general procedures for all employees in each department. If English was a second language for an employee, he was told to have someone translate the regulations for him. That way there would be "no possibility of misunderstanding," said Brown. "We take all the pains possible to help our employees to hold their places, but we require absolute obedience to our rules, and will not accept any neglect of duty."

A force of two hundred cleaners—160 women, and forty men—reported to Brown. There were cleaners on duty twenty-four hours a day, but the bulk of the janitorial work was done after normal business hours. All the floors were cleaned at least once a day. All except the terrazzo and marble floors were cleaned by vacuum cleaners that were hooked up to a central system; the stone floors in the public halls were mopped during the day and cleaned by power scrubbing machines at night.

Brown was quick to point out that no hand scrubbing was done in the Empire State Building. Nevertheless, in 1932, *The Evening Graphic* told of "lonely charwomen toiling in the hours between dusk and dawn, old women, broken and bent like a bow, looking down upon the beauty and laughter that no longer is theirs. . . . The glitter and gayety in the street far below is not for them. . . . All that belongs to the kingdom of youth. . . . It is not for old women who scrawl their dreams on marble floors."

"The spectacle of emaciated, poor old women on their knees in a mass of soap suds and dirty water will never be seen in the Empire State Building," said Brown, nor were there any "broken and bent" workers employed by the building. All applicants had to prove to the management that they were in good health before they were offered a job. They had to obtain a certificate of health from the health department, then pass a physical examination by the house doctor.

Brown tried to keep his staff busy, while assuring a certain income for the building. Tenants could plug in a lamp or change a lightbulb themselves, but that was about the limit. For more substantial work, he would hire out his force of in-house mechanics at what he described as a nominal charge. For tenants to bring in their own mechanics was perfectly acceptable to management, but Brown stressed that tenants did so at their own risk, and he made the point that it might ultimately cost more. Brown's argument was that house employees were familiar with every inch of the building, that they knew the intricacies of the wiring and piping. Somewhat akin to the old extortion scheme offering "protection," Brown pointed out that time and money were saved by using his staff. The outside mechanic would "of necessity" lose valuable time in searching for the place to make a connection, for example, and would most likely be obliged to call on an in-house mechanic—an "attaché of the management," as Brown euphumistically described the role—to assist. The tenant would then be billed for both workers.

Before the building opened, the New York Fire Department's Fire Prevention Bureau tested the fire pipes and discovered, with the exception of a workman's glove found in a standpipe that clogged a pipe, that water spurted from the nozzles with a pressure of between 50 and 80 pounds a square inch, as required by the fire department. The inspection was started by turning on a motor in the subbasement that pumped water at the rate of 750 gallons a minute. The system was designed to provide a pressure of more than 50 pounds a square inch all the way up to the mooring mast, through a series of pumps and reservoirs about every twenty floors. The building maintained a force of retired city firemen twenty-four hours a day—twenty-five during the day, sixteen at night—under the command of a former captain in the city's fire department, just in case a wastebasket fire got out of hand.

By 1937 the Empire State Building had a "compact truck of emergency fire-fighting equipment" that had been specially designed for the building by Walter Kidde & Co. This truck was hardly a Mack truck, but more a small platform on wheels that fit neatly in an elevator. The truck carried four carbon dioxide extinguishers, several water extinguishers, an ax, two crowbars, rubber and asbestos gloves, a blanket, a first-aid kit, and a gas mask.

The building nurse on staff was Brooklynite Marie de Chantal Kavanagh, who had been hired a month after the building opened to be on duty during the usual business hours. She was in charge of what was described as a "miniature hospital," which was fully equipped to dispense first aid. She was the nurse who treated the tourist who was frightened of riding the elevator down from the eighty-sixth to the first floor, but that was exceptional. The average injury was not the result of fear of elevators, but frustration with them. Most of the accidents the nurse treated were scrapes and bruises, the result of tripping on stairs. The victims were usually tenants who had only one or two flights to go and decided not to bother waiting for an elevator but to dash up or down the stairs, thereupon to slip. It must have seemed odd to the elevator experts that anyone could have been frustrated by their service. One of their specific goals had been to diminish long waits.

The elevators were the signal-control elevators that Otis had first installed in 1926 in the Standard Oil Building at 26 Broadway, elevators that soon became the standard in first-class buildings. Signals dispatched cars at carefully spaced intervals. Long, frustrating waits for short trips were abrogated because it was the signals, not the operators, that controlled the movement of the cars, and the signals were, theoretically at least, omniscient.

To operate an elevator, an operator simply had to press a button and start the elevator by pushing the handle, which he could then release, and the car would stop automatically at the desired floor. The operator's second important function was to press the "pass-by" button if the elevator was full, whereupon the elevator would travel nonstop to the next floor he had called for. If he did that too frequently, however, passengers who were

waiting for an elevator were left stranded and without service, and su-
pervisors would reprimand the operator who fell into the habit of skipping
floors unnecessarily.

The operator had become more an attendant riding in the car than an
actual operator. Acceleration and retardation were designed to be smooth,
with no sudden jerks or dizzy drops. The car automatically stopped at the
desired floors, the car leveled itself, and the doors opened automatically.
Innovations such as the self-leveling feature eliminated the time wasted
"jockeying" to a level, and made elevator travel more comfortable. What
might have been regarded simply as a comfort feature by passengers was
a boon to management and its insurance premiums. Tripping while getting on or off an elevator accounted for more than 70 percent of elevator
accidents, according to the insurance companies.

The likelihood of a door closing in the face of a passenger who was entering from the operator's blind side was also diminished, since there was
no blind side. The elevators were equipped with "periscope" mirrors manufactured by Ann Anzell, whose company was the largest manufacturer
of specialized mirrors in the country. She had conceived the idea of adapt-
ing the ground optical glass mirror manufactured for dentists for use in
elevators and other forms of transportation.

Elevator operators were obliged to buy their own uniforms, and to have
them cleaned and pressed. The operators had to pass muster as a matter
of course, and standards for decorum were high. Reading on the job, a favorite citywide pastime for elevator operators when things were slow, was
done on the sly, since it was officially discouraged. The quality of litera-
ture ran the gamut from belles lettres to pulp fiction, but, according to
*The Times*, journalism had no more-devoted supporters. Many an operator read as many as a dozen different papers in the course of a day. Tenants, having finished their newspapers, would hand them to the operator
before heading to their offices.

When elevator operators went on strike, as they did in 1935, precautions were recommended to assure that no walker overexerted himself.
Sufferers from high blood pressure, chronic heart or respiratory problems
were encouraged to test their reserve and recuperative powers before
tackling a long walk upstairs. They had to gauge how long it took, after
they had climbed a flight of stairs, to get their breath back and to feel
comfortable. If it took one minute to climb a flight and two minutes to return to normal, their resistance schedule made them a "three-minute-per-
flighter." They should set aside forty-five minutes to climb fifteen flights.

Four times a night, between midnight and 8 A.M., night watchmen
made the rounds of the skyscraper from the top of the tower down to the

basement. The watchman responsible for the building from the eighty-sixth to the fiftieth floors would walk down from the eighty-sixth. Along the route, he would "punch the clock" by turning a long key in a cylinder on almost every floor to record his presence, and he would try office doors to make sure they were closed and locked, extinguish lights, check the mail chutes for any jams, inspect the passes of any late workers, and watch for fires. When he had completed one tour, he would take an elevator back up to the eighty-sixth floor and start all over again.

Window washers, unlike the watchmen who worked alone, worked on the buddy system, a precaution that was started when one washer who had been working alone found himself locked out while on a ledge. To gain entry he did the only reasonable thing—he kicked in the window. Window washers had begun washing the building's windows in March 1931 in preparation for the grand opening. (They were part of an army of two thousand professional window cleaners operating in the city, where there were over a million windows, and, as one wit expressed it, a billion panes.)

Wind and rain had a natural scouring action and removed a great deal of the external dirt (the experts called it "dirt precipitation"); the greatest, if least dramatic, problem was the grime on the inside of window-panes. Building managers knew that dirty windows could reduce lighting efficiency by as much as 50 percent, and managers in well-run buildings had the windows cleaned an average of twice a month, inside and out. For the large buildings, this was an unrelenting task. In 1927, eight men worked full-time at keeping the Equitable Building's 5,500 windows clean; the Metropolitan Life tower and annex had fourteen full-time cleaners for its 5,275 windows; the Woolworth Building, with its 2,500 windows, used six window cleaners; and a force of five men cleaned the Graybar Building's 4,350 windows. The Empire State Building's 6,600 windows were cleaned to high industry standards. Eight window washers, working in four teams, were assigned different levels. The schedule was plotted on a chart, and every window was cleaned at least once every two weeks.

Window cleaning was arguably the city's most dangerous job, and, like ironworkers, window washers would not go up in bad weather—they'd hang around in their locker rooms and play cards waiting for the weather to clear. Eighty window cleaners were killed in the twenties, with eleven deaths in the first nine months of 1929 alone. The workers struck for better working conditions, and their two most important conditions were won: Windows had to be equipped with safety hooks and they, the workers, had to be outfitted with satisfactory safety belts. The safety belt was to a window washer what a parachute was to an aviator. The belt was made of heavy harness leather, kept pliable by the use of neat's-foot oil. The belt had inner and outer sections. The inner belt was firmly fastened, the outer belt fit more loosely. It had leather straps attached to it, with eight-inch brass safety catches, or "hooks," that fit to anchor studs in the side of the window about three feet above each sill. The studs in the Empire State went straight through the facing and were embedded in the steelwork itself.

On the job, the window washer carried his rags inside his shirt, a chamois over his shoulder, his sponge in a bucket, and the eighteen-inch-wide brass squeegee attached by a chain to his belt (brushes could be used only on the lower five floors because of the danger of their being dropped). Only water was used. No ammonia, no magical window-washing compound.

"All you do," said Richard Hart, the head of the window-washing team in 1937, "is to be sure your belt is jake, then slap on the water with a big sponge, and give the glass the old swipe with the squeegee. After that you finish up the corners and give the whole thing a polish with your 'shammy.' " When washing the outside of a windowpane, the "schmearer" had to leave his bucket inside the window, within easy reach. When he was through, he did not try any fancywork like edging across on the outside to the next window. He reentered the building. "The whole job takes about four minutes (per window)—three if you're racing—and when you've washed seventy-five windows you can call it a day. There's nothing to it."

The modern design of the Empire State Building created a problem for window washers not found in old-fashioned buildings. Older buildings had deep sills. "The sills here are only an inch and a half deep," said Hart, "and we have to stand with our feet turned outward—like Charlie Chaplin."

There was always the wind to contend with. "Air currents [come] whooping up and down the wall surface like express trains!" said Hart. "I'll be working away, and a gust will come screaming up from Thirty-fourth Street and for a moment I'll be doing a tap dance on nothing. Then, as my feet find the sill again, maybe another blast will come from above and make my knees buckle. Anyway, it keeps me interested." Despite the problems unique to the Empire State Building, in the first five and a half years there was not a single accident.

With windows that were regularly cleaned, natural light—the element that powered the building's design—flowed into offices. But daylight is a two-edged sword. The intensity and direction of sunlight are hardly constant. If the sky is clear and the light is bright, the only relief from glare is found in objectionable shadows; if it is overcast, the light might be even, but its intensity is probably so low that artificial lights are needed anyway.

The building itself cast a doozer of a shadow. Unlike the latter part of the twentieth century, when protesters would stand in a long line in Central Park with raised black umbrellas to protest the shadow cast by a building proposed for Columbus Circle, and when community planning boards would regularly send building proposals back to the drawing boards because the projects were too big, there was very little protest against the size of the Empire State Building in general or the shadow it would cast in particular. The *New York Sun*, in an upbeat of optimism, claimed that there were positive attributes in the Empire State's shadow during those hot, pre–air-conditioned summer months. Thousands of office workers in nearby buildings would "enjoy cool spots afforded by the [Empire State Building's] shadow as it veers around as the sun moves to the west."

Workers in the Empire State Building were said to benefit from the building's shadow because they could tell the time of day by the "heroic sundial." They could also watch other shadows as a result of the movement of the sun, shadows that other buildings created on themselves. In late afternoons or early mornings, the traditional trim on neighboring buildings cast deep shadows, and the buildings did not take the same form at nine o'clock as at five. Some observers of the cityscape found few things more intriguing than the way buildings were carved and recarved by the changing lights of different hours, days, and seasons. The city scene, as Monet showed at Rouen, is hardly the same twice.

There is also the effect of "secondhand light," the result of light reflecting onto the streets or other buildings from the Empire State's windows, or even off its metal trim. The light differs according to the season and the time of day. On a sunny February afternoon, cool dappled light reflected by the Empire State Building lies across Fifth Avenue south of the building. On a summer evening, the light reflected off the metal trim can be golden. Even before the building opened, *The Times* appreciated this light and called the building "a shining tower." *The Times* said that "as the ferries leave downtown Manhattan for points west and south at sundown, an unusual sight sometimes presents itself to the passenger who casts a backward glance at the city's ramparts. In the mid-town section there appears what seems to be a tower of flaming gold. For a full five minutes it gleams, a torch of fire in the midst of faintly glowing candle lights. It is the Empire State Building, ablaze with the reflection of the setting sun against its windows and bare metal strips."

A story in *The Evening Sun* in the summer of 1930 portrayed a paradisiacal daily life for women who would go to work in the Empire State Building. *The Sun* described a breeze-swept terrace high above the sidewalks of Fifth Avenue and Thirty-fourth Street, where women strolled along the parapet to view the towers of mid-Manhattan, or they comfortably draped themselves in window seats or steamer chairs. They might be chatting or reading the day's newspapers or one of the latest novels. Spacious quarters—half a floor with an adjoining terrace—would be furnished by the management and provided free of charge as a special rest and recreation suite for the exclusive use of the women who called the Empire State Building their business home. The suite would be open weekdays, from 8 A.M. 'til 7 P.M. Here the tired businesswoman could find relaxation in a large club room, and several small rooms with designated smoking and no-smoking areas—all furnished with cushioned chairs, rugs, tables, and reading lamps. Magazines and newspapers would be set out, and a lending library would stock the latest books. The inviting terrace would have wicker furniture and outdoor tables with sun umbrellas, and there would be specially outfitted dressing rooms, where women who wanted to freshen up and change from work clothes into "evening finery" could go, or if they needed "forty winks" they could rest undisturbed in a soundproof room. And to make sure that everything operated properly, several matrons and a trained nurse would be in attendance. This picture was not supposed to depict an exclusive preserve of the idle rich. It was an idyll of the publicists, and although management would allow women into the tony Empire State Club, and the building would maintain a nurse, the exclusive preserve for working women never came to pass.

Work in the Empire State Building would be work. The average worker went in, served his time, and went home. A worker—male or female—was hardly pampered. Nor was working there comparable to being an occasional visitor or a tourist whose only interest was the view from the top. Familiarity might not have bred contempt, but the excitement of the place would soon wear off, and although the view might still be staggering, life would take on a workaday nature.

Employers were happy to be there, because the address brought a certain panache. S. Samuel Wolfson, general agent of the Berkshire Life Insurance Company, formally opened his new offices with a reception for friends and relatives on the day the building opened. His offices, said *The American*, "like the building, are up-to-the-minute in every respect and the growing business of this comparatively new agency now has the advantage of ideal location as well as up-to-date management." And when Ward, Wells & Dreshman rented space on the thirty-first floor, the firm sent a general invitation to all their clients to come and visit them in the world's tallest building. Not only would the visitor get to see their new digs, but Ward, Wells & Dreshman would treat them to a visit to the top.

The offices were furnished in all styles and tastes, but the vast majority of those that were "decorated" were decorated traditionally. The modernity of the building was lost on the average interior decorator. The advocates of "modern" interiors—the Bauhaus designers in Germany, the Anglo-Irish expatriate Eileen Gray in France, and America's Donald Deskey, for instance—were hard at work designing modern furniture and arguing their case in the early 1930s. Sleek tables in burled ash, chairs upholstered in beige-gray wool tweed with chromium legs, unadorned paneling of sycamore, black lacquer tables, canopies projecting into rooms with back lighting—that was what the designers urged. But modernism frightened off all but the most daring and avant-garde, even those who wanted to work in a modernistic building. The general public simply did not like modern furnishing. It made them uncomfortable. It was too brave a new world.

What people wanted, especially people who were comfortably settled or those who just wanted to appear that way, was the tried and true. Fifth Avenue apartments were regularly transformed into pseudo-Georgian homes of "comfort and charm," complete with a fireplace in the living room with a carved mantel and a Grinling Gibbons swag used as decoration over the mantel. So it would go in the Empire State Building.

It was to the building's advantage to encourage tenants to invest as heavily in decorating their offices as they invested in decorating their homes, as renting director H. Hamilton Weber let slip. Tenants would be reluctant to move out at the end of their leases if they had spent a lot on decoration. To encourage this, Altman's was provided space on the sixth floor of the building where a model display of office decoration was mounted at the building's opening. Altman's ran an ad saying the display would "inspire all executives who contemplate a change in their official surroundings. Altman decorators in charge would be glad to explain how even the smallest suite of offices could be made effective through the intelligent plan and design services of Altman's staff." Altman's model offices hardly made any stylistic sense for a "moderne" building. The offices were conservative, indicative of the vast preponderance of decoration that would be found in the Empire State Building.

The Model Brassiere Company, one of the stars in the building's firmament, occupied offices on the forty-first floor—the highest of the occupied rental floors in the summer of 1931—and each of the offices in the suite was decorated in different styles, all but one of them "traditional."

The reception room's walls were paneled in walnut, its furnishings neo-Renaissance, its artwork faux Velasquez. One of the salesrooms was modeled on an English drawing room, with chintz draperies and "restful" tones; another of the salesrooms was decorated in American Colonial, which was equally comfortable and, frankly, difficult to distinguish from the English room.

The average top executive was said to have become so spoiled by 1930 that he was not content unless his office was furnished on the same sumptuous scale as his home, which was hardly anything new. Frank W. Woolworth, for instance, had a remarkable private office installed on the twenty-fourth floor of the Woolworth Building that was modeled after Napoleon's throne room in the château of Compiègne. The walls, panels, and wainscoting were of Vert Campan marble, with pilasters of mahogany-colored marble. The Empire-style capitals were covered with gold. The clock on the mantel was said to have belonged to Napoleon himself, and a facsimile of the painting of Napoleon in full coronation regalia that hangs in Versailles hung on the wall. The chairs were reproductions of Napoleon's throne chairs from Fontainebleau, and Woolworth's desk chair was, anachronistically enough, a swivel chair in the Empire style.

In the twenties there were penthouse offices with antique paneling on the walls and Aubusson carpets on the floors. One boardroom in a building in the Grand Central area was a replica of the taproom of an olde English inn, complete with rafters and worm-eaten panels. In some of the offices innocent-looking bookcases were known to swing back in those pre-Repeal days to reveal a neat bar where the visiting client could be entertained. The cost of decorating one of these offices might run from $40,000 to $60,000. That would have been a piddling price, something a piker might have paid, compared with what John J. Raskob and Pierre S. du Pont planned for their offices. Raskob and du Pont would occupy more than half the floor space on the eightieth floor for their private suite.

Francis B. Wadelton, head of the interior architectural firm of T. D. Wadelton's Son, had handled all of Raskob's work for more than twenty-five years, and he had worked about fifteen years for du Pont. He decorated the Raskob–du Pont offices in the Georgian style, featuring hand-carved paneled walls of imported and domestic oak paneling, flooring and trim of English oak, India teakwood, and American walnut. The paneling alone would cost more than $120,000. Wadelton said that he had set out to include practically every one of his clients' ideas, that the drapes and rugs throughout, for instance, were designed and made at the express order of Raskob and du Pont, with no two pieces similar.

One feature of the building that Wadelton wanted to exploit will no doubt come as a surprise to anyone considering how an office building built at the end of the first third of the twentieth century was equipped. The Empire State could accommodate wood-burning fireplaces, and Wadelton installed working fireplaces with elaborate Georgian-designed mantels supported by Ionic columns and topped by broken pediments—a symbol of domestic architecture—to take advantage of the possibilities.

When the faithful went to see Raskob in his capacity as chairman of the Democratic party in these offices—"Democracy's Palatial Headquarters," said one newspaper—and took a look at the rare wood in which they were finished and the general richness of the surroundings, they would hardly leave imbued with the spirit of starting a heated campaign against plutocracy. Any man who sits down with a political leader and smokes a campaign cigar in the presence of $120,000 worth of paneling, the paper pointed out, would hardly find himself in a frame of mind to go out and attack the robber barons of Wall Street.

The press pointed out that only one office in the building was decorated in the modern style in 1931, and it was in the Model Brassiere Company. In its suite of traditionally designed offices was one "modernistic" room, with walls of aspen wood, and draperies on simple straight lines in keeping with the vaguely uncomfortable-looking modern furniture.

By 1937, one major office reflected the modernity of the building. It was only fitting, since the theme of this office was modernity itself. The executive offices of the New York World's Fair of 1939 had moved in. The board of directors' room on the twenty-fourth floor, which was decorated by Miriam Miner, and executed by W. & J. Sloane, was described as "moderne," or in the "modernized classic motif." There were chromium fittings for the legs and arms of the chairs, cushiony, mouse-colored rugs, and a sleek table big enough to accommodate thirty-five directors. Just as impressive was the office of Grover Whalen,[1] the president of the fair, whose office was the same size as the boardroom, and contained an enormous flat-topped desk, a table, a couch and chairs, a globe, and a radio. All of it was modern and all was bathed in light, which was an especially important feature—models of the fair in various degrees of development had to be examined and approved.

Before the building opened, the management set in motion plans for a luncheon club modeled on the luncheon clubs of the Financial District,

---

[1]Whalen, who had started his career with Wanamaker's, was tapped by Jimmy Walker to be police commissioner, and then he served the city as its official greeter and front man, not unlike the role Al Smith played for the Empire State Building.

clubs that attracted businessmen who appreciated the collegiality of their own kind and who demanded service, as well as cuisine, that was low key but always attentive to detail. There was no comparable club in Midtown at the time—as evidenced by the incorporators' having to meet at the Vanderbilt Hotel—a fact that convinced the directors that the business life of the district made a social headquarters a necessity. The founders included the Fifth Avenue Association's Captain William J. Pedrick, Altman's president and building director Col. Michael Friedsam,[2] Best & Company's Philip Le Boutillier, real estate broker Lewis W. Flaunlacher, department store heads Bernard F. Gimbel and Jesse Isidor Straus, and the Empire State's Robert C. Brown. Not surprisingly, it was called The Empire State Club, and its first president was Al Smith.

The club, which would occupy about twenty-seven thousand square feet of space on the twenty-first floor, offered a choice of dining rooms. The main dining room—the largest and most formal—was presided over by Theodore Meye, who for many years had been at the Waldorf-Astoria and was back on the old site as headwaiter. Smaller, more intimate rooms included the grill room, an oyster bar, and nine private dining rooms for group luncheons and midday conferences. There was also a lounge, part of which was set aside as a library and reading room.

The club was situated at a setback level, and management decided to take advantage of the opportunities the setback provided. In the only effort in the Empire State Building to put the setbacks to any use other than as an accession to the law, the setbacks would serve as sunporches, and terraces for outdoor dining. Recognizing that there were women in business in Midtown who too might enjoy a similar environment in which to meet and dine, the officers and directors of the club established what they described as an "attractive feature"—a separate but equal women's dining room and private conference rooms. They thought that women were entitled to special facilities.

Mrs. Harmon, the wife of the architect, conceived the color schemes and all the interior decorations. For the main dining room, she selected chairs of French walnut upholstered in an apricot frieze, with draperies that carried out the theme in a striped, silky fabric. The walls of the ladies' dining room were a blending of silver and gold, with the ceiling framed in a reeding of blue. In all, $400,000 was spent on the B. Altman furnishings. Al Smith hosted a luncheon for the press to meet Mrs. Har-

[2]By the time the building opened, Friedsam was dead, but his name lives on as the benefactor of Central Park's carousel; in his place at Altman's and in the club was the store's new president, John S. Burke.

mon and to show off the club's luxurious appointments and accommodations. The day the club opened it already had five hundred members, most of them, it seemed, friends of Smith, or colleagues whose arms he could twist. They, in essence, underwrote the rent on half a floor.

The Empire State Club fed the five hundred. To feed the masses within the building there was the Empire State Pharmacy, which had opened by the fall of 1931. The pharmacy devoted far more of its floor space to food counters than to pharmaceutical matters—its lunch counters were 113 feet long, a rather outstanding feat for a store that measured only thirty-eight by fifty-three feet. The length of the counters was achieved by building an island counter around the center posts of the store, occupying a space about thirty-three feet by ten, into which were set three complete fountains for soft drinks, refrigerators for salads, toasters, steam tables, sinks, coffee urns—all the paraphernalia needed for a quick lunch. The other fountain, thirty-seven feet long and set against a wall, was similarly equipped.

Unless you went to the tearoom on the eighty-sixth floor, for which you paid a dollar admission, or to the Empire State Club, which required a membership fee, or to the Empire State Pharmacy's lunch counter, which meant sitting on a backless stool at the counter for a quick bite, the choice of places to eat within the building was limited. There was a wide choice of restaurants catering to middle-class customers in the neighborhood, including representatives of the city's most famous restaurant chains. There was a Schraffts at 15 West Thirty-fourth Street, and a Childs at 36 West Thirty-fourth Street. Following the practice of giving supplementary names of local landmarks to identify branches, Childs was calling this outlet the "Empire State" by the fall of 1931. You could get a lunch there from 50 cents and dinner from 60 cents. The Exchange Buffet offered a modest lunch at 5 West Thirty-fifth Street, and Gimbel's offered a prix fixe luncheon for 70 or 90 cents. Macy's, true to its image of bigness and bargains, offered less expensive fare in a dining room on the eighth floor that was ordinarily crowded and bustling. Its capacity was twenty-five hundred.

More stores and restaurants would gradually open within the building, but the renting proved slow, and the tenants found themselves having to leave the building to satisfy some of their most basic needs. That was the case for almost all office buildings, except the few that were in the orbit of a larger sphere. The Empire State Building was not part of a series of undercover pedestrian passageways such as the network linking buildings rimming Grand Central Terminal, nor was it ever a "city within a city" the way Rockefeller Center would bill itself, where undercover passageways allowed people to explore beyond the immediate walls without having to venture out. They could stay dry in the wet and warm in the cold, but still be offered the chance to get away from the immediate environs. The Thirty-third Street passageway that linked Gimbel's with Pennsylvania Station was expected to be extended east from Sixth Avenue, which would also have provided access to the Greeley/Herald Square area, but it never materialized.

What many people did for a quick lunch was to send out for it. Soda fountains reserved a counter and assigned a delivery boy for "out" orders, and simple meals went out from many places in paper bags, with sandwiches in wax paper and coffee in pasteboard containers. But there was also a relatively new phenomenon, one that had started on a much higher level than the corner sandwich shop sending up a corned beef on rye with a side of slaw and a regular coffee, two sugars. Restaurants established "out" service on a grand scale in the mid-twenties when a bank president found himself too busy to leave his office for his usual luncheon spot. He had his secretary telephone the restaurant to ask the special favor of being served a meal—fresh and steaming hot—at his desk. The restaurant manager obliged, and the onetime favor became a habit that mushroomed into a phenomenon during the boom, when brokers could not bring themselves to be torn away from the ticker long enough to chow down.

One of the oldest rules of trade is that the seller follows the buyer. It was true when dreaded commerce invaded the Astor preserve in the late nineteenth century, it was true when the Waldorf-Astoria presented the neighborhood with millionaires who were looking for ways to flaunt their money, and it was true with the coming of skyscrapers like the Empire State Building. Peddlers who had once traveled the countryside door to door, town to town, started traveling skyscrapers office to office, floor by floor. A single building might house a daytime population considerably greater than that of a good-sized town, so the potential profits from a route limited to a single building such as the Empire State Building could be enormous. Office supplies salesmen had long done business by direct canvass, but by 1931 shirtmakers, tailors, and jewelers had started to maintain a corps of salesmen whose sole responsibility was to visit clients in their offices. Some merchants abandoned business behind the counter altogether to take to the hustings, and each salesman would carve out his route and jealously guard his clients.

Shops within the building would try all sorts of gimmicks to interest the employees in their wares, and in turn to try to discover what the employees were interested in. For instance, the Sally Gown Shop sent out about two thousand questionnaires to the female employees in the building, asking them what their clothing preferences were. What they learned was that hard times and tight money were reflected in the choice of clothing. The most useful dress was one simple enough to wear to the office yet dressy enough for evening wear. Black silk crêpe with a touch of white was recommended for this type of wear. Frocks whose appearance could be changed by different accessories such as collars and cuffs, scarves, clips and other accessories were liked; detachable washable collars and cuffs were absolute necessities. The workers liked dresses that were "simple, tailored, but not too severe," as well as two-piece woolen sport dresses, because the skirt could be worn as a separate with sweaters or blouses.

The average office in the building was a two- to four-person operation, usually consisting of a secretary, a sales force of one or two, and a boss. Al Smith's office in Suite 3200 was typical of the scale, but not of the personnel. Smith, like the average boss, had the window office—it was on a corner, with one window facing east, the other south. His secretary shared the inner office, or the reception room, with Smith's longtime bodyguard, a former New York City policeman named Bill Roy, who generally sat near the watercooler and—according to Smith's secretary—served to scare away the more eccentric visitors.[3] Magazines devoted to big business were strewn on the tables of the waiting room just as they might have been set out in any business's reception area, but Smith's own office was hardly the ordinary office of an executive. You did not find much evidence of the buttoned-down, gray-flannel mind here. The nature of the man precluded it, and his role did not require it.

Smith's duties were largely ceremonial, but he showed up every day in his office on the thirty-second floor and sat behind his desk in the highbacked leather chair from the Executive Mansion in Albany. He got to work between ten and ten-thirty in the morning, frequently skipped lunch if he had eaten a late breakfast, and usually knocked off at about three or four in the afternoon. He often walked the twenty-two blocks to and from home and work when he lived on Lower Fifth Avenue. The staff handled all the rental and maintenance problems, while Smith served as attention getter, greeter, and publicity man extraordinaire.

Smith still drew a crowd in 1931. Wherever he went, people stopped,

[3]It was just like Smith to have Bill Roy around. Roy was born in the old Fourth Ward and had known Smith long before he became governor. Roy joined the police force, one of the few avenues for legitimate upward mobility open to an Irishman, and rose through the ranks to become a first-grade detective. He became known to the political correspondents in Albany during the eight years he served as Smith's bodyguard there, and he became known to almost every political writer in the country when he toured with Smith during the presidential campaign. After twenty-nine years on the force, he retired to become Smith's special guard in his office at the Empire State Building.

stared, and said: "There's Al Smith." When he entered a theater, he would always get an ovation, and between acts he would be pressed for handshakes and autographs. After he was working late at the Empire State Building one night a group of charwomen spied him. They stared a while, and finally one of them walked over and asked that if it wasn't too much, would he please shake hands with them. Smith grinned, shook hands all around, and said he was pleased to meet them. But fame had its drawbacks, too. He enjoyed lingering in the lobby to smoke an after-luncheon cigar, but word got out and he had to abandon that practice.

Nobody could ever accuse Smith's office of being "decorated." The most anybody said was that it was informal. His desk was in one corner, and behind it was perhaps the most noteworthy piece of furniture in his office—the chair he had sat in as governor, which carried with it the imprimatur of authority. The place was chockablock with mementos of the good old days, things that served "to bring back pleasant memories," as Smith said. One of his most recent acquisitions, a piece of memorabilia that was given a place of honor in his office, was the chair that he had sat in as a member of the New York Assembly. When the Assembly was redecorated in the fall of 1931, artifacts were sold off. Smith paid $4.50 for seat No. 44, from which he had begun his political career. The walls and tables were covered with photographs of his family, with cartoons and what might be called "oddities." Smith had been given souvenirs and mementos for years, which he made a point of always describing as "unsolicited," and from which he said he could never part. That he appreciated them all was attested to by the fact that he kept them all. Smith said that he had been sent several pen trays with recumbent tigers, and a model of the Empire State Building in anthracite coal that looked like marble, "all kinds of things cut out of wood, walking sticks, statues, replicas of the brown derby. . . . Blankets knitted as replicas of the American flag, hooked rugs, fancy bedspreads, . . . old newspapers, theater programs, books, old prints of New York and Albany, fire hats, stuffed birds and animals of all kinds." He said he kept track of every one and would squawk if any were moved.

Smith did many of the things himself that other executives would have relegated to others to do for them. If he knew he was going to be late for dinner, he would call his wife himself rather than have his secretary do it for him. He kept a little red book in which he had entered the birthdays of all members of his family and close friends. He referred to it every day, and went about buying presents himself.

His secretary, Mary Carr, had been working for Smith for about three years by the time the building opened. It was her job to read the hundreds of letters that arrived every day, sort them, and answer as many as she could. She was also the gatekeeper. Some of the visitors that Carr kept out were "just plain crazy. Usually the sergeant [referring to Bill Roy] takes care of them but some get to me and I have a terrible time." "She's good," said Smith. "She attends to her business, which means attending to my business. She knows who I'll see and who I won't. She's familiar with the people who write to me. And she's got a good memory." She admitted that her memory was actually less than perfect—some days she lost track of how many white lies she had told from the time she took off her hat at nine-thirty until she put it on again at five-thirty, her official quitting time.

Many business offices were no longer the "ugly, cheerless and uninviting place," claimed Mohawk Carpets in an advertisement heralding the fact that Mohawk had carpeted Altman's model offices in the building. Offices were nicer environments, which made for more efficient spaces. More important, perhaps, carpeted floors absorbed noise, hence were a profitable investment.

There was a direct correlation between noise and efficiency. Professor Paul E. Sabine, an authority on acoustics with the Riverbank Laboratories, Geneva, Illinois, said that fatigue was 25 percent higher for typists working under noisy conditions than those working under quiet conditions, which translated into a 4 percent difference in typing speed. There was also a direct correlation between noise and where your office was situated. The Empire State Building started with an advantage that the average building did not have—above the sixth floor, the walls started at least sixty feet back from the street wall, so offices were not part of the usual street canyon, where it is the noisiest. Once the height of the building cleared its neighbors—and there was no building taller than twenty-five stories in the immediate neighborhood of the Empire State Building, as the *American City* reported—it was not just the degree of the noise but the character of the noise that changed.

Where the offices were part of the street canyon, the principal source of noise was the traffic from the streets directly below, the sound of rubber meeting the road, of honking, and the occasional squeal of brakes. When the office was above the canyon, the noise was more the general roar of the city. One heard muffled traffic noises from all the streets around, elevated-train noises, tugboat whistles, airplane engines, even the drone of the occasional dirigible. The higher above the break in the buildings, the quieter the space, until you reached the eighty-sixth-floor observatory, where the roar was muffled into a low hum, where the sensation on a foggy day was described as being wrapped in cotton batting and suspended between earth and sky.

There was only one exception to the higher-you-are-the-quieter-you-are rule in towers. The floors on setbacks were better shielded from outside noises than floors on the face. The reduction in noise was so marked that floors with setbacks were quieter than two floors above.

Breathing less contaminated air was another attribute of skyscraper life, according to architect Alfred C. Bossom, who held that from his Fifth Avenue office he could see the exhaust gases rising to about the third story of buildings. Occupants of taller buildings were removed from the carbon monoxide gases and fumes, and the higher they were, the better off they were. These lucky workers, said the perhaps overly optimistic Bossom, added years to their lives by living in the sky where the air was purer.

The view was certainly better above the sixteenth floor, which was the line where most setbacks began, as was made perfectly clear from the view provided by architect Cass Gilbert's office at 244 Madison Avenue. In the passes that lay between the peaks was where you could see how architects treated what was essentially the same space, how they carved their buildings' forms within the allowable envelope determined by the zoning law. Starting far back from a major terrace the way Shreve, Lamb & Harmon had done was the exception. Usually the building was sent up in regular terraces, reminiscent of nesting boxes arranged by a child—a series of steps like those of the great pyramids. It was on any of those setbacks that you could make gardens and sunning places.

The Empire State Building made a short-lived attempt to use the setback on the level of the Empire State Club, and there had been the story about using a setback for the women's club. However, management never properly took the opportunity of planting on terraces, it never created hanging gardens or brought the "outside in" so that office workers could look out and see a bit of nature. The biggest opportunity—creating a greensward on the sixty-foot-wide setback on the sixth floor—never even seems to have been discussed.

The average roofline of Manhattan was still surprisingly low—four or five stories for the island as a whole—and from the heights of some of the offices in the Empire State one could easily believe in the vision of a city climbing toward the light. Management might have chosen to believe that nobody should look down from the building, only up and out. Or maybe it was purely economic. Although the Empire State Building was viewed as a symbol of American achievement and general ascendancy, and it served as a beacon in the dark economic night that had fallen, so much money had already been expended that perhaps management was simply not prepared to pay for plantings. Times were hard.

# 15

# THE BUST OF THE THIRTIES

The leasing of the Empire State
Building is proceeding rapidly.

—Al Smith, December 17, 1930

**G**eneral Motors stock was selling at
67 ½ on October 1, 1929, the day demolition began on the Waldorf-Astoria. A few weeks later, on Black Thursday, the stock market crashed.
Less than a year and a half later, on the day the Empire State Building
opened, GM stock had lost more than a third of its value and was selling
at 40 ¼. Compared with other blue-chip stocks, GM seemed a winner.
Other stocks that were likewise considered the backbone of the American
economy had fared far worse: United States Steel, down from 221 ¾ to
114 ¼; du Pont de Nemours, down from 190 to 81; New York Central,
down from 218 ¾ to 95 ½.

The pre-Crash multimillionaires of 1929 in all likelihood still had a few
post-Crash millions left, and some did not seem to be reeling as much as
others. However, the stock market figures were electrifyingly real for investors who had sunk their pitiful life savings in stocks, especially those
investors who had bought on margin and had put up only a percentage of
the purchase price in the belief that the value would rise and make up the
difference. They were left holding the bag.

Smith was not among those ruined by the Wall Street crash. He had never played the market in a big way.[1] And his job was safe. Once the project had begun in earnest there was no turning back. The building's backers, for the most part, had not been caught short in the market crash either. Raskob had pulled out of the speculative side of the stock market in the fall of 1928, although he still encouraged investors to enter the market as late as the spring of 1929, when he floated an idea that would allow the small-time investor to buy into the market over time, much as he had advocated that people buy automobiles with financing. But not even Raskob, the financial wizard, foresaw how devastating the Crash would be to the national psyche.

As the Empire State Building rose story by story, higher and higher, the country's hopes sank lower and lower. Among the professions hardest hit within the first year of the Depression were architects and engineers, the very workers who had planned and worked on the Empire State Building. Overall construction dropped 50 percent within the first year, and although the government had promised new construction, progress was slow. Architectural firms had learned to be cautious with the government—many had been burned because a contractual t had not been crossed—and the bureaucratic wheels on the government side were moving with their usual glacial rapidity.[2] By December 1930, the situation was so bad that a committee representing practically every architectural firm in New York established an office only a few blocks away from the Empire State Building, in the Architectural League Building at 115 East Fortieth Street, where unemployed draftsmen could register for work.

Architects and builders realized they had to carve out new markets. Andrew Eken cast about for ideas to keep Starrett Bros. & Eken afloat, and he came up with the notion of building new six-story dwellings on the Lower East Side, a suggestion that apparently shocked William Starrett. When challenged by Eken to come up with a better idea, Starrett couldn't.[3]

In November 1930, William Starrett announced that industrial morale

---

[1]Smith's sons and a nephew were caught in the market squeeze. Smith assumed their debts and met their notes over a period of a few years.

[2]This was a problem that Smith said had to be overcome. "It takes 20 minutes to let a contract for an 85-story building if you do it in private life," Smith told a group of service clubs. "It would take two or three months to do by law what I can decide with a contractor in less than half an hour."

[3]Eken's notion of putting up large-scale housing would eventually give his company the inside track in a new and profitable field. His company went to work for Met Life in developing the East Bronx community of Parkchester, then, after the war, Stuyvesant Town and Peter Cooper Village.

had suffered such a severe shock that it would take a long time before people could get over their hesitancy to undertake new ventures. But if ever it was to be done, this was the right time. Prices were the lowest they'd been in ten years, and supplies could be delivered quickly. There was an abundance of efficient labor, money was cheap, and demand for new structures with all their obvious advantages over old-fashioned buildings was high. In December 1930, Julian Clarence Levi, who chaired the Architects' Emergency Committee, agreed with Starrett. He estimated that a building constructed at the end of 1930 would cost 15 to 30 percent less than just a few months before, and the time was ripe. "The majority wait until prices are again on the up-grade before venturing to buy," he said. "They all jump in at once and the bargains disappear."

The Empire State Building had already taken the plunge. If you take a skewed and shortsighted perspective on the Crash, what was bad for the American economy was good for the Empire State Building. Although its leasing future might have looked bleak indeed—as Smith's daughter Emily said, Smith was "gravely concerned" as early as 1930, because businessmen were giving up offices rather than taking new ones—nevertheless, the final accounting for construction costs showed that Starrett and Levi knew what they were talking about. The anticipated cost of $43 million for the construction of the building did not materialize. It cost $24.7 million. The original estimates had been made in 1929 dollars. The building was constructed with 1930 and 1931 dollars.

News story after news story in 1930 had proclaimed the irony of the Crash for realty circles on another level. The Crash would aid realty and prove once and for all that liquid investments are literally liquid whereas real estate investments are truly permanent; thus went the line. On the first Sunday of January 1931, with the nation in the depths of the Depression, *The Times* real estate section ran the usual end-of-year/beginning-of-new-year overview. Four of the headlines that day were just as upbeat as the other realty stories had been for the former year: REALTY BUSINESS ON STABLE BASIS, BIG GROWTH AHEAD IN NEW YORK CITY, BRIGHT YEAR AHEAD IN MORTGAGE FIELD, and FUTURE PROSPERITY BASED ON CONFIDENCE. Illustrations showed 500 Fifth Avenue, the San Remo apartment house on Central Park West, the City Bank Farmers Trust on William Street, the Irving Trust Building at 1 Wall Street, and "New York's Newest Tower," the Empire State Building. Only the story headlined THE REALTY MARKET'S RECORD FOR 1930; ITS HOPES AND PROSPECTS FOR NEW YEAR told a more realistic story in keeping with the times. Even without the 1929 market crash, the 1930 real estate market would have fared no better than it did, and the situation would get worse because of the simple market economics of supply and demand. The undertaking that would prove the greatest culprit at the supply end, reported *The Times*, would be the Empire State Building.

A week later Al Smith said, "When the public was first told of our plan to erect a structure 1,250 feet high, . . . the man on the street, the business man, and the engineer wondered at the architectural and structural possibility of such a great pile of stone and steel. As this mighty structure reared skyward, wonderment changed to astonishment as the eye discerned actual accomplishment. . . . While it is a fact that the office renting market has been somewhat inactive generally, it is also a fact that a sizable volume of office space was rented in Empire State from plans long before a finished office unit could be shown." Smith's hyperbole continued. In April he said that it was "a trite statement to make at the present time that the Empire State Building was not erected for the sake of mere bigness, even though its dimensions equal the total of a dozen ordinarily large sized office structures, but because the logic of events pointed to the region from Fortieth Street to Madison Square and from Broadway to Park Avenue as the compelling new office zone. A large percentage of the space in many new office buildings within this area is rented."

Leo Rosten's fictional Hyman Kaplan,[4] who took courses in English as a second language in night school, gave the principal parts of the verb *to break* as "break, broke, bankrupt." For those who had bought on margin and were "overextended," or for those who were simply owed money but simply could not collect, the Crash meant more than "broke." It meant bankruptcy, first of the pocketbook, then of the spirit, that ultimately led to such widespread despair that when hotel guests requested a single room on a high floor the staff wondered whether the room was for sleeping or leaping.

One suicide affected Smith and Raskob directly. It was the suicide of their friend James Riordan, the head of the County Trust Company, in November 1929. Riordan had established the County Trust Company in the early 1920s with a group of Irish-Americans for whom the journey from ditchdigging to banking had been long and painful, but they had made it, which made the Crash especially painful. Raskob and Smith, both of whom were serving on the board, took over the reins of management—Raskob as president, Smith as chairman of the board.

It's not as if the Crash had come without warning, especially in real estate, where there was a known building cycle, a known correlation between boom and bust. Major financial panics, or crashes, as Professors George F. Warren and Frank A. Pearson pointed out, came one to four years after a building cycle reached its peak. When the vacancy rate is low, several years are required to build the buildings that will satisfy the market. With that momentum come bigger and bigger office buildings, with the largest of them frequently erected near or after the peak of the building cycle. The big latecomers are the ones that sow the seeds of their own destruction.

After a boom in building comes a boom in vacancies. Buildings last— they are durable goods—and if there are too many, it takes years to work off the surplus. Millions of feet of office space were added to the Grand Central zone alone in the late twenties, and although New York's vacancy rate was not as bad as the nation's, its future in 1929 was already clouded. On the same day that demolition of the Waldorf-Astoria began, the National Association of Building Owners and Managers announced a vacancy rate of almost 12 percent in space in the nation's twenty-three largest cities, but construction was still booming along unabated. By January 1, 1930, the vacancy rate stood at almost 15 percent, and the association was predicting, judging by past absorption rates, that a probable vacancy rate of 16 percent would be faced on May 1, 1930. The field was simply overbuilt.

The average office building in the twenties opened 52 percent rented, and usually took five years to reach 90 percent. That was considered normal, and the original financing had to take those five lean years into account. Although there was already the beginning of a glut on the market in 1929, some buildings were doing extraordinarily well. The unfinished New York Central Building stood at 80 percent rented early in the year, the unfinished Chanin Building at 40 percent. The Adler Building at 530 Seventh Avenue, which replaced the Pictorial Review Building, would not be ready for occupancy until 1930, but by June 1929, it was already fully rented from the second to the thirtieth floors. And Louis Adler had found a major tenant for the main floor. The Chatham Phenix Bank would occupy twenty thousand square feet of space in a specially built banking concourse, which would make it the largest banking quarters in Midtown. Adler had only the top three floors of his thirty-three-story building to worry about.

By the end of 1929, Chrysler had already rented about 186,000 square feet of the building's 890,395 square feet to Crucible Steel and another industrial firm—they took the whole of the eleventh floor and from the sixteenth to the twenty-ninth floors. With those two leases, the building was deemed well on its way to success.

When 500 Fifth Avenue opened in 1930, developer Walter J. Salmon admitted that it might take some time to absorb the approximately 500,000 square feet of office space in his building. Salmon's building was built as the wave was cresting. By May 1931, he had managed to rent the fifteenth and sixteenth floors to a firm in the coal business, and the twentieth floor to a hotel-management consulting company, but that was about it.

Smith and his colleagues might have been despondent in private by 1931, but in public they projected a scrappiness. Smith said that many real estate men had stopped boosting and selling, and had joined in the general wailing. "But . . . those who continued boosting and working when selling was hard work have found profit and success. They are the men who know that the average real estate investment is far more sound than the average stock investment." H. Hamilton Weber, who was only twenty-five when he took the job as the Empire State's renting manager but had already had a hand in renting the Equitable at 393 Seventh Avenue (aka Montgomery Ward, or 11 Penn Plaza) and New York Central Buildings, revealed that renting early in 1931 had been "comparatively inactive" but that an increasing number of inquiries were being made. Many large and small units of space had been taken, he said, and several large rental contracts were pending. Once floors had assumed definite forms, and prospective tenants could at last get a definite idea of layouts and conveniences, the theory was that a more rapid absorption of the office and store space could take place.

Weber said that the Empire State was fortunate to be nearing completion when the renting situation was showing definite signs of improvement. "In proportion to its size and the time still to elapse before opening, the Empire State is renting as rapidly as could be expected of any large new building. It will share largely in the activity of the spring leasing season." As opening day passed, Weber said that rentals had been "made at a gratifying rate and opening of the building has served to increase the number of inquiries for space." He was another who was a master at dissembling.

Not the president himself nor all the president's men and women could put the renting picture together. When the building opened, its occupancy was nowhere near the approved 50 percent. The figure made public was 23 percent. Twenty percent was the figure that was bruited about.

Compared with 1 Wall Street, which was charging as much as $8 a square foot, the Empire State was a relative bargain. A rate of $2.85 a square foot was set for the seventh floor, which had the advantage of already being part of the tower and of being set back sixty feet, which was quite enough to shield it from the usual roar of street noises. Weber was quick to point out that the rents had not been determined simply to be competitive in the marketplace. Weber claimed that he had set rents based on the costs of manufacture, maintenance, and a fair return on the investment, computed in a manner similar to setting prices in other businesses. Having said that, he went on to say that 6 percent on the cost of the land value was the standard return on ground-floor rentals. The site had cost $17 million, and he figured that about 70 percent of the plot was rentable, so it had cost over $250 per square rentable foot. The standard 6 percent return would run the rental price up to $26 a square foot, but he upped it. He put the average ground-floor rate at about $29.75 a square foot. Instead of the ground-floor rentals amounting to the usual percentage in land value, he priced them to bring in 7.5 percent. The aggregate ground-floor rentals, he figured, would be approximately $1.5 million, which would have been getting off to a flying start.

Once those costs were determined, the rents were fixed. Weber ignored the arguments of prospective tenants who told him that other buildings were offering concessions; he turned a deaf ear to the prospects who wanted to hondle. He said grandly that he did not believe in putting himself in the position of a peddler quoting an initial price and finally striking a bargain. He likewise refused to go along with the common practice of making concessions to a large tenant who might serve as a bellwether to attract other firms. He did not buy the theory that concessions could be charged to advertising, or could succeed in merchandising terms as a loss leader. It was bad business, he claimed. So far as he was concerned, the principles of office-building renting had been founded upon immutable principles.

If for no other reason than the fact that the Empire State Building was the largest building in the world—and size was a qualifying factor in leadership—Weber said it was natural that its policies were worth heeding. Weber had seen rental schedules, as he couched it, "cast asunder and totally ignored in some cases." The result was that owners were not making a return on their investment.

Smith and Raskob did their best to have their colleagues, their friends, and the friends of friends move in, as well as any institutions with which they were affiliated. The biggest lease of 1931 came in the spring when E. I. du Pont de Nemours & Co., Inc., took the ninth, tenth, and eleventh floors for several subsidiaries that had been scattered in Manhattan.

The County Trust had recently moved into its new head office in a twenty-story building at 82–90 Eighth Avenue at Fourteenth Street. As early as September 1930, under the direction of Smith and Raskob, the

County Trust applied to the State Banking Department for permission to open a branch office in the Empire State Building. The bank moved into offices on the second floor in April 1931.

Belle Moskowitz, who would handle the building's public relations, moved into an office on the Thirty-first floor. The Andrew Cone Agency, which would handle the building's advertising, took offices in the building. Colonel Pedrick's Fifth Avenue Association moved in. Starrett Bros. & Eken took a full floor. The United States Steel Corporation, another supplier, likewise took a floor. Raskob hired the John Price Jones Company to prepare the campaign to pay off the Democratic debt in October 1931, and Jones moved in the same month.

Dr. John J. Jaffin, who for years had been the dentist for the likes of Fanny Brice, Florenz Ziegfeld, Ethel Barrymore, and Eddie Cantor, moved in the month the building opened. (Dr. Jaffin was also well known for his charitable work, and hundreds of chorus girls, stagehands, and bit hams were said to have blessed his hands and his generosity.) Another who went to Dr. Jaffin was Smith, who selected the new office for Jaffin in person and had it outfitted as befit the dentist of the stars.

Louis Arico, the personal barber of Raskob's and Smith's friend William F. Kenny, was given the barbershop concession, and Arico moved in as soon as the building opened. It was reported that Kenny had backed the venture with an investment of more than $100,000, and Arico would be the boss of one of the largest barbershops in the city, "a big-time tonsorialist," as one reporter described him.

Leases dribbled in. The Buffalo Clock Company leased space; the Taylor Company, manufacturers of unfermented grape and wine juices, took offices; the Hotel and Travel Information Bureau; the law offices of C. Edward Benoit; the Emergency Secretarial Bureau, public stenographers; the H. F. Seff Advertising Company of New Jersey; and C. Edward Benaith, publicity associates, signed leases.

As much as management had tried to distance the building from the garment industry, many of the tenants had links with it. Parker Shirts rented Room 1523. Reed-Cook, manufacturers and importers of fancy leather goods and novelties, moved into 601. Office space on the thirtieth floor was leased to George P. Wakefield, manufacturers of boys' apparel, and a large suite on the thirty-ninth floor was leased to H. C. Aberle, manufacturers of ladies' hosiery. Underwear mill agent Richard S. Lillienthal; Walter Fred Hosiery Mills; shoe distributor Edmund S. Kormond; the Excelsior Shirt Corp.; Warren Leather Goods; the Model Brassiere Co.; and B.V.D. all leased space. Textile firms, including some owned by du Pont, took space. Jentzen Knitting Mills; Clifton Yarn Mills; the Armstrong Knitting Mills; the Carlton Mills Co.; and the Spool Cotton Co. took space. The New York house of Mitsui & Co., Ltd., the Japanese trading and import-export house, consolidated two of its departments and moved from 180 Madison Avenue and 65 Broadway to the seventh floor, where it occupied twenty-one thousand square feet. Another half floor was reserved for the Dai Ichi Company, Japanese raw-silk brokers.

Insurance firms were represented. Berkshire was the first to lease space, then New York Life rented space on the seventh floor, Travelers Insurance took offices on the thirteenth, and Connecticut Mutual, Mutual Life of New York, New England Mutual, and Northwestern Mutual Life all followed. By January 1933, when Guardian Life moved in, there were eight insurance companies in the Empire State Building.

H. Hamilton Weber recognized the importance of trade centers. In February 1932, the American Iron and Steel Institute, whose president was Charles M. Schwab of the Bethlehem Steel Company, signed a lease, which made it the ninth organization related to iron and steel in the building. In the hope of developing more, Weber announced the launch of a drive in July 1935 to establish a housewares, china, and glassware center in the Empire State Building. Failing that, he announced plans for a toy center in April 1936.

As early as February 1931, a full three months before the building was scheduled to open, the promoters tried to lure people into the building and create traffic. They had arranged with B. Altman & Co. to install a suite of model executive offices (or "chambers," as the ad called them), in exhibition spaces on the sixth floor. The interiors, boasted the ad, "were constructed of the most advanced materials, built with a practical appeal to varied interests, and furnished in individual manner." (These were the "model" offices that were so traditional.) To increase traffic more, the du Pont Cellophane Company opened a permanent Exhibit Salon where manufacturers were invited to see the company's newest developments in packaging.

If Weber could not find long-term tenants who would create traffic, he cast about for short-term tenants. The Real Estate Board of New York held a three-day exposition for building managers on the nineteenth floor. The entire floor was devoted to a display of merchandise used in the operation and maintenance of apartment houses, loft buildings, and office buildings. The National Drapery Association took the third floor and remodeled it for their annual curtain and drapery show in 1938. The display rooms were a minimum of six hundred square feet, they were furnished, and the walls were painted a soft cream color as a foil for the merchandise.

Perhaps the most intriguing early lessee took over the entire twenty-eighth floor in 1932 in a renting plan that reflected the insecurity of the times. The Executive Office Leasing Corporation partitioned the space into large and small offices that were fully equipped and furnished for immediate use, offices that the corporation would then sublet to anyone who needed an office but wanted to avoid making a commitment by signing anything beyond a month-to-month lease. All services were included in the monthly rent—light, heat, towel service, ice water, the use of the reception room, and a telephone answering service—and the switchboard would handle phone calls in the tenant's absence. The only extra charge was if a lessee wanted to use one of the organization's staff for dictation, which would be billed at an hourly rate.

A local newspaper story claimed that many signs up in Midtown and Midtown West read, REMOVED TO EMPIRE STATE BUILDING. Other stories claimed that the Empire State Building would be a commercial failure because the location was ill-advised, off the "main stem." They claimed the building was too large, and would immediately be declared a white elephant. The truth lies much closer to the negative stories than to the positive ones. The leasing of much more than a single office or a suite was rare. The state of renting was so conspicuously bad that by December 1931, only six months after it had opened, the Empire State Building was known as the "Empty State" Building.

Management was lucky that the building's assessment was low when it opened. In June 1931, the Empire State Building was still paying taxes on only the old valuation of $12 million for the site. Management's argument that the building was not finished, and therefore not liable for full taxation, did not last long. By the fall of 1931 the Empire State Building was assessed at $42 million, the highest valuation for any single piece of real estate. (It eclipsed the $33 million assessment on the Equitable Building at 120 Broadway, which had held the distinction of being the most valuable building in Manhattan in 1930.) Smith, derby in hand, appeared before the Board of Taxes and Assessment to contest the assessment in January 1932. He said that slow rentals—he admitted that the building was only about 25 percent rented—had reduced the building's earning value, and that although the mortgage was being paid, taxes deserved to be lowered.

He lost face, but he won the reduction. Assessment was reduced to $40 million in February, when the valuation for six other buildings was likewise reduced.[5] Such reductions in assessments would hurt the city's coffers. By 1933, over $3.4 billion had been reduced from the total taxable real estate valuation since the Depression began. Property values in the city had declined $1 billion in the preceding twelve months alone—from $17.7 billion in 1932 to $16.7 billion in 1933.

Foreclosures were the most important index used by economists to measure urban real estate trends, and the news was not good. In the first eight months of 1933, over $200 million worth of Manhattan property—1,235 pieces—was foreclosed. That was $20 million more than was foreclosed during the corresponding period in 1932, which in itself was a bad year.

Smith had hoped that state agencies would move into the Empire State Building, and at the dedication he said about as much. In his speech to Franklin Roosevelt he said that "this building is named after the Empire State of our Union. . . . The State of New York can use this building any time it wants to. The Governor can have a meeting up here, and if the session lasts into the warm weather he can bring the thirty-day bills up on the roof here and we will provide him with lemonade, and he can dispose of the State's business at the highest point on the continent." It wasn't all puff. Smith needed tenants. After no state agencies moved in and Roosevelt had moved from the Governor's Mansion in Albany to the White House in Washington, Mr. Smith went to Washington, derby in hand, in October 1933.

Perhaps the only similarity between the two men socially was that they had both married women of their own class. The differences were legion. Roosevelt was the scion of a long line of American aristocrats, Smith a first-generation American of Irish emigrant stock. Roosevelt was the product of Groton, Harvard, and Columbia Law, Smith of St. James School. When pushed, Smith might admit to being an F.F.M. grad—the Fulton Fish Market. Roosevelt was the country squire, Smith the Dead End Kid. Roosevelt had acre upon acre of lush Hudson River Valley forest from which to cut his presidential timber, Smith had only a few scrawny sumacs growing out of the cracks in the cement of the Lower East Side.

Despite the differences, political observers were convinced that Smith would be given a high post in Roosevelt's first administration, but noth-

[5]The other buildings whose assessments were reduced were the Lincoln, from $20 to $19.5 million; the Savoy Plaza, from $17.5 to $17 million; the Commodore, from $17 to $16.5 million; the Biltmore, from $14 to $13.65 million; the Chrysler Building, from $12.5 to $12 million; and the Chanin Building, from $12.5 to $12 million.

ing was forthcoming, and he was clearly above asking. Smith did not like being put in the role of the supplicant—he preferred granting wishes to requesting favors—and the reception he received on his mundane journey to attract tenants to his building only exacerbated his discomfort. *The New Yorker* reported that Mrs. Roosevelt was in the room the entire time the meeting was held, and Smith did not have a minute alone with the president.

By the time Smith went to Washington, the economic climate was acknowledged as a full-blown Depression, and it was being described with the indefinite article and a capital *D*. Everyone had known about it for a long time. Arthur Brisbane pointed out in his column in the summer of 1931 that Frederick Ecker, head of the Metropolitan Life Insurance Company, "an able man, acquainted with American conditions," said at the Empire State Building's dedication that the country was to be congratulated on having gone through two years of depression "without violence." Only a few months later, rioting in Chicago resulted in several killings and 150,000 Chicago blacks asking for protection.

In the opening days of the building, the unemployed were everywhere. They were sitting on park benches or just milling about on Sixth Avenue. Some looked hopefully at the notices posted in front of employment agencies, but most just looked lost. The apple sellers who had appeared overnight and became a symbol of the Depression were the only ones who appeared more prosperous and cheerful to Columnist Walter Trumbull, as if what had begun as a temporary expedient had developed into a steady job. He reported that they had a new brand of apples, darker red and more tempting. But the sidewalks of Broadway were thronged day and night with those who apparently lived without working, a solid crowd filling the sidewalks from building line to curb, a crowd that seemed to sway back and forth with nowhere to go.

People who were lucky enough to have a roof over their heads frequently did not have enough money to pay the rent, so they started throwing rent parties. Even before Repeal they would put out some cheap alcoholic beverages and invite in their friends and neighbors at two bits a head in order to stave off the landlord's demands for another month's rent. Columnist George Ross reported that a variation was to have people over for a rubber of bridge. The host would collect a tithe from each game and thus make up what he dubbed "the domicile deficit."

The only neighborhood place that seemed to be doing any real business in early 1932 was the Nedicks in the holdout building at the Thirty-fourth Street corner of Macy's. No matter that the orange drink really wasn't orange—a case taken to court on the purity of the orange drink claimed that the drink was in fact more carrot than orange; it was thrown out on the technicality that nobody had ever called the drink "juice." People still flocked to Nedicks' counters anyway. Bastardized orange drink or no, it was cheap.

The problem was that even if the rents at the Empire State Building were affordable for the average business, hardly anyone was willing to move to fancier digs in such an uncertain economic climate. The coming of the likes of Dr. Jaffin and Louis Arico and all the attendant hoopla served only to highlight the reality that rentals were slow. A tough selling job of Sisyphean endurance would be required—not just the usual buttonholing of prospects, but heavy public relations and advertising. Just as Starrett had said that a builder has to consider himself a general, with his staff and the workers his lieutenants and soldiers, so public relations and advertising people felt that they were the generals in a war, their only allies the media. Advertising people even talk in military terms. They target audiences, they mount campaigns, they blitz.

The advertising campaign for the Empire State Building was low key beginning in 1931. It was always on the corporate level, never retail. The approach always took the high road, with only the slightest intimation that perhaps, if you were very lucky, there was space to be had. There was never an actual office cited, never an actual rent quoted, only an occasional hint that the move might not cost as much as assumed, that it might actually be economical.

The opening salvo from the Empire State Building was a polite shot across the bow. Four months before the building opened, New Year's 1931, the Empire State Corporation ran a three-column, half-page ad in the general news section of local newspapers. GREETINGS, said the headline. "The officers and directors extend the Season's Greetings and best wishes for the coming year to tenants and tenants-to-be, and to the great business neighbors of Empire State," the copy read. "We hope this greatest structural achievement of 1931 will do much to further the prosperity of the uptown business district of which it is an integral part." It was signed by Al Smith.

In March, they stepped up the pressure and placed an ad—again in the general news section—with the headline: SERVICE. The copy made the point that "trained personnel of every department will provide for the needs of each tenant from the planning and building of the office to the maintenance and protection of its contents." When du Pont de Nemours, "one of America's greatest industrial organizations," signed a lease for three full floors,

the building's one-word headline was CENTRALIZATION. This was the building's first success at renting major space to big business. The management
hoped that the du Pont move would be the wedge, that other large firms
would follow. The space du Pont took, the ad said, was the equivalent of a
modern twenty-two-story office building covering a plot one hundred feet
square. "Big business recognized in Empire State the economy of mass
production of high grade office space, and the resultant saving in rentals."
The ad was signed: Empire State—An Internationally Famous Address.[6]

The Empire State Building never went head to head with its competition; it didn't even run ads in the real estate sections of local papers. The
competition did, and got their message across fast. They got in, they said
what they had to say, they got out. They even talked prices. The RCA (aka,
GE) Building at 570 Lexington Avenue on the southwest corner of Fifty-
first Street offered units on the thirtieth floor that were subdivided and
ready to inspect. "See for yourself what practicable layouts they make.
They are far above the noise and dust of the street—with superb outlook
and assured light. The partitions are of heavy steel and glass, finished with
a special rich walnut graining. The quality and tone are far more than you
would expect in such moderately priced offices. Three-office suite, each
with a window, $2,500. Three-office suite, two offices with a window and
reception hall without, $2,400. This year it's the RCA Building!"

The Fred French Building had "Choice Offerings." On a tower floor
was an office with an "unobstructed view with 23 windows and four exposures. Exceptionally well planned floor area. Carpets and cabinets included. Offered for sub-lease at reduction in rental value of $17,000.
Long-term lease can be arranged."

The Nelson Tower, a neighbor of the Empire State two blocks west on
Thirty-fourth Street at 450 Seventh Avenue, advertised a whole, four-
thousand-square-foot "Tower Floor with permanent light on all sides, not
just part of a floor as in the other skyscrapers in this district. [This was
perhaps a barb aimed at the Empire State Building, where, if you wanted
only four thousand square feet, you would have to settle for "just part of
a floor."] These Tower Floors are perfect for offices, sales- or showrooms." The Chrysler Building simply said that it was "Rich in Advantages—Reasonable in Price." The building at 295 Madison Avenue said
that it was "Best Service; Moderate Rents."

The Empire State corporation stayed above the fray. On April 29,

---

[6]This ad blew up in their faces. *The Times* said that the "whole building must be equal to
a flock of perhaps a dozen 22-story buildings. We have already learned by experience what
such a building, when fully occupied, does to movement in adjacent streets."

1931, a few days before the building opened, they ran quarter-page teaser ads. The artwork was in the form of a broadside, with a banner headline that said FOR SALE. With no other explanation, the copy said:

To be SOLD,

A new and convenient houfe, barn and feveral out-houfes, together with twenty acres of land, very pleafantly fituated in the heart of New York Ifland, along the Middle Road, near the 3 mile ftone, about ½ mile North from Chelfea Village. The land is fertile, partly wooded and well watered, and eminently fuitable for the raifing of various produce, profitably difpofed of to the opulent families of the City. It is confidently expected by thofe whofe opinions are conceded to be found, that the rapid growth of the City and of the Villages of Greenwich and Chelfea will foon caufe the value of the Aforefaid Land to be greatly enhanced.

The fubfcriber's only motive for difpofing of the above place is that circumftances require his removal to the City. For further particulars, enquire of the fubfcriber on the premifes.

Jno. Thompson

A few days later, six-column ads ran. This time the artwork showed a series of buildings that had stood on the site, as if they had been revealed by pentimento. Standing in front of the Empire State Building, and drawn close to scale to show perspective, was the Waldorf-Astoria, in front of it the paired Astor mansions, and in front of them the Thompson farm. The FOR SALE broadside in reduced scale was reprinted as an integral part of the layout, and the copy told the story of the purchase of the farm by William B. Astor, the original Astor Mansions, and the Waldorf-Astoria Hotel—"for more than a generation the pinnacle of hotel construction, luxury and service. AND NOW—the EMPIRE STATE, an office building, taking its logical position on this site, whose tradition is perfection. A building designed to be a worthy follower of its historic predecessors—in dignity, in size, in beauty of architecture and in efficiency of service to the great business population that will occupy it."

Follow-up ads on May 7 showed a rendering of the building with the headline trumpeting the EMPIRE STATE: ON A SITE INTERNATIONALLY FAMOUS, . . . the outstanding addition to the great group of modern uptown office buildings. Convenient to all points of transportation. . . . Thoughtful business leaders see in the selection of this site the broad scope of the development of modern office facilities in the city's most accessible area." On May 29, ads said that it was ". . . a building that evokes admiration . . . a board of directors that inspires confidence."

Almost a year later, in February 1932, an ad said that "a medium-sized business concern recently planned to locate a selling staff in New York." The sales manager told his broker that if he could fill their requirements "without exceeding the rental budget," his first choice was the Empire State Building. "He could . . . and did. There is no premium asked for the outstanding advantage of Empire State. Its unqualified economy was real news, and good news, to the sales manager. Perhaps it will be good news to you."

Another headline said obliquely: EVERY NEED AS PER SPECIFICATION . . . EVERY DETAIL AS PER REQUEST. The copy said the "tremendous range of unit-sizes in Empire State presents a real advantage to every user of office space. There is no need to lease excess area and pay for unnecessary footage. The flexibility of Empire State floor plans is an equally vital asset— because office space can be enlarged or reduced as desired."

Having charted their advertising campaign, management stuck to it. It was almost impossible to hear their despair from these ads, impossible to realize that floor after floor sat vacant and unfinished, and it was only those unfinished floors that enabled the building to boast about so much flexibility.

The Empire State Building would have received press coverage as a matter of course. The building would be a major record holder, it would be an important piece of architecture, and it would change the face of the city. As a result, it would fall in the bailiwick of several news beats, and the terrain did not have to be softened by a public relations bombard-ment, it was. Belle Moskowitz was hard at work in public relations long before the building opened. Moskowitz had been a social worker when Smith met her during his first gubernatorial campaign. Although she deprecatingly described herself as "sort of a secretary to the Governor. Sort of a literary secretary, perhaps," she was his chief strategy maker and speechwriter during his years in Albany, and the director of publicity for his presidential campaign. As Smith told Joseph Proskauer in 1926, when Mrs. Moskowitz had no news there wasn't any around. When Smith retired to private life, Moskowitz followed. She opened Publicity Associ-ates, her own public relations firm in New York City, and she got herself a major client right off the bat. Smith charged her with the publicity for the Empire State Building and she got into the act immediately.

One of the first things Belle Moskowitz decided was to have a photo-graphic record of the construction made. She hired Lewis Hine, a docu-mentary photographer who, like Moskowitz, was a sociologist (he had studied at Chicago, Columbia, and New York Universities). Hine had started using the camera the same way that Jacob Riis had—as a journalist—and when the National Child Labor Committee sent him to survey the conditions of child labor throughout the United States in 1908, his camera became a powerful muckraking tool.

Hine's work for the Empire State Building was different. In this instance he had not been hired by an outside agency to expose working conditions; he had been hired by management to glorify them. He was not a crusader against a corporate entity; he was an advocate of it. One of his goals was to show the workmen in action. "Day by day, floor by floor, he followed the steel work upward," said Beaumont Newhall in *The Magazine of Art*. "With the workmen he toasted sandwiches over the forges that held the rivets; he walked the girders at dizzying heights, carrying over his shoulder not a pocket-size miniature camera but a five-by-seven-inch view camera complete with tripod, or a four-by-five Graflex. When he reached, with the workmen, the very pinnacle of the building, he had them swing him out over the city from a crane, so that he might photograph in midair the moment they had all been striving for—the driving of the final rivet at the very top of the mooring mast." It was clearly an act of bravado, and management would not have approved. Hine wrote a note on the back of a photo he had taken of a worker doing something similar. The worker was "riding the ball"—literally putting your feet on the ball at the end of the lift and hanging on as the derrick swung. "This is against the rules, but the men often do it," he noted. The shot went on to become one of his most famous and most frequently reproduced photographs.

The show that was mounted as a result of Hine's photographs—"The Human Element in Skyscrapers"—became the model for industrial portraiture. In July 1930, *The New York Times* placed several of his photographs in their Times Square windows, Namm's on Fulton Street showed the photographs in their windows, and the Hastings Building & Loan Association at Hastings-on-Hudson, New York, displayed the exhibit in front of a large cutout of the building.[7] Naturally, the Empire State Building mounted a show of the photographs in their Fifth Avenue windows.

The progress of the building was newsworthy, and press releases would go out on the wire services one day to have newspaper readers in the tiniest of towns reading the same story on the same aspect of the monumen-

---

[7]Why Hastings? Hine lived there, Shreve lived there, Homer G. Balcom, the building's steel consultant, lived there, and Charles E. Andres, who supplied the window frames, lived there. Also, Shreve, Lamb & Harmon designed the town's municipal building. Somebody knew somebody there.

tal undertaking and looking at the same picture the next day, or at least within the same week. Press releases would go out when the steel skeleton had reached the thirtieth floor, when the building was topped out at the eighty-sixth story, when the building's cladding had reached the fifty-fourth story. When there was no "hard" news, a photograph of Smith dreamily gazing on a six-foot-high model of the building would be sent out. The photograph was widely syndicated by the press associations—nearly a hundred papers carried it, as well as the rotogravure section of *The New York Times*. To lend as much prestige as possible to the release, the captions always identified Smith as "Governor Smith."

Publicity Associates placed photographs of Al Smith looking over the plans of the building with Lord Vincent Astor, who remembered both his father's and uncle's houses that had stood on the site. "Very impressive," said Astor of the plans for the "magnificent new edifice."

In accordance with Smith's requests, Publicity Associates used their personal contacts at Paramount News to get the building in newsreels. Some of the news was genuine. Paramount Newsreels made "talking movies" of Governor Smith the day the building opened. Some of it was staged. Paramount took pictures of Lanny Ross singing a song from *Melody in Spring* in the observatory, then spliced them with film of New Yorkers listening to the song as if broadcast from the observatory to various parts of the city. The newsreel would appear in several hundred theaters throughout the country.

Publicity Associates arranged the following voice-over as a special production of Paramount newsreel:

[Al Smith and two other men standing on roof of building, the Empire State Building in background.]

ANNCR: We have a right to look forward to the time when the ingenuity of man will allow the *Los Angeles* to anchor from the mast of the Empire State Building, and as I look up at it . . .

[Tilt-up shot of Empire State Building.]

ANNCR: I believe we have the right to form in our mind's eye, the picture of that great airship landing its passengers on the corner of Thirty-fourth Street and Fifth Avenue.

[Scene in Broadcast Studio with Ward Wilson talking into mike.]

ANNCR: And so, my friends, even though it may be impossible at
the present time for you to land on the Empire State Building
from the air, I sincerely trust that you will at least pay us a visit
in the tower observatory on your next trip to New York City. I
thank you.

The publicists were always on the lookout for a deal. They might
arrange for Al Smith, for instance, to be featured in advertisements for
the New York Central Railroad's campaign "Who's Who on the 20th Century Limited," or they would place an ad in a magazine and have the
magazine include a guest "article" by Al Smith. In *Our Westchester*,
Smith wrote that "on a clear day we can look from the Empire State
Building all the way out to Westchester." He reinforced this sense of
neighborliness by reminding the magazine's readers how easy it was to
live in Westchester and work in New York City's Empire State Building,
a short walk from Grand Central Terminal.

In January 1932, an ad was placed in *Private School News* that talked
about "Geography on New York, Lesson 1. Take your pupils to see the
greatest city spread at their feet like an animated map." By November
1934, sixty-five hundred schoolchildren had visited the observatories. To
encourage more, Al Smith wrote to 1,257 principals of public and
parochial schools. "Part of the geographical education of every child
within fifty miles of New York [should be] at least one geography lesson
from the top of the Empire State Building," he said. "Under the guidance
of his instructor he will see States, Cities, Rivers, Islands and Mountains
laid out in one grand map."

The publicists bought the back cover of an issue of *The Tourist in New
York*. In the copy they urged people to visit "the highest man-made peak!"
As a quid pro quo, the building was featured on the cover, and it was featured as the leading point of interest for the tourist. The text was almost
identical to the articles "written" by Smith. The Empire State Building had
"become the logical sight-seeing goal of New York's millions of visitors. . . .
At its top, the tourist can visualize in a few minutes what would have taken
hours to study through maps. The city, in an instant, becomes an open
book. . . . The whole of New York and its environs are brought to his feet.
It has therefore become of inestimable importance and the first place to
visit on his arrival."

Moskowitz's firm twisted arms and inveigled suppliers and contractors
to buy space in trade journals that touted their contribution to the monumental undertaking. Josef Israels II, one of Belle Moskowitz's two sons

by her first marriage, worked for his mother. In late spring 1930, he wrote a memorandum spelling out some of Publicity Associates' results to obtain publicity:

The P. F. Corbin Company, manufacturers of locks and hardware, are using pictures and description of the building in full page advertising in the *Literary Digest, Saturday Evening Post,* and newspapers throughout the country.

The Allegheny Steel Corporation is using pictures and descriptions of the building in pamphlets, trade paper publicity and magazine advertising. [They made the ornamental metal used on the outside of the building.]

The Campbell Metal Window Company make the building the feature of their promotion pamphlet.

The Indiana Limestone Company features Empire State in the house organ and trade publicity, and will use it in general advertising in the fall.

The Otis Elevator Company is using the Empire State as a feature of advertising in business magazines in July and as the feature of a promotion campaign in August.

The Carnegie Steel Company will do national and trade paper advertising in August.

A number of companies have been approached and will, no doubt, cooperate with us.

Israels was right. Corbin came through with an ad that said, "Good buildings deserve good hardware." As promised, Otis ran an ad saying that it had installed "58 signal control elevators," and Carnegie Beams lived up to its promise ("Carnegie Beams form the steel framework of this modern Colossus"). Ads that featured the building were run by the American Sash Chain Company ("for perfect window operation"); the Spencer Turbine Company (Spencer-equipped buildings were "quickly purged of dirt and even the finest of dust"); the Orangeburg Underfloor Fibre Duct System ("forming a hidden network of wireways beneath the floor—the fibre ducts can be easily tapped to make outlets exactly as desired"); Structural Gypsum Corporation ("over 100,000 bags of Gypsteel Gypsum plaster will be used"); Allegheny Metal ran a two-page spread in *Architectural Forum* headlined FROM THE 5TH TO THE 85TH STORY OF THE EMPIRE STATE BUILDING PILASTERS [*sic*] ARE OF UNRUSTING, UNSTAINING, UNTARNISHING ALLEGHENY METAL; and the Campbell Metal Window Corporation (Campbell seemed to provide windows for every major building

erected in New York, Chicago, Cincinnati, Detroit; fifty-seven were illustrated in their ad, but the photograph of the Empire State Building was
the biggest and most prominent structure).

In 1931, Israels was riding the subway and noticed a car card that advertised Del Monte coffee. Its message: AS MODERN AS TOMORROW. He
called Del Monte's advertising agency, McCann-Erickson, and told the
Del Monte account executive that the "As Modern As" series could not do
better than use that chief symbol of modernity, the Empire State Building. The result of the call appeared in May 1931, wherever Del Monte
posted its bills in the country.

Sometimes Publicity Associates adopted a lighthearted tone. The Empire State Building hosted a séance in 1932 at which spiritualist Wil-
helmine Werner was supposed to raise the ghost of Thomas Alva Edison.
Sir Arthur Conan Doyle had insisted that the failure of many mediums
to receive the spirits was mostly due to the activity of the wireless waves
used for radios, so the séance was held on the eighty-second floor of the
building, where the participants were, theoretically at least, far above any
interference from the radio sets. Josef Israels explained that the Empire
State Building had entered into the spirit of the thing because nobody
looked at blimps anymore, and ghosts were, at least, a dignified form of
publicity, not like chorus girls walking up the stairs on a bet with Earl
Carroll. And anyway, since Israels believed that every historic building
had a ghost, he had a lease ready for signature by the wraith. One writer
who covered the séance was A. J. Liebling, a staff writer for *The World-
Telegram* at the time.

In the summer of 1934, one of "The Three Jacksons," an acrobat
team, was walking down Fifth Avenue and wondered if his touring act
could perform up on the observatory. Management said "okay," Paramount Newsreel took pictures of them on the eighty-eighth-floor ledge, and
the next gig for The Three Jacksons was two weeks at the Roxy. It was the
first and last time a stunt like that was allowed on the building, and too
late for Alvin "Shipwreck" Kelly, who had sat atop a flagpole in Baltimore
for twenty-three days and seven hours, and wanted to "flagpole-sit" atop
the Empire State Building. It was Smith who said no, in all likelihood because he did not want the building associated with the endurance-contests-
for-cash mania such as marathon dancing.

One story that had the seeds of having been planted appeared in
James Aswell's syndicated column "My New York" in July 1932. Several
detective-story writers had gathered at a side-street restaurant table to
discuss ideal spots where a murder might be committed in Manhattan.
They included a dungeon in Chinatown, an empty theater auditorium,

and Times Square at rush hour, with the fiend screened by the multitude of witnesses, and the observatory of the Empire State Building—the victim to be done away with while everyone was absorbed in the view.

Some stories were so Pollyanna-like that they taxed one's willing suspension of disbelief, so artificial that the only explanation for the words and phraseology was that someone had handed the reporter releases still hot from the publicists' typewriters. A story ran in the *New York Journal* in June 1931, with the headline: 2 GIRLS CITY'S HIGHEST PAID OFFICE HELP.

Frances Sillman, a stenographer, and Margaret Wood, chief clerk, are the highest paid office workers in New York City.

There's a catch in that statement, so don't start to argue until you hear the rest of the story. Frances and Margaret work for a brassiere company which happens to be the topmost tenant in the Empire State Building, the world's tallest office structure.

The only possible error in the statement is referring to these two lucky girls as "workers," for according to their own views, working in such an office is not really work at all. There are no street noises up there near the clouds and if one did not look out the windows from time to time it would be just like working at some quiet countryside, where refreshing breezes waft their way through the windows. "We have a grand view, bracing air and perfect light," said Miss Wood. "It's just like being up in the mountains."

"And the view we get during idle moments is the most entrancing in the whole world," interjected Miss Sillman. "The whole city is spread out before us like an aerial panorama. On clear days we can see fifty miles of land and ocean."

If the publicists couldn't wangle a story on the building, they would arrange for contractors, workers, or even themselves to be the subjects in ads or planted as editorial content.

One headline must have stopped some people in their tracks. In 1934, Venus pencils ran an ad with the headline, THE WORLD'S TALLEST BUILDING WAS STARTED WITH A PENCIL. No, Venus was not referring to the graphic device that was used to demonstrate how the building should look, they were referring to the more obvious fact that draftsmen use pencils, and that "in the extensive offices and drafting rooms of Shreve, Lamb & Harmon—each architect and draftsman chooses his own equipment. We are proud of the fact that a majority of the pencils used are Venus Drawing pencils."

The Waldorf-Astoria, built on the site of a pair of Astor mansions on Fifth Avenue between Thirty-third and Thirty-fourth Streets, was the city's largest, most socially prestigious hotel when it opened in the late 1890s. By 1929, it had outlived its usefulness and was expendable. Down it came to make way for the Empire State Building.

The first, new substantive plan for the Fifth Avenue site was put forward by the Bethlehem Engineering Corporation in 1928. Architects Shreve & Lamb originally designed a fifty-story office-and-loft structure that was dubbed the Waldorf-Astoria Office Building. It would not have added to the charm of the neighborhood.

By the summer of 1929, the property was in the hands of new owners—the Empire State Building Corporation—who asked Shreve & Lamb to design a more refined building for the site. They wanted an office building, pure and simple. The first plan for the Empire State Building called for a sixty-five-story structure.

The owners decided that they wanted something taller, even more refined, so Shreve & Lamb started carving away from the base and adding to the height to create a slimmer, more elongated tower. Experts considered eighty stories the highest a building could seriously be considered, and that was the height of the building when it was announced at the end of August 1929.

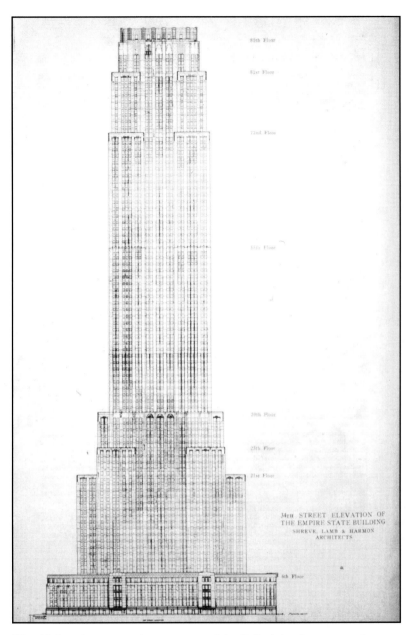

The chief catalyst among the owners was John J. Raskob, who, among other things, had been the chief financial officer for General Motors. He wanted a building taller than the one erected by competitor Walter P. Chrysler. Architects Richmond H. Shreve and William F. Lamb were joined by Arthur Loomis Harmon in partnership, and they went back to the drawing boards. The plan that won the day called for an eighty-six-story building that, from the sixth floor up, was all tower. It was a design that was true to the ideals of the great skyscraper thinkers—the building soared—and, at 1,050 feet high, it would rank as the world's tallest building, beating Chrysler by two feet. The architects were given eighteen months from the presentation of the plan to the opening of the building.

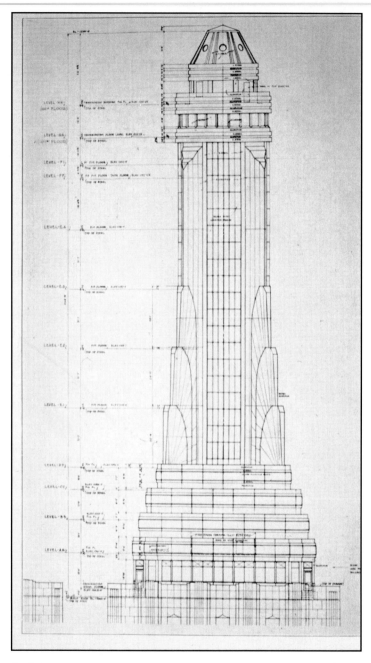

By December 1929, John J. Raskob decided that he wanted to ensure that nobody would best his building by any hanky panky. The proposal was to build a two hundred-foot-high dirigible mooring mast atop the building, which would take the building to a height of 1,250 feet. The dirigible mooring mast was the folly of all follies, but it provided one of the most distinctive crowns that a building ever wore.

The race against time was on. Starrett Bros. & Eken, arguably the best builders in the business, were selected as the general contractors for the demolition of the Waldorf-Astoria Hotel and the construction of the Empire State Building. By March 15, 1930, just about all that remained of the once-proud hotel were the vaults extending under the sidewalks, which were shored up and put to use. This view is northwesterly from Fifth Avenue and Thirty-third Street. Every building shown here on Thirty-fourth Street still stood virtually unchanged in 1995.

By April 21, 1930, the sign on the "sidewalk" heralding the coming of the building had been painted and the 210 steel columns were set in place, some of which would support a weight of more than ten million pounds and rise uninterrupted to the eighty-sixth floor. Fifth Avenue traffic flowed unhampered by the construction.

By May 26, 1930, the steel framework for the building had risen to the twelfth floor. The building would rise at an average of four and a half floors a week, toppling every construction record in the books for a comparable undertaking. This view is southwesterly from Fifth Avenue and Thirty-fourth Street.

By July 21, 1930, the steel was up to the thirty-ninth floor, the stainless steel mullions to the thirtieth, and the facing to the twenty-fifth. One of the secrets to the speed at which the building could be erected was the use of the mullions to cover the joins between the windows, the spandrels, and the limestone. It cut down on finish work at the site.

Lewis Hine, a photographer more naturally in the muckraking tradition than the business of glorifying a corporate undertaking, was hired by the building's public relations firm to record the work and the workers, a job he accomplished with panache, as exemplified by this perfectly framed view of ironworkers casually going about their task hundreds of feet up. This southward view shows, in the foreground, the campanile-like Metropolitan Life Tower, the world's tallest building in 1908, and the Flatiron Building, the prow-fronted building cutting through the right-angled grid of the city's streets.

The architects and engineers considered the construction little more than the repetition of the same specialized task, similar to assembly line production. The difference in this case was that the product was stationary and the workers moved from task to task. Here, a riveting gang is at work on a spandrel girder.

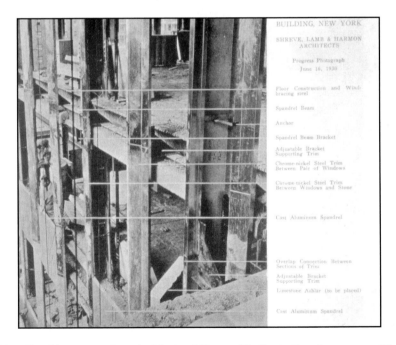

BUILDING, NEW YORK

SHREVE, LAMB & HARMON ARCHITECTS

Progress Photograph
June 16, 1930

Floor Construction and Wind-bracing steel

Spandrel Beam

Anchor

Spandrel Beam Bracket

Adjustable Bracket Supporting Trim

Chrome-nickel Steel Trim Between Pair of Windows

Chrome-nickel Steel Trim Between Windows and Stone

Cast Aluminum Spandrel

Overlap Connection Between Sections of Trim

Adjustable Bracket Supporting Trim

Limestone Ashlar (to be placed)

Cast Aluminum Spandrel

Literally taking a page from *Architectural Forum*, this illustration shows some of the revolutionary elements that comprised the construction of the Empire State Building.

The last pieces of structural steel were hoisted into place to top off the dirigible mooring mast November 21, 1930. The builders of the Empire State Building had thrown fifty-three thousand tons of steel into the sky not just higher but faster than almost anybody had ever dreamed possible.

By December 15, 1930, the scaffold protecting pedestrians was down and workmen were incising the name EMPIRE STATE in an elegant serif typeface above the Fifth Avenue entrance. The ghostly blur on Thirty-third Street is a truck entering one of the four temporary entrances to the building designed for the delivery of construction materials. In a public relations coup, there was no missing the ultimate disposition of the windows—many bore an "ES" within a circle.

Some of the last objects to be installed—the swinging and revolving doors—were already in place by April 6, 1931. The light from the three-story-high windows is reflected off the marble walls of the Fifth Avenue lobby, and the ceiling's delicate filigree work (since covered) is subtly lit by reflected light.

The Empire State Building, as a Gulliver in Lilliput, soared majestically above the skyline. Only the finishing touches remained by March 1931, when this photo was taken by the architects.

The former Governor of the State of New York proudly shows the view from the eighty-sixth floor to his successor, Franklin D. Roosevelt. The two men, one with his political life behind him, the other with his glory days ahead, were not the best of friends. FDR was slow in giving Smith the real estate patronage he had hoped for.

Opening Day, May 1, 1931. Alfred E. Smith, the president of the building, the presidential standard bearer for the Democratic Party in 1928, and former governor of the State of New York—the Empire State—acted as the congenial host and majordomo for the consecration of the house. Here he stands in the lobby, wearing his emblematic derby hat and holding the hands of his two grandchildren, who had just cut the ribbon to open the building officially.

John J. Raskob, a financial whiz kid before becoming Al Smith's campaign manager and chairman of the National Democratic Committee in 1928, built the building in part to give his unemployed friend a job. It would cost Raskob more than he had ever dreamed.

Lewis Hine's photographs, on display here in the windows of unrented shops on Fifth Avenue, drew crowds of admirers. The windows are topped by elegantly updated volutes and framed by aluminum and black granite that—except for the struts—cleverly mask the housing for the awnings.

The banding atop the window frames was continued in the side-street marquees, whose gently rounded corners became a signature of the period. New York architects in the early thirties did not cotton to the hard-edged Bauhaus look, and similar motifs were used in the entrance to Raymond Hood's McGraw-Hill Building and in the marquees of the RCA (now GE) Building.

The marble-lined lobby and crisply designed stairs resemble more a floating palace of the 1930s than an office building, as if you could take those stairs to the grand salon instead of to a bank or a stock brokerage.

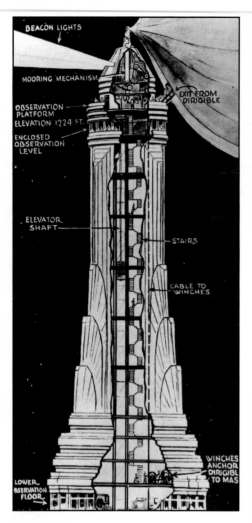

BEACON LIGHTS

MOORING MECHANISM

EXIT FROM DIRIGIBLE

OBSERVATION PLATFORM ELEVATION 1224 FT.

ENCLOSED OBSERVATION LEVEL

ELEVATOR SHAFT

STAIRS

CABLE TO WINCHES

WINCHES ANCHOR DIRIGIBL TO MAS

LOWER OBSERVATION FLOOR

The space that would have been used by the dirigible passengers on the eighty-sixth floor was metamorphosed into a tea room by the time the building had opened. The fountain was designed by Shreve, Lamb & Harmon in the tradition of the marquees. Almost as soon as Repeal came, the fountain became a bar.

This artist's fanciful rendering of the dirigible mooring mast has the passengers exiting from the belly of the beast instead of from the dirigible's gondola, where they would have been riding. The view serves to show the open observation platform on the 102d floor, which would have doubled as the embarkation and disembarkation platform. However, it never served either of the roles and has never been open to the public. Only the enclosed observation level on the 101st floor is open to the public.

The posted sign and the elevator's annunciator are misleading, since this view shows the 101st floor (the 102d floor was reached only by the stairs). The original elevator cabs serving the mooring mast were designed with geometric patterns in inlaid wood in the tradition of other exuberant buildings of the period, such as the Chrysler Building.

The "man in the street" liked the Empire State Building, which was easily assimilated into the streetscape. This is explained in part by the appeal of its human scale—only its lower five floors come to the building line and are readily apparent, and they define the space. Pedestrians were soon taking the building in stride, passing by without a second look.

The view from the top was dizzying; from a plane, even more so. This view, looking down and east, shows the modest scale of the neighboring buildings. The cleared site on the northwest corner of Park Avenue and Thirty-fourth Street would soon be home to one of the last of the apartment houses of the thirties, Ten Park Avenue.

As late as 1939, when this photograph of St. Gabriel's Park was taken, there was still Belgian block paving First Avenue and a watering trough for horses (St. Gabriel's Park had become St. Vartan's playground by 1995, and the block north had vanished to make way for an entrance to the Queens-Midtown Tunnel). Huddled at the foot of the Empire State Building are (left to right): Two Park Avenue; the Vanderbilt Hotel; the Florentine Renaissance–like tower of the Seventy-first Armory (demolished); Seven Park Avenue; Ten Park Avenue; and, between Thirty-fifth and Thirty-sixth Streets, 200 Madison Avenue, where the Empire State Building Corporation had its first renting offices and Al Smith had his office until the Empire State opened. *(Department of Art and Antiquities, City of New York, Parks & Recreation)*

One foggy Saturday morning in July 1945, while World War II still raged in the Pacific, a two-engine, ten-ton B-25 crashed into the north wall of the Empire State Building between the seventy-eighth and seventy-ninth floors, killing fourteen. New York Airway Traffic Control Center could find no flight plan for the pilot, who was trying to return to Newark Airfield. *(Ernie Sisto/The New York Times)*

Queen Elizabeth, the Queen Mother, visited the building in 1954. She threw her trip planners into a tizzy by requesting to stay longer than the itinerary had called for. The three big buildings on the left are, from bottom to top, Cass Gilbert's New York Life Insurance, Harvey Wiley Corbett and D. Everett Waid's Metropolitan Life's North Building, and Napoleon LeBrun's Metropolitan Life Tower.

In 1951, the building sprouted a television antenna to accommodate the growing demand for the relatively new medium. The RCA Building, the slab tower to the right, was the Empire State Building's only serious competition for observatory visitors from 1933 until the coming of the World Trade Center in 1972.

In 1995, the mooring mast bristled with electronic equipment for radio and television. Although the bulk of TV and radio transmissions emanated from the World Trade Center, the Empire State was still home to fourteen radio stations and seven TV stations. *(John Tauranac)*

In 1936, Josef Israels was asked by *The News'* Inquiring Photographer what the strangest place was that he had ever visited. Israels said "when the Empire State Building was just a mass of steel framework, a companion and I journeyed to the top of the mast on New Year's Eve. Here we were, a thousand feet above the noisy sidewalks with millions of lights below, and only a single steel wire around us. It was like dropping in from another world."

In July 1936, Julia Chandler had "the highest job in the world." She was the new general manager and press representative of the Empire State Building observatory. She had been the press agent for David Belasco and for the Selwyns, public relations counsel for several major department stores, drama critic for the *Washington Herald* for five years, and a syndicated writer. Julia Chandler was made the subject of a Bromo-Seltzer ad. She was photographed climbing the aerial atop the building. The layout had a balloon from her mouth: "I'm much too busy to indulge in headaches or frazzled nerves. Bromo-Seltzer leaves me feeling fit."

Camel cigarette ads claimed, CAMEL'S COSTLIER TOBACCOS ARE SOOTHING TO THE NERVES. They featured a window repairer "101 stories up on the world's tallest office building. Sidney Evert swings in the wind with only a frail scaffold between him and—well, it's 1100 feet to the street. His work is to repair windows in the tower of the Empire State Building. Nerve straining, you bet, but as Sid Evert says, 'A fellow with jumpy nerves wouldn't last long on my job. So I ease the tension on my nerves whenever I can. I let up—I light up a Camel. I find Camels are soothing to the nerves.' "

The public affairs department printed two-color folders in 1932 that showed the views from the top, and in 1934 a new folder was issued for the spring campaign. They sent thirty-two thousand to railroad ticket agents all over the country, they used eight thousand locally, and even provided ninety-four Bakelite holders specially designer for the purpose.

Joe Bolton, who was appointed the head of the observatories and charged with increasing attendance in March 1934, sent letters to one hundred "friends," asking them to be boosters for his new work. Bolton wrote letters to two thousand railroad agents informing them that they were entitled to "The Courtesy of the Road" and would be given a free trip to the observatories. "Just let me know when you will be here, and I'll take you up there and show you around myself, and it won't cost you a cent."

Bolton made arrangements with American Express to provide clients with "slips" that entitled them to a free trip to the top. Bolton had a form letter for arrivals from Europe, which he would personalize and send to the arriving guests at their hotels. He explained that the observatories ticket office was right near the Thirty-fourth Street entrance, where the guests should exchange their "slip" for a ticket. "When you arrive at the Observatory on the 86th floor," he said, "if you will ask for Mr. Walsh or Mr. McGuire, you will be met with every courtesy, and it will be a pleasure to do everything we can to make your visit here a most enjoyable one." Bolton sent a letter to all commanding officers when the fleet was in town, saying that that all sailors—officers and seamen, alike—who were in uniform would be admitted to the observatory at half price.

In July 1934, the observatories had yet another new brochure, this one with a gatefold map that showed "a few of the points of interest to be seen from the Empire State Observatories." In a public relations coup, the *New York World-Telegram* picked up the map in August and ran it to illustrate an article on tourism in the city. The same month, the observatory spent $1,000 advertising in the amusement, hotel, and restaurant sections of *The Times, The News, The Herald Tribune, The Evening Post, The Evening Journal*, and *The Brooklyn Eagle*. The ads, which were prepared by the Andrew Cone Agency, were headlined TIP FOR A TALL EVENING.

In June 1934, Walter Witko and his Empire Statesmen started playing music in the tearoom for dancing from nine to midnight at a cost to the building of $135 a week. No cover charge. *The World-Telegram* ran a story saying that the restaurant in "Al Smith's steel and stone and chromium nest is the coolest and most towering dinner and supper club in New York. . . . The terraces are spaciously wide, especially the one toward the east, which also is equipped with dining tables and dancing facilities. An attractive bar is inside and beyond that the dining room. Dinner is served on the terrace as well."

The advertising and public relations were proving effective. By 1936, evenings at the top were so popular that people were arriving at sunset, imbibing what were described as a "wide selection of long, chill drinks," dining leisurely, and lingering till midnight or later, while James Vincent (late of the Stork Club) and Norbert Ludwig (from the Sherry-Netherland) wandered around casually with their violin and accordion, producing "no end of pleasant atmosphere," according to one review. The dinner, which cost about $1.25, was called one of the miracles of the ages. It was served up without benefit of any perceptible kitchen.

As effective as the print medium could be sometimes, it was becoming old hat. Just as FDR was the first president to exploit radio, so the Empire State Building would be the first real estate venture to do so. Even before the building was finished, a broadcast was made from the setback on the eighty-first story. The roofing was not yet finished as sixteen carolers stood on planks to sing carols on Christmas Eve 1930. They were introduced across America by the voice of George Hicks of the National Broadcasting Company, whose dramatic cadence enveloped listeners:

> We are speaking, ladies and gentlemen, from the outdoor balcony of the eighty-first floor of the Empire State Building in New York City, in the first broadcast from this still incomplete building. Above us is the bare steel skeleton tower of this skyscraper—the mooring mast— actually built to be a terminus for trans-oceanic dirigibles. A revolving beacon soon will top it to guide air liners to their destination—up 102 stories—over one quarter mile in the air. Its base, only partly stoned, reveals the top—still gaunt, black steel against the sky—looking without peer over all the spires of the city, a virtual ruler of all it surveys— the wonderful, awesome, grotesque and beautiful island of Manhattan. And from this most modern setting, approximately eleven hundred feet above Thirty-fourth Street and Fifth Avenue, the site of the old Waldorf-Astoria, the carolers stand singing one of the old and simplest Christmas carols, "The First Noel."

NBC broadcast the *RKO Theatre of the Air* from the eighty-sixth floor on opening night. The guest speaker, introduced by Floyd Gibbons, was Al Smith, who was joined "on the world's most lofty broadcast" by showmen Weber & Fields and actress Helen Morgan. The program reviewed social, civic, and theatrical life that had passed in review "past this historic site during the past and present generation."

The contribution of the oil industry to the erection of the Empire State Building was "strikingly dramatized" when a Mobiloil Concert Hour was broadcast from the Empire State Building over NBC soon after the building opened, in June 1931. The drama hinged around the part played by Mobil in furnishing the oil that kept the machinery for building the great structure running smoothly. The keynote of the program was the orchestra's rendition of Rube Bloom's "Manhattan Skyscraper," a composition said to have been inspired by the rising tower of the Empire State Building. Nathaniel Shilkret led the orchestra in playing Bloom's new piece, which was dedicated to Shilkret.

Lowell Thomas, who was renting an office in the building, conceived the Tall Story Club, whose members told their wildest yarns from an NBC studio on the eighty-second floor. About fifty celebrities held their first dinner in October 1931. Lowell Thomas, also the toastmaster, told a "tall story" or two, and was joined by the likes of Robert Ripley, of Ripley's "Believe It or Not."

*Manhattan Melodies* was regularly broadcast from the building over WOR every Wednesday at 10 P.M. in 1932. The Do Re Mi Trio, with each singer singing from the tower of a different skyscraper, made radio history when the first four-point broadcast was staged by the Columbia Broadcasting System. "Do" (Evelyn Ross) was in the Empire State, eighty-six stories in the air; "Re" (Mabel Ross) was on the seventy-first floor of the Chrysler Building; and "Mi" (Ann Balthy) was on the roof of the Manhattan Bank Building. The pianist, Ray Block, was in a CBS studio at 485 Madison Avenue. Engineers, said CBS, blended the voices of the three singers into a perfect harmony.

A variation on this theme had Ben Grauer, comfortably ensconced in his NBC studio, interview some Empire State Building window washers perched on the edge of the building as they cleaned the windows. The interviews were accomplished by the use of special shortwave pack sets that the cleaners wore as they hung out the windows.

Ben Grauer's interviews with the building's window washers was not the first time the window washers had been featured on the air. In the summer of 1935, the longest song title in radio history was featured by the Dorsey Brothers Band: "Serenade to a Lonely Window Washer on the Seventy-third Floor of the Empire State Building."

In 1936, a fifteen-minute radio program on WOR was broadcast from the eighty-sixth-floor observatory every afternoon except Sundays. Its sole purpose was to bring the building alive in the minds of the American public. Julia Chandler teamed up with Earl Harper, whose usual broadcasting beat was the play-by-play for the Newark baseball team. Harper had been doing a "sidewalk interview" show for WNEW, but he moved over to WOR to do the show with Chandler because everyone agreed it had a more intriguing angle. Harper would pick four or five interesting-looking visitors from the crowd at the observatory and take them before the microphone to give their impressions of New York and New Yorkers. An announcer would step onto a platform and on the stroke of one o'clock speak into the mike:

> WOR takes pleasure in presenting again "The Microphone in the Sky" from the pinnacle of the world's tallest man-made structure, the towering Empire State Building in mid-town Manhattan.
>
> At the Empire State Observatories, 1,250 feet in the air in New York City, Earl Harper interviews travelers from all over the world and every day some question that you submit will be discussed and answered by these interesting people from everywhere. Julia Chandler tells you unusual stories about the Empire State Observatories and its many dis-

tinguished visitors. These stories are packed with fact and fancy . . . and now "The Microphone in the Sky" featuring Earl Harper, Julia Chandler and the visitors to the Empire State Observatories today.

Julia Chandler made certain that visitors knew there was no extra charge for attending a broadcast of *Microphone in the Sky* by regularly inserting stuffers in the current flyers. She was also a master at damage control. *The Boston Post* reported in October 1937 that one minute before a broadcast was to begin a man standing less than six feet from the microphone suddenly leaped to the parapet and hurtled to his death below. Although the broadcasters were stunned by the suicide, they remained calm, and pleaded with the crowd not to become hysterical. The program went on the air as usual, with no mention of the suicide.

Chandler would take reporters such as the *World-Telegram*'s Helen Worden to lunch at the Empire State Club (Worden had already written her book, *The Real New York*, by then). Chandler and Worden had luncheon in the room "for gentlemen who take ladies." It was "done in gold." Chandler told her that the du Ponts "always eat here when they're in town." So did Al Smith, she was told, but Worden imagined that he ate in another room. The flack might even have reached as high as the White House. Eleanor Roosevelt wrote in her "My Day" column in 1938 that she had "lunched with a friend high up in the Empire State Building. . . . We sat at a window looking out over the city, which always takes my breath away when I stop to realize what a beehive of human beings it is."

Some efforts at publicity were entirely too much. Hy Gardner reported in his syndicated column, "Broadway Newsreel," in May 1938, that "to this desk comes the third telegram inviting us to the observation tower of the Empire State Building to witness the release of two carrier pigeons bearing the first reservations for the June Honeymoon Month at the Scaroon Manor Country Club." Although Gardner thought the story did not qualify as news, the publicists nevertheless succeeded in getting the name of their client in his column, which, in the tradition of the I-don't-care-what-you-say-about-me-as-long-as-you-spell-my-name-right brand of publicity is what counts, and the banality of the idea did not keep the *New York Journal* or the *New York American* from covering the "story" of Jack Dempsey releasing one of the pigeons (a "love bird").

Some promotions did not work out as well as the publicists might have hoped, through no fault of their own. On Groundhog Day 1933, the subject groundhog escaped the publicity it would have had by seeing or not seeing its shadow atop the Empire State Building by leaping from its transport basket on East Fifty-second Street while on the way to the building. Willie, who was to have been "interviewed" on NBC, was killed by a taxi.

From the earliest days, Smith had said that the height of the Empire State Building would make it a splendid place for a radio station, but he probably never dreamed in 1929 that by the fall of 1931 people would be looking toward another medium. There had been radio, which might have been called "soundies," there had been flickers and talkies, but soon there was going to be something called "lookies." The National Broadcasting Company had been operating an experimental television transmitter for more than a year atop the New Amsterdam Theater Roof on Forty-second Street. However, the higher the antenna, the greater the range and the better the broadcast quality, which made the Empire State Building the most alluring place in town. (CBS would use the twenty-third floor of the Columbia Building at 485 Madison Avenue, from which they would experiment.)

In July 1931, the National Broadcasting Company leased the eastern half of the eighty-fifth floor for the erection of an experimental television and sound station, from which television images would "jump" into space. NBC would have a large studio, a control booth, dressing rooms, several reception rooms, a transmitter, and the first of a series of aerials. This one would be little more than a one-inch copper tube in a six-inch aluminum shielding pipe that would extend upward from the eighty-fifth floor through the center of the building's dirigible mooring mast. It would pass through the roof and hover fourteen feet above the weather vane.

The antenna, as high as anything in the city, gave rise to a new fraternal lodge, "The Top Nutters Club." The initiation was limited to a single feat—one had to climb a ladder atop the building and touch the nut that topped the mooring mast. The original Top Nutters were NBC engineers and members of the special broadcast events crew, but it came to include Lowell Thomas, and Julia Chandler, whom *The World-Telegram* described as one of the most obliging press agents the Empire State Building had ever had. She established what was known in the press as a "freak first"—she was the first woman to climb to the top of the antenna. She said it made her feel as if she wanted to fly.

Television did not fly at first. As NBC President Merlin H. Aylesworth said, the reason for acquiring the highest laboratory in the world was to bring television out of the laboratory and to begin experimentation with sight and sound broadcasts. He predicted that after about a year of intensive experimental tests under actual working conditions television would be developed for public use. In June 1936, NBC started broadcasting to more than one hundred observers—engineers and executives—

over a thirty-five-mile radius, who would report on reception. What was perhaps a first in television journalism took place soon after. A telecast of the presidential candidates was made from the Empire State Building. Scenes of Roosevelt talking from the observation platform of a train and Alf Landon addressing a crowd were filmed, and the "telefilm," as the process was described, "was run through the television transmitter atop the Empire State Building for broadcasting on tiny wave lengths."

There would not be any regularly scheduled broadcasts until April 1938, when NBC started broadcasting test charts and still pictures from 4 to 5 P.M. on Tuesdays, Wednesdays, and Thursdays, and dramatic and educational features, as well as music, from 8 to 9 P.M. Tuesdays and Thursdays. There were no television sets on the market, and the broadcasts were received in the homes of executives and a few families that had agreed to participate in the experiment. The laboratories were still laboratories in 1939. As *The New Yorker* described the scene, there were "panels with dials, radio tubes, miscellaneous coils of wire." But there was a new aerial that was "really something special, . . . a circular band of steel which gives off the sound waves. Below this are four stubby, torpedo-shaped arms of stainless steel at right angles, which send out the visual waves."

Although NBC's plans for television did not immediately pan out, renting one-half of the eighty-fifth floor was a coup in 1931, and Smith could only have wished for more activity like that. In 1934, when Smith appeared as a petitioner for relief before the New York City Tax Review Board and won a substantial reduction of taxes, the building was operating at a loss of more than a million dollars a year.

In 1936 things were so bad that developer Seymour Durst remembered going to lunch at the Empire State Club with his father, who owned the building on the northwest corner of Fifth Avenue and Thirty-fourth Street. Durst noticed that there was hardly any elevator service for the floors above the club, and none from the forty-fifth to eightieth floors. Except for the Raskob–du Pont offices on the eightieth floor and the NBC television laboratories on the eighty-fifth, the building was untenanted above the Model Brassiere floor—from the forty-first floor up was empty. Real estate experts claimed that unless the top forty-five stories were cut off, the building would lose $3 million a year for life.

"We rented up to the 21st floor," recalled H. Hamilton Weber, "because we had to run elevators up to the Empire State Club. Then we rented up to the 41st." The remaining forty floors in the building were bare, without partitions, unfinished and untenanted. The only sign of life in them was at night, when the building kept lights burning on the empty floors.

"The idea was to keep the tower from looking as if it were just floating," said *The New Yorker*. As long as the mooring mast tower was lit, the floors between the tenanted floors and the eighty-sixth floor were illuminated. "What with the first forty floors being fairly well lighted by cleaning women and belated office workers, the whole effect from outside is imposing and probably worth the expense; somebody who wanted an office might happen by, think 'What a fine building!' and rent some space in it. If this somebody should want one above the fortieth floor, the smallest amount of space the management would rent him would be four floors. As things are now, the express elevators marked '45–55,' '56–57,' and so on, aren't in use, and it wouldn't be financially worth while to operate them unless they were to serve at least four floors."

Perhaps the only glimmer on real estate's horizon had been the repeal of Prohibition in the spring of 1933. Landlords started being offered $100, $200, $300 more per month than they had been getting for stores, offers made by anyone who wanted to sell bottled liquor, and who could prove to the State Alcoholic Beverage Control Board that they had a lease or a deed to the property they intended to use for that purpose. Unfortunately, no liquor store owners were interested in renting in the Empire State Building, despite the natural publicity in having Repeal's strongest ally in residence. Anheuser-Busch, however, took advantage of the publicity angle. At noon on April 6, 1933, six Clydesdales pulling a brewery wagon clip-clopped up to the Fifth Avenue entrance of the Empire State Building, where Al Smith was handed a case of beer specially packed in cardboard to make it lighter, instead of the old heavy wooden cases. The beer had been flown in from St. Louis by Anheuser-Busch, which just happened to maintain its eastern sales office in the Empire State Building. Smith's speech hardly reflected the smile on his face. "Surely," he said, "it is a happy day for all because it will in some measure deplete the ranks of the unemployed and promote happiness and good cheer."

A day later, the Society of the Silurians, a group of retired reporters whose beat had been New York, held its first "constitutional dinner since 1920." The same night, Al Smith and Nicholas Murray Butler, the president of Columbia University, spoke at a Prohibition Repeal Dinner held at the Manhattan Club on Madison Avenue at Twenty-sixth Street. Two hundred attended the dinner, and although it was not reported, the odds are that all went home a little happier than they had arrived.

When the Empire State Building was erected, it was assumed that the ground-floor business sites would be leased immediately. The mezzanine level boasted branches from the County Trust, Irving Trust, and Chatham Phenix Banks, two of which had direct ties with the building's management. But six months after the building opened, only one major street-level store was rented, and the rest of the storefronts presented a cheerless face. O. O. McIntyre, who regularly wrote upbeat stories for his syndicated column "New York Day By Day," said that the vacant stores created a "bleakness," that the first-floor windows, "save for one brilliantly lit exception, were a study in funeral black so none may see its emptiness."

To relieve some of the dreariness, Smith twisted more arms. Du Pont took over two windows and provided them as a service to stores selling its products in an example of hands across the sea between manufacturer and retailer. The first display was of apparel, yard goods, and accessories sold at James McCutcheon & Co. An etched-glass sign in each window announced DU PONT RAYON IN FABRICS OF FASHION. The rationale for the display was to give stores exposure.

Displays were frequently installed that related to the building, especially a link with the observatories. Some were simple. Emil Coleman, in a letter to the *New York Sun* in January 1936, wrote that he had just learned that the vast majority of visitors to the building's observatories were from points outside New York City, which he considered a "sad commentary on our civic pride." So did the management, which was doing its best to encourage more New Yorkers to visit the top. The Empire State Building made an enlargement of his letter and put it in the window on Fifth Avenue at Thirty-fourth Street.

The following March, a grander window display was installed. The "Mighty Monuments of Man" rounded up the usual suspects: the Pyramid of Cheops, the Sphinx of Giza, the Leaning Tower of Pisa, the Eiffel Tower, the Washington Monument, and the Empire State Building. Two months later, a "Landscape" window was installed. It had a Lionel train (*The Empire State*), an airplane, an ocean liner, and a dirigible from Hobby Craft, all set before a model of the building.

In October 1936, the Thirty-fourth Street corner window held a display of toy trains that was oxymoronically billed as the "world's largest miniature railroad." The building had linked up with the Chesapeake & Ohio Railroad and mounted signs telling how many visitors the railroad had brought a month to New York to see the observation tower—a hypothetical figure at best. The exhibit was first shown at the Century of Progress Exposition in Chicago, and showed the growth and development of the railways in the Midwest and border states. The miniature railroad set contained over six hundred feet of tracks, and included exact replicas of famous trains. Landmarks were reproduced, including hotels in Virginia and West Virginia, and the grand railroad station in Cincinnati. It played to packed sidewalks.

In March 1937, an exhibit on the New York World's Fair of 1939—whose executive offices would move into the building the following month—was installed in the corner store location at Thirty-fourth Street and Fifth Avenue. It occupied about five thousand square feet of space, and included fourteen window displays.

A Stetson Hat Store opened in June 1931, followed by the menswear shop Kepple & Kepple, which took a large store and basement in July 1931. Kepple & Kepple had a sentimental association with the site. The original store in the chain had been established in the old Waldorf-Astoria.

Contrary to every one of H. Hamilton Weber's articles of faith on renting, Ed Sullivan reported that the Empire State Building had begun to rent out stores on percentage, with no minimum rental, in November 1931. A week later Weber admitted that it was true, "but the policy was restricted to only those concerns that were recognized by the public."

By December, Davega, which specialized in radio products, sporting goods, and sports apparel, had moved into two large street-level stores and four arcade shops. At the opening ceremony Smith acknowledged the obvious. Davega's "great courage in adding to their chain of stores at a time like this is deserving of the confidence and consideration of the public."

Negotiations for renting another shop were going on in the winter of 1931–32. Coward Shoes were interested in twenty thousand square feet on two levels—the store would have a frontage of fifty-six and a half feet on the Thirty-third Street side, in addition to eleven thousand square feet on the second floor. To get stock into and out of the store, they realized that they had to build an escalator from the Thirty-third Street freight entrance, where the shoes were to be delivered, up to the second floor, where they were to be stored. From there a specially designed chute was erected to take the shoes down to the main-level store as needed.

Coward then realized they had to install a passenger elevator from the ground-floor store to the second floor, which stumped the planners, because there was not adequate space for the elevator's housing. The negotiations lasted for three months, and it wasn't as if there were not other sites that were beckoning. When a broker interceded and told Coward that a nearby Fifth Avenue site had undeniable elements of appeal, and was in move-in condition, Smith interceded and worked his magic. He let it be known that his mother had bought him shoes when he was a lad in a small shop on Greenwich Street presided over by James S. Coward, the Scotch-English shoemaker who was introducing new ideas in the construction of footwear. That bit of publicity sealed the deal, and at the signing of the lease, Coward Shoes provided Smith with a pair of square-toed shoes with copper toeplates—a reproduction of the campaigning boots his mother had bought for him half a century before. The store was opened March 3, 1932.

Wallach's, the New York distributors of Hart Schaffner & Marx clothing, signed a ten-year lease on the Thirty-third Street corner in February 1934. The men's store occupied an eighty-five-foot frontage on Fifth Avenue and sixty-five feet on Thirty-third Street. Furnishing and accessories were grouped on the main floor, and the clothing department was on the lower level. The clothing department was ninety-five by ninety feet and had a ceiling high enough to fly a kite—it extended beyond the building line under the sidewalk to the curb, taking advantage of the vault space that Hardenbergh had created and Starrett had preserved. The store was air-conditioned, and its indirect lighting was said to make it light and airy, even on the lower level. A plan for the lower level was to install an entrance from the underground arcade planned for Thirty-third Street from Fifth Avenue right through to Penn Station, but the right of way had to be settled first (the arcade never was built).

Finally, in December 1937, a lease was signed for the prestigious Thirty-fourth Street corner that had remained vacant except for an occasional promotion since the building was built. Longchamps, which was the most stylish and prestigious of the city's restaurant chains, signed a twenty-one-year, $2 million lease for its twelfth branch. The restaurant, like Wallach's, occupied space both on the main floor—eighty-four feet square—and in the basement. It too would be air-conditioned, it would be decorated like other Longchamps restaurants in a "moderne" style, and it would have a capacity of about a thousand customers. It opened seven years to the day after the building had opened.[8]

The building catered to its few retail tenants during the 1936 Christmas season by running ads in the *New York Sun* that were set in Times Roman type and were cleverly masked to appear as if they were regular editorial columns. The ads were headlined FROM THE OBSERVATION TOWER, and the only hint that they were paid advertising was either the small word ADVERTISEMENT at the top of the column, or ADVT. at the bottom.

> Two giant Christmas trees, a-glitter with lights and beautiful as only
> a regal Christmas tree can be, invite your admiration and your inspec-

---

[8]Visitors to the Duane-Reade Drug Store in 1995 could still see the elegant wood paneling on the walls, and the Art Deco hand railing to the lower level that Wallachs had originally installed; likewise, visitors to the restaurant that occupied the Longchamps space in the Thirty-fourth Street corner could find a touch of Longchamps in the hand railing.

tion on the lobby of the Empire State Building. Every shop in the Building is gaily bedecked with Christmas decorations, and if you're at all lacking in a proper Christmas spirit, a short trip through the building and its smart shops will give you the spirit. . . .

Would she like a robe for Christmas? She would! The Canterbury Shop . . . is featuring . . . a Juilliard all-wool flannel robe at $5.95, warm as a goosedown puff, light as a zephyr.

Is he difficult to please? Kepple and Kepple will make everything easy. They offer an ensemble of robe, slippers, pajamas and traveling kit, or any one of the items. . . .[9]

Convincing lessors of the sagacity of moving in was rough going. Aside from the observatories, Smith was the building's biggest source of publicity, the publicists' greatest selling tool, and management's greatest hope. Working both ends of a deal became one of Smith's ways of getting things done, his modus operandi. He was fast to be the honorary head of fund drives or committees. He would publicize an immediate pet project by hosting a meeting in his offices in the building, or by pulling a stunt on the eighty-sixth-floor observation deck, or by holding a luncheon in the Empire State Club—all of which made the papers and brought publicity for his long-term pet project.

Smith got himself appointed to Mayor Walker's Emergency Work Committee, as an honorary chairman of the Family Welfare committee, and he chaired the Housing Association of New York City, all of which held regular meetings in his office. Mrs. Joseph M. Proskauer, wife of the judge who had been one of Smith's premier advisers, had been leading the fight for better homes for the city's poor for years, and she was then heading the Welfare Housing Council Section. Smith arranged for both housing groups to hold a conference at the Empire State Club, where they could discuss plans for a housing institute, with offices that he believed should be set up at the Empire State Building.

He was frequently photographed plugging a cause, always with the intention of plugging the building at the same time. As an honorary master of ceremony for a Salvation Army benefit at Madison Square Garden, Smith released an army carrier pigeon from the eighty-sixth floor to the military commander on Governors Island with an invitation to attend the benefit. Photos of Smith, *cum columbae*, ran in the *Herald Tribune* and the *American*. He was pictured with two American Red Cross volunteers in full regalia pinning a Red Cross pin to the lapel of his coat. He had just

[9]This is an amalgam of columns from December 10 and 21.

joined the drive, and the photo showed him on the eighty-sixth-floor observatory. That photograph ran in the Kellog, Idaho, *News*. And Smith was photographed hoisting aloft a Family Welfare banner from the top of the building. That photo ran in the *Herald Tribune*. Raskob, Smith, and Maryland's Governor Albert C. Ritchie met in Smith's office in the Empire State Building in November 1931, and decided that the major thrust of the Democratic plank would be unemployment. That made the news. The Democratic Victory Committee that Raskob headed discussed business over lunch at the Empire State Club in December 1931. That too made the news.

Smith, who was said to have met and shaken hands with more tourists than any New Yorker during his run as president of the building, was regularly summoned to perform the task of being photographed with whichever celebrity or aspiring celebrity was in town. He did it with such frequency and regularity that he came to describe being photographed the "chief American outdoor sport." He was escorting dignitaries around the building even before it opened. One unlikely party included dirigible expert Dr. Hugo Eckener, whose comments dashed Smith's hopes for an endorsement for the dirigible scheme, teamed up with Mrs. Winston Churchill and her son Winston, Jr., in March 1931.

In the first few years, Smith was photographed at the top with former heavyweight boxing champion Max Schmeling, who had a "knockout view," according to the *Mirror*. Smith was photographed with members of the 1936 American Olympic team; with Captain James A. Millison, the first person to fly solo westward across the North Atlantic; with Dr. Allan Roy Dafoe, who had delivered the Dionne quintuplets; with Princess Toshino and Prince Tsunenori Kaya, a cousin of the empress of Japan; with King Prajadhipok of Siam, who had come to the United States for an eye operation; and he was photographed with the duke of Windsor.

When the French premier was in town a headline reported simply, LAVAL TO BE GUEST OF AL, and everyone understood what it meant. Smith genially extended himself and escorted Mlle. Josée Laval, the premier's nineteen-year-old daughter, to the top, where, by waving her hand over a silver globe, she turned on a new floodlighting system for the Statue of Liberty. The link, of course, was France.

Smith's escort service was just another form of the latter-day escort service, a level of professionalism far removed from amateurism. Events were staged, press releases were sent out, and hokey publicity photos were frequently taken. Smith went to the top with nineteen-year-old Robert Wadlow, who at eight feet, five and a half inches tall seemed almost as tall as the Empire State Building. Three years later he was eight feet eleven, ranking him as the world's tallest man and securing a place in the *Guinness Book of Records*. Smith was photographed looking up at Wadlow through a telescope.

Smith always seemed to be exchanging his famous derby for someone else's headgear. He swapped his derby for a full Indian headdress with Sitting Bull, Jr., who appeared at Madison Square Garden while touring with the Ringling Brothers, Barnum & Bailey Circus. He swapped his derby for a ten-gallon cowgirl hat with Irene Caldwell, aka Miss Blue Bonnet, the winner of a beauty contest in Texas (whose state flower is the blue bonnet). She extended an invitation to Smith to "come on down, y'all" to Dallas to celebrate the Texas centennial. He traded his brown derby for the sombrero of Miss Texas, who was in New York as an ambassador of goodwill.

Some of the people he escorted to the top might have interested him by dint of their personalities. Amelia Earhart teased Smith about the view and told him that he really had not witnessed the view until he had seen it from the air, to which he responded that there was not much chance of that. Smith was a notorious homebody, and liked to keep his feet on the ground.

Not every celebrity or event was photographed with Smith. He missed Douglas "Wrong Way" Corrigan, who had set out to fly solo from New York to Los Angeles in the summer of 1938, only to wind up in Dublin because of what he called a faulty compass. Just out of habit, he got lost again on the top. Standing on the observation tower of the Empire State Building, the curly-haired flyer pointed straight at the Queensboro Bridge when he was asked to find Newark Airport.

Some joint promotions proved too crass and transparent even for the president of the corporation. To plug the rodeo that was being held in 1933 at Madison Square Garden, bronco buster Bryan Roach went to the top, and took his horse "Billy Sunday" with him. Smith was absent. Peggy Coleman, who won the Graphics 1931 Beauty Contest and the title "Miss New York," was photographed perched on the wall of the eighty-sixth floor as she "looked the city over." Smith was absent for that one. He also missed the Hollywood Stars Doubles troupe that stopped at the Empire State Building on its way to appearances in London and Paris. The troupe's members were billed as bearing startling resemblances to famous cinema stars Greta Garbo, Marlene Dietrich, Loretta Young, Joan Crawford, ZaSu Pitts, and Mae West.

Smith missed the genuine Mary Pickford, who released hundreds of balloons from the top bearing the stamp of the Nursing Service, for whom a benefit performance of Ringling Brothers was being held. Balloons presented by children at the Nursing Service's headquarters were good for two tickets to the opening performance.

He might have befriended only one of the many guests he met in an official capacity, and that was Winston Churchill, who visited the city several times before the war. On one of his trips, Churchill was hospitalized after being hit by a taxi. Smith went to visit him and asked permission to be alone with him for a while. "I suppose that you think of me as a politician, though I naturally hope that you may also think of me as a statesman," he said to Churchill. "But just now I am a diagnostician, and I have brought you a little medicine," with which he produced a bottle of Scotch.

Smith missed some visitors whom he might have enjoyed meeting. He liked children, so he would have had a good time with the baseball team from St. Mary's in Baltimore, which had been Babe Ruth's orphanage. The boys of St. Mary's had played sandlot baseball in the Polo Grounds with New York's All-Stars of the Police Junior Athletic League, after which they were treated to a trip to the top of the Empire State Building. A few years later Smith seemed to have a genuinely good time hosting a group of newsboys. He regaled them with tales of his having been a "newsie" himself.

Smith had always had a sincere belief in the greatness of the city's future, as well as a deep and abiding understanding of the man in the street, the ordinary, powerless citizens. One side of his personality still regarded himself as the voice of the people, as the reformer, and many people continued to think of him that way. With the onslaught of the Depression, Smith received thousands of letters from people asking for his help in getting a job. Some of the letters were simply addressed "Al, New York." They landed on his desk at the Empire State Building.

When Smith heard in January 1932 that Jimmy Blake, who had written "The Sidewalks of New York" thirty-four years before, was down and out, he placed some phone calls to make sure that Blake and his family were cared for. "We can't let the man who wrote that song find out that the streets aren't just for dancing any more," said Smith.

Smith had traditionally twisted arms or used psychological extortion to get his way. When he headed the Christmas Seal drive in 1929, among the subchairmen he appointed to head special groups was Colonel W. A. Starrett, who was in a difficult position to refuse. And Smith expected arms twisted to further his own cause. In November 1929, he was elected to the Chamber of Commerce of the State of New York, nominated by Eugenius H. Outerbridge, first chairman of the Port of New York Authority, who owed his job to Smith. His nomination was seconded by Frederick H.

Ecker, president of the Metropolitan Life Insurance Company, to whom the Empire State Building owed $27.5 million.

But Smith's attitude had started to change, in part because his own circumstances had changed. He had come to realize that he no longer had the power he had once held, that he could no longer wheel and deal the way he once had. Even the most powerful politicians can be frustrated, but Smith found that as an ex-politician, the shoals were ever more treacherous and navigating them ever more elusive. As a former politician heading up a major corporation, he could have the worst of both possible worlds. He was still regarded as fair game, he still had to suffer the outrageous slings and arrows. Smith was assailed by South Carolina Senator Coleman Livingston Blease in November 1929, for instance, because a major supplier of local pine complained that Smith had ordered supplies of comparable wood from Russia, not from South Carolina, and what was good for South Carolina was good for the USA. It didn't matter to the complaining senator that he and Smith belonged to the same political party, nor that the party's former standard-bearer would be embarrassed; what mattered was making political hay back home. Smith pleaded "nolo responsibilere." He said that he had nothing to do with specifying where materials came from. That was Starrett's job. "I am the president of the Empire State, Inc. We do not build buildings. We do not buy materials. We do not buy brick. We do not buy mortar. We do not buy steel and we do not buy lumber. I know nothing about the materials which enter the building. Our contract is with Starrett Brothers, who for a given fee are to deliver a finished building."

In April 1930, Smith learned that a twenty-five-year-long feud had erupted again, one that, like the lumber fiasco, would come to involve him. Despite a promise by Starrett that subcontracts be rewarded only to closed shops, which would make the construction of the Empire State Building 100 percent union, Post & McCord, the steel erectors, ran an open shop. Smith resumed the role of mediator in labor disputes that he had so frequently taken as governor. He met with the International Association of Bridge, Structural and Ornamental Iron Workers in an attempt to settle the dispute between the union and Starrett Brothers. The conference was held in Smith's office at 200 Madison Avenue. He brought all the weight of his past office to bear on the proceedings—he sat in the high-back leather upholstered chair, with its inscribed silver plate proclaiming that he had occupied it while governor of New York, flags and pennants stood draped in the background, political mementos were strewn about—but the trappings were hollow. His offer to mediate was rejected by the union, which, although it did not strike the Empire State

Building, struck at a dozen other sites where buildings were being erected by Starrett. Having failed, Smith washed his hands of the whole affair. He said that his company had entered into only one contract, and that was with Starrett. He said he had known nothing of the contract between Starrett Brothers and Post & McCord, nor had he ever seen, he said, any of the contracts or other agreements said to have been entered into with any of the subcontractors.

While some New Yorkers were hosting rent parties, the Smiths moved into a triplex penthouse at 51 Fifth Avenue. A story on the apartment ran in *The Times*'s Rotogravure Picture Section in 1930. The photographs were courtesy of B. Altman & Co., the source, no doubt, of much of the furniture. One could not say about the Smith home what was said about his office. This was decorated. The living room was in the English Georgian manner, the entrance hall in the style of the Renaissance. A wrought-iron gate separated the foyer from the living room. The solarium, high above the sidewalks of New York, was Smith's built-in porch, containing flags and personal mementos as part of the decorations. After living on Lower Fifth Avenue for about a year, the Smiths moved to Upper Fifth Avenue, to a fourteen-room, six-bath apartment at 820 Fifth Avenue at Sixty-third Street. This was a far less bohemian Fifth Avenue—there had never been such a thing as a Mabel Dodge salon in this neighborhood—only bankers and titans of industry. The Smiths attended St. Vincent Ferrar Church, which was to the Roman Catholic community what St. Thomas's or St. Bartholomew's was to the Episcopalian community. He would take Sunday strolls up Madison Avenue, and he was known to stop when he heard a crying baby to make inquiries concerning the child's well-being. "Whatssamatta, baby? Bellyache?" he would ask in his oddly kind avuncular way as he peered into the carriage.

Smith was still a popular figure in the myth of the city as late as 1935. *Times* reporter and city raconteur Meyer Berger said that although the Little Church Around the Corner was the tourists' favorite place from the perspective of sight-seeing guides, Al Smith was the most popular personage, in part because the guides made him so. They pointed out the house where he lived, opposite the Central Park Zoo, the house he used to live in on Lower Fifth Avenue, the church where he served as altar boy, and the house in Oliver Street where he grew up. They even pointed out the house on South Street under the Brooklyn Bridge where he was born, which Meyer Berger pointed out was rather a neat trick, because 174 South Street had been torn down many years before. A gasoline station and all-night diner occupied the spot, but the building the guides showed was just a few doors down, which was close enough.

As early as the summer of 1931, reporters were saying that Smith was already living the life of an affluent businessman. Charles P. Stewart, a reporter for the Waugatuck, Connecticut, *News*, wrote that as chief executive of the state—the job Smith held when the reporter had seen him last—Smith was unique. As manager of the Empire State Building, he was simply one big businessman in a whole city of them. His surroundings were a thousand times more magnificent, but not so dignified. He looked older and more subdued than he had only a few months before his nomination—older out of proportion to the few years that had elapsed since then. He lacked the air of "pep" that he had worn as governor. The suspicion was that business, as a substitute for public life, bored him.

Smith usually succeeded in masking his true feelings, but the warmheartedness that had been so much in evidence was not quite so near the surface anymore. He was deeply troubled by some past events. One that came to haunt him had not been any of his doing, but it had been done on his behalf. The suicide of his friend James Riordan so soon after Black Thursday was not precipitated exclusively by the Crash. There had been complicating factors. Unbeknownst to Smith, the County Trust under Riordan had lent the Democratic Party $1 million for the 1928 election. Election laws said it was improper for a banking institution to make political contributions, and Riordan had gotten around the law by putting the money forward as personal bank loans, for which friends, including the future owner of the New York Football Giants, Tim Mara, had signed. Riordan assured his friends that they would not be called on the loans. With the Crash, the assurances evaporated. Somebody had to make good.

At the same time, the 1932 political race was tugging for Smith's attention. Observers questioned whether the deep impression Smith had made as a man of the people—the product of the Fulton Fish Market—could be obliterated so quickly in the minds of the voters. The electorate had not forgotten him. Voters still liked him. Smith announced that he would not campaign for delegates for the nomination, but he would accept the nomination for the presidency if it were offered. After the nomination went to Roosevelt, Jon McCue wrote a letter to the *Brooklyn Eagle*, in which he said that Smith had made three major mistakes in his life. One was launching a man like Walker for mayor, the second was trying to block FDR's nomination, and the third—no more or no less—was the Empire State Building.

In 1933, the fifty-five-year-old Belle Moskowitz suffered a massive heart attack and died. Smith was visibly shaken by the news, and perhaps never recovered. With his chief strategists dead, people said that Smith became politically brain dead. After meeting with FDR in October 1933, Smith started talking more and more like a businessman and less like a man of the people. He talked about the "baloney dollar" and the "alphabet soup" of government agencies, although Roosevelt's agenda at the national level was philosophically the same as Smith's had been at the state level. Critics said that he had lost touch with the average man, that elevators had driven from his memory the creaky stairs of the tenements he had climbed as a boy. He had been hanging around with the rich and powerful too long, and he was no longer concerned with the well-being of the workers, only mouthing the sentiments of owners of empty buildings. He had swapped headgear again, this time permanently. He had traded in his derby for a top hat.

Even when Smith managed to look like a benefactor to his employees, he was merely reinforcing relationships in the old-boy network. In 1935, he announced the adoption of a cooperative group life insurance program covering the employees of Empire State, Inc. Within the first week, 80 percent of Empire State's eligible employees were enrolled in the plan, with the proviso that new employees would become eligible to join the plan after a short service period. The insurance was placed through the insurance brokerage operated by Smith's friend William J. Pedrick, who had offices in the Empire State Building, had been the head of the Fifth Avenue Association, and was one of the founders of the Empire State Club. The company that underwrote the insurance was, of course, Metropolitan Life.

The building's management was naturally distracted by economics in the mid-1930s, but none more so than John J. Raskob and Pierre du Pont, who found themselves in hot tax water over a scheme Raskob had hatched after the Crash. They had sold each other large blocks of stock well below the original price each had paid in 1929. Then they sold the stocks back to each other after the first of the year. The brief swap, which involved gross sales totaling nearly $30 million, left the two men only $46.86 apart. The glory of the deal, so far as Raskob and du Pont were concerned, was that the sales involved deductible losses under the income tax laws—or so they argued. In January 1936, Internal Revenue disallowed the tax saving, which amounted to about $2 million. The investigation had begun under the Hoover administration, and although it wasn't easy for a Democratic administration to prosecute a case against one of its own, it did. That fact was difficult for Raskob to reconcile, but it was indicative of how topsy-turvy things had become in his world.

With the Depression, both du Pont and Raskob were disoriented. The world that they knew, the society that they had thrived in and were comforted by, was crumbling, disintegrating within their very grasp. Du Pont no longer sought Raskob's advice on stocks and had never taken an active interest in the workings of the Empire State Building. It was simply another venture turned sour. Although the two grew ever farther apart, du Pont and Raskob banded together against what they viewed as a greater enemy. They formed the American Liberty League in 1934, which ostensibly was created to root out "un-Americanism," but which was little more than an attempt to discredit Roosevelt and his New Deal. Smith was with them. In January 1936, he gave a speech before the American Liberty League in which he said that if Roosevelt's policies were to continue, he would "take a walk."

When newsmen asked Smith about the Liberty League speech immediately after he had given it, he brushed them aside, saying that he had to "go back to work." He was worried about something else. The Empire State Building was threatened by a building-service employee strike of 320 of his employees. The union's demands were the restoration of a 25 percent wage cut that had been applied to all service employees in the building receiving more than $25 a week, and they wanted a workweek of forty hours. "Mr. Smith's speech before the American Liberty League in Washington last Saturday was a complete contradiction of his attitude toward his own men in the Empire State Building," said union president James J. Bambrick. Smith had said that the first danger he saw in American society was the arraignment of class against class. "It has been freely predicted that, if we were ever to have civil strife again in this country, it would come from the appeal to passion and prejudice that comes from the demagogue that would incite one class of our people against the other." During times of labor unrest in the past, reporters had noticed a half dozen or so goons lounging around the lobby of the Empire State Building. One report had them directly in the employ of Al Smith. There had been no trouble at the Empire State Building in the past, and there would be none this time. The strike was averted.[10]

While the workers prepared to strike, Raskob was sending out letters from his office in the Empire State Building on behalf of the Liberty League to "root out the vicious radical element" that threatened the destruction of the government. He said that he had started out as a poor boy to become successful, success that came "from accomplishments made possible under our form of government, accomplishments impossible under a socialistic, communistic or other form of government which fails to encourage initiative."

By the fall of 1936, Al Smith, the Happy Warrior, was the Unhappy Warrior. Something had "taken place in this country," he said. "There is

---

[10]Mayor La Guardia intervened in the strike; workers were granted a $2-a-week raise, but the forty-eight-hour week remained.

some certain kind of foreign 'ism' crawling over this country. What it is I don't know. What its first name will be when it is christened I haven't the slightest idea. But I know that it is here." His "take a walk" speech had been interpreted as taking a walk out of the convention, but he walked away from the Democratic Party.[11] In 1936 Smith endorsed Republican Alf Landon, prompting a cartoon in the *Mirror* that showed Smith in the gondola of a blimp floating away from the building's mooring mast. The blimp was not quite the usual blimp—it was a Republican elephant, and Smith was carrying his anti–New Deal speeches. The caption read: AL TAKES OFF: HAPPY LANDON.

Smith announced in 1936 that it had been the worst renting season in thirty years, that real estate had been the last to feel the effects of the Depression and would be the last to recover. But he remained confident. "It affected the Empire State Building, of course, but it did better than other buildings of that kind in the Grand Central zone. I have faith in the building because I have faith in the City of New York. Would I build it today? Certainly!" But he stressed that capital would not flow while taxes remained so high. A few days after his Liberty League speech, Smith had asked the Board of Taxes and Assessments for a reduction of the tentative $28.5 million assessed valuation placed on the Empire State Building for 1936. He explained his actions as just a routine matter in an effort to adjust what he and his directors regarded as an exorbitant assessment. The inevitable question was how the taxes that were assessed on the building were being paid when the occupancy rate was so low; how, in fact, the mortgage was being paid with a vacancy rate so high. One of the greatest sources of income was the observatories. All those millions of dollar admissions contributed to the coffers of the Empire State Building, especially after King Kong had been depicted climbing to the pinnacle of the Empire State with a disheveled Fay Wray in his grasp. But even King Kong was not enough.

With the real estate trade in the doldrums, the Empire State Building Corporation desperately struggled to stave off bankruptcy. The total income was not enough to pay the interest on the mortgage, and the building found itself in default with the mortgagor. Smith and Brown went to work, and succeeded in persuading Met Life to halve its mortgage rate from 6 to 3 percent. Met Life also agreed to carry the interest payments that had been missed; it agreed to help with taxes; to advance money to

[11]At the opening of the "world's largest miniature railroad," Smith threw the switch that started the show. The headline in the *American* was A DISTINGUISHED SWITCHMAN, no doubt a pun on his politics.

make some material changes in the building; it even agreed to advance money for some alterations for tenants to the tune of $250,000.

Met Life subsequently told the owners in 1936 that if they forked over $500,000, which would be applied to the principal, the interest rate would be dropped some more—to 2 ½ percent—and some of the accumulated interest that the insurance company continued to carry on its books would be canceled. Met Life Chairman Frederick Ecker defended his actions in 1940 by pointing out that he had not simply handed over the store. He had held out a carrot to make sure that future installments were made according to the payment schedule in the mid-1930s. The insurance company was willing to carry the building, but it did not forgive the debt; it did not write the entire unpaid interest off the obligation, but it would write off some of the debt providing the agreed future payments were met as they fell due. Interest was not in arrears. It was "readjusted." The building had been bankrupt in everything but name for years.

Ecker's justification for not foreclosing at the time of the first default was that Met Life would have owned the building if he had, and Met Life didn't want it. Ecker thought the present management perfectly capable and he could obtain no better results. By 1940, Met Life had received $3.8 million that it would not have received had they foreclosed, and although everybody might not have been particularly happy, they were satisfied, and he believed the building would be making money by 1943. Ecker did admit that even as late as 1940, the building was not yet yielding 2 ½ percent, and that there was a "contribution from someone" each time interest fell due to make up the payment the insurance company received. That someone, everyone assumed, was John J. Raskob.

Smith had always maintained that all the money needed for erection of the Empire State Building beyond the $27.5 million loan from Met Life had been advanced by four members of the owning company—Kaufman, Earle, Raskob, and du Pont—and that they had made up the balance. It turns out, however, that an additional $13.5 million had been received from Chatham Phenix, and an additional $4 million was underwritten by Manufacturers Trust, which by then had absorbed Chatham Phenix. Raskob revealed that when still further financing became necessary, the owners themselves put up out of their own pockets the sum of $22,150,000.

In the mid-thirties, Smith still took visiting dignitaries to the top to show them the view, but he did it less and less, and with less enthusiasm. In October 1937, he escorted Vittorio Mussolini, the eldest son of the Italian premier. Observers of Smith noted that he had taken on the tone of the spieler in his remarks. "Now on this side," he declaimed, "we have. . . ."

until somebody snickered. Smith cleared his throat. When he continued, it was in a lower and more personal tone. It could have been that these guests were seldom closer to real power than being someone's relative, people who had little stature in his eyes and no real authority, or perhaps he was simply sick and tired of his job. Whatever the cause, he had begun to be ornery and cranky.

In March 1938, Smith escorted the three sisters of Albania's King Zog to the top. He raised his voice, as if to make himself understood better by the Princesses Ruhije, Maxhide, and Myzejen, none of whom spoke English, and who, it had been reported, were in New York to find husbands for themselves. He would then turn to the Albanian minister to Washington and say, "Counsel, explain to the ladies." At one stage of the visit, Smith asked the princesses if they wanted a drink, only to be told that their religion forbade it. "What kind of a religion says you can't drink?" Smith asked incredulously. "The Mohammedan," he was told. He shrugged.

By 1938 the man selling views of the stars at night and the Empire State Building by day had a new daytime sign on his giant telescope on Forty-second Street near Sixth Avenue: SEE THE EMPIRE STATE OBSERVATION TOWER—86TH FLOOR—OCCASIONALLY AL SMITH—2 CENTS. Smith's visits were indeed becoming more occasional, so occasional that George Ross wrote about a skyscraper oddity in 1939. He said that "on a clear, fogless day from the top of the Empire State Building, Alfred E. Smith can't even see the Hudson River. That's because he doesn't go up there too often these days."

Smith was depressed and becoming withdrawn from it all. The day of the superskyscraper had been declared over by 1935. Vacant office space in New York early in 1934 had reached an average of 21 percent. Other cities were worse off. In Chicago the vacancy rate stood at 25 percent, Philadelphia at 31, Detroit at 38. Until those vacancies were reduced substantially, business would not improve and a resumption of skyscraper construction could not be expected.

Areas that had been eyed as the next development zones in New York were viewed differently as well. Park Avenue in the low Fifties had been regarded as the logical extension of the commercial field, according to Douglas L. Elliman & Co., but by 1933, the glut on the market created by the Empire State Building, by the numerous buildings on Forty-second Street and at Rockefeller Center, removed any possibility of a change from residential to commercial use, a change that would only begin in the 1950s. As it was, it took a world war to fill up the buildings that were already there.

# 16

# THE WAR

Almost from the day the Empire State Building opened, the nation seemed to be preparing for war. On May 24, 1931, the army air force sent 672 planes into the air over New York City to simulate an air attack on the city, an event covered by a host of radio announcers for stations WABC and WJZ. The tops of some of the city's best situated buildings were used as observation posts, with the Empire State Building the most favored. Peggy Hull, the first newspaperwoman granted a pass into a battle sector by the U.S. War Department in World War I, and James Wallington covered the air action for the radio from the 102nd floor. The publicists took advantage of the opportunity, reserving the entire eighty-sixth-floor observatory for politicians, dignitaries, military attachés, and the press. Perhaps the most deserving observer was former Brigadier General William (Billy) Mitchell, the great proponent of airpower who had been the head of the army air force before his infamously unjust court-martial, and a man whose name would come crashing into the building's later history.

Chairs were set out, and a buffet lunch was served. The partylike atmosphere was reflected in Lieutenant Governor Herbert H. Lehman's yachting costume—white cap, blue coat, flannel trousers—as if he were there to watch a Harvard-Yale regatta on the Charles. The show began at 2 P.M. with a radio speech from the Washington office of the chief of staff of the United States Army, General Douglas MacArthur. The armada was late in arriving, but there was plenty of banter atop the Empire State Building. Amos & Andy had been invited to entertain.

By the winter of 1939–40, the party was over, and mock attacks had turned into fear of the real thing. By January 1941, the eighty-sixth-floor observatory was one of ten observation posts in the metropolitan area that was used to spot the approach of enemy aircraft. In addition to providing the observatory, Smith provided quarters for the spotters on the eighty-first floor, where they could take coffee breaks and store their belongings. At the outset, the spotters were primarily World War I veterans—mainly American Legionnaires—but as the war progressed, a broader cross section of volunteers came to man the outpost twenty-four hours a day in shifts as long as eight hours. When a plane was spotted, its description and course was immediately called in to Army Interceptor Command.

In November 1941, Douglas Leigh had an appointment with the building management on a matter unrelated to war, but the war would be its undoing. Douglas Leigh had achieved fame in the mid-thirties by turning some walls in the city into flashing, multicolored electric signs—a carnival of animated electric lights—that he aptly dubbed "spectaculars." One of his Times Square productions was a block-long, seven-story-high spectacular for Wrigley's chewing gum that was lit by 29,508 lights and showed a sea of slow-moving, indolent fish. It proved so popular that the police were frequently obliged to encourage the gathering crowds to move along. Douglas Leigh was known to sigh when he thought of what he could do with the Empire State Building. He thought that the building had the potential for being *the* spectacular of all spectaculars in the New York night. His dream was to light it like a cigarette, with ashes at the top and smoke curling up into the heavens, an advertising colossus created by a million white electric bulbs, a few thousand red lights to paint a burning tip against the night sky, and the Lucky Strike name emblazoned in neon on all four sides.

But Leigh was not in the building in 1941 to pitch a simple spectacular. He was there to pitch a package deal he had worked out with Coca-Cola's director of advertising, Price Gilbert, and DeSales Harrison, one of the company's executives. Coke was sponsoring Andre Kostelanetz concerts from Liederkranz Hall on East Fifty-eighth Street, and Leigh thought that a better place for the broadcasts was the top of the Empire

State Building. He figured the building could use the publicity that would come with the performances, as well as the rent Coke would pay for the broadcasting sessions. To sweeten the deal, Coca-Cola had agreed to move its New York offices into the building. Douglas Leigh's special contribution was to erect lights in the form of Coke's distinctively shaped "Mae West" bottle atop the tower, which would change colors to forecast the weather. Leigh had the sketches with him that showed how the lighting would change, and he made an offer to the building of $120,000 a year for the whole package. Management was interested, but while preliminary papers were being drawn up, the U.S. navy was sunk at Pearl Harbor. Leigh's proposal sank with it.

Within ten days of the attack on Pearl Harbor, operating manager Chapin L. Brown appointed five air-raid wardens from the staff. A detailed engineering survey of the building had been made in May that allowed Brown and his staff to select the safest parts of various floors for use as air-raid shelters. Short of evacuation, their conclusion was that the center of the building was the safest. Brown held regular meetings to discuss how to get more than eight thousand people to the safest possible places in the shortest period in the event of an air raid. Every floor in the building was organized, with one person designated as a chief monitor and with assistant monitors for every sixteen persons. Building officials "suggested" that tenants and visitors go to the halls, stairwells, and fire towers that were grouped in the center of the building and stay there. (Brown explained that he used the word *suggested* because he did not think a building could go ordering its tenants around, even in wartime.) At the first sound of an air-raid alarm, visitors to the tower and all tenants above the eightieth floor would be taken by elevator to landings between the eighteenth and thirty-second floors, where they would remain. During an air raid itself, nobody would be allowed to use the elevators. Notice of the safe places had already been distributed to tenants. Venetian blinds had already been installed in all occupied offices to keep light from seeping out. The lights atop the mooring mast had already been extinguished for the duration. And nobody would be allowed in the observatories.

Real estate was beginning to pick up, and to encourage a faster recovery, Mayor Fiorello La Guardia alerted the federal government after a survey of building occupancy in January 1942 that the city offered ideal accommodations at a minimum cost to agencies. Three months later, Smith finally got what he had been waiting for. The regional office of the Office of Price Administration signed a lease on five floors, the forty-second to the forty-sixth, amounting to eighty thousand square feet, with options for several additional floors in case more agencies moved in.

That bit of good news came hard on the heels of having leased five floors to Schenley liquors, whose eight hundred employees made it the largest employer in the building. When the time came to choose a coordinator of civilian defense in May 1942, Smith tapped Schenley, and requested the services of John J. Hennessy, a former deputy chief inspector for the New York Police Department. Hennessy had written the department's *Book of Rules* and its *Manual of Procedure*, and he had been recognized as the most able officer on the force at handling large crowds. He was a natural. He realized that fire alarms, with their volume turned up, could serve as air-raid alarms. Porters' rooms on every floor had to be outfitted with pails of sand and long-handled shovels. Firefighting equipment, which included asbestos suits, had to be laid in. To keep tenants sharp, Hennessy held surprise alarms once a week, and soon the tenants were old hands at putting their papers away, letting down the blinds, and filing to their safety stations in the corridors. The average elapsed time: seven minutes.

Al Smith pointed out that since many of the more experienced employees were away on active duty or in war factories, particular attention had to be paid to instruction in safety precautions for the newer personnel, many of whom were women doing jobs that had formerly been exclusively male, such as operating elevators. His concern was two-pronged, of course—he did not want his employees injured on the job, and a safer working environment meant higher productivity. Chapin L. Brown, the building manager, estimated that about 260 special items of equipment and safety guards had been designed and installed in the building, which had resulted in a low percentage of accidents over the years. Safety goggles were provided for grinding and other work that might be dangerous, safety helmets were supplied for elevator mechanics, nonskid mats appeared in wet weather to prevent falls, and iron treads and guide rails had been placed on the steps of the observation tower. Management also gave out a book of safety rules, and Smith insisted that all employees read and abide by it.

Smith was still called upon to perform his official duties. His daughter said that a seemingly endless stream of national and foreign leaders invariably spent some of their time in the city, and rarely did any of those who headed missions fail to visit the Empire State Building. The "VIPs," as they came to be known during the war, called for special handling, and Smith, who was known at least by reputation to most of them, often found himself in his same old role, serving as a reception committee.

By April 1942, a citywide edict had all buildings blacked out above the fifteenth floor to protect shipping. Coastal glare had been silhouetting surface ships, making them visible to submarines. In addition to the windows in buildings being blacked out, the hours and minutes stopped flashing from atop the Metropolitan Life Tower, the lights in the Con Ed clock were extinguished, and the pencil lights of the Empire State Building were darkened for the duration. Writer William L. Shirer thought that precautions should be taken further. He feared that sunlight reflecting off the metal spires atop the Empire State and Chrysler Buildings made them a readily seen target from the sea and air, and he thought their surfaces should be dulled.

Columnist Dorothy Kilgallen blithely went to the top to see the view in the dimout, which she found "a thrilling—if spooky sight" in September 1942. A month later, columnist L. L. Stevenson was surprised by how much he could see from the tower in a dimout. In fact, he found the night view of the city "as fascinating as it was when all the lights burned brightly. Subdued instead of glaring, illumination seemed to bring out the natural beauty and mystic quality of the metropolis as it lay bathed in the light of the moon and the stars. There were still enough lights to get distances, but they were not so brilliant as to obscure the natural contour of the rivers and the far-flung countryside."

By May 1942, the observatory atop the Woolworth Building was closed because it was too close to the Brooklyn Navy Yard. Sightseers could still visit the observatories atop the RCA and Empire State Buildings, but no cameras or telescopes were allowed. With the aid of a telescope, anyone could record the comings and goings of troopships and great ocean liners. The *Queen Mary*, for instance, could be seen as far as sixty miles away. If a tourist looked down instead of out, he might have noticed a new style of rooftop messages. Reflecting the spirit of the times, the tourist would have read BUY U.S. WAR BONDS.

Servicemen in uniform were admitted free to the observatories on Wednesdays and Sundays, and at half price other days. The public relations department would regularly pluck a lucky serviceman and photograph him seeing the town, going to the top of the Empire State Building, and dining in the Empire State Club as a guest of the directors.

By September 1944, the public affairs department was girding for its 5 millionth visitor to the observatory. Al Smith was in St. Vincent's Hospital and could not attend the ceremony, but Mayor La Guardia stood in and presented a $100 U.S. War Bond to the lucky visitor. The 4 millionth visitor had been a pure setup. That "visitor" had been Jimmy Stewart, whose role in *Mr. Smith Goes to Washington* had just won him the motion picture critics' award for best performance by a screen star in 1939. The

5 millionth visitor was on the up-and-up, and a publicist's dream. He was charming, easygoing, articulate, but there was only one problem: He could not be described as "clean-cut and all-American." He was Sub-Lieutenant John H. Morris of the Fleet Air Arm of the British Royal Naval Volunteer Reserve, a young British flying officer who was training to be a torpedo bomber pilot in the United States, and who planned to return to his study of physics at Oxford University after the war. The downside to the story was that only United States citizens could hold U.S. War Bonds. What saved the day was that he had just married an American, and they were honeymooning in New York. The happy couple went downstairs to the Lawyers Trust Company, where the bank officials made out the bond in his wife's name.

Many offices were open five-and-a-half- or even six-day weeks during the war, and although the firms might have been at half staff on the sixth day of the week, the offices were still open, and filled with workers. Saturday, July 28, 1945, well after VE Day and just a few weeks before VJ Day, seemed a perfectly routine Saturday for the workers in the Empire State Building. They had to be at work when many of their colleagues were taking the day off, but since the weather was terrible, their jealousy quotient was down a notch. But something happened that day that people had often feared might happen, something that would make this less than a routine day.

The pilot of a ten-ton B-25 bomber who was flying contact—he had to keep his bearings visually because of the low ceiling—found himself in the fog. The top of the Empire State Building was the flight controllers' benchmark for visibility, and the pilot had been told to make sure that he could see it while maintaining a minimum altitude of fifteen hundred feet. However, he was in the fog and could not see anything, so he dropped the twin-engine plane below the fog to get his bearings. He would have avoided disaster almost anywhere within the metropolitan area except where he was. He had blundered into Midtown Manhattan and its maze of skyscrapers.

The plane was flying in a southwesterly direction and entered Manhattan's airspace at about Fiftieth Street, which put it on a direct line with the New York Central Building (today's Helmsley Building), which straddles Park Avenue at Forty-sixth Street. At the last moment, the pilot banked away to the west, only to put himself on a collision course with 500 Fifth Avenue at Forty-second Street. Again he banked away, with only seconds to spare. He was half in the clouds, half out of the clouds. Skyscrapers surrounded him on all sides, and just as he successfully cleared one tower, another seemed to appear, then a third, and a fourth. The veteran combat bomber pilot with thirty-four bombing missions to his credit was confused, he was desperate, and he knew that this time he was again flying for his life.

His greatest hurdle lay dead ahead of him. Instead of flak and Messerschmitts to contend with, he had to deal with the hulking mass of a building at twelve o'clock high. The pilot pulled the plane up and managed to climb to 913 feet while twisting away, but neither his responses nor the plane's were fast enough. Pedestrians who witnessed his desperate maneuverings took cover; office workers who could not see what was going on but who could hear the roar of the engines sprang to their windows to see what was the matter. Those who could see ran the other way.

Ten tons of B-25 smashed into the north wall of the seventy-eighth and seventy-ninth floors of the 365,000-ton Empire State Building, the plane's upper two-thirds hitting the seventy-ninth floor, the lower third the seventy-eighth, ripping a gash in the wall that measured eighteen feet wide and twenty feet high. The building shuddered, realigned itself, and settled. Probably instantly, although several witnesses said there seemed to be a moment's interval, came the explosion, and the top of the fog-shrouded Empire State Building was briefly seen in a bright orange glow. High-octane airplane fuel spewed out of the ruptured tanks and sprayed the building. While a sheet of flame dropped down the façade of the building as far as the sixty-fifth floor, torrents of flaming gasoline poured through the hallways of the seventy-eighth and seventy-ninth floors and down the stairways to the seventy-fifth floor, setting fire to everything combustible it encountered. The heat was so intense that partition frames within offices disappeared, and the shattered glass from windows and lamp fixtures melted and fused into stalactites. While the flames were contained between the seventy-fifth and seventy-ninth floors, choking fumes and smoke geysered upward to the eighty-sixth-floor observatory, where, because of the poor visibility, there were only a few sightseers.

The plane's wings were sheared off by the impact, and a propeller lodged in the building's limestone façade. The fuselage and other parts hurtled through the walls and windows. One engine, part of the fuselage, and a landing gear tore through the internal office walls, through two fire walls and across a stairway, through another office wall and out the south wall of the building, with the parts coming to a fiery rest at 10 West Thirty-third Street in the penthouse studio/apartment of sculptor Henry Hering, who was off playing golf in Scarsdale at the time. Metal fragments landed on the eighty-sixth-floor observatory and bits of jagged glass, steel, mortar, bricks, and "pieces" of fire cascaded onto the streets below, startling workers and scattering pedestrians. Some debris landed a block away on Madison Avenue, and one large chunk of the plane traveled as far as Fifth Avenue and Twenty-ninth Street, where it ripped into the façade of a building. The other engine fell into an elevator shaft and landed atop the cab. Piggyback, the engine and elevator dropped from about the thirty-fifth floor to the subbasement.

The crash demonstrated graphically and horribly that the war was not yet over. Stan Lomax, sports director of radio station WOR, had just left Penn Station and was walking up Seventh Avenue. As he was crossing Thirty-fourth Street, the plane hit the building. He immediately went to the nearest pay phone to alert the station that something had just happened—he wasn't quite sure what it was, he just knew it was something big. Some feared that it was a kamikaze attack, or speculated that it was the Japanese balloon said to have been sighted in Michigan, or it was a devilishly fiendish radio-controlled robot bomb similar to Hitler's buzz bombs. Despite the fears voiced or unvoiced, there was little panic. "The comparative order of the whole experience was remarkable," said Maurice Whitebook, the chief rent attorney for the Office of Price Administration. "Maybe the war had something to do with this—all the preparations for an air raid that never came." Workers left their offices and remained in the corridors, as they had been trained, but they felt trapped. There was a continuous crash of debris roaring down the tower elevator shafts, and when the emergency exit doors were opened a crack, workers heard the deafening noise of the debris banging against the walls as it plunged down—enough to warn anyone away.

The official time of the disaster was 9:49 A.M., when police received the first message of alarm. Jack Wernli, the staff photographer whose job was to snap celebrities or just plain folks who visited the observatory, was about to punch in. Wernli was frequently late and regularly getting "hell" from observatory manager Frank Powell, and he was late again. He got off the elevator at the eighty-fifth floor to sneak upstairs to the eighty-sixth to punch his time card surreptitiously. He arrived at the clock, and as he pulled the lever, the airplane hit the building just below him. He thought Frank Powell had rigged a booby trap.

Within eight minutes, four fire alarms had been sounded, bringing twenty-three fire companies and forty-one pieces of equipment, including a gasoline tender to refuel the engine companies. The skills of the city's disaster units were finely honed because of the war, and before the last fireman had jumped from his truck, two of Bellevue's disaster units and two Red Cross canteens were already on the scene. The city's hospital system rushed twelve ambulances, twenty doctors, twenty nurses, and twelve stretcher-bearers. St. Vincent's Hospital dispatched three ambulances, five doctors, four nurses, and one attendant. The police and fire departments set up field headquarters in the Schrafft's on Thirty-fourth Street, and an emergency hospital was established in the lobby of the Empire State Building. The disaster units made their way upstairs as the Red Cross dispensed coffee and doughnuts downstairs.

Mayor La Guardia, who was known for following fires, heard the fourth alarm sound while he was getting out of his radio-equipped limousine at City Hall. He recognized the number of the box as Fifth Avenue and Thirty-fourth Street and told his chauffeur that he'd better go. He thought it might be bad. He sped to the scene, to discover that his hunch was right. This was no ordinary fire—it would rank as the world's highest blaze, twice as high as the fire that had engulfed the scaffold at the Sherry-Netherland Hotel in 1929, and a few hundred feet higher than the fire that had ranked as the city's highest, a fire in the Woolworth Building that also took place in 1929. Although the Woolworth fire was hardly as spectacular as the Sherry-Netherland fire, sightseers were caught on the observation deck, and the height of the fire contributed to its drama. One of the sightseers had feared being "roasted alive," but the building manager said that the fireproof Woolworth Building had presented no real danger to the visitors in the observatory. Fire hose was accessible on all floors, the firemen readily reached it, and the fire was easily contained.

The Empire State Building fire was complicated by the fact that it was an airplane crash to boot. The first time an airplane crashed into a New York building had also taken place in 1929. Thirty-three-year-old Charles I. Reid, a booking agent with the likes of Prince Alexis Obolensky signed up by his lecture bureau, had learned to fly about a year and a half before. He rented a biplane from Roosevelt Field and took one of his lecturers for a joyride. As they were crossing the East River toward Manhattan the plane started to lose altitude. The pilot could not find a safe place to land in Central Park, and told his passenger to parachute. The crippled plane, sputtering and wheezing, crashed into the seventh floor of the south side of the not-yet-finished West Side YMCA on Sixty-fourth Street. In a selfless act, Reid cut the switch of the motor before the crash, which kept the crash from becoming a conflagration. Police Commissioner Grover Whalen urged new methods of dealing with the problems presented by the increase in flying by amateur pilots where there was more opportunity for negligence than with commercial airline pilots, who were tested to a higher standard and whose equipment was better maintained. Whalen found solace in one aspect of the crash—the plane had crashed directly into the Y, avoiding the tremendous loss of life that would have occurred if the plane had careened off. The same was the case with the Empire State Building. The bomber smashed smack dab into the building. But never before had so big a plane crashed into a building so high to start so big a blaze.

Elevator service was out above the sixtieth floor, which did not deter the Little Flower. The mayor walked up from there to witness the scene, which he described as a fiery furnace. The fire commissioner later said proudly that although a main eight-inch standpipe had been broken by falling debris, and firemen had been forced to trudge up the stairs carrying their coiled hoses and portable apparatus from the sixtieth floor in full firefighting regalia while dodging terror-stricken tenants in their flight downstairs, the blaze was nevertheless brought under control in nineteen minutes and was completely extinguished within forty. Where all the trained fire wardens were during all this is one of those unsolved mysteries.

The irony of the crash was its chief victim, the War Relief Services of the National Catholic Welfare Conference, an agency that had been aiding thousands made homeless and destitute by the war.[1] The agency's offices faced north on the seventy-ninth floor, the spot that received the greatest impact. The agency was there because Al Smith had been faithful to two masters—the building and the Church—and he had carried out his responsibility to both. A goal was to fill up the building with tenants. Even if it meant providing the space rent free, the space was not going to waste, and the building showed some life. At the same time, Smith could fulfill philanthropic obligations. He had already provided free office space for the Cardinal's Committee of the Laity, whose goal was to raise money for the archdiocese, and he did the same for the Catholic War Relief Office, for whom he served as treasurer in 1944. The understanding was that if the space on the seventy-ninth floor could be rented, other space in the building would be arranged.

A little more than half of the agency's usual complement of thirty were at their desks that Saturday morning, one of whom was nineteen-year-old Therese Fortier from Queens. She saw a big orange ball of flame, and black smoke come rushing at her. She escaped to a neighboring office in the southwest corner of the building, where she huddled with some colleagues. Although she was not yet officially engaged to her future husband, George, she was wearing a small ruby ring he had given her before going overseas. She was sure that she would not survive, and since she would no longer have any use for her ring, her gold earrings, or her watch, she tossed them out a window in the hope that somebody would find them

[1]The War Relief Services has been known since 1955 as the Catholic Relief Services.

and put them to good use. "It seemed a shame to let them burn up," she said thirty-two years later in an interview with Judy Klemesrud in *The Times*.[2] She had in the meantime married her George—George Willig— and had borne a son named George, the same George Willig of "human fly" fame who scaled the south tower of the World Trade Center in May 1977.

Most of her colleagues were not so lucky. Those who were on a direct line with the crash were either killed outright by the impact or by the explosion, mummified in the positions they had assumed when the crash occurred. Several who were running from the flames were overtaken by them and engulfed. Of the eleven who were killed from the office staff, only one was recognizable, and he had been thrown from his office and had landed on the setback of the seventy-second floor.

Searchers waded ankle-deep in water, often finding it difficult to distinguish between the charred bodies and the smoldering paper and office furniture that littered the floor. The firemen used shovels to sift through the mess, and when they found human remains, they tenderly placed the parts on boards, and then onto desks. There were two sets of shoulders, bloody and crushed, which the city medical examiner theorized were some of the remains of those in the plane—the captain, his engineer, or a navy hitchhiker. The others were blackened trunks and limbs. There was a head that was shrunken by the fire. There was a body, with part of an arm uplifted from the elbow, as if to ward off a blow. Most of the bodies were burned to the point where it was impossible to distinguish between male and female victims until chemical analyses could be made. Relatives of the victims were requested to bring dental records to Bellevue Hospital, but the coroners knew that the search was perfunctory at best. One victim was identified solely by a wristwatch that her father had given her, another by her wedding and engagement rings. "Identified" is a misnomer. The man who identified the woman by her rings was not allowed to view the body, only to verify that the rings had belonged to her.

Stories of heroism and selflessness abounded. Harold Smith, who was working in the War Assets Administration office on the sixty-second floor, knew the sound of revving engines, having served in the army in North Africa. He heard the sound, looked up, saw the plane about two hundred feet away and seemingly coming straight at him, and he ran. From the safety of the south side of the building, he looked up, and saw three women at a window high above him. Smoke was billowing out from behind them. He grabbed whatever first-aid equipment he could find, and started up the stairs, to be turned back at the sixty-fifth floor. He returned to the sixty-

[2]The story was titled "Tall—but True—Tales Run in Her Family."

second floor, looked out the same window again, this time to see only flames where before there had been the three women. Undeterred this time, he raced to the seventy-ninth floor, to encounter Lt. Edward Buchanan, of the New York fire department, and two firemen. Smith identified the office where he thought the three women were trapped. The wall was hot, the door hotter. The firemen doused both the door and Smith, knocked down the door, poured water on the fire, and Smith pulled two women to safety. The heat from the fire had been so intense that the nylon blouse of one of the women had melted onto her chest.

Another story, and another classic of heroism and humility, likewise stands out. A coast guard hospital apprentice saw the crash and rushed into the Walgreen Drug Store that was in the Thirty-third Street side of the Empire State Building, where he summarily ordered first-aid kits. Without hesitation, and with no financial transaction, the clerk handed over two hypodermic needles, eight grams of morphine, ten tubes of burn ointment, bandages, and alcohol, and the apprentice rushed out. The elevator cable in shaft six had snapped, causing the cab, with two female elevator operators aboard, to land in the subbasement. The hospital apprentice crawled into the cab to discover that the two women, although badly injured, were alive. And, as fate would have it, one had a fast quip. "Thank heaven," said she, "the navy's here." After applying first aid and carrying out the injured women, the hospital apprentice went up to the seventy-eighth and seventy-ninth floors, where he applied first aid to victims who were suffering from burn and shock. Then, like the Lone Ranger, he walked off without a word, with people wondering who that uniformed man was.[3]

By early afternoon, an official army car arrived on the scene. Out of the chauffeured car stepped a brigadier general whose job was public affairs and whose charge was damage control. He walked over to a clutch of reporters milling about on Thirty-fourth Street and said, "There's no story here, boys," whereupon, and without another word, he turned around, walked back to the curb, got back in his car, and was driven away. He was wrong on at least one count—not all the reporters were "boys." Betsy Luce wrote the lead story for the *New York Post* that Saturday afternoon, and the following Monday the *Post* ran a follow-up story by Barbara Klaw.[4]

Ernie Sisto, a photographer for *The New York Times*, managed to get his story too. He and a *Times* colleague, Bill Eckenberg, learned the news

---

[3] He was later identified as Donald Molony, who was seventeen at the time.
[4] Fifty years later, Barbara Klaw, still shudders when she describes the scene.

of the crash from a copyboy. They grabbed their 4 x 5 Speed Graphic cameras and arrived at the scene by the fastest means they could muster—they took the IRT Subway the one stop from Forty-second Street to Thirty-fourth Street. The elevators that were still in operation had been commandeered by the fire department, but Sisto managed to ride to the sixtieth floor. He walked the remaining nineteen floors to the seventy-ninth, where he surveyed the damage. "If he could get out on the parapet just above," related John Faber, the historian for the National Press Photographers Association, "he'd get a picture that would tell the whole story. He took two news photographers aside and explained his plan. 'All you've got to do is hold on to my legs while I get far enough to shoot back and down the building.' . . . He put a wide angle lens on his camera and climbed up on the ledge. The odor of burnt wood and flesh drifted up. With the photographers holding his legs, he inched out to arm's length. He made his shot. The men pulled him in. . . . After recording the damage inside, he returned to the Times Building."[5]

Hundreds of people, concerned for their loved ones, arrived at the scene, while thousands of the mildly curious gathered to gape. They could not see much at first because of the fog, and nobody could get very close because the police had thrown a cordon around the surrounding streets, a precaution well taken, since debris continued to fall throughout the day. Emergency vehicles still had to get through and run the gauntlet, however, and one suffered as a result—a large piece of debris crashed down and landed on a hearse of the Mortuary Division of the Department of Hospitals as it backed up to a doorway to begin carrying away the dead.

The building's architects, contractor, and elevator and steel engineers all reported the same news Monday morning: Despite massive holes in the northern and southern walls, despite both a supporting steel post and beam that were rendered structurally useless by the force of the impact (the beam was bent eighteen inches upward), and despite two floors that were totally destroyed by fire, there was no structural damage to the building as a result of the crash. "There must be many tenants of the Empire State Building," wrote Frances G. Guilford, who was at work on the thirty-fourth floor at the time of the crash, "who, like us, wish to pay tribute to the engineering perfection which enabled this magnificent building to withstand the assault of the bomber. . . . The grand building stood staunch and firm. This almost human steadfastness on the part of the structure itself was further impressed on me when later I returned to my

[5]The dramatic photograph (reprinted in the photo section) carried Ernie Sisto's credit line, an honor accorded only rarely by the editors.

office. There was the same stillness of any Saturday afternoon . . . no hint of the chaos not so many floors above and of the wreckage of the two elevators in the basement below." The building had been designed with redundancy, so there was no progressive collapse, no chain reaction. It was designed to be resilient, able to compensate for the structural loss it suffered, by redistributing its weight. The damage to the building was estimated at $500,000.

The day after the accident, a crew rigged a scaffolding below the stricken floors on the north and south sides of the building to ward off any more falling fragments, and a piece of green latticed canvas was drawn across the holes in the building's flank. Except for the observatories and the floors that had been damaged by fire, the building was officially reopened on Monday, and business was back to normal. Sort of. New Yorkers, who are ordinarily so blasé about their skyscrapers, took to their roofs to see the damage, and pedestrians actually looked up whenever there was a view of the building. Several enterprising entrepreneurs set up "shop" in front of Stern's Department Store on the north side of Forty-second Street between Fifth and Sixth Avenues, where they sold telescopic views of the damage from their vantage point. Ten cents a look.

The army estimated that claims totaling perhaps $1 million worth of property would be filed, and by July 31, sixty-six claimants had come forward. McCreery's Department Store, which was across the street from the Empire State Building, filed a claim for seven broken windows; the navy filed a claim for damage to a station wagon; and the sculptor Henry Hering filed a claim, but he could not yet estimate his property damage. He had lost almost his life's work, including the twenty-two-foot-high model of *Pro Patria*, which had been used to cast the largest bronze statue of its kind in the country when it was installed in Indiana's War Memorial in 1930 as part of Indianapolis's new Civic Center.[6] Harold Smith was not forgotten. Lieutenant Buchanan wrote a letter saying that Smith deserved to be reimbursed $87 for damage to his suit, shoes, and watch.

The final death toll was fourteen—the three occupants of the plane, and eleven civilians. About twenty-five more were injured. Everyone agreed that it could have been a lot worse. Mayor La Guardia, for one, pointed out that if the plane had hit at an angle and careened off from the height, bits and pieces would have rained down over a broad area of Midtown, and hundreds of people might have been killed. Miraculously, nobody on any of the surrounding streets or in any neighboring buildings

---

[6]When Hering viewed the still-smoldering remains of his studio, his only comment was "Holy smokes."

was hit by debris. It was early enough on a Saturday morning so that shoppers were not yet mobbing the streets, and most of the office workers who had to be at work had already arrived. The seventy-eighth floor of the Empire State Building was vacant at the time and being used as a storage area for building supplies. The staff of NBC's television laboratory on the eighty-fifth floor had not yet arrived, and the intervening floors were unoccupied. There were only about fifty sightseers on the eighty-sixth-floor observatory, and only two on the upper observatory on the 102nd floor. The building usually had more than ten thousand tenants on an average business day, and about the same number of transients. At the time of the crash, there were fewer than fifteen hundred people in the entire building.

A factor that minimized the damage to the Empire State Building was the size of the plane. It was a B-25, a medium bomber, the same type that Captain Jimmy Doolittle had flown from the aircraft carrier *Hornet* in 1942 for the first allied bombing raid on Tokyo. The plane was nicknamed the Mitchell Bomber in vindication of Colonel Billy Mitchell's belief in the superiority of airpower, the same Billy Mitchell who had watched the war games from the eighty-sixth floor in 1931. If the plane had been bigger—say, the B-17 that the pilot had flown in Europe, or a B-29—the results would have been far worse.

The pilot was Lieutenant Colonel William F. Smith, Jr., a West Point graduate who had served eighteen months in the European theater. Smith had 1,254 hours' flying time, he had piloted Flying Fortresses on thirty-six missions for the Eighth Air Force, and had been decorated with the Distinguished Flying Cross with one cluster, the Air Medal with three clusters and five battle stars, and the Croix de Guerre. There was only one problem.

Smith had never flown a B-25 until the Thursday before the accident, when he was "transitioned," a military term used to describe an already experienced pilot's initiation to a new plane. Smith was expected to be redeployed to the Pacific, where the war still raged, and the cross-country flight between Sioux Falls, South Dakota, and Newark, New Jersey, was designed as a navigation training flight, which incidentally acquainted him with B-25s, and kept his flight pay intact. The flight between Sioux Falls and Newark had a refueling stop in Cleveland. It was on the leg from Cleveland to Newark that Smith copiloted the B-25 under the tutelage of Smith's commanding officer, Colonel Harris K. Rogner, commanding officer of the 457th Bombardment Group.

With what Rogner described to the board of inquiry as a voice order, and with no official papers, Smith then made his first solo flight from Newark to the Bedford Air Force Base, about twenty miles west of Boston, where he spent Thursday and Friday nights with his wife. On Saturday morning at 8:55 he left Bedford with his technical sergeant and a navy hitchhiker to rejoin his crew at Newark for the final leg of his journey back to Sioux City.

Smith knew the weather was bad, and he told his wife that flying conditions would be poor. He requested clearance, flying instrument control at one thousand feet to Newark, but Boston Airway Traffic Control would not approve the flight for less than four thousand feet. Bedford Air Force Base refused permission to fly contact—navigating by visual observation—to Newark, but gave him clearance to fly contact to La Guardia Airport, which served as the major civilian airport for the New York area, and which, like Newark, had a military base attached to it. Smith signed a form saying that he was "familiar with the danger areas" on his line of flight, and that he had official business with the 1338th Base unit at La Guardia.

Smith had no official business at La Guardia, but he figured that if he could reach La Guardia, his ingenuity would somehow get him to Newark. He was so eager to get back to Newark that, in his haste, he took off with the keys to the family car. By the time his wife discovered them gone, Smith had either flown beyond radio contact or he simply chose to ignore the call from the Bedford control tower.

Having been cleared for La Guardia, he knew that Newark was closed to him as a destination. But he had to get there. If he called Newark himself he would have to identify himself, and he would surely be told that he was not following his flight plan. He figured he'd let La Guardia call Newark and let him off the hook. At about 9:40 A.M., Smith made radio contact with the tower at La Guardia Air Field.

Although he had claimed official business at La Guardia and had been cleared by Bedford for La Guardia, Smith now told the La Guardia tower that he had official business at Newark and would appreciate as little delay as possible in being cleared. He identified his position as fifteen miles south of the field and requested the weather at Newark, which made no sense to the tower, since Smith's coordinates put him almost directly above Newark.

La Guardia Tower told Smith that as far as they knew, Newark was fogged in, but they would check further, and he should report back. Within about two minutes, the B-25 showed up at La Guardia. By then, the weather at Newark had been confirmed—the altitude was six hundred feet. In the meantime, La Guardia Tower had reported Smith's presence to the New York Airway Traffic Control Center, which found no flight plan for Smith. To compound Smith's problem, he had entered La Guardia's traffic pattern unannounced.

The controllers were furious. They wanted Smith to bring the B-25 into La Guardia, and they told him to fly in a holding pattern while awaiting further instructions. Despite Smith's plane having been retrofitted for noncombat use, in the eyes of the tower it was still a bomber, and the controllers wanted the Army Advisory Flight Control to grant authority for the civilian airport to bring in the plane.

Accounts contradict each other about what precisely happened next, but it seems the army told the tower that its information was wrong, that Newark had a thousand-foot ceiling with visibility of two and a quarter miles. Although the board of inquiry report claimed that the Army Flight Service Center did not change Smith's flight plan from La Guardia to Newark, nor that it had given clearance, the tower claimed that the army said the decision to fly on to Newark was the pilot's, and told Smith so. La Guardia Tower advised him to reconsider, and although the army required its pilots to observe civilian rules and regulations, the custom was to grant the military considerable latitude. Smith opted for Newark. From the vantage point of the tower, the top of the Empire State Building was not visible. The tower told Smith if he could not maintain contact flying operation, with three miles visibility at a minimum of fifteen hundred feet—which meant that he had to be able to see the top of the Empire State Building—he had to return to La Guardia. The tower gave Smith a tentative okay. "Roger," came Smith's response.

Smith, who had been circling the field, turned his plane south and headed for Newark, about fifteen miles southwest of La Guardia. He lost visibility in the heavy fog, and dipped below the overcast. A theory is that flying west he mistook the East River for the Hudson River. Thinking that Manhattan was behind him to the east, and that to the south were Jersey City, Newark Bay, and the safety of the airport, he turned left and lowered his wheels in anticipation of landing. Instead of the safety of the Jersey swamps under him, the towers of Manhattan lay in wait ahead of him.

Few witnesses thought that pilot error was to blame—the general assumption was that the plane had suffered a malfunction, that Smith was experiencing engine trouble or rudder problems. All operations, however, were "go," as evidenced by the tight control he had over the plane and by the fact that the plane was climbing when it hit. The B-25's engines were operating normally, and the roar of its engines was recorded on a dictating machine. Mr. Jagger, an employee of the American Society of Civil Engineers, whose office was on the fifteenth floor of 33 West Thirty-ninth Street, had paused in his dictation when the plane roared over. When he returned to dictating, he noticed that he had failed to turn off the dictating machine. He ran the record back to pick up where he had left off, and realized that the machine had recorded the sounds of the plane's engines. *The New Yorker* reported that Jagger spent two days trying to get through to the Army Board of Inquiry, but as soon as he did there were six members of the board on their way over to listen to the record.

Just as the New York City Police Department closes ranks to present a blue wall to protect its own, so the army closes ranks to present a khaki wall. The three-officer board investigating the crash heard sixty witnesses. Their conclusion was that Smith showed misjudgment, but that the culprits were the officials at La Guardia Field, who should never have allowed him to proceed to Newark. The army needed a scapegoat, and the civilians at La Guardia were an easy target. In the spirit of good-old-boyishness, the army chose to ignore that Smith had lied to Bedford, that he had continued to lie to La Guardia, and that it was the army that had told La Guardia that the final decision was the pilot's.

Whether Smith had indeed been given his commanding officer's blessing to fly to Bedford in the form of a verbal order, which Rogner told the board of inquiry was the case, or whether Smith had acted unilaterally and was officially AWOL, which would explain his actions, was a subject that was never reported. In cases where a soldier dies, superiors will frequently be compassionate, if only to preserve the widow's benefits. Finding Smith guilty of any further malfeasance might also have opened the floodgates of litigiousness and insurance claims. It certainly would have brought more bad press, and the army would have found worse mud on its face. Smith had already paid the ultimate penalty, and he would have made a poor scapegoat and a worse example. Misjudgment on behalf of Smith simply seemed easier. Anyway, there was a war on.

Elmer Haslett, the city's director of airports, was up in arms over the report that mildly chastised Smith's behavior yet rebuked La Guardia personnel. And Mayor La Guardia, who had been a pilot in World War I and whose advocacy of civilian aviation had led to the city's major airport being named for him, was enraged by what he considered military high jinks over the city. An army Flying Fortress had buzzed Yankee Stadium at 275 feet during a World Series game in 1943, and he had protested then. And here he was protesting again. "I told them not to fly over the city," he complained to the commissioner of Marine and Aviation at the scene of the accident, while he gestured angrily with his fist. "If the pilot had been up where he belonged, there would have been no problem."[7]

Within a month of the accident, the army banned its planes from flying over the city except under certain unspecified conditions, but there was general agreement that further civil-aviation legislation was required. The practice for instrument flying over Manhattan, according to the Civil Aeronautics Administration, was to bring in airliners at an altitude of twenty-five hundred feet, with a minimum of one thousand feet from the nearest obstruction both vertically and horizontally, while the practice among noncommercial pilots was simply to keep to a minimum altitude of one thousand feet. Commercial pilots generally avoided anywhere between the Battery and Fifty-ninth Street even in good weather, and as a rule they tried to avoid flying over Manhattan south of 110th Street. Those heading south from La Guardia Airfield first crossed the upper reaches of Manhattan and continued northwest until they were over the Jersey Meadows before turning south; coming in from the south, the course lay to the west of Coney Island and in over Brooklyn and Queens.

Fire Commissioner Patrick Walsh had urged federal agencies to agree on a total ban on all air travel over congested sections of the city. Although the Civil Aeronautics Administration, the predecessor of the Federal Aviation Administration, would not go that far, three months after the crash, the CAA set an altitude of twenty-five hundred feet as the minimum to be maintained at all times by private and commercial pilots flying over Midtown and Lower Manhattan,[8] regardless of the flying conditions.

But pilot error is pilot error. The May after the crash, as Yogi Berra might have said, it was a case of déjà vu all over again. Again there was a heavy overcast, again a military plane was en route to Newark, and again the pilot, this time flying a coast guard twin-engine C-45, was groping his way through the soup. The pilot had opened a flying manual to the

---

[7]There is a particular irony to the crash. Fifteen years before, at a Sons of the Revolution dinner at the Waldorf-Astoria, on the very site of the Empire State Building, Captain E. S. Land, U.S.N., declared that among the chief problems of aviation were the need of overcoming fog, better control of planes at low speed, and a means of determining the height above ground when "flying blind."

[8]Lower Manhattan was defined as going as far south as Governor's Island and the Statue of Liberty.

page that gave instructions for landing at Newark in fog. He wasn't on course for Newark; he was headed straight for the fifty-eighth floor of the Bank of Manhattan Building at 40 Wall Street. The crash created a ten-by-twenty-foot hole in the north wall of the building, killing the pilot and four others.

# 17

# SINCE THE WAR

I am not just a landmark. I am not
just a relic of the past. I am not just
an exercise in nostalgia. No. I am still
at the center of New York.

—Louis Phillips, a letter on the Empire
State Building to *The New York Times*,
December 15, 1977

By the time the war was over, rent-
ing manager H. Hamilton Weber sensed that the Empire State Building
was on its economic feet in ways that were not reflected on the books.
Prospective tenants had started asking whether he was interested in a
Cadillac, or if his wife wanted a new fur coat. In 1944, the building was
85 percent rented. By 1946, the building was home to about five hundred
organizations and about fifteen thousand office workers—two thousand
of them in twenty-one federal agencies—and it was said to be fully tenanted. By 1950, *Time* magazine said the building was "jammed to the
rafters." It was grossing $10 million a year, and netting close to half that,
which made it one of the world's most profitable buildings. It was fulfilling its destiny.

There had been changes. Al Smith died in the fall of 1944. From his
thirty-second-floor window he had continued to look down on the city he
loved, the city of which he felt such an inalienable part. He was still called
upon to front for the building and to fulfill countless charity functions,
but he had begun to perform them perfunctorily. Smith was no longer a
political force. He had quarreled with his party, he had opposed its can-

didates for national office, and the doors to the corridors of political power had swung shut in his face.

Lieutenant General Hugh A. Drum, a long-term friend of Smith, was the only person considered for Smith's position, according to Raskob. Drum had been Pershing's chief of staff in World War I, deputy chief of staff under MacArthur between the wars, and the head of New York State's national guard.[1] "The army is a business too," he said in response to his inexperience in building management. "The only difference is that instead of trying to make a dollar, you try to run your organization efficiently and, in peacetime, at the least possible expense." Although Drum did not have the panache of Smith, he had an occasional sense of drama. When he commanded the First American Army at the start of World War II, Drum realized that he had to show his superiors how poorly equipped the army was. He trained his soldiers with broomsticks to simulate guns, and had them driving trucks to simulate tanks.

Drum was given his first crack at real estate glory in 1946, when the United Nations Committee for New York, headed by Grover Whalen, was seeking temporary offices for the United Nations until its headquarters were built.[2] Some members of the United Nations secretariat general voiced an interest in the Empire State for its large size and central location, but the building was chockablock with tenants. What Whalen could not accomplish by himself was achieved by presidential directive. Truman ordered government agencies to lend all possible help to the UN. Quicker than you can say "Shazam!" the War Assets Administration vacated about sixty-three thousand square feet on the sixty-first through sixty-third floors, and about seventeen foreign nations moved in their offices.

A phenomenon unrelated to the coming of UN tenants was a rash of suicide attempts in 1947. Between 1931 and 1947, nine people had jumped from the tower, and six from offices on various floors. Between May and July 1947, there were two suicides from the tower. Between October 20 and November 9, there were five attempts. The eighty-sixth-floor observatory had few physical restraints. The parapet wall was about four feet, six inches high, except where ornamentation added another foot or so. By December 1947, management had installed a seven-foot-high stainless steel fence laced by diamond-shaped mesh that allowed people to

---

[1]Camp Drum in upstate New York was named for him.

[2]The Whitelaw Reid home at 451 Madison Avenue, which is also known as the Villard mansion and is now part of the Palace Hotel, was planned to be used temporarily for the Security Council, and the now-demolished Rockefeller Center (Roxy) Theater was considered for the General Assembly.

stick their heads through but not enough room to squeeze their bodies through. The fence was topped with sickles curving inward to thwart climbing up and over.

Jumping to one's death was not the goal of everyone who wanted to jump from the top. The summer before the protective fence was installed, three young paratroopers showed up on the eighty-sixth floor in full uniform. Five hundred dollars was riding on whether the one toting a parachute pack had the gumption to jump. Soon, he and his pals picked up an escort. A guard was on to them by their antic behavior—one of the soldiers kept waving the five $100 bills—and the guard let the soldiers know that he was not about to stop tailing them until they called off the bet.

For the Christmas season, 1947, the building installed what was billed as the loudest carillon in the world. It was not a true carillon at all, but a machine invented and manufactured by George J. Schulmerich. The "bells" were actually bell-metal tone rods struck by hammers tuned to approximate the sound of carillon bells, which gave forth their sound through "stentors" on the eighty-ninth floor.[3] Reception was better at a distance from the building, which explained why the sound was heard as far as sixteen miles away at Coney Island, but poorly, if at all, in Times Square, less than a mile away. Despite the admitted need for adjustments, when the first of two daily performances took place at noon on December 19, 1947, mystified pedestrians in Midtown stopped and tried to locate the source of the national anthem and twenty minutes' worth of hymns and carols they were hearing.

One of the building's improvements begun after the war deserved encomiums from the planning community. The Department of Traffic needed help in relieving traffic congestion, and management was among the first to take action. It was hardly the grand scheme of an underground truck delivery system that Floyd de L. Brown had conceived for the building or that Rockefeller Center introduced, but it would approximate the scale of off-street deliveries that Lawrence Veiller had advocated in the 1920s. There was already a truck-loading facility on Thirty-third Street, but it had proved inadequate—trucks stacked up and contributed to the already congested streets. In 1948, General Drum announced a new off-street loading platform and trucking facility on a plot adjoining the building on Thirty-third Street that would triple the building's facilities. Management had already purchased the property from the Astor estate in 1929, but the project did not come cheap. The demolition of the six-story loft building that occupied the site had to

---

[3]The stentors were no doubt named for Stentor, the loud-voiced herald in *The Iliad*.

be underwritten; the loss of revenue generated by the building, which was assessed at $80,000, had to be absorbed; and the $50,000 construction cost had to be paid.

The new loading bays were not an entirely selfless act to reduce the city's traffic. The building benefited by increased tenant satisfaction, and the improvement itself could be publicized as part of the building's $1.25 million modernization program in general, which included air-conditioning to the forty-second floor by 1951.

The loading dock and air-conditioning would hardly be noticed by the average passing pedestrian, but the likelihood of missing management's next plan was pretty slim. Management wanted a taller television antenna so that more stations could use the building and more revenue could be generated, and on the horizon was the most visible alteration to the Empire State since it opened—a 222-foot-high television antenna atop the building, which would take the height of the structure to 1,472 feet above the street, 1,522 feet above sea level. It was not just the best possible site in New York for television transmission. It was, said engineers, the best location in the world.

NBC-TV had sewn up exclusive rights to transmit programs from atop the building in 1931. By the late 1940s, the station then called WNBT was making regular broadcasts, including the popular children's show *Howdy Doody*, whose "peanut gallery" entered the nation's lexicon. Unfortunately, NBC's transmitters, limited by the Federal Communications Commission to a mere 5,000 watts, provided snowy pictures to New Jersey. E. Fredy Warns, a transmitter engineer who worked on the eighty-fifth floor for NBC at the time, says that when *Howdy Doody* came on, he and his colleagues from New Jersey "cranked the emissions up to the maximum the transmitters could handle" so that kids in the western suburbs would not miss their favorite show.

Business was booming for television in general, but, even with the FCC's restrictions on WNBT's power, no other TV station could hope to compete successfully while transmitting signals from lesser buildings. WJZ-TV, owned by the American Broadcasting Company, transmitted from the top of the Hotel Pierre; the city-owned WNYC-TV broadcast its UHF signals from the top of the Municipal Building; WPIX, the station of the Daily News ("The Picture Newspaper," hence PIX) broadcast from the top of the Daily News Building. Their signals struck other buildings, bounced around, and created ghosts. Transmission from atop the Empire State would exorcise the ghosts, while at the same time allowing individual receiving antennas in homes to be directed toward just one transmission point instead of several.

NBC decided to forgo its exclusive rights to the Empire State Building for the benefit of the television industry, and agreed to allow other television and radio stations use of the building as a common transmission point on a share-the-cost basis. The building underwrote the cost of the antenna's design and construction, because it stood to profit from the ensuing rentals. The upper observation deck was closed for the duration, a temporary antenna was installed, and NBC's existing four-and-a-half-ton, sixty-two-foot tower was removed. The usual procedure would have been to erect a scaffolding around the antenna, disassemble the tower piece by piece from the top down, and lower each section individually. Management asked Andrew J. Eken to be the contractor for the job.[4] Eken said that dismantling the old antenna in the traditional method was too hazardous and time consuming. He decided to turn the usual way of doing things on its head, and he devised a plan that was almost the reverse of the construction of the Chrysler Building's tower. Just as Van Alen had raised his tower in sections from within the building, Eken lowered the antenna into the building, where he could disassemble sections as they descended.

The building's frame had been designed to withstand the pull of a dirigible, so Eken reasoned that it could readily absorb a sixty-ton addition that would be little more than dead weight. To make the new TV tower structurally sound, however, it should be an actual part of the building's structural frame, an extension of the building itself. Erecting a television tower from a base measuring seven feet square, or an area about the size of a pitcher's mound, and having it rise through a hole in the top of a building 1,250 feet up in the air, posed other problems. "We'll lug the steel up from the street in an elevator open at the top," said Eken. "That'll be slow, but better than taking the chance of dropping a steel girder a thousand feet into Thirty-fourth Street." The tower was made in sections that were assembled and disassembled at the steelworks. The holes were already reamed when the steel arrived at the site, and it was simply a matter of setting the steel in place, lining up the holes, and hoping the members were set plumb. Workers from the International Association of Bridge, Structural and Ornamental Ironworkers were accustomed to working in high places, but nobody had ever worked as high before, where the winds would "rattle your slats," said Eken. "We thought of using a protective scaffolding, but the steel-erection people just laughed." The

---

[4] Both Starrett brothers were already dead. Colonel William Starrett suffered a massive stroke and died a year after the building was finished. Paul Starrett had a nervous breakdown, after which he retired. The building in all likelihood killed them both.

workers wore safety lines that encircled their waists. "If a man gets blown off one of the highest beams a man ever walked," said Eken, "he'll fetch up with a jerk but he won't get hurt." As the tower grew taller, working space diminished to the point where delivering rivets to the gunmen became almost impossible. Eken solved the problem by heating the rivets at the building's top level and shooting them skyward through a pneumatic tube to arrive at the top red-hot.

A variation on the traditional ground-breaking ceremony took place in July 1950. A shaky, narrow scaffolding was built jutting out from the top of the building's tower for the ceremonial driving of a 14-carat gold-plated rivet. Mayor William O'Dwyer, John J. Raskob, David Sarnoff of the Radio Corporation of America, Grover Whalen, General Drum, and other dignitaries climbed to the top to peer out over the fifty-two-mile radius that the new television tower would serve, where 10 percent of the national television audience lived. The Police Department Band serenaded from the eighty-sixth floor with "The Sidewalks of New York" and the national anthem, while flags and bunting added a festive air to the "Foundation Riveting Ceremony." Mayor O'Dwyer wore a safety helmet and held a compressed-air gun against the gold-plated rivet while he posed for photographers. Fortunately, he did not shoot. A riveting gun operated by an inexperienced hand could very well have knocked the mayor and all his friends off the building, said a steelworker for the American Bridge Company. Two hundred balloons, ten of which carried lifetime passes to the Empire State observatories and to the city's television studios, were scheduled to be released, but the helium in them expanded in the noonday sun and most of the balloons burst before they could be sent off. In the meantime, the gold-plated rivet that was to have been presented to the mayor disappeared. A consolation-prize rivet went to Hizzoner, along with a framed drawing of the tower as it would finally appear.

With the antenna up and operating in 1951, five stations started paying $70,000 each per annum for the use of the tower, in addition to $7 per square foot for transmitter floor space, realizing about $500,000 a year for the building. By the mid-1950s, New York's eight television stations—WCBS (2), WNBC (4), WNEW (5), WABC (7), WOR (9), WPIX (11), WNDT (13), and WNYC (31)—transmitted from the Empire State, which had become the television capital of the world.

Much to H. Hamilton Weber's delight, one of the building's largest tenants had made major improvements, which indicated they intended to stay a while. Soon after the war, Schenley imported three rooms from Europe to house the firm's dining rooms on the thirty-seventh floor. One room was from the 335-year-old Rugeley Manor in Stafford, England (it came with the room's original green mullioned windows threaded with lead); the second was a Georgian room made for London's Guildhall in 1730; the third was a chamber from a château near Dax in Gascony. Each room had its own fireplace, which did not work except, as *Times* reporter Meyer Berger said, "with electric trickery." The hand-pegged chairs, tables, and sideboards that had stood in the chambers long ago, on the other hand, were used daily at company luncheons.

Almost six years to the day after Smith's death, in October 1950, Raskob died. He had lived long enough to have his confidence vindicated in the nation's growth and the potential of the Empire State Building, which had become one of the most profitable single-building operations in the world. Raskob had already provided his children with individual trust funds. The bulk of his remaining estate went to the Raskob Foundation for Catholic Activities, Inc., which had been chartered in Delaware in 1945 and had offices in Wilmington and the Empire State Building. Two of Raskob's sons were appointed to the Empire State board, but theirs was not to be the pride of wearing the mantle, of continuing the tradition. Theirs was to sell, and it did not take long. Their father had already held preliminary negotiations with Chicago's Colonel Henry Crown, but Crown felt that the Empire State Building was too rich for his blood, too much to take on individually, and he bowed out. By the end of May 1951, the blandly named Realty Associates Securities Corporation had made a $50 million offer.

The buyers of the Empire State Building in 1951 were all out-of-towners. Two of the buyers, Roger L. Stevens and Alfred R. Glancy, Jr., were from Detroit. The third, Ben Tobin, was from Hollywood, Florida. Glancy, forty-three, the son of the former head of the Pontiac Division of General Motors, was a vice president of the National Bank of Detroit. Tobin owned the Hollywood Beach Hotel and the eleven-hundred-room Hollenden Hotel in Cleveland, and served as the president of the Bank of Hollywood. Roger L. Stevens, only forty-one, was embarked on a second career as a Broadway producer, with *Peter Pan* already under his belt. A director of the American National Theatre Assembly, and a member of the Playwrights Company, he would go on to be a major force in arts management and to head the Kennedy Center in Washington. Two years before the Empire State deal, the three men had acquired Realty Associates, which brought them the Brooklyn Paramount Theater, the Printing Crafts Building, and a substantial interest in the Taft Hotel.

The closing took place in December 1951, in the boardroom of the Bankers Trust Company offices at 16 Wall Street. It had been preceded by an all-day rehearsal the day before to check and seal the hundreds of documents required to consummate the transaction. A second closing at the Empire State Building that had all the hallmarks of a Hollywood first night was staged for the benefit of the press. The checks were already safely deposited in vaults in the Wall Street offices of Bankers Trust, but for the public record Stevens handed a token check to representatives of Raskob's heirs. Flashbulbs popped, television cameras whirred, and the principals—clutching little models of the building—posed again and again.

By then the total purchase price had swollen by a million dollars to $51 million, the additional $1 million charged up to greater commissions and fees than had been bargained for. More than fifty lawyers and financial experts were brought in, and all got their fees. Four title companies joined in insuring the title to spread the risk, and each got its fee. The lion's share of the commission—a cool million—went to the brokerage firm of Charles F. Noyes Company. The firm got half, and vice president George A. Hammer, who had set the gears in motion and had made the deal, personally received the other half, which was amortized over ten years for tax purposes. An extra plum for Hammer and Noyes came in the form of a ten-year management-consultant contract that stood to bring in another million.

Many brokers worked all their lives for less money than Hammer received for negotiating this single change of ownership, a deal that had conveniently dropped in his lap. He had been asked to appraise the building, which he confessed made him privy to information before an offering of the sale was made. Hammer was the only one outside of the owners who knew that Raskob had advised his executors to dispose of the structure as soon as an offer of $50 million had been made. Hammer also knew of the television transmission deal that he estimated would easily grow to $600,000 annually. "All I had to do was find a buyer willing to pay $50 million and accomplish that before the 'cat was out of the bag.' This was easier than perhaps you would imagine," said Hammer. In a matter of weeks, he had obtained an exclusive option for Realty Associates. Within two months a contract was executed.

Realty Associates did not enter into the deal alone. They made an equity investment of $13.5 million, but the Prudential Life Insurance Company bought the land for $17 million, which would provide handsome returns from a long-term ground lease of $1.02 million yearly, and the insurance company put up most of the balance with a $15.5 million mortgage. The Raskob estate stayed in to the tune of about $4 million. Of the old guard, only Mary Carr and H. Hamilton Weber remained on active duty.

In 1951, the city's assessment on the building was a paltry $34.8 million, but with all the publicity surrounding the $51 million sale price, the city took a second look at its assessment, which shot up to $45 million. Not surprisingly, the owners went to court. In 1954 they argued that even the 1951 assessment of $34.8 million had been too high. They thought that $27 million was more like it. As their star witness, the owners trotted out George A. Hammer, who was in the peculiar position of trying to convince a judge that property he had said was worth one price for sales purposes was worth considerably less for tax purposes. The owners conceded that the building was producing substantial income, but they contended that the revenue-producing and very lucrative observatories and television tower should be classified as "specialties" that were operated as separate businesses. An appraiser for the city disputed the owners' claim, calculating the gross income at $11.3 million, the net at $6.8 million. With new leases at higher rates, the appraiser forecast an even greater earning capacity for the immediate future. The assessment stood.

Despite the profitability of the building, the Stevens group was in over its head. Clancey and Tobin sold out to Chicago's Colonel Henry Crown. Stevens, however, did not sell to Crown immediately. According to Peter L. Malkin, the building's managing partner in the mid-1990s, first offered to sell the building to Lawrence A. Wien, who analyzed the building and made an offer. Stevens did not take the offer, according to Malkin. Instead, Stevens took the price that Wien had concluded was appropriate, and without word of appreciation, Stevens used Wien's figures as a basis for an offering to Crown, who bought out Stevens's interest at the rate of Wien's offering price.

In October 1954, Crown became the second person to own the building personally. He purchased the building for $49.5 million, which on paper looked like a loss for the sellers, but which was viewed as a gain because of operating profit and depreciation. According to real estate writer Richard J. Anderson, real estate operators benefited from federal tax laws that permitted substantial depreciation deductions on improved real property. And under accelerated methods of depreciation first allowed in 1954, realtors could take the highest possible write-offs in the early years of ownership.

Henry Crown was the chief executive, and, with his family, virtually the sole owner of the Material Service Corporation, a company valued in 1955 at $80 million. Few buildings in Greater Chicago had gone up between 1930 and 1955 without Crown building materials going into them, and although Crown played down his role by calling himself a "sand-and-gravel man," he had his fingers in diversified pies. Crown was the second-biggest coal producer in Illinois, and eleventh in the nation; he and two associates owned 25 percent of the Rock Island Line; and only Conrad Hilton owned more stock in Hilton Hotels. Crown had started work selling matches door-to-door after school as a nine-year-old. He never went to high school, but went to work full-time as a Western Union messenger and newspaper office boy. He took bookkeeping classes at night school, learned something about freight rates, and by twenty-one was treasurer of a small company. Two years later he had his own company, and he was on his way. During World War II he served as the chief of procurement for the Army Corps of Engineers in the Chicago area, which earned him his colonelcy and the Legion of Merit. He received the Horatio Alger Award in 1953.

As his publicist, Crown hired Ben Sonnenberg, who described himself beyond earshot of his clients as "a cabinetmaker who fashioned large pedestals for small statues." One of Sonnenberg's first clients was the Fifth Avenue Hotel, for whom he garnered tremendous publicity in 1926 by promoting the presence of newsworthy guests, paying or otherwise. He soon learned that a more lucrative way to operate was to represent a few big corporations and their chiefs, so he hooked Lever Brothers, Lipton Tea, Squibb, Pan Am, CBS, and Philip Morris, among others. His house at 19 Gramercy Park South, which he turned into one of the grandest homes in the city for entertaining, came to be an extension of his personality and his business. Perhaps the only thing in Sonnenberg's life that received little publicity was his death, which occurred during the 1978 newspaper strike in New York.

One of Sonnenberg's bright ideas was hatched with Raymond Loewy and given the in-house name "Operation: Light Up the Sky." For the rest of the world the project was known as "The Freedom Lights"—four mighty beacons, each weighing a ton apiece, set at the foot of the Empire State's television tower. In 1955, almost 925,000 persons came to New York by ship, but half again as many passengers arrived by air. The Freedom Lights were designed to provide an "air-age symbol of welcome and freedom" to air passengers, serving the same role for the age of aviation as the Statue of Liberty's beacon had been serving for the steamship age. The publicists were quick to point out that they were not so vainglorious as to think that the beacons would supplant the Statue of Liberty's torch; they would only supplement it. With a total of 2 billion candlepower, the lights were "the brightest continuous source of man-made light in the world," powerful enough to be seen under ideal conditions from as far away as Boston and Baltimore. The beacons turned 180 degrees every minute, and their angle was set above the horizontal, the slight upward tilt designed to avoid dazzling pilots. The counterclockwise motion added to the safety measures for pilots—airport beacons move in a clockwise fashion. As the lights made their full arc and turned to the building, they tilted back and were angled upward to sweep across the television antenna, exposing it to a brilliant path of light at all times. At the end of each night's operation between midnight and sunrise, three of the lights were extinguished, but the beacon facing the harbor remained steadily on.

Sonnenberg regarded the "Light Up the Sky" project as a "complete star project" requiring the services of all the agency's disparate departments to assure maximum publicity, from the movie and TV-radio magazine departments to the financial and business news departments. Sonnenberg's office prepared a press conference where a working model was displayed. A press party was planned for the first illumination, an affair that Sonnenberg's staff thought might start well before sundown with a cocktail party for the press and celebrities. Since Herbert Hoover had thrown the switch that opened the building in 1931, they thought that he might be called upon again. Failing that, perhaps ex-President Harry Truman, or even a descendant of Al Smith would do the trick.

Sonnenberg's office requested a proclamation from the mayor's office declaring "Empire State Building Week—or Day," and a bronze plaque carrying inspirational text by a writer the stature of Carl Sandburg or Robert Frost. They thought that a suitable paperweight modeled after the plaque would make a nice souvenir of the party. Earl Wilson had written a column about a recent trip he had taken on a New York sight-seeing bus, and they wanted to get him to write a comparable story on the building. The publicists said they would provide some of the better jokes and anecdotes about the building for a John Crosby feature on the TV tower, and they wanted to "dig up" some material for Louella Parsons on all the movies that had featured the building for her movie column. They wanted a movie star to talk about the night view (preferably a star who had appeared in a movie that featured the Empire State Building). The publicists wanted Faye Emerson to serve as Mistress of Ceremonies and to write a piece for her radio-TV column. They would supply her with a "virtually written" column with plenty of anecdotes. Sonnenberg would supply the "unusuals" for Ed Sullivan's column; they wanted him to do a film clip on the lighting for his Sunday night show *Toast of the Town*, and they hoped he would devote a full-hour Sunday night TV show to the "Eighth Wonder of the World." They planned newspaper ads, window displays for the stores in the building and displays in the lobby, a postmark bearing the message "Light-Up-The-Sky At The Empire State Building" on all mail sent from management's office, a handbill for all tenants, and a contest to find "Miss Tower" or "Miss Observatory," who would become the official hostess for all "Light Up the Sky" activities. Contestants would be "restricted to those young women between the ages of eighteen and twenty-five, and over six feet tall. Because of her abnormal size, she simulates—in effect—the world's tallest building."

Some of it came to pass. Governor Averell Harriman issued a statement on the "Freedom Lights," and Mayor Robert F. Wagner's office did indeed issue a proclamation. The publicity agents did not get Sandburg or Frost, although they lined up MacKinley Kantor, who had written "Andersonville," to write "The Empire State Lights." His words:

Whence rise you, Lights? **** From this tower built upon Manhattan's native rock. Its roots are deep below forgotten musket balls, the moldered wooden shoe, the flint, the bone. **** What mark you, Lights? **** Our Nation's doorway. **** Who sleep or toil beneath your good warm gaze? **** All who love this Land: they who are of the Land's stout seed, and they who love the Land because they chose to come. **** Sing you a song, Proud Lights? **** We sing silently. We chant a Mass and Spiritual, Doxology and Kol Nidre, battle hymn and ballad. We tell of village and of jet—Of wheat and cotton, turbine oil and goldenrod, the wildest mountains and the cities' roar. **** This is a strange new time. Strong Lights, why never do you fear? **** There is something more powerful. The heart and soul of all Mankind. **** What build you with your beams? **** A bridge to the stars. **** What offer you to God, O Lights? **** America's devotion.

The poem never won the recognition of Emma Lazarus's sonnet, nor did the beacons win equal recognition with Liberty's torch as a symbol of welcome, but the lights brought the building yet another superlative—the beacons made the building the ultimate achievement in pharology, a term derived from the Pharos of Alexandria, the lighthouse that was one of the seven wonders of the ancient world. It was a link with the building's traditional publicity that Sonnenberg somehow overlooked.

The Freedom Light beacons brought the building more criticism than praise. Even before the lights were lit in May 1956, complaints were pouring in. The lights would be a nuisance for just plain folks who wanted to sit back on their backyard chaise longues and enjoy the nighttime sky without having someone's idea of how to promote a building intrude upon their pastoral nighttime scene. But the problem for astronomers was more serious. The glow of London by night had made it necessary to move the Greenwich Observatory, the glow of Los Angeles had interfered with the work of the Mount Wilson observatory, and the glare from New York City was bad enough as it was. A professor at Yale called the Freedom Lights "diabolical" for anyone seriously studying the heavens with a telescope or photographic equipment. The lights would fog long-exposure photographic plates and distort star-measuring photoelectric counters. And the Freedom Lights would be to birds what lights are to moths. Night flyers migrating along the Atlantic flyway would be attracted to them, become disoriented, and smash into the building by the tens of thousands. The deaths of the small birds common to field, forest, and garden—warblers, thrushes, vireos, tanagers, finches, and others—would create a furor. In an arrangement worked out with the National Audubon Society, the building agreed to turn off its Freedom Lights from mid-April until June so that the north-flying birds would have safe passage, and to turn them off again from September 15 to November 1 for the trip south.

Crown understood the power of the press, and the gentle persuasion of money. Bernard Gimbel was chairing the New York Convention & Visitors Bureau in 1954, to which Crown sent a check for $5,000 on behalf of the Empire State Building for the "good work" the bureau was doing (roughly translated: The Empire State Building was regularly placed at the top of the bureau's list of the city's "must see" attractions). Crown followed up with a proposal to Gimbel in 1955 that H. Hamilton Weber, then the chief executive officer of the Empire State Building, join the bureau's board of directors. A note, probably from Ben Sonnenberg, was attached to Gimbel reminding him of Colonel Crown's generous contribution to the bureau some months before.

In the fifties, the observatories were still packin' 'em in—the income from the observatories for the tax year 1952–53 was $727,824. Regardless of the weather, somebody always showed up and paid his way to the top every day the observatories were open. The record low attendance for one day was eight visitors, and the supposition was that the weather must have been something fierce that day. Visitors on bad days were usually tourists who had procrastinated until they ran out of time. But they were determined. Going to New York City and not visiting the top of the Empire State was like going to Venice and not seeing the canals.

The visibility at the top was posted in the ticket office downstairs, which carried with it the voice of authority, but the standard was unscientific at best. The visibility was judged by what landmarks the guards could spot. The south end of Central Park was counted as one mile, the Cathedral of St. John the Divine was counted as three miles, the Statue of Liberty, five. Theresa McKeon, the restaurant manager at the top, used a slightly more scientific standard for ordering supplies. She called the weather bureau and acted accordingly. On a good day, McKeon would order ten loaves of bread; on a bad day, two. "A cook's got to keep a weather eye peeled up here," she said.

Under Frank Powell's supervision during the fifties, the staff at the observatories was kept crisp. The summer uniforms for the guides and those who worked at the souvenir stand—smocks for women, shirts worn outside the trousers for men—were the responsibility of the workers. The unisex material had images of New York's tourist attractions printed on it, with the competition given equal billing with the host building. (In 1995, the summer staff at the observatories wore a unisex uniform—crisp khaki slacks and blue-and-white shirts with white collars.) Students were hired to supplement Powell's regular staff as relief elevator operators and guides in the summers, and some of them were inventive. Wayne Carhart, who worked as a summer guide in the late 1950s, discovered that children would frequently get a little bored, so he devised a game for them to play. He would tell them to look for a yellow cab that was about to enter the Queens Midtown Tunnel on the Manhattan side at Thirty-eighth Street. When they had spotted one, Carhart would then point out the exit in Queens and tell them to watch for their yellow cab as it exited. The kids would be enthralled, time would pass that the adults could spend looking at things that interested them, and after a while a yellow cab would appear. It was not necessarily the same yellow cab that the child had seen entering the tunnel, but the kids never caught on. They were happy.

The eighty-sixth floor was still being used to broadcast radio specials. In 1956, the Voice of America directed a radio show called *From Tower to Tower,* which linked the world's four greatest TV and radio towers—New York's Empire State Building, Paris's Eiffel Tower, Berlin's radio tower, and Stuttgart's TV tower. From atop the Empire State Building, Joseph Schildkraut, star of the Broadway production of *The Diary of Anne Frank*, chatted with his counterparts in the Berlin and Stuttgart productions of the play, and Caterina Valente sang selections from her nightclub act.

The usual mixed bag of celebrities visited the top in the fifties. Sir Edmund Hillary, who scaled Mount Everest in 1953, gave caption writers a line that none could resist as he made it to the top of New York's "man-made Everest" in 1954. A whole series of Lassies posed prettily, usually with one paw on the parapet. Las Vegas dancing girls, the winners of the crowns for Miss Ireland and Miss Maid of Cotton, contestants for the titles of Miss World, Miss Universe, and Miss Exquisite Form, the three finalists for the "coveted" title of America's Most Beautiful Greek Girl for 1956—they all strutted their stuff.

The building was still the chosen destination for visiting dignitaries. In May 1956, Ben Sonnenberg sent a release to the assignment editors of newspapers, wire services, and newsreels. Dr. Sukarno, president of Indonesia, was scheduled to visit the Empire State Building at 9:30 A.M. on Wednesday, May 23. "As usual," said Sonnenberg, "we will make any arrangements for photographers, etc. that you wish."

Visiting British royalty was perhaps given the "reddest-carpet" treatment. Although the building had been host to innumerable government leaders and celebrities, the only time in the building's history that a red carpet was actually laid was when Queen Elizabeth II and Prince Philip visited the building in October 1957. The building did not have a carpet and was obliged to borrow one from the Waldorf-Astoria Hotel. (The Waldorf was by then a Hilton Hotel, with Crown a major stockholder in the chain. The hotel also provided red-coated waiters, old English silverware, and its gold china.) The carpet stretched from the curb at Thirty-fourth Street, where potted palms and yellow chrysanthemums flanked the queen's way, and into the lobby and to the elevator that would whisk the royal couple to the top. The carpet was laid on the eighty-sixth-floor observatory, and on the eightieth floor from the elevator leading to what had been Pierre du Pont's offices, which were then serving as the executive lounge. The elevator cabs that the queen and her consort rode in were also outfitted with red carpet.

Ben Sonnenberg made sure that there was at least one human interest story attached to the royal event. They chose Edward A. Quinn, a veteran Empire State Building employee, to operate the honored elevator to the eightieth floor. In the early 1920s, Quinn had been a bobby whose duty tours for Division A of the London Metropolitan Police Force included St. James and Buckingham Palaces. Quinn recalled one blistering hot July day in the 1920s. He was patrolling the palace gardens, when Queen Mary, Elizabeth II's grandmother, noticed that he was suffering in the heat. She said to him, "I am sending out a chair. You must sit down and rest." A palace servant brought out a chair and set it in a garden path. Constable Quinn remained stiffly correct in his tightly buttoned uniform, and sat in it only briefly. "It was embarrassing," Quinn explained. No constable on duty has the right to sit down and rest, but the constable knew that one may not argue with a queen either. With the wisdom of Solomon, Quinn tried to placate both camps. For the rest of his tour, he marched around the chair.

Management had thoughtfully fixed the coin-operated telescopes in the observatories so that nobody had to fish for a dime to pay for a close-up view. The building got its money's worth in free publicity. The queen said that the view was "the most beautiful thing" she had ever seen. She and Prince Philip were then guests at a reception in the executive lounge. Escorted by Colonel Crown and his wife, the couple was introduced to the Empire State Building directors and their wives, and, quite inexplicably, to Miss Virginia Warren, daughter of Chief Justice Earl Warren. The queen occupied the same chair that her mother had sat in on the occasion of her visit to the Empire State Building three years before. (The queen mother had created a stir on her visit. She decided to stay longer than her itinerary called for because she wanted to see the view at night.)

The queen was unable to take advantage of one of the benefits that comes with travel—to eat local ethnic cuisine such as bagels, cream cheese and lox, or a Reuben sandwich, or even a Coney Island hot dog. The luncheon consisted of fingertip tea sandwiches, French and Danish pastries, crumpets, petit fours, champagne, cocktails, tea, and coffee. The queen had Twining's Earl Grey's Finest—milk, no sugar—while the prince had a Scotch and soda (no brand reported). The queen was presented with a model of the building that was not the sort you pick up at the souvenir counter on the eighty-sixth floor. This one was from Tiffany's. The model was gold-plated, the TV antenna was solid gold, and the red beacon was a ruby. Management made sure that Princess Anne received a silver charm bracelet, and Prince Charles a silver key ring, both with images of the building.

In addition to a New York police inspector, a Scotland Yard inspector, and a State Department representative, who were constantly by the couple's side, two hundred policemen were on duty outside the building, fifty more uniformed policemen were inside with the building's full security staff, and sixty-three city detectives were stationed throughout the building. When Prince Philip saw all the police he said that the place looked like police headquarters.

In 1961 came the third change in ownership, when the building and the leasehold upon the land were purchased from Henry Crown by a syndicate called Empire State Associates for $65 million, a sale that earned a place in the record books. Together with the $17 million previously paid by Prudential for the land, the total of $82 million was the greatest sum ever paid for a building, and the negotiations were commensurate with the price. The purchase was initiated by Lawrence A. Wien, who had created Empire State Building Associates. He had been interested in the property ever since his "appraisal" for Roger Stevens in 1954, after which he and his broker, Harry Helmsley, had maintained contact with Crown, who on several occasions had indicated interest in selling, only to change his mind and back out. What finally precipitated the sale came when Crown learned that Congress might amend the tax code by taxing long-term capital gains at the substantially higher rate of ordinary income tax as of January 1, 1962. In September 1961, he agreed to sell, with one major proviso—that the sale be consummated by the end of 1961. The transaction kept batteries of lawyers, accountants, tax experts, and title insurance companies hard at work for the rest of the year. The contract and exhibits ran over four hundred pages, with about one hundred legal documents that had to be signed in precisely the right order. Eight dry runs were required before the final signing took place in the board of directors suite of the Prudential Insurance Company of America in Newark, New Jersey. It took from midmorning until midafternoon.

Wien, a graduate of Columbia College and Columbia Law School, was already an experienced hand at real estate, having acquired hotels such as The Plaza and The Taft, and office buildings such as the Lincoln Building on Forty-second Street, the Graybar Building on Lexington Avenue, the Equitable Building at 120 Broadway, and the International Toy Center at 200 Fifth Avenue. He would go on to become a major benefactor to his alma mater, and to Brandeis University, WNET/Thirteen, Lincoln Center, and various performing arts groups. His colleagues in the venture were both partners in his law firm, Wien, Lane & Klein, who represented Empire State Building Associates in the purchase and continued to represent the building in the 1990s as Wien, Malkin & Bettex. Henry W. Klein was a graduate of Cornell College and Harvard Law School, and twenty-seven-year-old Peter L. Malkin was a graduate of Harvard College and Harvard Law School. This was a new breed of management class.

No sooner had the ink been blotted on the contract that gave Wien control of the building than he turned around and arranged for partial financing by revising the existing arrangement with Prudential. The insurance company increased its investment by $29 million and took legal title to the building. Wien then leased back the structure for five terms totaling 114 years—through January 2076—a sale-and-leaseback deal that represented the most spectacular orchestration of a practice that had only been introduced after World War II. The sale returned Wien's money to him immediately, and the lease brought him control of the building. Prudential realized immediate income in the form of rent. Prudential's investment was treated as a mortgage that would be paid in full with interest at 5 ¾ percent per annum over the initial thirty-year term of the lease. Prudential could also depreciate its investment over the initial thirty-year term of the master lease, thus sheltering part of the rental income from corporate income taxation. It was rather like both parties having their cake and eating it too.

Under a master lease on both the land and building, the Wien group received the Empire State's annual income, which was about $10.5 million at the time. It would pay Prudential yearly rentals of $3.22 million for the first thirty years, with the right to renew the lease for four additional twenty-one-year terms. The annual rent was scheduled to drop to $1.84 million for the first twenty-one-year renewal, and to $1.61 million for the last three, with no adjustment for inflation or participation in the profits for Prudential. But Wien and Malkin recognized that some major improvements might have to be made, and they convinced Prudential to agree to put up the necessary capital for one of them, in return for an increase in rent upon completion of the job. The major improvement that was settled on was to upgrade the elevators, a job that would cost $3.5 million in 1966. It would send the rent from 1991 to 2013 to $1.97 million, and from 2013 to 2076, to $1.72 million.

Wien paid $3 million for legal fees and brokerage commissions, $500,000 of which went to the primary broker, Helmsley-Spear, Inc. Wien then established the Empire State Building Company, a second partnership consisting of Helmsley and himself. The company would actually manage the building and operate the property, paying a net rent plus 50 percent of its profit in excess of $1 million a year to Empire State Building Associates, who would in turn pay the master lease rent to Prudential and distribute the profits.

Wien raised some cash by issuing $33 million of stock ("partnership participations") in the Empire State Building Associates in units of $10,000 each. The shares were designed to return $900 yearly—9 percent—on each $10,000 share. It was a good investment. The return on the original investment has never been less than the projected 9 percent, and, through a combination of monthly distributions at a rate of 11 percent and year-end distributions through a profit-sharing arrangement, the yield has averaged far higher.

Prudential knew it was getting a good deal. The city was experiencing a building boom that put to shame the boom of the twenties. In 1930, there was about 26 million square feet of office space in all of Midtown. In the five years between 1956 and 1961, new construction accounted for over 27.5 million square feet of office space in Manhattan, virtually all of which was rented, and there was another 12 million square feet under construction. John G. Jewett, who headed Prudential's mortgage loan and real estate investment department, said that the Empire State Building could not have been duplicated under the city's revised zoning laws, nor could it have been reproduced economically, given the costs of the day. "Structurally," he said, it was "better than many of the newer buildings in the city." The twenty-three stores on the ground floor were flourishing, and the eighty-five floors above were filled with 850 tenants, many of whom had links with the neighboring garment center. Owen Aldis's prescription for success included an abundance of small tenants. Du Pont, which occupied 100,000 square feet in 1961, was the building's largest tenant. No single tenant occupied more than 5 percent of the building's rentable area or accounted for as much as 5 percent of the annual rent collections. Other good portents were that the building was 97.7 percent tenanted in 1960, and on July 1, 1961, the average rental rate per square foot was $6.70, up almost a dollar from only five years before. Management was collecting $10,914,000 a year in rent, a figure that did not include the more than $2 million in revenues from the observatories and the $770,000 from antenna license fees.[5] It added up to over $13,684,000 a year.

A program of improvements was quickly undertaken by Empire State Building Associates. All the setbacks were reroofed, and contractors Albert Rogell and Abraham Best, who had restored the concrete surfaces of Yankee Stadium and redecorated the Fifth Avenue lobby of the Plaza Hotel, gave the exterior its first cleaning and restoration. The crews operated from baskets to clean the mooring mast. To clean the rest of the building, they used electrically operated scaffolds that traveled at a rate of eighteen feet a minute (the conventional method, which was to jack or winch the scaffolds up and down by hand, would have been too slow and enervating). The crews worked on one face at a time, in each case beginning at the eighty-sixth floor and working their way down. In addition to recaulking, the refinishing work was designed to restore the limestone's original color, which had become a charred brown. The metal window frames were first cleaned with wire brushes, then rust-inhibitor paint was applied and coated with a lead-and-oil-base paint. The stainless-steel mullions were restored to their natural brilliance with a metal cleanser and solvents.

While the façade was being cleaned, changes took place on the second floor. Banking halls filled the east end overlooking Fifth Avenue—Manu-

---

[5]These figures are from a press release the Empire State Building Associates sent out in August 1962. Having in-house counsel check PR releases and all advertising copy is standard operating procedure, but Wien and Malkin went one step further on the release that told of recent renting—they cleared it with the SEC.

facturers Trust was in the northeast corner, Irving Trust was in the southeast corner. In a classic demonstration of concentration of industry, two brokerage houses were down the hall—Shearson, Hammill & Co. and Reynolds & Co. However, the building had never fully utilized the west end of the second floor, which had been a storage area for Coward Shoes for over thirty years. When Coward vacated the premises in 1964, management decided to upgrade the space, and make it more accessible by installing a pair of high-speed escalators. Escalators traveling at 90 feet a minute and able to carry four thousand persons an hour were much more efficient than elevators for moving traffic one floor. Furthermore, escalators take up less lobby space, and since they rise on a slant, some of the area beneath them can be rented out to high-traffic, low-ticket operations such as newsstands.

The removal of Coward Shoes and the coming of the escalators meant converting about seventeen thousand square feet of limited-use space into prime space. About five thousand square feet of it was turned into an art exhibition area in 1965 that stayed open the same hours as the observatories, from 9 A.M. to midnight. Unlike the corporate galleries operated by the likes of IBM and Time, Inc., which ordinarily had their own curatorial staffs, the Empire State Gallery invited museums and other cultural institutions to mount monthly exhibitions with their own staffs. The first to take advantage of the offer was the Spanish Pavilion of the New York World's Fair, which opened a show of contemporary works by Spanish painters and sculptors. At the same time, an "Introduction to New York" was installed on the second floor where tourists assembled on their way to the observatories. At the height of the summer season, as many as fifteen thousand persons a day passed the display cases that highlighted attractions at twenty of the city's cultural institutions.

The building was still used as a tactical observation point. In 1965, as part of a campaign to reduce air pollution, the Consolidated Edison Company posted "rangers" to the eightieth floor, who kept a lookout on seven Con Ed electric generating stations from 6 A.M. to 10 P.M., seven days a week. At the first hint of smoke, a ranger telephoned the superintendent of the offending plant to report the condition.

A change in the day-to-day working environment came in 1966, when the manually operated high-speed elevators serving the first eighty floors were changed over to automatic operation, a job that Wien and Malkin had foreseen. Gone were the elevator operators who frequently spoke for New York and who had provided the comfort of knowing that someone was in charge; they were replaced by a plate of buttons. As usual, the changeover came with a superlative—the job of converting the fifty-eight elevators required more than 9 million feet of insulated wire, 250,000 feet of conduit, 30 miles of rail, and 120 miles of wire rope, and was said to be the largest elevator automation ever undertaken. The new Millar elevator cab walls were paneled in rosewood and laminated with Formica, so even though they might really have been wood they still looked like plastic. In exchange for easier maintenance, a sense of place was gone.

In response to the city's first major power failure, the new elevators had a recall system so that they would not be stranded between floors in the event the power failed again. At the same time, an emergency lighting system was installed.

The blackout had hit the city at 5:27 P.M., Tuesday, November 9, 1965. People stood on street corners in wonder as they watched the lights go out progressively from north to south, and stories started to fly. A bewildered stranger on the corner of Lexington Avenue and Forty-fourth Street asked advertising executive Ann Lynn Puddu what was going on. She jokingly said that it was a communist plot. She then told someone else that the lights were out along the entire eastern seaboard. Unbeknownst to her, they were. This was the "good" blackout, and the mood early turned festive. On the eighty-sixth-floor observatory, about two hundred visitors enthusiastically enjoyed the best view in town. "You should see the full moon shimmering in the East River," said a Columbia student from Sweden. "I've never seen anything like it." A group of French tourists sang "La Marseillaise," and tried to teach it to some Americans. A group from the South led the singing of "Dixie," and an improvised barbershop quartet took up "Sweet Adeline."

The blackout was no joke for the nearly 800,000 persons trapped for hours in elevator shafts, subway trains, and commuter trains. There were moments of panic in disabled elevator cars, but most of those trapped were quickly extricated, and the fear melted into joviality. Many of the city's elevators were already equipped with the safety device that automatically lowered them to the next floor, where the doors could be opened manually. The recall system had not yet been installed in the Empire State Building, and in extreme cases walls had to be cut through to reach stranded passengers. McCandlish Phillips, one of *The Times*'s great local writers, reported that a fireman finally reached a stranded elevator in the Empire State Building. The fireman's first question was whether there were any pregnant women in the car. One wag in the elevator was quick to reply, "Pregnant? We've hardly even met."

The blackout came in the middle of testing the most dramatic change in the look of the building since the decision was made to add the dirigible mooring mast. Wien was testing the floodlighting of the upper stories of the building, an idea that management liked but would not be implemented without first gauging the public's reaction. In the wake of the blackout came a response nobody had banked on. As a precaution against overloading the system, the city's residents were requested to curtail their use of electricity the day after the blackout, but the Empire State Building turned on its floodlights anyway, until an indignant resident of Stuyvesant Town called to complain. The next day, after Mayor Robert Wagner announced that normal service had been restored, the lights went back on.

The decision to transform the building's nighttime face into a solid block of white light was made the following spring—in time to be unveiled for the opening of the 1964 World's Fair—when floodlights were mounted on the setbacks above the seventy-second floor. At the same time, the four revolving beams on top of the building—the "Freedom Lights"—were turned off. The floodlighting cost $250,000 to install, but the 360 kilowatts required to make the building gleam cost relatively little to maintain. Commercial light bills were calculated by the amount of current used and by the time of day it was used. Since the floodlights were on when most office lights were off, they cost only about one penny a kilowatt-hour. With 360 kilowatts, the bill came to $3.60 an hour; with the lights on seven hours a night, it cost about $25 a day. Management was hoping that enough lights would be turned off below the seventy-second floor to create a block of light that seemed to have no visible support, "like a chandelier suspended from the sky." This new philosophy manifested the change in the rental situation. In the thirties, management was running around turning on lights on unoccupied floors to keep the lights in the mooring mast from seemingly floating and to create the illusion that the building was tenanted. By the sixties, management did not have to create any illusions about tenancy rates.

Management had something else to worry about in the sixties, and suggestions have been made that the concept of the lighting program was perhaps a way of reasserting the Empire State Building's preeminence on the New York skyline. Plans for a world trade center had been announced by the Port Authority of New York & New Jersey in 1961, the same year that Lawrence Wien took control of the Empire State Building. The rationale for the project was that the dominance of the port would be enhanced if firms engaged in international trade were concentrated in one project. The original plans for the complex did not pose a threat to the sovereignty of the Empire State Building. The tallest buildings in the center were to have been seventy-six stories. But by 1964 the city was in for a surprise—the twin seventy-six-story towers had stretched to 110 stories, to 1,350 feet, a height that would eclipse the Empire State Building by 100 feet and allow the World Trade Towers to lay claim to being the world's tallest buildings. Although many prominent real estate people in Lower Manhattan had originally supported the idea, some were getting nervous at the prospect of what 10 million square feet of space would do to the real estate market. The towers alone, each over two hundred feet square, would provide 7.9 million square feet of rentable floor space—the equivalent of about fifty 200-by-800-foot blocks, or roughly the area of the blocks bounded by Thirty-fourth and Fifty-ninth Streets between Sixth and Eighth Avenues. Realtors were afraid that the already existing glut on the market would be exacerbated. Worse, when the new space was filled it would be at the expense of buildings that were privately owned and operated.

Owners of older buildings who had tried to woo tenants with costly modernization—80 percent of the Empire State Building had been fully air-conditioned by 1961—would have their tenants lured away by the sleek 110-story towers downtown. And newer buildings offered other in-ducements. Tenants could take advantage of the new style of office planning that older buildings could not readily offer. Instead of the fixed layout of corridors and small, permanently partitioned spaces in buildings of the Empire State's vintage, the modular open-plan style dictated the creation of large, column-free areas capable of being easily rearranged to suit tenants' needs. The World Trade Center offered unobstructed sixty-foot spaces from the elevator banks to the outside walls, thanks to a new method of construction that replaced the traditional cage skeleton with a variation on the old-style load-bearing wall.

It is a given in government circles that government is not to perform tasks that private industry can perform, that the public sector is not to compete with the private sector. However, the Port Authority placed itself squarely in competition with private industry, and the quasi-governmental agency would have an unfair competitive advantage. It would pay only $3 million a year in lieu of real estate taxes versus the $30 million a year in real estate taxes a private developer would be obligated to pay for a comparable project; it could issue tax-exempt bonds with an interest rate that was about one-half what a private developer would pay for a conventional mortgage; and the project would be repaid in part by revenues generated by tolls on the region's bridges and tunnels that should have been invested in the port that the authority had been designed to serve.

Tenants involved in world trade who were interested in moving to the center were not easy to find, and by 1966 the notion of the buildings serving as a true world trade center began to unravel. The response by the Port Authority was to woo corporate tenants with no specific connection with world trade whose needs would ordinarily have been filled by the commercial marketplace, as well as other governmental agencies such as the Metropolitan Transportation Authority. Officials of some of the city's largest realty concerns, including Robert V. Tishman, president of Tishman Realty and Construction Company, opposed the project, and Lawrence Wien's Committee for a Reasonable Trade Center, which attracted realtors such as Seymour Durst, advocated that the Port Authority scale down its plans to reflect the size required for a true world trade center.

The second area where the World Trade Center found itself in competition with the private sector was an accident of birth. It was the issue of television reception. The glory of transmitting from the Empire State Building was that it was the tallest transmitter around. Suddenly there would be two taller buildings that, unlike the Empire State Building, which gets thinner as it gets higher, were big square objects all the way to the top. Signals from the Empire State would bounce off the buildings and the ghosts of reception past would return. If transferring transmissions to the World Trade Center could salvage reception, a quasi-governmental agency would again be competing against the private sector. The leases for the masts were profitable for the Empire State Building, and management did not want to lose the revenue. By the 1960s, nine stations were paying $720,000 a year for the use of the antenna and $100,000 a year to house their equipment, with leases running to May 1984.

The broadcasters said that they'd rather switch to the World Trade Center than fight to stop the project. However, they maintained that it was the World Trade Center Towers that had caused the problem, and the broadcasters refused to assume responsibility for the move. They said that the Port Authority should pay for the new antenna and the cost of relocating, and they got a court order to that effect. The Port Authority had to construct a mast to accommodate television and FM broadcasting antennas on the first building scheduled to be completed (the north tower). The Port Authority had to provide space above the one hundredth floor for transmission equipment, the equivalent space to what the broadcasters then had in the Empire State Building. And the Port Authority had to install the new transmitting equipment, pay the $40 million relocation costs, and pick up the leases the television stations had with the Empire State Building until 1984, when the existing leases with the Empire State Building expired. The transmission shifted in 1971. After

1984, the Empire State Building found itself high and, with the exception of a few stations, dry.[6]

Port Authority Executive Director Austin J. Tobin claimed that the real reason Wien opposed the World Trade Towers was that the Empire State Building stood to lose its title as the world's tallest building, and with the loss of the title would go all the public relations appeal that had been so assiduously cultivated over the years. Tobin was hardly politic in his condemnation of Wien. He said that from the moment the 110-story towers were announced, "Mr. Wien and his publicity agent, Mr. Robert Kopple, have applied every conceivable political pressure, every propaganda device, every distortion and every mis-statement of fact that would serve their narrow and selfish objectives." Tobin asserted that the "time of Mr. Wien's opposition puts the finger on his motives and his callous disinterest in the Port of New York, its future and the 400,000 people who earn their living in the operation of the port."

With the "world's tallest" title gone to the World Trade Center in 1972, and with Chicago's Sears Tower on the horizon, Robert W. Jones, an architect with the successor firm of Shreve, Lamb & Harmon, started noodling with how to make the building once again the world's tallest. He thought the solution was to tear down the dirigible mooring mast and the top six stories and replace them with a new thirty-three-story structure to make the "new" Empire State Building 113 stories high, taking it to a height of 1,494 feet—144 feet higher than the Twin Towers and 44 feet higher than the Sears Tower. Jones created two versions of the same proposal: One had the top tapering upward from two sides; the other was an updated version of the original roofline for the eighty-sixth floor. He would have adapted the World Trade Towers' "skylobby" idea by running express and local elevators in each of the existing shafts to accommodate the thirty-three additional floors. On the eightieth floor would be a transfer point to elevators inside the new structure, most of which would have been used for office space in the style of the open plan, less like the long halls and small offices in vogue when the building was built and more like the interiors of the World Trade Center. On demolishing the topmost sixteen floors to make way for the addition, Jones

---

[6]In 1995, fourteen FM radio stations, including WQXR, New York's only remaining classical radio station, were broadcasting from the top of the building, as were seven television stations. The building was also equipped for "ENS," or electronic news gathering. When mobile television news units are broadcasting live from the field, the mobile unit sends its signals to the Empire State Building, which relays the signals to the broadcast studio.

said that if you can get it up there, you can get it down. *The Times* said that "each man kills the thing he loves." The building's "characteristic silhouette stands for the city of New York almost uniquely; there is no stronger symbol in the twentieth century. Its Art Deco tower is not just the most important local landmark, still upstaging the graceless new flattops that outbulk it; it is also an undisputed artistic monument of international stature. The architects make it clear that it could not be reproduced. That unmistakable tower . . . is New York."

The story broke in a front-page story in *The New York Times*, and was followed up by the editorial comment above, but Jones had never submitted his concept to management. According to Peter Malkin, Wien's immediate response to the proposal when apprised of it by a reporter was that the plan would prove uneconomic—the floor sizes would simply be too small. He laughingly suggested an alternative plan—the additional thirty-three stories should be inserted at the base of the building, which could be jacked up to accommodate the new floors. Wien had unwittingly struck upon an idea that had a historical precedent. City Hall was declared redundant in the 1890s, and was up for demolition or grabs. Alfred Ely Beach, the editor of *Scientific American* and a pioneer in rapid transit, realized the value of the building as a landmark as well as the necessity for providing more space for the expanding bureaucracy. Beach proposed slipping an iron floor under the foundation of City Hall and raising it bodily by means of hydraulic jacks. With City Hall up in the air, a new municipal building could be constructed under it, and then the venerable and architecturally worthy building could be lowered to sit atop the new building. Neither suggestion went anywhere.

The building's PR department had to reconcile itself to the fact that the Empire State was no longer the "world's tallest." It started touting the building as the "world's most famous," and, judging by the number of visitors that continued to flock to the observatories, the claim was justified. In May 1976, the building had its 50 millionth visitor. Robert Tinker, the manager of the building, acknowledged that he and his staff did not really know when the magic number would come up, so they arbitrarily set a day and agreed that to the person purchasing the hundredth ticket that day would go the honors. These might have been inflationary times, but the gifts were hardly in a league with the hundred-dollar war bond that was given to the British Navy's Sub-Lieutenant John H. Morris, the 5 millionth visitor. Helfa Eilers, of Bremen, West Germany, was given an official key to the city, a sterling silver lifetime pass for the observatory, a Paul Revere sterling silver bowl, a silver pen set, a silver desk model of the Empire State Building, a Steuben glass "Big Apple," a week's stay for two at the St. Moritz Hotel, and sight-seeing tours by helicopter, boat, and bus. And the building was named for Mrs. Eilers for the day.

The year of the 50 millionth visitor—1976—was also the year the city hosted the National Democratic Convention and participated in the Bicentennial. Douglas Leigh, the "spectacular" lighting impresario, had not forgotten the Empire State Building.[7] Leigh was serving as New York's chairman of City Decor for the Convention and the Bicentennial in 1976, and he was looking for ways to celebrate the city and the nation. He thought he'd start at the top. He asked Lawrence Wien and Harry Helmsley if they'd like the building to join the celebration by flying the red, white, and blue. They liked the idea, and not just because their wives shared the Fourth of July as their respective birthdays. They said that by celebrating the city's individual parts, a contribution was made to the city as a whole. What's more, Helmsley said it was "a great advertising gimmick. It certainly makes your building stand out and makes people think of it when they're looking for space."

Gone was the white floodlighting on the Empire State, replaced by the nation's colors. As architect Charles Linn said, "the Empire State Building became the toast of the town." The one-shot scheme to light the building turned into a way to celebrate festive occasions and holidays—"color with meaning," said Leigh. The top started being bathed (in calendar order) in red, black, and green for Martin Luther King Jr. Day; in red and white for Valentine's Day; in red, white, and blue for President's Day; in green for St. Patrick's Day; in white and yellow for Easter Week; in blue as a Police Memorial; in red, white, and blue for Memorial Day, Independence Day, and Labor Day; in blue and white for Steuben Day; in red and white for Pulaski Day; in red, white, and green for Columbus Day; in red as a Fire Safety and Firefighters Memorial; in blue and white for United Nations Day; in the autumn colors of red and yellow from Halloween to Thanksgiving Day; and red and green for what was originally called Christmas but which by the more politically correct 1990s was the Holiday Season. These colors became traditional as did celebrating specific events. When the New York Yankees won the World Series in 1977, the team's blue-and-white colors decorated the top. Two years later, Pope John Paul II visited the city and the papal colors of white and gold lit up

---

[7]Coca-Cola had told Douglas Leigh to try his idea for lighting the tower as a weather station again after the war, and he brought up the subject with General Drum when he "was running the show. But the Empire State Building was doing fine, and wasn't so desperate any more," said Leigh.

the upper floors. In the same year, Bob Tinker came up with the creative solution for celebrating the Camp David peace accord—two sides of the building were lit in the state colors of Egypt, the other two in the state colors of Israel. When there was no specific holiday or celebration, the building returned to being bathed in white light.

New Yorkers sometimes forgot the civic nature of the lighting and viewed the colors as an ideal way to make a personal statement. "Some woman would write in and say, 'It's my husband's birthday on such a date and his favorite colors are such and such,' " Tinker said. "We always had to write back and say it's not done that way."

Not everyone was happy with the lighting. *Times* critic Paul Goldberger said that although "it sounded like the sort of lovable civic gesture that no one could argue with," the change was dramatic enough to make the building an altogether different presence on the city's nighttime skyline. The Empire State Building was already a great icon, and playing games with colored lights added nothing to its meaning, no different from painting it red or yellow or green or purple. It was a violation of the design.

The renting public did not seem to care that the subtleties of the design had vanished in the colored lights. In 1981, only 24,000 square feet were vacant, and the building stood at 99 percent occupancy, with rents ranging from $22 a square foot on lower floors to $32 on upper floors. The building that had been planned to attract blue-chip corporations had never attracted many—du Pont and Schenley had been the major exceptions, and du Pont was the only one still there. Ironically, many small firms engaged in international trade occupied space in the building, and there were lawyers and accountants, but the vast majority of the tenancy was still related to the garment industry—in menswear alone there were 302 tenants occupying 748,000 square feet. The majority of the 850 tenants occupied midsize offices in the range of 2,000 to 3,000 square feet. There were more than two hundred tenants with a full bay—a bay was between building column and building column—and almost two hundred tenants with a half bay.

Tenants did not seem to care that by 1984 the antenna atop the building was shorter than it had been. WNBC had used its own fifty-two-foot-high antenna at the top of the antenna, but it had been declared redundant when transmission was moved to the World Trade Center. In 1984, radio station WWHT wanted to transmit from the Empire State Building, but adding to the already existing mast and extending the antenna beyond the station's technological needs, combined with the weight of other communications equipment on the mast, would have required expensive structural reinforcements. Down came NBC's fifty-two-foot antenna. In its place appeared a thirty-four-foot antenna to share the mast with fifteen FM radio stations and WNYC-TV, bringing the height to 1,454 feet.

Life as a landmark is not a simple one. Before any "alteration, reconstruction, demolition, or new construction" affecting a landmark can begin, approval has to be granted by the Landmarks Preservation Commission, a notoriously conservative commission that is ordinarily reluctant to grant changes of any sort. And this case was the worst example. Part of the officially designated structure—the "original fabric"—had been removed without notifying the commission. Despite the fact that the case had not even been reviewed, commission officials barely raised an eyebrow. They concluded that the decrease in the mast's height of eighteen feet wasn't "going to make a difference in the integrity or perception of the building," and they granted permission after the fact without so much as a slap on the wrist. Kent Barwick, the chairman of the Landmark Preservation Commission when the Empire State Building had been designated and president of the Municipal Art Society when the antenna was altered, concurred. He did not think that the change in antennas would harm the building one bit. As far as he was concerned, the building had "gained the affection of New Yorkers not because of its great size but because of its great beauty." The building—not the television antenna—was the thing.

On the building's fiftieth anniversary, *Times* critic Paul Goldberger said that the building was "about height, it is about commerce, it is about entertainment, it is about views, it is about the very meaning of the skyline itself." Visitors were as enthralled by the view fifty years after the building opened as on opening day. Some of the objects in the line of vision had changed, as had some of the cultural icons. Mary Cantwell wrote in *The Times* that "Manhattan seemed squeezed between its rivers and buildings pushed into space. Central Park sprawled before us and helicopters whirred past. And I suddenly thought of something that Cagney had shouted at the end of *White Heat*, under very different circumstances. 'Top of the world, Ma,' I said to myself. 'Top of the world!' "

To celebrate the building's golden jubilee, architects Prentice & Chan Ohlhausen hosted a three-layered party. Their penthouse office on the fifty-ninth floor of Shreve, Lamb & Harmon's Salmon Tower provided an unobstructed view of the building and its celebratory light show, and *King Kong* was shown nonstop on an office wall while Rolf Ohlhausen and Tim Prentice, alternating in gorilla costume because neither could stand the heat, mimicked the film. As Rolf Ohlhausen later said, it was "a series of collaged images. Best party we ever had."

The official promotions for the fiftieth anniversary were not such happy events. Upon removing the time capsule in preparation for the celebration, management discovered that the seams of the copper box had not been properly sealed. The box had filled with water, and most of the contents had disintegrated. The celebratory lighting that had been installed was not the anticipated extravaganza of a laser-light show—birthday candles had been promised, but they fizzled. The only exciting thing the red and amber lights delivered came when fog rolled in. The combination created the illusion that the building was on fire, which prompted calls to the fire department. The lights were turned off.

The biggest disappointment, perhaps, was the celebration of the fiftieth anniversary of *King Kong* in April 1983. An eighty-four-foot-high balloon replica of King Kong was tied to the mooring mast, the big idea of Robert Keith Vicino, president of a company that manufactured "cold air giant inflatable advertising displays." He spent $100,000 of the company's money on King Kong, believing that the stunt would result in the greatest bit of publicity his product could get. The eight-story balloon suffered a blowout during a test, and developed a hole in its left shoulder while being inflated, which left it in a heap on the side of the building's mast. The big ape was finally inflated sufficiently to warrant keeping him up there a few days, but this time it was not beauty that killed the beast. Along came wind gusts of 100 miles an hour to tear a fifteen-foot hole along the balloon's seam. In ignominy, a deflated Kong came down.

Almost four decades after a parachutist was dissuaded from practicing his craft from the top, two amateur parachutists from London succeeded in eluding the guards and foiling the fence. Twenty-eight-year-old Alistair Boyd, a landscape artist who worked on subterranean gardens in buildings, and twenty-five-year old Michael R. P. McCarthy, a part-time computer programmer who had already jumped off the Eiffel Tower, jumped from the eighty-sixth floor and made a safe landing two blocks down Fifth Avenue in April 1986. Just as Everest had been climbed because it was there, so they made the jump, they said, because it had never been done. They had planned for months, studying photographs of the building and making practice jumps from airplanes and an antenna tower. The day of the jump, Boyd and McCarthy bought their $3 admission tickets and went upstairs just as any other tourist might do, only they had blue aerofoil parachutes hidden under their coats. Their decision was to jump from the Thirty-third Street side. McCarthy went first. Boyd followed ten seconds later. The parachutes they used were highly maneuverable and could be manipulated in the same manner as hang gliders. Without modern technology, the story of these parachutist might not have had such a happy ending. They had to negotiate what they dubbed the Thirty-third Street "corridor" with its setbacks, then the avenue with its lampposts, trees, awnings, and traffic on their way to a safe landing, but they did it. McCarthy was arrested on the spot, but Boyd left the scene of the crime by hailing a taxi, a fact that was more startling to some observers of the Midtown scene than the fact of the jump. McCarthy was taken to the Midtown South station house on West Thirty-fifth Street where he was charged with reckless endangerment and parachuting within city limits. A few days later his partner turned himself in. Faced with the same charges, he promised to go straight.

The parachutists had been able to foil barriers that had been intentionally set to achieve their goal, unlike some visitors to the top who could not overcome barriers that had been unintentionally set, since the building was built when little thought was accorded to people with disabilities. Telephones were mounted too high for anybody in a wheelchair, the bathrooms and concession stands on the eighty-sixth floor could be reached only by negotiating a short flight of stairs, and, worst of all perhaps, the outdoor observation deck could only be reached by yet another flight of stairs. The Americans With Disabilities Act mandated that architectural barriers to wheelchair accessibility be removed in places of public accommodation, and the Empire State Building was clearly one of the city's most desirable places of public accommodation. As a symbol of its preeminence, in 1992 the building was picketed in an attempt to demonstrate the need for improving accommodations, a place to draw attention to the new legal obligations toward people with physical impairments. By the spring of 1995, the entire eighty-sixth floor was reconfigured and fully ramped, the height of the protective barriers was reduced, and new binoculars at wheelchair height were installed, all at a cost of over $1 million.

By 1991, the Prudential Life Insurance Company of America had recovered its original investment, and the insurance company decided to sell the land and the building subject to the existing master lease. With the annual rent at $1.97 million until 2013, and then at only $1,723,000 through 2076, Prudential expected bids in the range of $25 to $30 million, so they were pleased when interest was shown at $32 million. It came from the Empire State Building Associates' Peter L. Malkin, the managing partner of Empire State Associates, who in 1995 had an interest in nineteen major pieces of Manhattan real estate. He believed that the price was justified because the company that operated the building would actually own it.

Ada Louise Huxtable, the architecture critic for *The Times* who dealt with urban issues as much as architectural affairs, said in 1977 that "feelings ran high on the Empire State Building, because every New Yorker believed that he or she personally owned or was responsible for that enduring symbol of the city." The same held true in the 1990s, and Prudential was sensitive to the significance of the property as a local and national symbol, especially in light of the recent sale of 80 percent of Rockefeller Center to Mitsubishi Estates, which had received bad press. When Prudential's agent, Salomon Bros., received an offer of $40 million from a Japanese company that was controlled by an investor with an unsavory reputation, Prudential refused to sell. The few New Yorkers who knew of the investor's thwarted plans heaved a sigh of relief. They did not want the building in the hands of a reputed Japanese mafioso. When Oliver Grace, Jr.—great-grandson of former New York mayor William R. Grace—quietly bought the property for $40 million under the corporate name E. G. Holdings in 1991, those in the know felt secure that the building, like the promise of another insurance company, was in good hands. To say that the sale received very little publicity is an understatement. According to *The Wall Street Journal*, all the parties involved signed agreements pledging not to disclose the buyer's identity. But all was not as it seemed. Bryan Burrough reported in *Vanity Fair* that one week before Grace and Prudential closed, Grace received a wire transfer of $29.5 million from a corporation in Japan controlled by the same man to whom the Prudential had refused to sell, and Grace had also received other transfers from affiliates. In 1993, Grace turned around and sold the property to the enigmatically named NS 1999 American Company, a "group of Asian and European investors," for about $42 million. That was when New Yorkers started wondering what was happening with *their* building.

The bidders to whom Prudential had refused to sell were identified as Hideki Yokoi, his daughter Kiiko Nakahara, one of Yokoi's many illegitimate children, and her husband, Jean-Paul Renoir (no relation to Auguste or Jean Renoir—this Renoir's real name, says Burrough, was Perez before he changed it). *The New York Observer*'s Charles V. Bagli described Hideki Yokoi as a "former war profiteer and stock manipulator . . . embroiled with organized crime in Japan." The eighty-one-year-old Mr. Yokoi was by then serving a three-year sentence for involuntary manslaughter in the 1982 blaze at his New Japan Hotel that killed thirty-three people. He had repeatedly ignored orders to install and upgrade the hotel's fire equipment. And son-in-law Renoir, the former chairman of Lehman Brothers Asset Management in Tokyo, was prosecuted by French authorities in 1992 for stripping antiquities from historic châteaux that belonged to Yokoi but were protected under French law.[8]

The sale of the building was "sure to bewilder the New York real estate community because the entire 102-floor building remains encumbered [through January 2076] by a lease," pointed out *The Wall Street Journal*. Russell Miller wondered in *The London Times Magazine* why an investor would want to buy the building. "The property is leased on a fixed rent until the year 2076," said Miller. "This represents a return of 4.5 percent for the next 19 years and only 4 percent thereafter. If Yokoi had put up the money, he would have done rather better to deposit it with the Post Office savings bank." NS 1999, an "offshore" operation, almost immediately took on an "onshore" adviser in the person of Donald J. Trump, who claimed to have acquired a one-half interest in the Empire State Building without having invested a dime of his own money. As late as the spring of 1995, what Trump had actually acquired, however, was far from clear. It seemed that a company controlled by him had entered into an agreement with a company controlled by Nakahara and Renoir, which stipulated that if Trump was successful in obtaining an increase in the master lease rent or a sale of the fee title for more than $42 million, Trump would receive one-half the profit. It meant negotiating a deal with the Empire State Building Associates or managing to break the master lease, and neither seemed likely.

Peter L. Malkin pointed out that even as a fee owner, Trump would have no voice in the day-to-day operation of the building, and no interest in operating results, facts that did little to slow Trump from maintaining that he would "take those actions necessary to restore the building to its rightful position as a world-class operation." Trump floated the idea of converting the upper floors to condominium apartments, turning the building into a mixed-use building akin to Trump Tower. A "tenants' association" of two claimed that the building lacked adequate security, and was crawling with vermin and rodents. The association's membership swelled to three tenants, but the third member had joined only to find out what all the fuss was about, and quickly dropped out. He was Jack Brod, a tenant of sixty-three years. He considered the building in as good shape as when he had moved in, and the builders had "put very fine materials in at the start." He told *The Observer*'s Charles Bagli that the tenant

---

[8]Among other charges, Renoir stood accused of dismantling a garden temple and putting it up for auction. Perhaps Renoir had read *Unbuilding*, David Macauley's fable for our times, in which New Yorkers allow the Empire State Building to be taken apart, labeled, and reerected in a mythical Arabian desert.

group was a "tool of Donald Trump." According to Bryan Burrough, Trump even provided the printer used to crank out press releases.

And the plot thickens. On November 1, 1994, Yokoi and his company Nihon Sangyo sued his own daughter and son-in-law, claiming that they had defrauded him by naming themselves as beneficial owners of the interest in the Empire State Building rather than as trustees for him and his company. And Yokoi maintained that since Trump had made his deal with parties who did not really own any interest, Trump was dealing with stolen property and had not in fact acquired any interest in the Empire State Building. Regardless, NS 1999's only real hope of making any money on the building was by breaking the master lease, by evicting Harry Helmsley and his partner Peter L. Malkin, and that was the tack that Trump took. "Trumped up" or otherwise, Trump's charges were filed in a $100 million lawsuit contending that under the Malkin-Helmsley management, the building had become "second-rate, [and] rodent-infested." In March 1995, a New York State Supreme Court judge granted Malkin and Helmsley an injunction to prevent Trump and his affiliates from terminating the master lease until Trump could prove his allegations. If Trump succeeded, Malkin and Helmsley would still have a reasonable opportunity to remedy the alleged violations and to protect their "valuable leasehold on one of the most famous buildings in the world." In May 1995 came the countersuit.

In the meantime, a spokesman for the building management had said that since 1990, a $65 million modernization program had been under way that included computer-controlled elevators, fire and security systems, renewed heating and air-conditioning systems, and all new windows and window frames (the new windows were given the same tomato-red color as the originals, a nice gesture on behalf of management for the integrity of the landmark building). Between 1988 and 1994, during which time there was a stock market crash and a recession, the average occupancy rate was 94 percent. In the same period, the observatories were still attracting over 2 million visitors a year, and the building won three awards from the Building Owners and Managers Association of America for "management, maintenance and historic preservation." This is less the stuff of real estate failure and more the stuff of dreams, precisely the intent of the original builders, which in part explains the wrangling.

As the city of yesterday merges into the city of today, and today into tomorrow, the Empire State Building remains an enduring and beloved symbol, secure in its place in New York's past, present, and future. The building's chief protagonists—John J. Raskob and Al Smith; Shreve, Lamb, and Harmon; and the Starrett Brothers and Eken—are all dead, but the good they did is hardly interred with their bones. Their building lives after them. "Look at that World Trade Center over there," says long-term Empire State tenant Jack Brod from his window on the sixty-sixth floor. "What is it? Nothing but a couple of shoeboxes standing on end. But this place, this is special, a landmark building."

# BIBLIOGRAPHY

SELECTED MAGAZINE AND NEWSPAPER ARTICLES

*American City,* "Height Limitations," September 1926, 318.

*American City,* "New York's Population," May 1926, 557.

*American City,* "Noise Level in Skyscrapers," June 1930, 118.

Anderson, Richard J., "Real Estate Equities for the Average Investor," *Financial World,* September 13, 1961.

Atterbury, Grosvenor, "Our Monster City and Its Life," *The New York Times,* January 13, 1929, V, 1.

Bent, Silas, "Danger Stalks the Building Wrecker," *The New York Times,* January 17, 1926, IV, 9.1.

Berger, Meyer, "About New York: Ex Bobby from London to Operate Elevator Queen Will Use in Empire State Building," *The New York Times,* October 18, 1957, 20.2.

Berger, Meyer, "About New York: Three Storied Rooms from Europe Tucked Away High in Empire State Building," *The New York Times,* December 14, 1955, 54.1.

Berger, Meyer, "O. Henry Returns to His Bagdad," *The New York Times Magazine,* November 24, 1935.

Bernstein, Victor H., "Elevators Vital to City," *The New York Times,* March 8, 1936, IV, 10.3.

Beugge, Walter J., "Round the Town, *Brooklyn Central,* March 1, 1935.

Bossom, Alfred C., "City of Future Likely to Grow Higher Still," *The New York Times,* May 15, 1927, VIII, 14.1.

Brock, H. I., "Architecture Styled 'International,' " *The New York Times Magazine*, February 7, 1932, V, 11.

Brock, H. I., "The City That the Air Traveler Sees," *The New York Times*, March 11, 1928, V, 14.

Brock, H. I., "Our Towers Take on Decoration," *The New York Times*, January 16, 1927, IV, 9.

Bruner, Warren D., "Office Layouts for Tenants," *Architectural Forum*, June 1930, 905–908.

Brutschy, Fred, "Plumbing (Empire State Building)," *Architectural Forum*, June 1930, 645–646.

Burrough, Bryan, "Trump's Tower?" *Vanity Fair*, May 1995.

Cantwell, Mary, "Welcome to—and in—New York," *The New York Times*, May 1, 1981, I, 30.1.

Carmody, John P., "Expediting the Empire State Building," *The Construction*, Baltimore, Md., July 1931.

Carmody, John P., "Field Organization and Methods (Empire State Building)," *Architectural Forum*, April 1931, 495–506.

Cary, Elizabeth Luther, "Architectural and Allied Arts Show, Grand Central Palace," *The New York Times*, April 21, 1929, X, 3.1.

*Christian Science Monitor*, "Tattoo of Riveter's Hammer Quiets Along Line of New York's Skyscrapers," March 2, 1931, 5.4.

Clavan, Irwin, "The Mooring Mast," *Architectural Forum*, February 1931, 229–233.

Clute, Eugene, "Lighting the World's Tallest Building," *Electrical World*, July 18, 1931.

Coates, Robert M., "Packmen Who Use the Skyscraper Route," *The New York Times*, September 30, 1928, V, 16.

Coley, Clarence, "Office Buildings, Past, Present and Future," *Architectural Forum*, September 1924, 113–114.

Corbett, Harvey Wiley, "America's Great Gift to Architecture, *The New York Times*, March 18, 1928, V, 4.

Corbett, Harvey Wiley, "The Limits of Our Sky-Scraping," *The New York Times*, November 17, 1929, V, 1.

Coyle, David C., C.E., "Skyscrapers Vibrate Like the Tuning Fork," *The New York Times*, March 31, 1929, IX, 13.1.

Demorest, William J., "Millions of Feet of Office Space Added to Grand Central Zone," *The New York Times*, January 20, 1929, XI, 1.4.

Dowswell, H. R., "Materials of Construction," *Architectural Forum*, May 1931, 625–632.

Dubin, Susan Schraub, "The Man Who Lights Up New York," *Town & Country*, September 1984, 239–240, 291–295.

Duffus, R. L., "The New York of 1965: A Colossal City," *The New York Times*, June 2, 1929, IX, 1.

Dunlap, David W., "Trump Plans Revitalization of Empire State Building," *The New York Times*, July 8, 1994.

Edwards, J. L., "The Structural Frame (Empire State Building)," *Architectural Forum*, August 1930, 241–246.

Eken, Andrew J., "The Empire State Building," *Scientific American*, May 1931.

Faber, John, "The Empire State Building Plane Crash," *Silurian News*, New York, November 1993.

*Fortune*, "Governor Smith of the Empire State," September 1930, 52–53.

*Fortune,* "Skyscrapers: The Paper Spires," September 1930, 54–59, 119–126.

Fowler, Glenn, "A Very Tall Lady Is Gainly and Gainful at 40," *The New York Times,* May 9, 1971, VIII, 1.1.

Friedsam, Col. Michael, "Empire State's Effect on Neighborhood," *The New York Times,* May 4, 1930, XIV, 1.8.

Glueck, Grace, "34th Street Vernissage," *The New York Times,* August 1, 1965.

Goldberger, Paul, "A Symbol of Grace Unsullied by Time," *The New York Times,* April 23, 1981, II, 1.4.

Goldberger, Paul, "Design Notebook: Colored Lights Turn the Empire State Building into a Toy," *The New York Times,* December 8, 1977, C 10.

Goldberger, Paul, "Design Notebook: 5 Ideas to Redo Empire State's Deck," *The New York Times,* April 5, 1979, III, 22.1.

Goldstein, Matthew, "Helmsley Wins Eviction Suit Delay," *The New York Law Journal,* March 22, 1995.

Gray, Christopher, "A Red Reprise for a '31 Design," *The New York Times,* June 14, 1992, X, 7.1.

Harmon, Arthur Loomis, "The Design of Office Buildings," *Architectural Forum,* June 1930, 819–820.

Harmon, Arthur Loomis, "The Interior Architecture of Offices," *Architectural Forum,* June 1930, 863–865.

Horowitz, Louis J., "The Towers of New York," *The Saturday Evening Post,* March 14 and April 25, 1936.

Huxtable, Ada Louise, "Editorial Notebook: Tinsel in the Sky," *The New York Times,* December 19, 1977, 30.1.

Ingraham, Reg, "Speeding Up the Climb of the Skyline," *Baltimore Sun,* December 21, 1930.

Jacobs, Harry Allan, "New Architecture Based on Utility," *The New York Times,* November 30, 1930, XII, 2.1.

Jones, Bassett, "Elevators (Empire State Building)," *Architectural Forum,* January 1931, 95–99.

Kahn, Albert, "Designing Modern Office Building," *Architectural Forum,* June 1930, 775–777.

Kahn, Ely Jacques, "Our Skyscrapers Take Simple Forms," *The New York Times,* May 2, 1926, IV, 11.

Keller, Allan, "They Build New York," *New York World Telegram,* February 18, 1938.

Keller, Helen, "The New York That Helen Keller Sees," *The New York Times Magazine,* January 31, 1932, V, 3.1.

King, Wayne, "An Artist Sees Icon of the Age in Empire State," *The New York Times,* July 25, 1989, II, 1.1.

Klaw, Spencer, "The World's Tallest Building (Woolworth)," *American Heritage,* February 1977, 86–99.

Klemesrud, Judy, "Tall—but True—Tales Run in Her Family," *The New York Times,* September 27, 1977, 44.1.

Lamb, William F., "The General Design (Empire State Building)," *Architectural Forum,* January 1931, 1–8.

Lamb, William F., "The Ground Floor Lobbies and Shops (Empire State Building)," *Architectural Forum,* July 1931, 42–46.

Lescaze, William, "Building in the Spirit of the Age," *The New York Times,* October 14, 1928, X, 10.2.

Linn, Charles, "Douglas Leigh: Creating New Visions for Great Cities," *Architectural Lighting,* May 1987, 30–37.

*Literary Digest,* "Personal Glimpses: Sky Boys Who 'Rode the Ball' on Empire State," May 23, 1931, 30–31.

Mandel, Henry, "Big Building Units Need New Financing," *The New York Times,* January 6, 1929, XIII, 2.2.

Margery, Mrs. Lewis, "I Married a Steeplejack," *Sunday Mirror Magazine Section,* August 2, 1936.

Matthews, Henry, "The Promotion of Modern Architecture by the Museum of Modern Art in the 1930s," *Journal of Design History,* vol. 7, no. 1, 1994, Oxford University Press.

McCormick, W. B., "The Empire State," *The New York American,* May 15, 1931.

McDonald, William H., "Thermal Inertia and Nostalgia Increasing Markets for Indiana Limestone," *Pit & Quarry,* September 1979.

McGoldrick, Joseph, letter on "The Skyscraper: A Study of Its Economic Height," *American City,* May 1930, 130.

McInerney, John, "The Empire State," *Herald Tribune,* July 20, 1930.

McNally, Edward E., "Grand Central Zone Presents No Cause for Pessimism," *The New York Times,* February 3, 1929, 1.7.

McQuade, Walter, "A Skyscraper You Could Love," *Life,* April 30, 1971.

Meyer, Henry C., "Heating and Ventilating (Empire State Building)," *Architectural Forum,* October 1930, 517–521.

Miller, Russell, "The Empire Strikes Back," *The London Sunday Times Magazine,* December 18, 1994.

*The New York Times,* "75 Story Buildings Found Economical," September 22, 1929, II, 1.7.

*The New York Times,* "A Shining Tower," December 14, 1930, V, 30.3.

*The New York Times,* "Smith to Build Highest Skyscraper," August 30, 1929, 1.4.

*The New York Times,* "Tallest Building in World for Waldorf-Astoria Site," *The New York Times,* November 20, 1929, 1.5.

*New Yorker,* "Highest with Steel," October 21, 1951, 24–25.

*New Yorker,* "Interruption," September 1, 1945, 15–16.

*New Yorker,* "Limited," July 28, 1951, 13–14.

*New Yorker,* "Two Unveilings," May 14, 1979, 31–32.

Newhall, Beaumont, "Lewis W. Hine," *Magazine of Art,* Washington, DC, no. 1, 38.

Newman, James B., "Factors in Office Building Planning," *Architectural Forum,* June 1930, 881–890.

*Newsweek,* "Lighting the Empire State Building," March 26, 1956.

Palmer, C. F., "Office Buildings from an Investment Standpoint," *Architectural Forum,* June 1930, 891–896.

Phillips, McCandlish, "Blackout Vignettes Are Everywhere You Look, *The New York Times,* November 11, 1965.

Polk, Grace, "Sire of the Skyscraper (Buffington)," *The New York Times,* November 21, 1926, IV, 15.

Poore, C. G., "Greatest Skyscraper Rises on Clockwork Schedule," *The New York Times,* July 27, 1930, IX, 4.1.

Poore, C. G., "The Riveters Panorama of New York," *The New York Times,* January 5, 1930, V, 8.

Poore, C. G., "Watching a Skyscraper Grow Out of a Hole," *The New York Times,* February 17, 1929, V, 19.1.

Price, Clair, "An Older and Wiser New York," *The New York Times Magazine,* January 19, 1941.

Ralston, Louis T. M., "The Engineers' Problems in Tall Buildings, *Architectural Forum,* June 1930, 909–913.

*Real Estate Record and Guide,* "The Empire State Building," August 16, 1930, 7.

*Real Estate Record and Guide,* "Facts and Figures from the Records of the Builders of the Empire State Building," May 9, 1931.

*Real Estate Record and Guide,* "The Fifth Avenue District," October 4, 1930, 7.

*Real Estate Record and Guide,* "Fifth Avenue Preeminent as Shopping District," February 21, 1931, 10.

Reinitz, Bertram, "Wreckers Tackle the Skyscraper," *The New York Times,* October 7, 1928, X, 2.1.

Richardson, H. F., "Electrical Equipment (Empire State Building)," *Architectural Forum,* November 1930, 639–643.

Robertson, Stewart, "Paneful Experience," *Family Circle,* November 19, 1937.

Shepherd, Thomas Edison, "Exposition of the Architectural League of New York," *Architectural Progress,* July 1931.

Sherburne, E. C., "The Skyscraper as an Invention," *Christian Science Monitor,* May 2, 1931.

Shreve, R. H., "Organization (Empire State Building)," *Architectural Forum,* June 1930, 771–774.

Shreve, R. H., "The Window-Spandrel-Wall Detail and Its Relation to Building Progress," *Architectural Forum,* July 1930, 99–104.

Shreve, Richmond, "The Architect's Fee in Getting Business," *Architectural Record,* vol. 69, May 1931, 423–424.

Slagle, Alton, "Empire State: 60 and Still Glowing," *The New York Daily News,* April 30, 1991.

Smith, Al, "A View of the Month," *Property, The National Realty Mart,* May 1931, I, 1.

Smith, Alfred E., "Empire State Nears Completion," *The New York Times,* January 11, 1931, XI, 1.4.

Spencer, Clifford W., "Practical Floodlighting," *Architectural Forum,* November 1930, 627–634.

Sullivan, Ed, "Ed Sullivan Sees Broadway," *New York Graphic,* June 5, 1931.

Sullivan, Ed, "Ed Sullivan Sees Broadway," *New York Graphic,* November 13, 1931.

Taylor, Deems, "The City That Died of Greatness," *Vanity Fair,* November 1928, 74.

Turner, H. C., "The Selection of the Builder," *Architectural Forum,* June 1930, 522.

Wilson, Nathan, "Manhattan Realty Yields Big Profits," *The New York Times,* September 2, 1928, X, 1.1.

Winchell, Walter, "On Broadway," *New York Mirror,* March 17, 1934.

Woolf, S. J., "An Architect Hails the Rule of Reason (Raymond Hood)," *The New York Times,* November 1, 1931, V, 6.

SELECTED BOOKS

Allen, Frederick Lewis, *Only Yesterday*, Harper & Brothers: New York, 1931.

Alpern, Andrew, *Apartments for the Affluent*, McGraw-Hill: New York, 1975.

Alpern, Andrew, *Luxury Apartment Houses of Manhattan*, Dover Publications: New York, 1992.

Ballard, Robert F. R., *Directory of Manhattan Office Buildings*, McGraw-Hill: New York, 1978.

Battersby, Martin, *The Decorative Thirties*, revised and edited by Philippe Garner, Whitney Library of Design, Watson-Guptill: New York, 1988.

Carr, William H. A., *The duPonts of Delaware*, Dodd, Mead & Company: New York, 1964.

Chandler, Alfred D., Jr., and Stephen Salsbury, *Pierre S. duPont and the Making of the Modern Corporation*, Harper & Row: New York, 1971.

Chrysler Corporation, Department of Public Relations, *Chrysler Corporation: The Story of an American Company*, Detroit, Mi., 1955.

Condit, Carl W., *American Building: Materials and Techniques*, University of Chicago Press: Chicago, 1981.

Connable, Alfred, and Edward Silberfarb, *The Tigers of Tammany*, Holt, Rinehart & Winston: New York, 1967.

Conway, Donald J., ed., *Human Response to Tall Buildings*, Dowden, Hutchinson & Ross, Stroudsburg, PA, 1977.

Dunlap, David W., *On Broadway: A Journey Uptown over Time*, Rizzoli: New York, 1990.

Empire State, Inc., *Dinner Commemorating the Completion of the Empire State*, New York, 1931.

Empire State, Inc., *Empire State: A History*, New York, 1931.

Farley, James A., *Jim Farley's Story: The Roosevelt Years*, Whittlesey House, McGraw-Hill: New York, 1948.

Federal Writers' Project, *The WPA Guide to New York*, Random House: New York, 1939.

Gibbs, Kenneth Turney, *Business Architectural Imagery in America, 1870–1930*, UMI Research Press: Ann Arbor, Mi., 1976.

Goldberger, Paul, *The Skyscraper*, Alfred A. Knopf: New York, 1982.

Gordon, J. E., *Structures: Or Why Things Don't Fall Down*, Plenum Press: New York, 1978; DaCapo Press: New York, 1981.

Graham, Frank, *Al Smith: American*, G. P. Putnam's: New York, 1945.

Handlin, Oscar, *Al Smith and His America*, Northwestern University Press: Boston, 1958, 1987.

Horne, Charles F., ed, *Source Records of the Great War*, National Alumni, 1923.

Huxtable, Ada Louise, *The Tall Building Artistically Reconsidered: The Search for a Skyscraper Style*, New York: Pantheon Books, 1984.

Irace, Fulvio, *Emerging Skylines: The New American Skyscrapers*, Whitney Library of Design, Watson-Guptill: New York, 1990.

Josephson, Matthew and Hannah, *Al Smith: Hero of the Cities*, Houghton Mifflin Company: Boston, 1969.

Krinsky, Carol Herselle, *Rockefeller Center*, Oxford University Press: New York, 1978.

Lehman, Arnold, *The New York Skyscraper: A History of Its Development, 1870–1939*, Ph.D. diss., Yale University, 1975.

Leich, Jean Ferriss, *Architectural Visions: The Drawings of Hugh Ferriss*, Whitney Library of Design, Watson-Guptill: New York, 1980.

Levy, Matthys, and Mario Salvadori, *Why Buildings Fall Down*, W. W. Norton & Company: New York, 1992.

Moore, Charles, *Daniel Burnham: Architect, Planner of Cities,* Boston and New York: Houghton Mifflin Company, 1921.

Mujica, Francisco, *The History of the Skyscraper,* Archaeology and Architecture Press: New York and Paris, 1929.

O'Connor, Harvey, *The Astors,* Alfred A. Knopf: New York, 1941.

O'Connor, Richard, *The First Hurrah: A Biography of Al Smith,* G. P. Putnam's Sons: New York, 1970.

Perry, Elizabeth Israels, *Belle Moskowitz: Feminine Politics & the Exercise of Power in the Age of Alfred E. Smith,* Oxford University Press: New York, 1987.

Rider, Fremont, *Rider's Guide to New York City,* 2nd ed., Macmillan: New York, 1924.

Robbins, Yale, and Henry Robbins, *Manhattan Office Buildings: Midtown, Midtown South, and Downtown,* Yale Robbins, Inc.: New York, 1985.

Robins, Anthony, *The World Trade Center,* Pineapple Press and Omnigraphics? Englewood, Fl., 1987.

Robinson, Cervin, and Rosemarie Hagg Bletter, *Skyscraper Style: Art Deco New York,* Oxford University Press: New York, 1975.

Shultz, Earle, and Walter Simmons, *Offices in the Sky,* Bobbs-Merrill: New York, 1959.

Smith, Alfred E., *Up to Now, An Autobiography,* Star Books, Garden City Publishing Company: Garden City, N.J., 1929.

Starrett, Colonel W. A., *Skyscrapers and the Men Who Build Them,* Charles Scribner's Sons: New York, 1928.

Starrett, Colonel W. A., U.S.A., *Building for Victory,* Thompson-Starrett Company: New York, 1919.

Starrett, Paul, *Changing the Skyline: An Autobiography,* Whittlesey House, McGraw-Hill: New York, 1938.

Stern, Robert A. M., Gregory Gilmartin, and Thomas Mellins, *New York 1930: Architecture and Urbanism Between the Two World Wars,* Rizzoli: New York, 1987.

Vlack, Don, *Art Deco Architecture in New York,* Harper & Row, Icon Editions: New York, 1974.

Ward, David, and Olivier Zunz, eds., *The Landscape of Modernity,* Russell Sage Foundation: New York, 1992.

Ward, James, *Architects in Practice in New York City, 1900–1940,* for the Committee for the Preservation of Architectural Records, J & D Associates, Union, N.J., 1989.

Warner, Emily Smith, with Daniel Hawthorne, *The Happy Warrior: A Biography of My Father, Alfred E. Smith,* Doubleday & Company: Garden City, N.J., 1956.

Weingarten, Arthur, *The Sky Is Falling,* Grosset & Dunlap: New York, 1977.

Willensky, Elliot, and Norval White, *AIA Guide to New York City,* 3rd ed., Harcourt Brace Jovanovich: New York, 1988.

Williamson, Roxanne Kuter, *American Architects and the Mechanics of Fame,* University of Texas Press: Austin, 1991.

Wilson, Richard Guy, *The AIA Gold Medal,* McGraw-Hill Book Company: New York, 1984.

REPORTS

Landmark Society of Western New York, "Times Square Building (aka Genesee)," n.d.

Robins, Anthony W., *Report on the Empire State Building,* Landmarks Preservation Commission, New York City, May 19, 1981.

New York Telephone Company, Public Relations Office, "The Story of Central Office Names," n.d.

United States Army Air Force, Headquarters, Atlantic Overseas and Local Service Command, "Report of the Collision of TB-25-D Type Aircraft, #41-30577, . . . with the Empire State Building, 7 August, 1945," Port Authority, Newark; releasable portions provided by the Department of the Air Force, Headquarters Air Force Safety Agency, Kirtland Air Force Base, New Mexico.

# INDEX